Black, White, and Catholic

Black, White, and Catholic:
New Orleans Interracialism,
1947–1956

R. BENTLEY ANDERSON

Vanderbilt University Press ■ Nashville

Printed on acid-free paper
Manufactured in the United States of America
Design by Ellen Beeler

Library of Congress Cataloging-in-Publication Data

Anderson, R. Bentley, 1959–
Black, White, and Catholic : New Orleans interracialism, 1947–1956 /
R. Bentley Anderson.— 1st ed.
    p. cm.
Includes bibliographical references.
ISBN 0-8265-1483-9 (cloth : alk. paper)
 1. New Orleans (La.)—Race relations—History—20th century.
 2. Catholics—Louisiana—New Orleans—Attitudes—History—20th century.
 3. Catholics—Louisiana—New Orleans—Social conditions—20th century.
I. Title.
F380.A1A53 2005
305.8'0097633509'041—dc22
2005005034

Publication of this book has been supported by a grant from the Louisiana
Endowment for the Humanities, an affiliate of the National Endowment of
the Humanities.

Material from Chapters 5 and 9 appeared previously in slightly different
form as "Black, White, and Catholic: Southern Jesuits Confront the Race
Question, 1952," *Catholic Historical Review* 91 (July 2005): 484–505. Used
with permission of the American Catholic Historical Association. A portion
of chapter seven appeared in "Prelates, Protest, and Public Opinion: Catholic
Opposition to Desegregation, 1947–1955," *Journal of Church and State* 46
(summer 2004): 617–44. Used with permission.

TO MY PARENTS

ROBERT BENTLEY ANDERSON, JR.

AND

JANET RIVET ANDERSON

CONTENTS

ILLUSTRATIONS

ACKNOWLEDGMENTS

I would like to acknowledge my professors, colleagues, and friends who read and commented on my work and encouraged me during the development of this project. A special note of thanks to my professors at Boston College: Andrew Bunie, Mark Gelfand, and James O'Toole; to my colleagues at Saint Louis University, especially Lewis Perry, Jose Sanchez, Daniel Schlafly, and Silvana Siddali; to my friends at Loyola University, New Orleans: Mark Fernandez, Peter Rogers, S.J., and Larry Moore, S.J.; to Jesuit historians: Mark Lewis, S.J., Mark Massa, S.J., Leo Nicoll, S.J., Charles O'Neill, S.J., John Padberg, S.J., and David Suwalsky, S.J.; and to SLU friends Teresa Harvey, Erin Couch, Barney Barry, S.J., and Shannon Schlafly. Particular mention goes to Cynthia Stachecki, graduate research assistant at SLU, who did a yeoman's job during the editing process.

A note of gratitude to all the archivists who have assisted me in my research: Joseph DeCock, S.J., and Thomas Reddy, S.J. (Roman Archives of the Society of Jesus); Art Carpenter (Loyola University of New Orleans); Lester Sullivan (Xavier University of New Orleans); Marguerite Brou, O.P. (St. Mary's Dominican College, New Orleans); Joan Marie Aycock, O.S.U. (Ursuline Academy, New Orleans); Thomas Clancy, S.J. (Archives of the New Orleans Province of the Society of Jesus); Elizabeth Farley, R.S.C.J. (Archives of the Society of the Sacred Heart, St. Louis); Mary T. Clark, R.S.C.J. (Manhattanville College, New York); Dorothy Daues, O.P. (Archives of the Dominican Sisters, New Orleans); and Charles Nolan (Archives of the Archdiocese of New Orleans).

I would like to thank the superior general of the Society of Jesus, Peter-Hans Kolvenbach, S.J., for granting me permission to examine the files of the New Orleans Province of the Society of Jesus located in the Roman archives. Without his permission, I could not have written a substantial portion of this story. Likewise, I am indebted to the former provincial of the New Orleans Province, James P. Bradley, S.J., who allowed me to examine the province records in New Orleans, and to John Armstrong, S.J., former assistant to the provincial, who assisted me in conducting that portion of my research.

One could not ask for a better group of folks to work with than the staff at Vanderbilt University Press. Special thanks to Betsy Phillips, acquisitions editor, for her interest, enthusiasm, and encouragement throughout this process; to Dariel Mayer, editing and production manager, for enduring a "long-distance relationship" as I lived and worked in India and Sri Lanka during a good portion of the editing process; George Roupe, copy editor; and to Sue Havlish in the marketing arena. Of course any errors or misstatements of fact found in this work are of my doing.

Funding from the following organizations and bodies allowed me to produce this book: the Marchetti Fund, Saint Louis University; the Jesuit community at Saint Louis University; the New Orleans Province of the Society of Jesus; the Jesuit community at Loyola University, New Orleans; and the Louisiana Endowment for the Humanities, a state affiliate of the National Endowment for the Humanities.

To all those who granted me interviews, especially members of the Southeastern Regional Interracial Commission and the Commission on Human Rights, I am grateful. These men and women helped shape the modern South. By challenging the social mores of their day, they have made this world more just.

PREFACE

> Never doubt that a small group of thoughtful, committed
> citizens can change the world. Indeed, it is the only thing
> that ever has.
>
> —MARGARET MEAD

The activities of a small group of Catholic interracialists in the 1940s and 1950s
had repercussions that went far beyond their immediate circle. By 1956, the archbishop of New Orleans, the Jesuit provincial of the New Orleans Province, and
the Roman superior of the Society of Jesus, as well as the city of New Orleans and
the state of Louisiana, had been drawn into the controversy that the Commission
on Human Rights (CHR) and the Southeastern Regional Interracial Commission
(SERINCO) unwittingly had provoked. How the seemingly innocuous meetings,
lectures, and newsletters of a relative handful of idealistic Catholics convulsed the
entire archdiocese of New Orleans is the subject of this story.

In the 1940s, the Roman Catholic Church had not yet come to terms with
its complicity in maintaining racial segregation in the southern United States,
and, it is fair to say, had not adequately challenged race policy within or without
the church. Yet, early in the post–World War II period there were nascent signs
of change: Archbishop Joseph E. Ritter of St. Louis desegregated his archdiocese
in 1947, and Archbishop Patrick A. O'Boyle of Washington followed suit the following year. Then in the 1950s southern bishops issued individual pastoral letters calling for an end to segregation within the church: Joseph Francis Rummel,
archbishop of New Orleans, and Vincent S. Waters, bishop of Raleigh, did so in
1953, and Bishops Robert E. Lucey of San Antonio and Peter L. Ireton of Richmond followed in 1954. In 1958, a representative group of United States bishops
issued a pastoral letter regarding the race question titled "Discrimination and the
Christian Conscience." Nevertheless, in the postwar period, a majority of the
Roman Catholic clergy and laity did not challenge social mores concerning race
relations. For most Catholics, segregation, if it was a problem at all, was a social,
political, and/or legal problem but not necessarily a moral one.[1]

In New Orleans, a small but dedicated group of Catholics in the postwar
period set out to challenge the racial practices of the day. Through interracial
cooperation, black and white Catholic college students, black and white adult
Catholic laity, black and white Catholic religious men and women, and black and
white Catholic clergy, worked together to undermine the practice of racial segregation in the church. Catholic New Orleanians used the principle and practice

of interracialism—organized interaction and cooperation between black and white Catholics to promote racial harmony and advance racial justice—to oppose segregation. Prayer, study, and reflection, leading to action, was an interracialist's plan of attack.

Interracialism influenced and informed Catholic opinion and practice through most of the twentieth century; it dominated the Catholic response to the race question. Interracialists' efforts to end Jim Crow Catholicism resulted in some successes and many disappointments; ultimately New Orleans Catholic interracialists were suppressed at the hands of ecclesiastical and secular forces. Theirs is a complex story of religious principles clashing with social practice, of Christian charity conflicting with racial norms, of moral conviction succumbing to political expediency.

Under the auspices of the National Federation of Catholic College Students, Catholic collegians established SERINCO in 1948, which was comprised of students from St. Mary's Dominican College for white women,[2] Loyola University of the South for white men,[3] Ursuline College for white women,[4] and the College of the Sacred Heart,[5] also for white women but located in Grand Coteau, Louisiana, and male and female students from the only black Catholic institution of higher learning in the United States, Xavier University.[6]

The mere fact that black and white Catholic college students met together on equal footing to discuss racial issues aroused fierce opposition. In fact, the meetings and other activities these Catholic college students undertook led church officials at Loyola University of the South to try to disband the group early in its history. Of the two Catholic interracial groups in Louisiana, SERINCO was the more active and provocative.[7]

The other group, the CHR, a subcommittee of the Catholic Committee of the South, made up of adult Catholics of the archdiocese, averaging one hundred members a year, was established in 1949. Invoking Catholic principles to promote their cause, members of these organizations found kindred spirits who believed in racial equality and strove to foster it; in doing so, however, they incurred the wrath of their fellow Catholics who would not accept the change in the racial mores of the day. The CHR had great difficulty meeting and worshiping as an integrated body. While some might argue that the organization was insignificant because it had a small membership and did not seem to accomplish much, the very existence of an interracial organization in the South, no matter how small or "insignificant," subverted Jim Crow society and was perceived as a direct threat to the existing social order.[8]

Both the CHR and SERINCO held monthly meetings, published monthly newsletters, attended social gatherings, and organized annual interracial affairs where discussions and presentations about the race question took place. Time and again these interracialists heard the message that Christianity and racial segrega-tion were incompatible and were encouraged to put their religious beliefs into practice—interracial activities were one way these Catholics could live out their faith. By participating in these events, black and white Catholics continually exposed the contradiction between religious convictions and social practices. In the study of Southern Catholic interracialism, one discovers that talking and meeting led to action.

These various endeavors generated a response from Catholics who were sat-isfied with the racial status quo, especially the faculty and staff at member school Loyola University of the South, which was run by members of the New Orleans Province of the Society of Jesus (Jesuits). The Jesuits, more than the other reli-gious orders that administered Catholic institutions of higher learning in New Orleans, struggled with the social and religious implications of maintaining racial segregation. The interracial activities became so contentious for the Jesuits that the order finally drafted a racial policy statement on integration in 1952. This principled stand, which took several years to implement, nevertheless, brought an end to segregationist practices within this religious order of men. Furthermore, this document would be used by the archbishop of New Orleans, Joseph Francis Rummel, to produce his own statement regarding segregation in 1956.

The negative reaction to desegregation efforts, both ecclesiastical and secular, was not anticipated by church or government officials. In the aftermath of the all-important 1954 *Brown* v. *Board of Education* decision,[9] Catholics who favored integration felt vindicated, while those who opposed it felt betrayed. Meanwhile, Louisiana state officials tried to reverse or nullify the Court's decision and, in doing so, attacked the Catholic Church. Archbishop Joseph Francis Rummel of New Orleans, in his 1956 pastoral letter dealing with the immorality of racial seg-regation, indicated that Catholic desegregation was forthcoming. The thought of black and white Catholics attending church services on an integrated basis, of black and white Catholic school children attending classes together, threatened most white Catholics. Organized resistance by New Orleans Catholics in the mid-1950s, albeit short-lived, laid the groundwork for resistance on a larger scale in the early 1960s. Only Rummel's threat of excommunication from the church ended the vocal opposition to Catholic integration.

The hostility expressed by New Orleans Catholics toward desegregation, cou-pled with the fear that further efforts at promoting integration would provoke more resistance, resulted in the demise of Catholic interracialism. Both SER-INCO and the CHR disbanded in the fall of 1956, victims of fear and intimida-tion. Catholic principle gave way to Catholic expediency. Nevertheless, Catholic New Orleans had promoted and participated in the civil rights struggle through the vehicle of interracialism and had brought about some social change.

While the activities of SERINCO and CHR might appear ineffective to many today, I argue that Catholic interracialism was the best method of direct action for bringing about integration in the Catholic South. Together black and white Catholics challenged racial segregation by making a connection between Christian belief and human rights; together they promoted Christian teachings: the unity of the human race and the dignity of the human person. In the aftermath of the Second World War, these Catholics wanted to live more authentic Christian lives, and they believed there was no place for racial segregation within the church. Had these biracial organizations survived into the 1960s, the church, as an institution and as a community of believers, could have served as a bulwark against those advocating segregation.

As these interracial groups attempted to effect change, the Roman Catholic Church in Louisiana, especially the archdiocese of New Orleans, was also coming to terms with racial segregation. This is the second major theme running through this work. The archbishop of New Orleans, Joseph Francis Rummel, began the process of desegregating the church in the late 1940s. In the later part of that decade he accepted his first black candidates for the priesthood and took a principled stand against state-sponsored segregation. In the early 1950s, Rummel called for an end to the practice of racial segregation within parish churches. By the middle of the decade, he was facing state interference regarding Catholic educational policy and open dissent from segregationist Catholics concerning changes in ecclesiastical race policy. Part of this dissent was fostered by the activities of the interracial groups. This open opposition to the archbishop from church members was significant, as it demonstrated, long before the more-celebrated challenges to authority following the Second Vatican Council, that Catholics were not uniform in their thinking on church policy and teachings. American Catholic dissent did not begin with *Humanae vitae.*

This overlapping or interweaving of southern Catholic interracial history with that of archdiocesan history as well as the histories of the religious orders working in Louisiana points to the complexity of the situation and confounds those who believe the Roman Catholic Church was a monolithic organization in the 1940s and 1950s, given its hierarchical structure. In the pre–Second Vatican Council church (i.e., before 1962), bishops and archbishops in their respective dioceses and archdioceses addressed church issues as they saw fit—they acted independently of each other. Rome did not meddle in local affairs, as the papacy concerned itself with matters of faith and doctrine. Prior to the Second Vatican Council there were no regular bishops' conferences, and except for occasional statements by select groups of bishops, they did not deliberate as a body. Hence the episcopacy did not speak with one voice. It did not act in unison. The race question in post–World War II America was informed by that reality.[10]

Given this complexity, the history of the Catholic response to the race question in the United States is a particular history, informed by the actions of a bishop, local clergy, religious men and women, and the Catholic laity of a particular diocese. In order to present a general account of the church and race in the South, one must examine each and every diocese and archdiocese. This work focuses on New Orleans and southern Louisiana, thus providing an important chapter for a complete story that has yet to be written. Histories of the modern Civil Rights Movement have followed a similar trajectory. To understand that movement fully, one must examine the work undertaken by individuals and organizations in various locals, for local people created the modern movement.

Histories of Roman Catholicism in the United States scarcely address the issue of Catholics and civil rights or race relations in post–World War II America and have even less to say about the church in the South. Thomas McAvoy in his history of the church devotes one paragraph out of 468 pages of text to the issue of civil rights—almost, one is led to believe, as an afterthought: "The intensified argument about civil rights was an important side issue for Catholics."[11] Priest and scholar John Tracy Ellis surveys the issue of Catholic race relations in a few pages. While he does acknowledge the existence of prejudicial feelings among some northern urban Catholics, he tries to mitigate these shortcomings by highlighting the fact that several hundred Catholics participated in the Selma-to-Montgomery march of 1965.[12] Noted church historian Martin Marty states in his account of American Catholicism that "[t]he Civil Rights Movement . . . called forth the best in the Catholic conscience" and nothing more.[13] Historian James Hennesey's *American Catholics* devotes a few pages to the issue of race relations and concludes that the "aftershock of *Brown* was felt throughout the Catholic community."[14] In their article concerning the church and blacks, Richard Lamanna and Jay Coakley address the church's reluctance to involve herself with the plight of black Americans.[15] Recent scholarship gives short shrift to southern Catholic history and the race question. In *American Catholic,* Charles Morris ignores the most Catholic of southern towns, New Orleans, and the most Catholic state in the South, Louisiana. While he does address the issue of nonsouthern racism in general terms, Morris does not address the impact of the Civil Rights Movement on the church.[16]

One possible reason for this lack of historical attention is the presumption by scholars and laity alike that the challenges to Jim Crow, and therefore the advancement of civil rights, were exclusively undertaken by the South's black and Protestant population. Moreover, the struggle for civil rights in the South has been framed in terms of time. For many, December 1955 marks the beginning of the modern Civil Rights Movement in the United States, when the Montgomery bus boycott began in Alabama. While there are valid reasons and arguments for framing the Civil Rights Movement in terms of race and religion (i.e., black and Protestant), this approach limits one's understanding of the development of civil rights agitation in the South. Historians now agree that for a more complete picture of the struggle for racial equality in the United States, one must examine the actions of black and white southerners prior to Montgomery, prior to the twentieth century. Only by considering earlier individuals' attempts to further civil rights can we come to see that the struggle was fought on many fronts by many people.[17]

What is the history of Catholicism and American race relations? One could argue that American Catholicism has promoted, fostered, and confronted racism in the United States. Contemporary American Catholic scholarship is now coming to terms with this reality. Some historians have addressed the issue from the perspective of the American parish, others from the diocesan or national organizational perspective, and still others from the viewpoint of the history of a religious order. Scholars have discovered that the parochialism of Euro-American Catholics contributed to the development of racist attitudes. Paradoxically, it was this same parochialism that fostered the strong sense of community, family, and faith necessary to survive in a hostile white, Anglo-Saxon, Protestant world. From this narrow and limiting world, American Catholics came to address the issue of race.[18]

Literature dealing specifically with southern Catholics and civil rights and race relations is scant.[19] *Black, White, and Catholic* seeks to expand this area of research. It complements the social and political works already undertaken by Adam Fairclough, Kim Lacy Rogers, and Liva Baker regarding the race question in Louisiana. Fairclough's *Race and Democracy: The Civil Rights Struggle in Louisiana, 1915–1972* is the definitive work concerning the Civil Rights Movement in Louisiana. While his work focuses specifically on the political and social developments of the civil rights struggle in twentieth-century Louisiana, Fairclough gives a brief, and rather critical, overview of Roman Catholic developments regarding the race question. Concentrating on political figures and social activists, Kim Lacy Rogers in *Righteous Lives: Narratives of the New Orleans Civil Rights Movement* cites, in passing, Catholic individuals involved in racial affairs but does not write about them. *The Second Battle of New Orleans: The Hundred-Year Struggle to Integrate the Schools* by Liva Baker is a legal history that focuses on the roles black New Orleans lawyer Alexander P. Tureaud of the National Association for the Advancement of Colored People (NAACP) and Federal Circuit Judge Skelly Wright played in desegregating New Orleans schools.

Black, White, and Catholic is based on the minutes and reports of both the Catholic college students' interracial organization SERINCO and its adult counterpart, the CHR; the papers of the National Federation of Catholic College

Students and the Catholic Committee of the South also form the basis of this research. This work is also based on material from the archives of the New Orleans Province of the Society of Jesus, located in New Orleans, and the Society's international archives housed in Rome. Most of the material found in these archives has not been available to earlier researchers. The letters and reports contained in the Jesuit archives provide a window into the contrasting values found among these twentieth-century religious men who grappled with the issue of segregation. The archives of Loyola University, Ursuline College, St. Mary's Dominican College, Sacred Heart College, and Xavier University explain how and why religious men and women took the positions they did regarding segregation. The public papers of Joseph Francis Rummel, archbishop of New Orleans, provide the official stance of the Catholic Church in New Orleans regarding race relations; unfortunately his personal papers are not available to scholars at this time.

Historian Leslie Tentler, among others, laments the fact that American Catholic history lies on the margins of general United States history. She believes religious history has much to contribute to one's understanding of secular history and that a person's faith can be quite instrumental in determining his or her course of action in life, with ramifications for society at large. As the research and scholarship develops, church historians will be contributing to the movement of American Catholic history from the margins to the mainstream of American history.[20]

Black, White, and Catholic contributes to the trend of mainstreaming American Catholic history. The actions of individuals motivated by religious convictions are just as worthy of historical investigation as the actions of individuals motivated by social, political, economic, or philosophical principles. Racial attitudes and policies cannot be evaluated solely on the basis of socioeconomic or political criteria. There are other underlying attitudes and beliefs that contributed to a peoples' tolerance or intolerance of "the other" in their midst.

Writing about this period of American life, historian David Goldfield calls 1945–1954 "a season of hope," and so it was in the South. The Supreme Court decision of *Smith* v. *Allwright* in 1944 held out the promise of opening the ballot box to blacks.[21] Southern progressives occupied key political offices from the statehouse to Congress. President Harry S. Truman's support for civil rights legislation and his decision to end segregation in the armed forces and discrimination in federal employment in 1948 signaled a shift in federal support for civil rights. The NAACP's legal assault on segregated education resulted in the 1954 *Brown* decision. Segregationists had not yet organized their counterassault on *Brown*. White backlash was still a few years away, so there was hope that permanent and long-lasting change could come without violence or recrimination. It was within this "season of hope" that southern Catholics acted.

New Orleans, the Land of Creoles and Catholics

TWENTIETH-CENTURY RACE RELATIONS in Catholic New Orleans can only be understood in terms of the mixing of the people and cultures of Europe, Africa, and America. First France, then Spain, and finally the United States and its citizens settled the lower Mississippi Valley, producing a people and culture unique in North America. For almost one hundred years, from the founding of the city in the early eighteenth century until the early nineteenth century, before English began to dominate the linguistic landscape, the French language was spoken both at home and in public. The people are of European and African descent, with Euro-Africans known as Creoles of color, many of whom were free people of color during the era of slavery.[1] Common and canon law as well as the Napoleonic Code inform Louisiana jurisprudence.

New Orleans is a Catholic city in the predominately Protestant southern United States. Prior to the Civil War and the great influx of Catholic immigrants to northern urban centers in the latter part of the nineteenth century, the Roman Catholic Church in the United States was a predominately southern institution. New Orleans, Mobile, Baltimore, Bardstown (Kentucky), St. Louis, Charleston, and Savannah all had significant Catholic populations, Baltimore and New Orleans being the largest. Only four years separate the establishment of the first diocese in the newly formed United States of America in Baltimore in 1789 and the establishment of the diocese of New Orleans in the French-settled territory of Louisiana in 1793. Some fifteen years later, in 1808, the dioceses of Bardstown, Boston, Philadelphia, and New York were all established. Charleston (1820), St. Louis (1826), and Mobile (1829) followed the eastern sees. In antebellum America, the vast majority of Catholics lived south of the Mason-Dixon line.[2]

As a largely southern denomination, American Roman Catholics were forced to confront the issue of race, first in the form of slavery and later in the development of segregation. The church accepted both practices with little protest. During the antebellum period, the church did not involve itself in the politics of the day, especially regarding the question of slavery. As a minority in a predominantly Anglo-Saxon Protestant culture, Catholics wanted to be accepted by the majority population. In the North and the South, Catholics adopted different strategies for survival, but, for differing reasons, a majority of Roman Catholics in both regions accepted slavery.[3]

Southern Catholics endorsed the "peculiar institution" as a way of demonstrating their loyalty to the region and its white population. Given that Catholics were taught to obey civil law and respect public officials, southern Catholics did not challenge the social mores of the region. The spirit of conformity also led southern Catholics to reject abolitionist positions. For the most part, southern Catholics accepted the institution of slavery; members of both the laity and the clergy owned slaves. Northern Catholics accepted slavery but for different reasons. As recent arrivals to the United States, European Catholics were readily welcomed into the Democratic Party, which favored slavery. Fear of black labor also influenced Northern Catholic opinion, especially among Irish Catholic workers. Freeing the slaves would result, many of them believed, in an influx of freed black laborers, creating unwanted competition. Catholic strength in the Democratic Party and the attendant political victories gave rise to a nativist and anti-Catholic movement, the Know-Nothings. Because of their proslavery sentiments, Northern Catholics were placed on the defensive by both the abolitionists and the Know-Nothings. For most Catholics the abolitionist movement was too radical and its ideas too threatening to the social order to be adopted regardless of one's attitude toward slavery.[4]

Unlike Protestant denominations such as the Baptists, Presbyterians, and Methodists, Roman Catholics in the United States did not suffer a sectional division over the slavery question. Because Catholics did not consider slavery to be intrinsically evil (e.g., not a matter that would threaten one's immortal soul), it could be tolerated and even accepted.[5] Black priest and historian Cyprian Davis notes that most white Catholics' acceptance of slavery was as much a result of racial prejudice as it was a reaction to abolition.[6] Regardless of their station in life, blacks were considered socially inferior by most white Catholics. This belief influenced white Catholics' attitudes in the postbellum period when racial segregation eventually became the law of the land.[7]

As secular society moved to segregate blacks in the decades after the Civil War, so did the Roman Catholic Church. Whereas the bishops of New Orleans, Charleston, Natchez, Baltimore, Bardstown, and Savannah were among the few prelates concerned with the spiritual care of blacks in the antebellum period, all the bishops of the United States became involved with the plight of the freedmen in the postwar period. In 1866 and again in 1884, the United States bishops took up the issue of black evangelization.

At the Second Plenary Council of the Roman Catholic Church in the United States, held in Baltimore in 1866, American Catholic bishops discussed the needs of black Americans. Because of a lack of priests, religious brothers, and religious sisters in the United States, the bishops called on European missionaries to come to America to work among the "Negroes." The bishops also went on record endorsing the establishment of a men's religious order to work with blacks, and they wanted a religious community of sisters to do likewise. Further, the prelates called upon existing religious orders to undertake the education of black children. The bishops did not mandate any policy concerning the establishment of separate parishes for blacks and whites; rather, they left decisions to the local ordinary. Their counsel was practical: bishops should establish separate parishes if the conditions so warranted and not if they did not.[8]

At the Third Plenary Council of Baltimore, in 1884, the bishops again took up the race question. Given the neglect and discrimination that many black Catholics were experiencing in predominantly white churches, the bishops strongly recommended the establishment of separate facilities for the two racial groups. The prelates hoped that by establishing separate churches, schools, and orphanages, black Catholics would have a more positive experience of the faith and that black parishes, in particular, would gain converts. The prelates called upon American priests to minister to black Catholics, and mandated an annual collection for the "Indian and Negro Missions."[9]

The issue of education was also discussed at the 1884 meeting. The bishops were concerned that the secular and Protestant influences found in U.S. public education were corrupting the morals and religious practices of the faithful. In order to counter this "American" influence and to perpetuate the faith, the bishops decreed that every parish should build a parochial school, and that parents should send their children to these Catholic educational institutions rather than public ones. The establishment of parochial schools would hasten the separation of the races.[10]

From 1718 through the 1890s, New Orleans parish churches were racially integrated. Throughout this period blacks (slaves and free blacks) and whites, though segregated in seating, all worshiped together. The fact that all races were under one roof reflected the concept of a catholic (i.e., universal) community. However, among Catholic institutions, only the churches were integrated; Catholic hospitals, homes for the aged, social and spiritual organizations, and schools were by law, tradition, and custom segregated. The development of segregated parishes, beginning in the mid-1890s, was the result of testing and experimentation by Archbishop Francis A. Janssens, not a deliberate policy decision on his part.[11]

In 1888 Francis A. Janssens became the fifth archbishop of New Orleans. Born and reared in the Netherlands in a devout Catholic family, he entered the minor seminary at the age of twelve to begin his studies for the priesthood. A speech he heard concerning the needs of the church in America given by John McGill, third bishop of Richmond, Virginia, convinced the young Janssens that, after ordination, he should go to the United States as a missionary. He was ordained in 1867 and arrived in Richmond in 1868. His ecclesiastical career took him from Virginia to Natchez, Mississippi, where he served as the fourth bishop of that diocese (1881–1888), and finally to New Orleans.[12]

While serving in Natchez, Janssens wrote "The Negro Problem and the Catholic Church" for the March 1887 issue of *Catholic World,* in which he advocated the ordination of black men to the priesthood. Janssens believed that black clerics should bring the Word of God to fellow blacks, and he believed, unlike many others, that black Catholic males were morally and spiritually capable of becoming priests and living a sanctified life. He cited the success of the church in Japan, Africa, and China in producing native clergy as one reason for advocating the development of a black clergy in the United States. His conviction that black Catholics wanted to conduct their own affairs influenced his policy decisions in New Orleans. As archbishop of New Orleans, Janssens was able to send two black youths to the Society of St. Joseph of the Sacred Heart (Josephites) in Baltimore to be trained for the priesthood.[13]

While the need to convert blacks to the Roman Catholic faith was not as pressing in New Orleans as it was elsewhere, the challenge facing the new archbishop was to prevent the desertion of black Catholics to the more welcoming black Protestant denominations. Within a year of taking office, the archbishop discussed with his advisors the idea of establishing separate racial parishes in order to stem what he perceived as the tide of the black Catholic exodus. Archbishop Janssens justified his experiment in establishing a separate parish on the basis of a decline in the number of black Catholics in the archdiocese; however, statistics that might support the archbishop's assertion of black Catholic desertion are difficult to interpret. The accuracy of the numbers is certainly in question, and the claim that black Catholics were leaving the church in large numbers prior to 1895 is subject to further evaluation.[14]

Janssens's suggestion that separate parishes be established for black Catholics was not new in late nineteenth-century America, as the archdiocese of Baltimore and the dioceses of Charleston and Savannah had already done so.[15] His intention in establishing separate parishes was a pragmatic one; Janssens wanted to give blacks a greater degree of autonomy in church life, a greater sense of inclusion within the church. The situation, he believed, called for experimentation; his was not a calculated policy of segregation. His proposal to establish black parishes, moreover, was rejected by his advisers. He wrote, "Among the priests I stand almost alone in desiring separate churches for them; and yet the more I consider the question, the more I feel the necessity of it in order to keep the *growing up generation* in the church."[16]

In his 1892 report to the Bishops' Commission for Catholic Missions among Colored People and Indians, Janssens expressed his fears about black Catholic defections and advocated the establishment of separate parishes.[17] "Separate churches would, I believe, prevent the evil [of the black Catholic exodus]." He noted that New Orleans black Catholics, "creole Catholics as they are called, are in language, manners, and ways of thinking quite different from the colored people elsewhere." They did not favor separation, he continued, because they imagined "that we wish to draw the line of white and colored upon them."[18] Given the passage of legislation mandating the separation of the races on railroad cars in 1890, Catholics opposed to segregation of the churches had reason to be troubled by Janssens's proposal. In 1894, Janssens again reported to the Commission for Catholic Missions among Colored People and Indians disapproval of his idea of establishing separate parishes. "Our colored Catholics who speak French," he wrote, "do not want a church for themselves. They imagine that I want to separate the races and widen the gap which exists between the white and colored population."[19] He also noted that members of the clergy continued to oppose the idea as well. It appeared that one of the reasons the clerics opposed removing black Catholics from their congregations was financial. Black Catholics were reliable benefactors of their respective parishes, and pastors did not want that monetary support diverted.[20]

Janssens pressed ahead anyway. The financial and personnel constraints that had prevented him from experimenting with the establishment of a black parish were overcome with the assistance of the Sisters of the Blessed Sacrament for Indians and Colored People (S.B.S.), a religious order of women founded by a wealthy Philadelphia heiress, Catherine Mary Drexel.[21] Drexel, who chose the name of Katharine upon entering religious life, established the S.B.S. for the sole purpose of evangelizing native and black Americans. The sisters, who did not minister to whites or in integrated parishes, provided a solution to the difficulties facing the archbishop of New Orleans with regard to both money and personnel, but their work added to the complexity of the racial situation in the diocese. Janssens also located a religious order of men willing to staff a black parish, the Vincentian Fathers. With the sisters' money and the priests' manpower, Janssens moved forward. Well-intentioned as it was, however, the establishment of a separate parish for blacks reinforced the segregationist mentality of the white population of New Orleans.[22]

In 1895 Archbishop Janssens dedicated a newly renovated church in the English-speaking section of downtown New Orleans, renamed St. Katherine's as a "national" church for blacks.[23] For black Catholics in New Orleans, the national church would provide a refuge from the discrimination and insults experienced by the faithful attending predominately white parishes. Black Catholics were not forced to go to St. Katherine's; they had the option of either attending services there or at their parish churches. The Catholic, French-speaking Creoles of color, descendants of free people of color, opposed the establishment of a national church for blacks, which they viewed as reinforcing the development of a segregated secular society. The *Comité des Citoyens,* a protest group made up of Creoles of color, informed Janssens that, as far as they were concerned, his idea of separate parishes was a violation of Catholic principles. They argued that instead of ameliorating conditions for black Catholics within the existing parish structures, he was sanctioning discrimination.[24]

Janssens could not be dissuaded now that he had the money and manpower to carry out the experiment, black Catholic protests notwithstanding. In his 1895 report to the Commission for Catholic Missions, he explained:

> Whilst here and there we are hampered by the prejudices of the white people; in the city we are hampered by a small portion of the colored people, most of them light mulattoes and politicians, who abuse me in public print for attempting to begin a new church for the colored people. These persons aim at a greater equality with the whites, politically and socially, and also in the churches, and they pretend that I wish to accentuate still more the separation between the churches.[25]

At the dedication ceremony for St. Katherine's, Janssens told the assembled crowd of black Catholics that "he was glad that the colored people had a church of their own, where they could come and take any seat in the house that they chose; where they could have a choir of their own, composed of their own people; where altar boys and acolytes could be of their own color; in fact a church for colored people." He explained that "the church was not built to exclude the colored people from other churches, but on the contrary, they were just as welcome to come to worship in the other churches as they have always been."[26]

After St. Katherine's Church opened, further efforts to develop black parishes came to a halt when Archbishop Janssens died in 1897. His successor, Louis P. Chapelle (1897–1905), was too involved with international affairs to spend as much time on local matters. Appointed apostolic delegate to Puerto Rico, Cuba, and the Philippines in the aftermath of the Spanish-American War, Chapelle spent a great deal of time overseas. It would be Chapelle's successor who would transform Janssens's experiment into a permanent reality.[27]

Separate parishes for black and white Catholics were firmly established in New Orleans under James H. Blenk, S.M., archbishop from 1906 to 1918. Born into a Protestant Bavarian family, Blenk and his family moved to New Orleans when he was a child. He converted to Roman Catholicism at the age of thirteen and eventually joined the Society of Mary (Marists). After studying for the priesthood in France and Ireland, he was ordained in 1886. Upon his return to the United States, Blenk served as a pastor, educator, and bishop of Puerto Rico before being chosen as the seventh archbishop of New Orleans in 1906.[28]

Moving to implement the educational directives of the Third Plenary Council (1884), Blenk systematized the Catholic school system in New Orleans. He unified and standardized the Catholic educational board and insisted upon establishing parochial schools in each parish. The establishment of parish schools coupled with a directive from Rome prohibiting the development of additional national parishes (which, from the beginning, were experimental and viewed as exclusionary and contrary to the universal nature of the church) resulted in a change of the status of separate churches. No longer designated "national" parishes, black churches became "territorial" parishes, which meant that blacks should attend services at these designated churches. Changing the designation of the black parishes did not change the fact that these churches were established to segregate. By the time Blenk became archbishop and these changes came into effect, opposition to the establishment of segregated parishes had faded. The outspoken and militant black Catholics were aging or had died, and the change in the political landscape had also taken its toll on black protest, as blacks had lost their political voice. The archbishop recognized that to keep black Catholics in the church, he would have to provide educational opportunities for their children, and blacks realized that if they wanted their children to go to parochial school, they would have to accept separate parish churches. Several new segregated parishes were established during Blenk's episcopacy.[29]

The success of black parishes was due to the availability of money and labor. By the time Archbishop Blenk took office, the Society of St. Joseph of the Sacred Heart had been established. This order of priests ministered exclusively to blacks and black Catholics and was invited to labor in New Orleans in the "Negro apostolate." The Holy Ghost Fathers, another religious order of men dedicated to working in the Negro apostolate, were also invited to the archdiocese. Religious women were also serving the black community. The Sisters of the Blessed Sacrament and the Sisters of the Holy Family, composed of women of color, labored as educators in the black apostolate.[30]

Archbishop Blenk laid a solid foundation for meeting the educational needs of all Catholic New Orleanians, and the Catholic Church, not the state, would provide quality education to blacks in Louisiana. The institutions founded during his tenure meant that black and white faithful could receive an education from the elementary level through college and professional training. Blenk's successors John W. Shaw and Joseph Francis Rummel built on that success.[31]

As archbishop from 1935 to 1964, Rummel inevitably played a role in the story of New Orleans Catholic interracialism. Born in Germany in 1876, Rummel emigrated to New York as a young boy. Ordained a priest for the archdiocese of New York in 1902, he served in Harlem before becoming the bishop of Omaha, Nebraska, in 1928. In 1935, Rummel was appointed the ninth archbishop of New Orleans, and he discovered that the Catholics there were not like the immigrant Catholic communities he had known in the Northeast and Midwest.[32] The Catholic Church in Louisiana was well established long before the American Revolution. Its faithful spoke English as their first language, were educated, held good jobs, and were a major element in the political, economic, and cultural leadership of the city. The racial norms of the region, however, mandated by law and practiced as social custom, were new to Rummel. As unpalatable as racial segregation might be, the new archbishop did not challenge or change the practice in the archdiocese until after the Second World War.

When Rummel finally did address the race question in the 1950s, white southern Catholics were taken aback because they did not believe that segregation violated the religious and moral code of the faith. Religious teachings had not focused on this issue. Among Catholics of the post–World War II period there was a clear understanding of good and bad, of the difference between right and wrong, and a strong sense of sin. One's ethical and moral development, the formation of conscience, was based on an understanding of and adherence to the Ten Commandments, the laws of the church, and faith-based cultural values. One did not lie, cheat, or steal. One did not kill. One did not commit adultery or covet another person's spouse or possessions. There was a sense of honor, integrity, decency, and propriety. There was also a sense of shame and guilt, which pervaded society and social behavior. Every act had a consequence, and each individual was held responsible and accountable for his or her actions. Many hungered for spiritual perfection, with particular value attached to the religious life of a priest, nun, or brother.[33]

For many, black or white, being a good Roman Catholic in post–World War II America consisted of observance of Holy Days and Sunday, scrupulous adherence to the dietary laws of the church, and maintenance of one's sexual purity. To miss Sunday Mass or a Holy Day of obligation was to commit a mortal sin. With exceptions only for the most serious reasons, a practicing Catholic was expected to attend services every Sunday and on all prescribed Holy Days of the church calendar. Catholics were forbidden to eat meat or meat products on Fridays under pain of mortal sin. A young man or woman was expected to remain sexually pure until marriage, and any sexual activity outside of marriage was considered a serious matter for confession. Catholics were also expected to marry within the faith and raise their children according to the customs, teachings, and traditions of the church.[34]

Most Catholics of the day participated in one or more religious devotional practices, such as reciting the rosary, participating in "Forty Hours" of adoration, and attending a novena to Our Lady of Perpetual Help. Devotion to the Blessed Virgin, to the saints, and to the Eucharist informed one's understanding of the faith. This emphasis focused one on individual spiritual development and individual sin, not necessarily communal (or "corporate") sin.[35]

Despite their devotional practices and adherence to disciplinarian norms, New Orleans Catholics were challenged in the official archdiocesan newspaper *Catholic Action of the South* to live their lives based on religious principles. In the weekly column "Keeping the Record Straight," the editorial writer argued that one could not separate religious faith and life. "Religion is not merely reciting a set of prayers, or visiting the church once a week, or attending some function," stated the writer. "It requires the putting into practice, day by day, and all the time the teachings of Christ and following the Christian philosophy of life." Whether in political, economical, or social affairs, the editorial declared, denying the "applicability of Christ's teachings to all phases of life is renunciation of Christianity."[36]

This is not to say that Catholics were unaware of the social issues of their day. The church had spoken to socioeconomic and political issues beginning in the late nineteenth century. Lay Catholic social movements of the first half of the twentieth century were based in part on the authoritative pronouncements of the papacy, such as Pope Leo XIII's encyclical *Rerum novarum* in 1891, Pope Pius XI's encyclical *Quadragesimo anno* in 1931, and many of Pope Pius XII's addresses. These pronouncements concerned labor issues, family life, and social justice, not the race question.

Given the legal reinforcement of segregationist practices in Louisiana and the establishment of segregated parishes in the archdiocese of New Orleans, however, most Catholics in the 1940s and 1950s might well have assumed that the social separation of the races was part of the natural order. Both the secular and spiritual worlds sanctioned racial segregation, and few, certainly not most white Catholics, thought anything was wrong. How could one imagine that the separation of churches for black and white Catholics, decreed by the bishops of New Orleans themselves, was sinful?[37]

New Orleans Catholics expressed prejudiced views of blacks through social activities, especially minstrel shows in the 1940s and 1950s. In these comic variety shows, white actors wore blackface as they sang songs and told jokes to a white audience. Especially under church auspices, this form of entertainment not only confirmed stereotypes of African Americans as childlike and inferior, but also gave white Catholics permission to ridicule blacks. Minstrel shows were regularly announced in the archdiocesan newspaper.[38]

Segregation among Catholics had other ramifications. Black Catholics were denied access to Catholic health care. The two Catholic hospitals in the city of New Orleans, Hotel-Dieu and Mercy Hospital, were for whites only. While a black Catholic could not receive medical attention at either institution nor benefit from the spiritual services offered therein, even if critically ill, a white Protestant was always welcome.[39] Catholicism therefore mirrored the segregation practices of the city and state.

Twentieth-century Catholic New Orleanians differed little from either their coreligionists in other parts of the country or their Protestant brethren regarding racial attitudes. The racial structures developed from the time of slavery through Reconstruction and the implementation of Jim Crow society reinforced an attitude of white supremacy. This was the given social order, which appeared to many foreordained. The results of a survey of Mater Dolorosa parish in New Orleans concerning race and Catholic education conducted in the late 1940s by Jesuit sociologist Joseph Fichter was indicative of this outlook. Only one-quarter of the white parents questioned would allow their children to attend an integrated grammar school, and almost 90 percent of those surveyed wanted to maintain separate parishes for blacks and whites.[40] The results from this southern parish were not an anomaly, given the general reaction to Catholic interracial groups in the 1940s and 1950s and, specifically, the rise of a prosegregation Catholic organization in New Orleans in 1956.

Given the history and development of race relations in New Orleans and southern Catholic Louisiana, the call to end racial segregation in the post–World War II church was perceived as a radical disruption of the natural order. The secular and spiritual worlds would be rent asunder, it was assumed, if the racial divide was disturbed. Separate churches, separate schools, separate spheres for socializing—separate worlds—such was the reality of Catholic New Orleans, and the rest of the South, in the mid-twentieth century. Separation had not always been the norm, but once it was in place, most people believed it to have been. The Catholic Church of New Orleans followed the example of secular society in establishing racial segregation in the archdiocese. Because the church promoted and sanctioned such an arrangement, many of the laity would be shocked and surprised when the leader of their church called for it to end, and attempts by lay Catholics to end segregation in the post–World War II period through interracial efforts were just as provocative.

CHAPTER I

The Genesis of Southern Catholic Interracialism, 1917–1947

IN TWENTIETH-CENTURY AMERICA, war, poverty, and idealism gave rise to Catholic interracialism—organized interaction and cooperation between black and white Catholics to promote racial harmony and advance racial justice. Catholic interracialists did not engage in mass protests or acts of civil disobedience to challenge racial segregation; rather they attempted to convert the hearts and minds of their coreligionists to bring about change. Though often criticized for this nonconfrontational approach, Catholic interracial activism did effect some immediate change as well as lay the foundation for further advancements in Catholic civil rights.

While the First World War and the Great Depression were the immediate causes for the development of the interracial movement, belief in human solidarity was the underlying principle. The roots of Catholic interracialism are found in black Catholic protest and grew out of the Catholic conviction that all people, as members of the human race, were due respect as children of God. Furthermore, the practice of racial segregation was eventually seen to be incongruent with the unifying message of Christianity.

THOMAS WYATT TURNER, JOHN LAFARGE, S.J., AND THE FEDERATED COLORED CATHOLICS

The first Catholic Interracial Council evolved from black Catholic protest during World War I. At that time, black Catholic soldiers received little social support and attention compared with white Catholic servicemen, who were cared for by the Knights of Columbus, a Catholic social and benevolent fraternity, under the auspices of the American bishops' National Catholic War Conference (NCWC). A delegation of six black Catholic laymen, headed by Howard University professor Thomas Wyatt Turner, meet with Cardinal James Gibbons of Baltimore to discuss the situation. Gibbons recommended they voice their concerns to the NCWC, which they did, and soon thereafter, black Catholic servicemen began receiving assistance. Black protest brought about change for black Catholics involved in the war, and that experience lead to the creation of a black Catholic protest movement.[1]

Thomas W. Turner, leader of the black Catholic protest movement, was born in 1877 in southern Maryland. Reared a Catholic, Turner graduated with a degree in biology in 1901 from Howard University. He began graduate studies in the natural sciences at the then-desegregated Catholic University of America, and then he taught in Alabama, Missouri, and Maryland before returning to Howard in 1913 to teach biology. Turner earned his doctorate in biology from Cornell University in 1921 and joined the faculty of Hampton Institute in Virginia three years later.[2] His interest in and devotion to his church led him to protest racial segregation. Based on his experience protesting the treatment of black Catholic soldiers during World War I, Turner and his coreligionists established the Committee for the Advancement of Colored Catholics in 1916, changing the name to Federated Colored Catholics (FCC) in 1924. The organization's purpose was to promote unity among black Catholics, to advance black Catholic interests within the church, and to involve black Catholics in the promotion of racial justice. Members of the FCC elected Thomas Turner its first president in 1924.[3]

From 1916 to 1932, these black Catholics ran their own organization. Led by blacks for blacks, the FCC regularly called upon the church hierarchy to address their needs and concerns, focusing on Catholic education, Catholic organizations, the priesthood, and race relations within the church. The lack of Catholic educational opportunities for black children was appalling, and members felt their children were being treated as though they were not Catholics and "not expected to share in the Church's blessings." The Catholic University of America, where Turner had briefly pursued graduate studies, no longer admitted blacks, thus denying black Catholics access to what was supposed to be America's premier Catholic institution of higher learning. Church organizations, such as the Knights of the Columbus, discriminated against blacks, and desegregating the priesthood remained problematic. Faced with discriminatory practices within the church, FCC members argued that racial intolerance was unjust and had to be ended.[4]

The FCC expressed displeasure with the state of Catholic race relations through resolutions passed at their annual gatherings as well as through letters to the United States bishops and clergy. On a regular basis, members called for Catholic education for black children, admission of blacks to Catholic University, representation and participation in Catholic organizations, and more black priests. The FCC was not the only organization concerned with race matters in post–World War I America as the National Association for the Advancement of Colored People (founded in 1909), the National Urban League (1911) and the

Commission on Interracial Cooperation (1919) also sought to improve the status of black Americans.[5] Until 1932 the FCC was a protest movement for black Catholics; after 1932, however, the federation became an altogether different organization.

In the early 1930s there was a clash of visions between the president of the FCC and its national chaplain. As an original founder and first president of the FCC, Thomas Turner wanted the federation to remain a black-only organization to agitate for reform. The national chaplain, John LaFarge,[6] a member of the Maryland Province of the Society of Jesus, and another Jesuit involved in Catholic racial affairs, William Markoe[7] of the Missouri Province, both white, wanted to see the FCC evolve into an interracial body, but for different reasons. For Markoe the FCC was a Jim Crow organization encouraging separatism and segregation. He argued that the federation should change to promote a universal and therefore Catholic perspective. LaFarge also wanted the focus of the group to be interracial with an educational emphasis because he believed that prejudice was the result of ignorance; if people were educated in the proper thinking regarding race matters, he believed, prejudice would disappear from the church and its members. In the meantime, he opposed the concept of black-only protest movements. These clashing perspectives would transform the nature of protest within the Catholic Church as it dealt with the race question.[8]

Even though Markoe's entire religious career had been with blacks and he served in an all-black parish, he did not support separate structures, an attitude he brought to the FCC. At the federation's 1929 convention, he advocated changing the composition and direction of the organization from an all-black organization to an interracial body that would promote integration. In an effort to influence and reshape the federation, Markoe offered his parish's newspaper, the *St. Elizabeth's Chronicle,* renamed simply the *Chronicle,* as the quasi-official publication of the federation with himself as editor. It was from that platform that he could advocate Catholic interracialism.[9]

At the 1930 FCC convention in Detroit, the constitution of the organization was changed. Now the federation was to become a form of Catholic Action (i.e., Catholic laity working in union with the bishop to promote faith and build up the church),[10] thus broadening its work to include such areas as Catholic education, the liturgical movement, young people's welfare, and the interracial movement. Agitation and protest by blacks for black causes would give way to analysis, discussion, and education, and lay leadership would be replaced by clerical oversight and control. The black lay Catholic organization Turner and others had founded would disappear in all but name.[11]

Two years later, in the fall of 1932, LaFarge orchestrated Turner's ouster as president of the FCC based on charges of "unwarranted assumption of power," "false publicity," and "imprudence." A split in the organization resulted: Turner supporters wanted the federation to remain a black-dominated body run by black laity, while LaFarge supporters wanted to transform it into an interracial organization. The latter evolved into a short-lived biracial body, the National Catholic Interracial Federation, which gave way to yet another interracial organization, the Northeastern Clergy Conference on Negro Welfare, founded in 1933, and finally in 1934 to the Catholic Interracial Council of New York (CICNY). This northern-based organization would influence all future Catholic interracial bodies in the United States, including those in the South.[12]

CICNY, CCS, CHR, NFCCS, AND SERINCO

The purpose of the CICNY was "to promote in every practicable way, relations between the races based on Christian principles, by creating a better understanding in the public as to the situation, needs and progress of the Negro group in America through the establishment of social justice and through the practice of mutual cooperation." The CICNY and LaFarge's vision of the Catholic response to racial discrimination would hold sway for more than three decades in the United States. Through dialogue, discussion, and interaction, black and white Catholics would resolve the race problem within the church, he believed, and through Catholic efforts they would advance the cause of interracial harmony in American society.[13]

As Martin Zielinski has noted, the major activities of the CICNY were publicity and education as means of reaching out to American Catholics regarding the race question. The *Interracial Review,* the name Markoe had given the *Chronicle* in 1930, became the official organ of Catholic interracialism. LaFarge and the CICNY now had a public platform from which to foster racial harmony and to educate Catholics on racial matters. Throughout its history, the CICNY addressed a variety of race issues such as the Scottsboro trial, antilynching legislation, the Fair Employment Practices Committee, blacks and the Communist threat, racism, and urban race riots. Even with the establishment of other interracial councils in cities such as Chicago, St. Louis, Detroit, Washington, and Philadelphia, John LaFarge, with the assistance of executive secretary George Hunton, dominated Catholic interracial activities until his death in 1963.[14]

Five years after the establishment of the CICNY, another Catholic organization was founded that also addressed the race question in America. This time, however, it was Catholics of the South, rather than the North, who established an interracial body. The genesis of the Catholic Committee of the South (CCS), originally called the Catholic Conference of the South, came from the impoverished conditions of the region itself. Reporting on the South in 1938, President Franklin Roosevelt identified the area as "economic problem number one." Based on their own knowledge of the region's problems and in response to the president's challenge, southern Catholics believed that they could assist in reforming the South by applying Catholic social teachings to its problems. At the second National Social Action Congress, held in Cleveland in 1939, Paul Williams, a young layman from Richmond, Virginia, coordinated two well-received forums regarding the South. The positive reaction in Cleveland convinced Williams and members of the southern clergy that a regional organization should be established. The result was the creation of the CCS, comprised of Catholics from the former states of the Confederacy under the sponsorship of the southern bishops. Williams served as the organization's first executive secretary, with Bishop Gerald O'Hara of the diocese of Savannah-Atlanta its first episcopal chairman.[15]

As stated at its first convention, the purpose of the CCS was to "bring the blessings of Catholic teaching, of Catholic tradition, and of Catholic culture to the solution of the South's economic, social and industrial problems."[16] The CCS concentrated on six major issues affecting the South: industrial relations, rural life, the lay apostolate, education, race relations, and youth, with individual CCS chapters determining the focus of their efforts according to the particular needs and circumstances of the area.[17]

Under the auspices of the CCS, the Commission on Human Rights (CHR) was founded in the archdiocese of New Orleans on 21 February 1949, when twenty-two New Orleans Catholics,[18] black and white, responded to the invitation of Dr. Vernon X. Miller, dean of the school of law at Loyola University of the South, to meet to discuss the race question.[19] The stated aim of the CHR was the "removal of prejudice, intolerance, segregation, jim-crowism and kindred evils from within the framework of *Catholic* life in New Orleans."[20] Like the Catholic Interracial Councils already in existence in the other parts of the country, the CHR was a lay Catholic organization made up of adult black and white Catholics, men and women, striving to end segregation within the church.

The driving force behind the CHR was its chaplain and founding member, Joseph H. Fichter, S.J., professor of sociology at Loyola University of the South, who had already played an instrumental role in establishing an interracial organization for Catholic college students the year before. Under Fichter's guidance and influence, the CHR was the only adult Catholic organization in the Deep South challenging racial segregation. With an annual membership of approximately one hundred individuals, the organization contested racial practices in the archdiocese of New Orleans on a regular basis. Its effectiveness, however, would be hampered by the intransigence of the white Catholic laity who did not want to see segregation dismantled. Catholic laity and clergy, unfortunately, were equally responsible for the persistence of racial intolerance and prejudice within the church.

Throughout the history of the organization, CHR members strove to put their faith and beliefs into practice. They did this through attending Sunday services as an integrated body, holding monthly meetings, publishing a monthly newsletter, organizing a speakers bureau, and protesting racial discrimination. Specifically, members advocated the following reforms within the church: elimination of segregated seating, signs, and notices in churches; removal of the "color bar" from Catholic universities, colleges, seminaries, academies, high schools, and elementary schools; admission to Catholic hospitals based on need rather than race; elimination of dual church organizations based on race and the complete integration of those organizations (e.g., Holy Name Society, Association of Council of Catholic Women, Association of Council of Catholic Men, and St. Vincent DePaul Society); and integration of all public displays of Catholic identity (e.g., religious processions, forums, and discussion groups). The CHR undertook all such efforts in recognition of the oneness of the human race through the Mystical Body of Christ.[21]

For CHR members, race relations were understood through the theological concept of the Mystical Body of Christ. This doctrine holds that members of the Catholic church comprise the visible body of the risen Christ here on earth while Christ, its head, reigns in heaven.[22] St. Paul told the people of Corinth, that "in one spirit we were we all baptized into one Body, whether Jew or Gentiles, whether slave or free."[23] In his letter to the Colossians, Paul wrote that Jesus the Christ is "the Head of the Body, the Church."[24] Separating out members of the church because of the color of their skin, southern Catholic interracialists held, was a violation of the Mystical Body; therefore, this broken body needed to be healed.

Most Catholic New Orleanians did not see the CHR and its interracial agenda as an attempt to repair the broken, or torn, Mystical Body; rather they accused the CHR of being dominated by "Northern whites" and faculty members from Xavier University, the only black Catholic institution of higher learning in the United States. If the charge that the commission was influenced or controlled by "outside agitators" could have been proven, CHR efforts to challenge racial segregation would have been dismissed. And if Xavier faculty had indeed controlled the organization, CHR detractors could have portrayed the body as representing black interests and not interracial ones. In reality, the CHR was a southern Catholic organization; 75 percent of its white members were southern-born. And while at that time several of the CHR administrative positions were filled by Xavier faculty members, one could hardly argue that the organization was controlled by Xavier.[25]

The first activity undertaken by the CHR was monthly attendance at Mass as an integrated group—a manifestation of members' belief that all are "one in the mystical body of Christ, regardless of race, color or national origin."[26] From the beginning, members envisioned attending church services at white and black parishes on an alternating basis as a sign of solidarity and witness to fellow Catholics; unfortunately, because of the negative reaction of white pastors and parishioners, CHR members were able to attend services at only two white parishes in the archdiocese. Reception at black parishes was always positive, and members were welcomed at convent chapels (i.e., chapels of religious women such as the Ursuline nuns and the Religious of the Sacred Heart), Xavier University, and the archdiocesan seminary. Following Mass members would have breakfast together followed by their monthly meeting.[27]

Because the group faced obstacles attending services at area parishes, members usually had Mass and breakfast at Xavier University or the diocesan seminary, both safe havens for interracial gatherings. Loyola University of the South, on the other hand, was not as welcoming. When CHR members asked Loyola University to host one of their first Mass and breakfast gatherings, they were turned down. The president of the university, Thomas Shields, S.J.,[28] explained that while he had no problem with the group attending Mass on an integrated basis, he did not believe it would be prudent for the group to eat together in the college cafeteria because "it would create an obstacle to better race relations." Given the negative reception he anticipated at Loyola, Shields justified his position by stating that "we have to adopt a course which will most expeditiously bring about the happy day when racial prejudice will be abolished."[29] Shields's rationale, however, is difficult to accept because the accompanying act of denying CHR permission to meet at Loyola appears to have endorsed racial segregation rather than opposing it.

In addition to the monthly Mass and breakfast, members gathered in the middle of the month for an evening meeting to hear guest speakers on American race relations. CHR members also produced a monthly newsletter called *Christian Impact,* furnished Catholic literature to those interested in the race question, supported local Catholic college students in their efforts to promote racial justice, and sponsored essay contests that focused on some aspect of Catholic race relations.[30]

Christian Impact, the official organ of the CHR, printed information regarding its activities as well as articles challenging the practice of racial segregation within the church and American society. The editorial board addressed such topics and issues as the Fair Employment Practices Commission, race riots, bigotry and desegregation.[31] Much like the Catholic college students' interracial newsletter, *Christian Conscience, Impact* argued that racial discrimination was contrary to Christian practices and beliefs and, therefore, should end. Together *Christian Impact* and *Christian Conscience* were the only Catholic publications in the archdiocese of New Orleans that advocated an end to racial discrimination; the archdiocesan newspaper, *Catholic Action of the South,* refrained from taking a stand on the issue until 1954, when state action threatened Catholic educational policy.

Initially the CHR was not a highly structured organization; it had neither a constitution nor bylaws. Lay Catholics were responsible for the success of the operation; while clergymen belonged to the organization, they did not control the commission. There were only two permanent offices, the moderator and the executive secretary, with rotating chairs for the five standing committees: the speakers bureau, the membership bureau, the program bureau, the finance bureau, and the bureau of information. Membership in the commission was restricted to adult Catholics because area Catholic college students had their own interracial commission. While restricting membership to Catholics precluded infiltration by "trouble-makers" or the uninformed, there were times when members disagreed on goals and objectives. The membership proscription limited the commission's effectiveness, restricting like-minded non-Catholics from contributing their time and talent to the organization.[32]

In an effort to present Catholic teaching concerning race relations to various church groups and clubs, the CHR established a speakers bureau. Through information and education, members hoped to break down the walls of ignorance and separation between the races. This was the ideal—in practice the speakers bureau was less than successful. Reflecting on the difficulties associated with their efforts, Patricia Ryan, executive secretary of the commission, would later explain to delegates attending the annual convention of the CCS that their major obstacle was "the general unwillingness on the part of so many white Catholics to hear what we have to say."[33] For over eight years most white Catholics in New Orleans would continue to refuse to listen, and eventually some of them would publicly dissent from church teachings regarding racial equality. During its existence, the commission achieved some of its objectives, but all too often it was frustrated in its attempts to end racial segregation and eliminate racial prejudice. Because of threats and intimidation, the CHR ceased to function by the fall of 1956.

No less controversial in New Orleans was the Southeastern Regional Interracial Commission (SERINCO) of the National Federation of Catholic College Students (NFCCS), which promoted interracial harmony and challenged the practice of racial segregation within the church. Established in 1948, SERINCO was one of the many interracial commissions sponsored by the NFCCS, itself founded in 1937 by New York–area Catholic institutions of higher learning. The genesis of the NFCCS was Pax Romana, the International Movement of Catholic Students, which sought American participation in its worldwide organization.[34]

In justifying the establishment of the NFCCS, student promoters argued that

Catholic college students needed to form their own organization; they "*simply do not count on the national level,* because they have no adequate national organization through which they can be effectively represented, through which they can speak, through which they can act."[35] The Protestants had the Christian Student Movement, they contended, and "the radicals use the 'American Student Union' setup in order to exert influence out of all proportion with their real strength," but the Catholics had nothing.[36] These Catholic students were aware of the social and political influence non-Catholic and "radical" students were exerting in society, and while the Catholic youth would not cooperate with either, they did not want to be left out. Once constituted, the NFCCS received ecclesiastical approval from the National Catholic Welfare Conference, which placed the student organization under the direction of the National Council of Catholic Youth. Within a year of its founding, the NFCCS had grown from eighteen member schools to thirty-eight. By 1947 there were 134 Catholic colleges in the federation.[37]

According to its constitution, the NFCCS was established for the purpose of developing Catholic student leaders. While in college and after, these individuals would be the vanguard for promoting church ideas, programs, and endeavors among the laity, as well as for training others to be leaders in the church community. Involvement in the federation would enable these student leaders to articulate Catholic opinion regarding issues of the day just as their non-Catholic counterparts did. In addition, a nationwide network of Catholic colleges would provide a mechanism whereby information and ideas regarding Catholic issues and concerns could be shared, explored, and developed.[38]

The governance of the federation was shared by a national congress, a national council, and national officers. The national council was empowered to charter councils and commissions, which would carry out the aims and objectives of the federation on a regional basis. According to the NFCCS constitution, regional intercollegiate associations were established "for study and action in relation to religious, cultural, social, political and economic problems, treated in light of Catholic teaching and from the viewpoint of student life."[39] Race relations was one such area of examination.

In cooperation with the CICNY, the NFCCS sponsored its first interracial symposium at Manhattanville College in December 1938. The CICNY had suggested that students institute an educational campaign in favor of interracial justice by publishing articles in college periodicals, by sponsoring lectures, forums, and debates on campus as well as by collecting and reading works by black writers. The council also encouraged students to support legislation that affected blacks, especially federal anti-lynching bills. In addition, students were asked to adopt the "Manhattanville Resolutions," which provided ways an individuals could improve race relations (e.g., acknowledging blacks as human beings entitled to the full measure of social justice, recognizing that they share membership in the Mystical Body of Christ, and engaging in some form of Catholic Action for the betterment of blacks, spiritually and materially).[40]

The result of this gathering was the decision to establish interracial council units at all federation campuses. Not until the 1944 annual meeting of the national council of the NFCCS at Loyola University of Chicago, however, did the collegians discuss establishing their own commission on interracial relations. Debate ensued over the propriety of undertaking such a commission. One delegate wondered if interracial work "was not too 'hot and heavy a question' for the NFCCS to get behind." The discussion revealed great hesitation about moving into this area. Without a clear statement of purpose and the types of activities to be sanctioned, approval would not be forthcoming from the national council. The delegates finally agreed to establish an interracial relations commission under the condition that it "would definitely be limited to the field of student activity and its purpose would be solely that of the study of Christian principles on this subject, the coordination of such study, and by practical application on the campus to break down prejudice in the schools among the students themselves." Catholic college students would not engage in "direct action" (e.g., demonstrations, protests, or acts of civil disobedience). Although the compromise allowed the commission to be formed, it limited the extent to which Catholic youth would act in the public sphere for several decades.[41]

At the Chicago gathering, delegates from the University of Detroit requested that their institution be awarded the chair of this newly established interracial commission, for "as far as the students of the University of Detroit were concerned they were 'sitting on a furnace'"—an obvious reference to the race riots of the previous summer, which required the dispatch of federal troops to restore order.[42] The Michigan students had been active in interracial relations and desired the national chairmanship, but despite their interest, the convention decided to award the national commission to Manhattanville College of New York. Delegates chose the New York institution because of its president, Mother Grace Cowardin Dammann, R.S.C.J., who was considered "one of the few people to be interested in this field." And with the chair located at Manhattanville College, the delegates argued, the interracial chairperson could call upon the assistance of the CICNY and the Reverend John LaFarge, S.J., its chaplain, when formulating policy and programs for the national federation.[43]

In New Orleans, the establishment of the Southeastern Regional Interracial Commission by a small but enthusiastic group of Catholic college students in the spring of 1948 had far-reaching effect. In talking and meeting to discuss the race question, students forced individuals and institutions to examine the race question and to state their respective positions. By broaching the issue, these collegians upset the status quo and incurred censorship and admonition. Attempts at suppression did not stop them or their faculty advisers from continuing to question the segregation practices of the 1940s and 1950s.

JOSEPH FICHTER, S.J., AND NEW ORLEANS CATHOLIC INTERRACIALISM

Joseph Henry Fichter, S.J., a member of the New Orleans Province of the Society of Jesus and a professor of sociology at Loyola University of the South, was directly responsible for the establishment of the Catholic college interracial commission in New Orleans. Armed with a newly earned doctorate from Harvard University, Fichter arrived at Loyola University in the fall of 1947 prepared to challenge the racial attitudes and practices of Catholic New Orleanians. He did not want the "Negro problem," sociologist Gunnar Myrdal's phrase for the quandary presented by segregation, to remain a problem for much longer.[44] Fichter wanted to desegregate Loyola University of the South and wanted to do so as quickly as possible. While his first attempt at change and reform within the Roman Catholic Church was not a complete success, he and those involved in the race question did effect change.[45]

There was nothing in Fichter's background to indicate that he would earn a doctorate from Harvard, publish over two hundred scholarly articles and three dozen books in his lifetime—let alone become a priest. Born into a working-class family in 1908, Joseph Fichter grew up in Union City, New Jersey. After two years of secondary education, he quit his studies and returned home to take a job in the building trades.[46] Eventually he became a brick layer, but there was a restlessness inside him, and as he used to tell his students, he decided to become a "builder of men rather than a builder of buildings."[47] In 1930, at the age of twenty-two, he entered religious life. Lacking the prerequisite training in classical languages, Fichter had been advised by authorities of the New York Province of the Society of Jesus to join the New Orleans Province because the presumption was that the academic standards in the South were less stringent.[48]

As a member of the New Orleans Province, Fichter spent the first four years of his new life in Grand Coteau, Louisiana, a small village in the southwestern section of the state. There he underwent spiritual and academic training in preparation for life as a Jesuit. At the conclusion of the first two years of spiritual testing and discernment, he took his first perpetual vows of poverty, chastity, and obedience, thus becoming a member of the Jesuit order. Afterwards he began a two-year juniorate stressing the liberal arts: classical and modern foreign languages, history, music, and English grammar and literature; the level of instruction was comparable to that found in the first two years of college.[49] In the fall of

1934 he began studying philosophy at St. Louis University, receiving a bachelor's degree the following year. After teaching at Spring Hill College in Mobile, Alabama, for two years, he returned to St. Louis to earn a master's degree in 1939. During his theological studies at St. Mary's College in St. Mary's, Kansas, he was ordained a priest in 1942.[50]

Fichter began his doctoral studies in sociology at Harvard University in 1945, where he studied under the noted sociologist Gordon Allport, and was awarded a Ph.D. in 1947.[51] His course work in Cambridge, especially the seminar "Group Prejudice and Conflict," prepared him for his work at Loyola. In this course students learned of the general theories involving group prejudice, the role of scapegoats (e.g., Jews and blacks) in American society, the factors influencing a child's acquisition of prejudice, and the significance of group prejudice. The graduate students also read Gunnar Myrdal's *An American Dilemma* and *Race Riot* by Alfred M. Lee and Norman D. Humphrey. Fichter would draw from this course and these readings when formulating his own ideas concerning race relations in New Orleans.[52]

In the fall of 1947 Fichter began his teaching career at Loyola University of the South. Already a prolific writer, he had published fifty articles and six books by the time he arrived in New Orleans. In those early years, his writing was biographical in nature with a focus on religious and social matters. Reflecting this interest, his first book, *Roots of Change* (1939), examined the role of fifteen individuals in the development of political, social, and economic thought in Western culture since the seventeenth century.[53] Each individual chosen, Fichter noted, harbored "the dream of contributing his little share in reshaping the mold [of society] somewhat closer to his own ideal." The book was for the person "who feels a divine dissatisfaction with things as they are; who is determined that his own life and striving must not go down the vortex of popular and hysterical movements; who believes that he can bend ever so slightly by his own efforts the onrush of a chaotic civilization."[54] Those who practiced racial segregation were about to encounter one who believed he could bend ever so slightly, if not totally reverse, its course.

Fichter's biography of Saint Cecil Cyprian (bishop of Carthage, martyred 258 C.E.) could, in retrospect, be viewed as partly autobiographical. "Above and beyond all else," Fichter wrote of the saint, "Cecil Cyprian was a man of practical action, with a clear view of affairs, an orderliness of ideas, an imperturbable coolness of decision. He could be reproached for having sometimes struck forcibly, never for having struck blindly."[55] The same could be said of Fichter regarding his outlook on race relations in the New Orleans Province of the Society of Jesus and the Roman Catholic Church in New Orleans. He had a clear view of the situation, he had an orderliness of ideas concerning what needed to be done, and he had a coolness regarding his decision-making process. Often Fichter would be reproached for having struck forcibly, but he never struck blindly.

Those Cyprianesque characteristics were manifest when Fichter formulated a policy for desegregating Loyola University of the South. While still a student at Harvard, Fichter outlined a plan of action for desegregating Loyola in a conversation he had with fellow Jesuit and dean of the College of Arts and Sciences, William Crandell. Fichter presented a proposal to the dean, which he believed to be sound and reasonable, the essence of simplicity and prudence, but in his overconfidence, he did not anticipate the responses his desegregation proposal would generate: some of his fellow Jesuits reacted with indifference, some even with hostility.[56]

According to Fichter's plan, Loyola would have been integrated over a period of eighteen months. As he explained to his mentor Gordon Allport, during the fall semester of 1947 students from Xavier University and Loyola University would meet to discuss race issues. The following semester these same students would register for a seminar on race relations similar to the one he had taken at Harvard; course credits would be granted by the student's home institution. "If the lid does not blow off, or the walls bulge out too dangerously, I do not see why I cannot run a mixed seminar on family problems during the summer session," he wrote Allport. The third phase of his desegregation plan called for the formal acceptance of black applicants to Loyola in the fall of 1948, thereby integrating the institution. Regarding these plans, Fichter acknowledged to his mentor, "prayer and the practice of virtue may be better tools than scientific knowledge."[57]

Had the university followed Fichter's plan, Loyola University would have been the first institution of higher learning, private or public, to desegregate in Louisiana.[58] The Jesuits would have anticipated by two years the federal court ruling ending the discriminatory admissions policy at Louisiana State University.[59] The impact of integrating a Jesuit-sponsored school in New Orleans would have been enormous; the Society of Jesus and its educational institutions there, Loyola University and Jesuit High School, exerted considerable influence throughout and beyond Catholic circles in the city.

Within months of beginning his university career in New Orleans, Fichter inquired about the admissions policies of Loyola's School of Law because he favored integrating the educational institutions beginning at the graduate level and working down to the primary grade schools.[60] When he asked Vernon Miller, dean of the law school, if Loyola could admit blacks, Fichter was told, "We can admit colored students to Loyola if we want to do it." Miller explained that the segregation laws in Louisiana were few in number and pertained "only to dwelling houses, street railways [streetcars], railroads trains and tent shows."[61] There was nothing except racial etiquette, custom, and tradition to keep Loyola from challenging the racial practices of the day.

Fichter underestimated the opposition his three-step plan to integrate Loyola would arouse and overestimated the support he could expect from the administration and faculty of the university.[62] Without prior consultation with the Loyola University administration, Fichter implemented step one of his plan and invited black Catholic students from Xavier University in the fall of 1947 to participate in a race relations seminar with white Catholic students of Loyola. However, William Crandell, dean of Loyola's college of arts and sciences, informed Fichter that credit could not be granted to the Xavier students attending the seminar and that he would have to discuss the issue with the president of the university, Thomas J. Shields, S.J., because it involved a matter of administrative policy.[63]

This matter was discussed at a Loyola University board of directors' meeting to determine what position or policy the institution should take.[64] Wanting "to avoid any prejudice against the negro [sic] race," board members, nevertheless, felt that Fichter was "moving entirely too fast in view of the conditions in the city." They advised that he "become more acquainted with the local feelings before attempting such a project as a university function." If these gatherings were to be a private affair where Fichter would preside, however, the board members believed "it might be tolerated."[65]

Only the first step of Fichter's three-phase plan for desegregation was implemented. The second phase, holding integrated classes with the Xavier and Loyola students, never came to pass. The integration of the undergraduate program at Loyola University of the South was still some fifteen years away. In the meantime, Fichter would have to improvise to meet his basic objective of getting black and white students together for academic and social interaction.

In response to the board's action, Fichter used the sociology club he advised as the basis for establishing an interracial commission at Loyola under the auspices of the NFCCS on 13 April 1948.[66] Subsequently the Loyola students invited the area Catholic colleges to do likewise.[67] Five days later, Loyola was chosen to chair the regional NFCCS Interracial Commission.[68] Because the charter institutions were from within the city, the organization was originally called the New Orleans Regional Interracial Commission, but the name was changed to the Louisiana Regional Interracial Commission with the addition of the all-white women's College of the Sacred Heart in Grand Coteau, Louisiana.[69] However, wanting to reflect a broader geographical territory within the region (by 1956 Jesuit-run Spring Hill College in Mobile, Alabama, was a member), NFCCS officials changed the name of the regional organization again from "Louisiana" to "Southeastern" in February 1950 when the interracial commission finally became known as the Southeastern Regional Interracial Commission.[70]

In their application for approval as a student organization, the Loyola founding members stated that the purpose of the organization was "to work for the removal of forced racial segregation." They argued that this particular organization was necessary because forced racial segregation was a social problem that could be overcome only by group action. For these college students, the race question was not only a social issue but also a religious one; they hoped this new organization would meet the needs of "those individuals who are sincerely interested in the interracial aspect of restoring all things in Christ."[71]

While SERINCO fell short of Fichter's integrationist plan, the interracial commission soon became a source of tension and irritation within and among the Catholic college communities. Promoting Christian unity, charity, and justice, the commission forced Catholic college students, faculty, and administrators to examine their own prejudices and biases. Members of SERINCO challenged authority, the status quo, and the social mores of their peers and elders.

CHAPTER II

Interracial Agitation:
Raising Awareness, 1948

THE ESTABLISHMENT OF a collegians' interracial commission in Catholic New Orleans occurred at a propitious time for dismantling racial segregation: democracy had triumphed over fascism in the Second World War, President Truman had established a committee on civil rights to report on race relations in the nation, veterans returning from the war with troubling questions about the structure of their own society had filled college classrooms, and in New Orleans the voters had just elected a reformer as mayor, DeLesseps S. "Chep" Morrison.

Under Morrison the people of the Crescent City anticipated a period of honest and effective government, and the new mayor strove to meet their expectations. Although he claimed to be "mayor of all the people," Morrison did not challenge the segregationist practices of his day, as such an act would have meant political suicide. Nevertheless, Chep Morrison's administration did integrate the New Orleans police force (albeit a token integration), undertake a new housing program for blacks, pave roads in black neighborhoods and keep their streets clean, and finance new recreational facilities for black youths as well as provide for a black municipal park and golf course.[1]

On the national level, the executive branch of the federal government took a principled stance regarding racial matters. In the wake of numerous incidents of racial violence in the post–World War II South, especially against black veterans, Harry S. Truman established the President's Committee on Civil Rights in December 1946 to examine the situation. In December of the following year, the committee submitted its report, *To Secure These Rights*. Based on the committee's finding, Truman sent a "Special Message" to Congress in February 1948 recommending the establishment of a permanent Commission on Civil Rights, a Joint Congressional Committee on Civil Rights, a Civil Rights Division in the Department of Justice, and a Fair Employment Practice Commission to prevent discrimination in employment. The president also recommended passage of legislation protecting voting rights, prohibiting discrimination in interstate transportation facilities, and prosecuting acts of lynching. Although there was no guarantee that these recommendations would translate into United States law, the possibility was there—this was a time of hope and progress.[2]

To Secure These Rights and the president's special message to Congress led southern conservative Democrats to organize in opposition. Unhappy with the positions their party was taking, especially regarding labor and civil rights, these disgruntled Democrats attempted to win control of their respective state political organizations to reverse what they saw as a dangerous liberal trend. Controlling their state parties and working within the national organization, southern Democrats hoped to block Truman's nomination and his civil rights initiatives or, failing that, to present an alternative Democratic candidate who would win enough states to force the presidential election into the House of Representatives.[3] This nearly happened in 1948.

After Minneapolis mayor Hubert H. Humphrey's challenge to his fellow delegates to "get out of the shadow of states' rights and walk forthrightly into the bright sunshine of human rights" led to the adoption of a strong civil rights plank at the 1948 Democratic National Convention, which the party nominee Truman endorsed, many southern Democrats bolted. Representatives from the former Confederate states convened in Birmingham, Alabama, to form the States' Rights Party, popularly known as the "Dixiecrats." On 17 July they selected Governor Strom Thurmond of South Carolina as their presidential nominee and Governor Fielding Wright of Mississippi as his running mate.[4] The first forces of resistance to racial equality were marshaling.

COLLEGE INTERRACIALISTS AND
ARCHBISHOP JOSEPH FRANCIS RUMMEL

Two days after the States' Rights convention, Joseph Francis Rummel, archbishop of New Orleans, attended a meeting of black and white Catholic college students, members of the Southeastern Regional Interracial Commission (SERINCO).[5] Although the archbishop's presence at this gathering publicly demonstrated his openness to interracial activities, Rummel did not favor an immediate end to Jim Crow society. At this July gathering the college students presented a resolution encouraging the archbishop to take a more dramatic step toward eliminating segregation within the church by integrating the Catholic school system. They also called upon the archbishop to endorse integration in Catholic graduate schools. To the president of Loyola University of the South, Thomas J. Shields, S.J., this meeting, held in his office, was an affront to the archbishop, the church, the Jesuits, and the university.[6] The meeting also cast suspicion on the role of the interracial commission chaplain, Joseph Fichter, S.J., whom the president blamed for stirring up the students.

The next day, President Shields drafted a memorandum to his religious superior the provincial of the New Orleans Province of the Society of Jesus, Harry L. Crane,[7] that recounted the meeting. According to that memo, the focus of the gathering was the reading of a SERINCO resolution that called for an end to the practice of racial discrimination in the archdiocese.[8]

Invited to respond after the resolution was read, the archbishop began by justifying the practice of racial segregation in terms of principles and practices. While the church upholds and maintains Christian principles, he explained, the church also adapts to "people, times and conditions." For Rummel, the acceptance of the practice of racial segregation in the South was one such situation. This tradition, "deeply ingrained in the people," he argued, had to be "respected" and could not "be overturned in a moment."[9]

Rummel gave three possible approaches to ending racial segregation in the church: to terminate it by proclamation, to do nothing and allow time to take its course, or to take reasonable, prudent, and constant steps to remove prejudice. The archbishop did not believe the removal of segregation by fiat would accomplish anything, "human nature being what it is." Allowing time to cure all evils, he reasoned, also was not an option because nothing would ever be accomplished. The third way, a nonviolent, reasonable approach, he concluded, would accomplish the goal of desegregation.[10]

Responding to the call to end segregation within the Catholic school system, the archbishop stated that such action "would be precipitate, imprudent and immature, that the carrying out of the resolution would do immeasurably more harm than good in that the parochial school system of New Orleans would be utterly destroyed." New Orleans black Catholics, he continued, "were not being deprived of any opportunity for their religious or intellectual life and that there is no immediate need for stressing the removal of segregation in the schools even if such is permitted by state law."[11]

After Rummel's comments, a number of students, mostly black, addressed the archbishop. Their comments concerned the introduction and use of racially sensitive textbooks in the school system, the formation of an interracial lecture bureau to speak to parochial school children on matters of race, the end of segregated seating in Catholic churches, the call for immediate action regardless of consequences, and the possibility of integrating Catholic graduate schools (especially Loyola University's School of Law).[12] The archbishop responded favorably on the subjects of textbooks and the lecture bureau. With regard to ending segregated seating in Catholic churches, Rummel stated that he had already ordered the removal of racial signs in all churches, and he pointed out that the continuation of segregated seating was because of the intransigence of ushers. President Shields noted that the discussion concerning segregated seating reinforced what he saw as the archbishop's main point: "namely that it will take considerable time and prudence to change the inherent prejudices of the people and that in the meantime the Negroes must be patient and prudent."[13]

The recommendation to take immediate action, regardless of consequences, provided a watchword that gained credence during the civil rights struggles of the 1950s and 1960s: action. The unidentified student recommending this course stated that "all great movements were made by proclamation and that what was needed were converts to the removal of segregation, which converts could be obtained only by strong and immediate action."[14] He and others at the meeting believed that a strong church stance would encourage others to take a similar stand, and as the movement gained strength, segregation would be ended.

Eventually the issue of integrating Loyola's law school was raised. Rummel did not voice an opinion, saying that that was an issue for the university to decide. The president of Loyola University of the South responded. Placed on the spot, Shields began his remarks by welcoming the members of the interracial commission to his office and stating that "he thoroughly agreed with everything the Archbishop had said." To bolster his own authority, he then commented on his history as an administrator. He told the students there was a "great difference between discussing a matter in theory, or talking about principles, and the application of these principles to daily life and to the people who constitute the world in which we live."[15]

He continued his presentation by comparing the Irish of Boston and the discrimination they faced at the hands of white Anglo-Saxon Protestants with the struggles blacks faced in the South.[16] And just as the Irish overcame oppression and injustice "to occupy a place of prestige in Boston," Shields believed that "the Negro people must help themselves" as well. Furthermore, he stated, "We must be realistic and realize that we are living in a world where other than in religious matters where charity urges us to help each other, there is keen competition for survival. This is exemplified in the business world." And then echoing Booker T. Washington's call for accommodation rather than agitation, Shields argued that "the Negro should begin by improving his own race and the most practical work for the Commission would be efforts to uplift their fellow Negroes."[17]

When the president finally addressed the issue of accepting a black applicant into Loyola's law school, Shields answered that no new student, black or white, would be accepted as enrollment was at capacity for the coming academic year. "As for the future," he stated, "I am not authorized to speak for the University[,] for its policy would be decided not only by the Rector alone but by the Board of Consultors and other prudent men." He did feel, however, that "they would do what was right and just." Shields ventured that "the real answer to this question is that the administration of Loyola will be guided by the principle that if it is for the greater glory of God, the good of the University, and the good of humanity, then and in that event Negroes will be admitted," but "if in the prudent judgment of those charged with the responsibility of the University such would not be for the greater glory of God and the good of humanity, they would not be admitted."[18]

In an attempt to justify Loyola's segregated admissions practices, Shields placed the burden of administrative decision-making on the students demanding change by asking, "Which one of you [black students] would apply for admission to the Loyola law school knowing that by your entrance into said school a vast majority of the students would depart from the school and go to Tulane or LSU law schools and thus you would take the responsibility of destroying the only Catholic law school in the entire South?" Shields wanted the students to understand and to appreciate the hard work the Jesuits had expended in building and developing a law program at Loyola. In his memorandum he explained, "it has taken many years of hard work against tremendous obstacles to build up the law school to its present position, that this law school is a definite help to the Catholic Church in this area and its future should not be placed in jeopardy."[19]

Accompanying the memo to his religious superior, President Shields sent a cover letter presenting his own view of the situation. He began by stating that the group of students in the interracial commission were "young, zealous, but definitely inexperienced in practical affairs and strongly in need of guidance from one who, while adhering to principles, knows how to apply same in a realistic manner." After dismissing the actions of the students as misguided but well-intentioned, Shields developed the main theme of his letter: Joseph Fichter's racial agenda. None too pleased at having been put on the spot with regard to integrating the law school, he continued:

> I do not know if this particular question [integration of Loyola] was premeditated and prepared and, therefore, I make no accusation; nevertheless, I call to your mind a very interesting sequence of events: (1) that Fr. Fichter made efforts to have Loyola admit Negro students with classes last fall . . . (2) . . . he caused to be inserted in the agenda for the I.S.O. [Institute for Social Order] meeting at Spring Hill a discussion on the matter of admitting Negro students to Loyola and Spring Hill [the other Jesuit institution of higher learning in the New Orleans Province, located in Mobile, Alabama]. . . . (3) Now the matter has been taken up before the Archbishop . . . someone might have anticipated the Archbishop would favor the admission of a Negro (which, of course, he not only did not, but absolutely rejected)

and thereby put the administration of Loyola University into a very embarrassing position before the Archbishop and sixty people in a public meeting.[20]

With this circumstantial evidence, Shields used this letter to build a case against Fichter. Moving beyond the issue of the interracial meeting, the president informed the provincial, "[T]here is an intense feeling against Fr. Fichter in this community" because of his stance on racial issues. More damaging to Fichter's reputation than the feelings of community members was the rector's evaluation of the young priest's candidness with superiors, a hallmark of a Jesuit's life. "It is to be regretted that Fr. Fichter is not more open and honest with superiors in the matter of promoting the cause in which he is interested." Here Shields was referring to Fichter's appearance on a radio program sponsored by the American Veterans Committee, which was considered a "Communist front organization."[21]

If Fichter did not change his ways, Shields informed Crane, then "we shall have to appoint another and more prudent director for the Interracial Commission."[22] The president wanted Fichter to behave more like fellow Jesuit Louis J. Twomey, founder and first director of Loyola University's Institute of Industrial Relations (IIR), who was involved in labor and racial issues and, unlike Fichter, had "been prudent, open to superiors, and obedient" and that his work had "the full cooperation and endorsement of the community."[23] For the president, it was "imperative" that Fichter moderate his position, "both from the angle of prudence and good order as well as from the constitutions of the Society [of Jesus]." Shields, however, assured Crane that he would not "obstruct any of his [Fichter's] endeavors which are in accord with right reason and prudence."[24]

In addition to his comments about the meeting with the archbishop and the chaplain of SERINCO, Thomas Shields wedged into his letter a one-sentence paragraph regarding the interracial commission's monthly newsletter, the *Christian Conscience:* "The propaganda sheet issued by the Commission is not written in a vein conducive to better relations between the races."[25] Jesuit displeasure with this newsletter would haunt the organization throughout its history and ultimately be the cause of its demise.

As the president of Loyola University reported the substance of the student meeting from his perspective, Carmelo Graffagnini, as acting chairman of the interracial commission, sent letters to the principals involved: Archbishop Rummel and President Shields. These missives were optimistic, conciliatory, and diplomatic in tone and nature. Demonstrating their respect for these church leaders, the college students addressed them in a dignified manner.

In his letter to the archbishop, Graffagnini thanked Rummel for participating in the meeting and for allowing such a "frank and open discussion" to take place. The acting chairman also expressed the group's concern that the archbishop not consider them either "zealots or radicals." Graffagnini explained that the interracial commission's resolution concerning race relations was intended to be "the minimum that could be said in the circumstances of our contemporary New Orleans community." The collegians, he continued, "had no thought of recommending immediate, drastic revision of the existing biracial arrangement." Should the archbishop suggest any measures to be undertaken to dismantle segregated society, however, the college students were ready to follow his counsel and direction.[26]

The collegian's letter to President Shields was also positive and expressed optimism about future endeavors. On behalf of the students, the acting chairman thanked the president for attending the meeting and for participating in the group discussion. Graffagnini noted that the collegians appreciated his willingness to allow them free expression of their views concerning race relations. They were encouraged by his "sympathetic understanding" of the work they were undertaking and believed that his views, expressed at the meeting, would "go far in maintaining among . . . [them] the positive spirit of Christian Charity and justice." Enclosed with the letter were copies of the *Christian Conscience.*[27]

A few weeks after meeting with the collegians, the archbishop attended the annual Jesuit dinner honoring Ignatius of Loyola, founder of the Society of Jesus, where he had the opportunity to speak to the president of Loyola University regarding the students and their activities. According to Shields, Rummel characterized the group as "fanatical" and advised closely supervising them "lest harm result." The students' fears were realized: Rummel did consider them to be radical. Recounting this conversation in a letter to John B. Janssens, S.J., the superior general of the order, Shields assured Janssens that the students would be watched.[28]

Jesuit provincial Harry Crane also kept Janssens informed of the developments at Loyola in his annual letter to his Roman superior. Crane reported that there had been "just a little tension at Loyola among the faculty over the [interracial] question as some of the older Fathers think that one or two of the younger priests are inclined to be radical in the matter." Crane and his advisers had discussed the race question but had not decided on any course of action; rather, at this point, he was just keeping his superior informed so that he would not hear of the situation "from other sources."[29]

Anthony Achée, S.J., a province consultor, was one of these "other sources."[30] Achée reported to Janssens that Joseph Fichter was "doing fine work in Family Life and Parish Relations and also in Race Relations." The latter issue, he noted, was "an explosive issue on which even some of our own Jesuits are not entirely orthodox." Realizing that Janssens might be called upon to provide direction to the university community regarding the race question, he provided his own evaluation of the situation. He noted that President Shields "has always been somewhat subject to groundless fears . . . and is afraid that Fr. Fichter is trying to go too fast in arriving at justice and charity in race relations." Achée assured Janssens that Fichter was "no radical" on racial matters and was even working with the Bishops' Committee of the Catholic Committee of the South on the issue.[31]

FIRST ATTEMPT AT SUPPRESSION

In September 1948 Shields wrote Fichter concerning the interracial commission; his comments were not surprising given the tone of his July letter to the provincial. The president began his letter by stating that he was writing "after due reflection . . . and after having consulted with the dean and other officials of Loyola University."[32] What followed was a three-point directive intended to curtail all interracial activities at Loyola.

While commending Fichter for his efforts to improve race relations, the president was concerned that the interracial commission "might very well become a group of malcontents thus hindering instead of helping race relations." Since the intention of the group, as Shields understood it, was the abolition of segregation in Catholic and public schools (a goal that he said "cannot be put into immediate actuality"), he recommended that "it would be more prudent that said group or any other similar group should *not* continue meeting on this campus."[33]

Furthermore, Shields banned the interracial newsletter from campus. "The publication of the *Christian Conscience* of [*sic*] any other such publication should not be connected in any way with Loyola University or printed, prepared or distributed here. From several inflammatory remarks in said publication, it is evident that no lasting good or genuinely improved relations between the races can result from such writings."[34] While Shields's letter did not mention any other reasons for suppressing the newsletter, the board of directors at Loyola, in a subsequent meeting, did: "no permission was obtained from either [the] president or dean to inaugurate this publication, . . . no censorship was sought or exercised over said publication, [and] the publication contained statements which were . . . contrary to Catholic dogma."[35] The specific statements that the directors found objectionable were never identified. "If the publication were printed elsewhere," the board members concluded, "there would be no objection of it being distributed to the members of the Interracial Commission of the Loyola student body or the members of the class of interracial relations."[36] The *Christian Conscience* survived outright proscription.

Shields also prohibited Fichter from inviting a black priest or "other distinguished member of the negro [*sic*] race to speak to a group of your students" without the permission of the president's office. Here, in part, Shields was referring to an incident involving Clarence Howard, S.V.D., a black priest. In February 1948, Howard had been invited to address SERINCO members meeting at Loyola.[37] Joseph Fichter, extending the usual courtesies and hospitalities shown a fellow priest, had invited Howard to eat with the Jesuit community prior to addressing the group.[38] The very day he had extended the invitation, however, Loyola University board members discussed the advisability of Fichter's deed, as the "delicate point of this matter is the fact that Father Howard is a negro [sic]."[39] Having informally surveyed the members of the Jesuit community, the president of the university discovered (as he told Fichter) that a "[m]ajority of Ours would have no difficulty or objection [in having Howard for dinner] but it is feared a small minority (but very vocal) might not only create unpleasantness in the community but might even be, to say the least, ungracious in presence of Fr. Howard. Regretable [sic]!" The president's solution was to be as welcoming and hospitable as possible to their guest lecturer when he arrived but not to have him partake of dinner: "Maybe this is the more prudent course in view of unreasonable and unjustified prejudice." Shields, however, did find something positive coming from this unfortunate affair; he viewed the solution as a step forward, "for it will be the first visit of a negro [sic] priest to Loyola."[40] The Howard incident notwithstanding, the president of Loyola University effectively proscribed black speakers from addressing the student body.[41] Censorship and control would be used to maintain the status quo at the university.

Shields ended his letter to Fichter by reaffirming Loyola University's commitment to Christian principles regarding race relations. While these principles were not stated, one may presume that they were antisegregationist. In what could be understood as a "gradualist" position, Shields called for understanding and prudence in these matters. A quick and easy solution to the difficulties surrounding race relations would not be forthcoming, and Shields was concerned that "[t]he precipitate, immature and imprudent words or actions of young people might well result in bitterness instead of better race relations."[42]

Fichter immediately replied to the president's letter, explaining the purpose of the student organization and the positive contribution it was making to improve race relations. The "*primary purpose*" of the interracial commission, he noted, was the attaining of "knowledge and understanding of each other by the individual Catholics of both races." He further explained that the means for realizing this objective was frequent personal contact among the students. The results, he noted, were gratifying, as the collegians were gaining knowledge in their racial perceptions of one another. They were growing in sympathy and charity as they learned of the plight of their fellow Catholics. Most important, Fichter pointed out, the interracial commission was putting Catholic teachings into practice.[43]

Given the interracial commission's purpose, objectives, and accomplishments, the moderator of the student group could not understand the president's assertion that its activities would lead to a deterioration of race relations. Fichter argued that problems would arise among the races if the organization were in the "hands of Dixiecrats, Communists, Wallacites [i.e., left-of-center Democrats], certain self-interest, quasi-military groups and various White Supremacy groups." That would not be the case, he informed the president, as the collegians have received "*prudent and conservative direction*" at Loyola. Fichter believed that the Loyola community would "soon reach the point where we need not be ashamed that Tulane University will continue to show us up; and especially secular, Protestant, or State schools (University of North Carolina, Louisiana State University, Arkansas, etc.,) will provide the moral leadership that Loyola, the only Catholic University in the South, should assume." He closed his letter by suggesting that Loyola officially and openly support the efforts of the interracial commission for bettering race relations.[44]

After responding to Shields, Fichter sent a copy of the president's letter to the provincial, Harry Crane, with a one-sentence commentary: "I pass this on to you without comment except to say that it stops cold the moderate and prudent progress that has been made in a small way in Catholicizing the social thought and behavior of our students."[45] Invoking the vow of obedience, the provincial of the New Orleans Province responded to Fichter's letter by encouraging the young priest to accept the restrictions on his interracial work "in a spirit of loyal obedience." Realizing that Fichter would be disappointed with this counsel, the provincial encouraged him to "offer up" his disappointment for the cause that he espoused.[46]

Two days before receiving the provincial's letter, Fichter wrote a follow-up letter to President Shields concerning rumors being circulated within the Jesuit community. Allegations had been made that Fichter had engineered the embarrassing 19 July exchange between the students, the archbishop, and the president. Not only was Fichter being accused of masterminding the incident, but he was also being accused of having "'instigated a Negro to apply for admission to the Loyola Law School.'" In his letter, Fichter flatly denied all of the allegations. He understood the 19 July meeting as a natural outcome of the discussions that took place at SERINCO's meetings. As far as encouraging a black student to apply to the law school, Fichter stated, "[T]he suggestion that I in any way at any time directly or indirectly encouraged Negro Catholics to apply for admission to Loyola in any college, school or department, is an outright distortion of the truth."[47]

Taking a line from his detractors, Fichter stated that he had "been a constant exponent of moderate and prudent thought and action in this whole field of race relations." All that he was asking for was "an opportunity to allow open discussion of race relations in an intelligent, above-board manner (as with any other social problem) without the need for self-defense against rumor-mongering, misinterpretation, unfounded allegations and general all-around sniping." He did not take such uncharitable behavior personally; rather, he saw it as impeding "any reasonable attempt to implement the directives of Very Reverend Father General [John B. Janssens] and the papal program for social enlightenment and improvement."[48]

Fichter made clear he would continue on his path. He had already advertised a night school course for the fall semester entitled "Race Relations." Over 160 prospective students, "all *white persons*," Fichter noted, had been contacted regarding this course offering; thirteen prominent black Catholics had been invited to speak to the class, a majority of whom had already accepted the invitation.[49] Among the thirteen was the only black lawyer in the city of New Orleans, A. P. Tureaud, who also served as counsel for the National Association for the Advancement of Colored People (NAACP); Charles Rousseve, author of *The Negro in Louisiana;* and Daniel Byrd, regional secretary of the NAACP.

In the fall of 1948, the president of Xavier University, Mother Mary Agatha, S.B.S., contacted Fichter thanking him for instituting the lecture series and for the selection of several Xavier graduates as speakers. She believed that such a program would have a positive effect on New Orleans and its people. "You recall what I told you before," she concluded, "that the holy Jesuits could change the face of the city if they will to. Thank you a thousand times, dear Father, for your efforts to do so!"[50]

PHILOSOPHICAL OPPOSITION TO INTERRACIALISM, 1948

During the presidential campaign of 1948, the Jesuits of Loyola University were far from silent regarding their political preferences. Martin Burke, S.J., professor of philosophy, made a public statement in favor of the States' Rights presidential candidate, Strom Thurmond, and the Dixiecrats.[51] The endorsement should not be much of a surprise given that Burke taught his philosophy classes that segregation was morally justifiable.[52] First Fichter and now Burke, two prominent Jesuit faculty members, invoked Catholic principles to reach diametrically opposed conclusions on the morality of segregation.

Born in New Orleans in 1886, Martin Burke entered the Society of Jesus in 1900. After following the normal course of formation for the Jesuits, he was ordained a priest in 1915. Burke began his teaching career at Loyola University in 1918 where he was an instructor of logic and metaphysics. After a two-year sabbatical (1923–1924) in Rome where he studied canon law, he returned to Loyola and taught for fifteen years, 1924–1939, before another teaching assignment took him to Spring Hill College in Mobile, Alabama, for the academic years 1939 through 1942. Burke returned to New Orleans in 1942 and remained at the university until 1957. At Loyola he was a much beloved professor. Tall, bespectacled, and full-faced with a mane of gray hair, Burke had a commanding presence and imposing personality. A persuasive speaker, his gravelly voice resonated with authority when he spoke.[53]

Gregory Choppin, one of Burke's former students, classified him as "an unreconstructed old Southerner." While Choppin did not recall any racist remarks made in or out of class, he remembered that during the presidential election of 1948 Burke was "an outspoken States' Rights person who even gave talks on the radio for Strom Thurmond." When Choppin and his classmates expressed their displeasure with Thurmond and the racist position espoused by the States' Rights Party, Burke gave them a lecture "on why it was not illogical for him to have certain opinions given when and how he grew up whereas he concluded we came from a different time with a different, changing culture and it would not be logical for us to have those same emotions and opinions."[54]

Also during the campaign season of 1948, Congressman F. Edward Hebert, a graduate of Jesuit High School of New Orleans and a States' Rights Party leader, spoke at Loyola.[55] While individuals favoring segregation were allowed to speak openly at the university, those opposed were not. Fichter, in particular, was counseled to be prudent in his efforts to improve race relations and advised to consult with his superiors on a regular basis while carrying out his objectives. When Fichter asked his provincial, Harry Crane, to speak to a sociology class on the "ticklish" question of the admission of black Catholics into religious orders, Crane declined the invitation. The provincial reasoned that "[s]omeone else could speak about the subject theoretically, but in my case there could easily be embarrassing practical consequences. It is hard to develop that subject without giving offense to one side or the other." Furthermore, the provincial stated, "I am not sure that it is yet time to bring the subject into the open in the south. I do feel that we are not yet ready to act upon this principle, that the time is not yet ripe, but I do hope that the time will come, and I think that it will."[56]

During the campaign of 1948, the students of Loyola debated the merits of the Truman-Barkley and the Thurmond-Wright tickets as well as the merits of the Democratic Party's civil rights platform.[57] SERINCO members participated in these debates as Pat Schott defended the Truman ticket and Harold Lamy supported enactment of the civil rights program. The other Catholic institutions of higher learning in New Orleans did not report any political activities taking place on their campuses during this period.

Although St. Mary's Dominican College did not report on the campaign, the November issue of its campus newspaper, *Veritas,* contained an editorial concerning the election results and civil rights titled "What Shall You Say?" Either the piece was written by a SERINCO member or the newspaper staff had access to an issue of the *Christian Conscience,* because quoting directly from *Christian Conscience,* the *Veritas* writer characterized Truman's election as "a hopeful sign to those of us who hope the question of unjust segregation will soon be, not whether it should be removed, but rather when and how it will be removed." The South, the reporter continued, "should readjust itself to some inevitable changes" regarding civil rights. And as for southern Catholics, the editorial wondered why they were prejudiced. Insecurity and ignorance were no excuse. Who was going to change the attitudes of society? The answer lay with Catholic college students— the same answer given by members of the interracial commission. The future leaders of the Catholic community were urged to come to terms with the problem of segregation and eventually do something about it.[58]

SERINCO ACTIVITIES AND INTERRACIAL SUNDAY

While national and academic politics dominated campus life in the fall of 1948, members of the Southeastern Regional Interracial Commission formulated their goals and objectives for the coming term. During their inaugural year, members decided to meet on the first Monday of every month, with the location of the meeting to rotate among the member institutions. This decision, while at first glance rather insignificant, had definite social implications, as it meant black and white students, especially black males and white females, would be meeting together as academic peers and social equals on black and white campuses. Unbeknownst to most New Orleanians, Catholic college students were violating the rigid code of racial segregation during their monthly gatherings.[59]

Maintaining interest in the commission was a problem early on in its history and remained so throughout its existence. One way commission members tried to attract attention and boost attendance was to organize and publicize the appearance of guest speakers and various presentations at the monthly meetings.[60] In addition to having a guest speaker address the group, members also made presentations themselves, such as brief talks, one-act plays, and radio skits.[61] Members also developed a list of projects they could undertake to maintain interest in the organization: encourage other students to attend the meetings, form a publicity committee to advertise the commission's activities, and meet with parish groups to talk about race relations.

Of the many suggestions made to recruit and maintain involvement in the commission, one called for college students to take an activist role: the suggestion of "petitioning for admission of Negro students" into the white Catholic institutions of higher learning.[62] Such a petition would have been the logical next step after the 1948 convention of SERINCO's parent organization, the National Federation of Catholic College Students (NFCCS), held in Philadelphia that spring, at which two key resolutions were passed. One resolution called for "a standard policy of non-discrimination in regard to the race or color of a student applying for admission to Catholic colleges."[63] The other endorsed the report of the President's Commission on Civil Rights and urged "enactment of its recommendations into law by the Congress of the United States."[64]

While there are no indications a petition drive was conducted, the college students did take an activist role in challenging racial attitudes and practices in the United States through their newsletter, the *Christian Conscience*. One area of particular concern to the students was racial stereotyping of blacks by whites. On one hand, the editors wrote, white Americans view the black man as "a good, kindly, jovial, and reliable person who does all the dirty work willingly for little reward," but on the other, whites view the black man as "a dangerous character, to be feared, hated, and distrusted—because he aspires to vote, or own his own land, or get more education." As long as a black "kept his or her place" in society, all was well, whites believed. Of course keeping his place, the newsletter authors explained, meant "that the Negro is supposed to continue to exist in the underprivileged, subservient (and hence slavish in all but name) status that has been his lot since the Civil War, when he was given nominal freedom and theoretical equality of opportunity."[65]

SERINCO editors understood that these biased and bigoted perceptions of blacks were the result of "pattern[s] of segregation within society, stereotyped thinking produced by news accounts, ignorance and prejudice, selfishness and greed, [and a] lack of charity and concern for others." One way to combat these attitudes and beliefs, the students argued, was to adopt and put into practice "a decalogue of race," and so they formulated an interracial version of the Ten Commandments:

Thou shalt not bow down before the false god of racial superiority.

Thou shalt not boast that only thy race is "pure."

Thou shalt not preach that whole races are at different levels of physical development.

Thou shalt not attach more importance to color of skin or other racial traits.

Thou shalt not establish racial groups as fixed and unchangeable.

Thou shalt not, to the detriment of thy neighbor, assert that cultural achievements are based on racial traits.

Thou shalt not look down upon thy brother because his appearance differs from thine.

Thou shalt not, because a man is of a different religion or nationality, say that he belongs to a different race.

Thou *shall* faithfully and sincerely act on the foregoing admonitions and then, indeed, thou wilt love thy neighbor as thyself.[66]

Adopting a Christian attitude toward others, they posited, would hasten the advancement of justice for all blacks. Furthermore, and perhaps more important, embracing these commandments would assist in the salvation of one's soul; eternal damnation for harboring racist attitudes and beliefs was a very real possibility.[67] Clare Boothe Luce, a prominent convert to Catholicism, reinforced the collegians' position on a visit to Loyola University in the fall of 1948.[68] "Racial prejudice is the spiritual leprosy of America," stated Luce. "We cannot cure ourselves, but Christ can help us conquer it in our hearts. . . . [U]ntil you have seen Christ in the face of your colored neighbor, you have never seen Christ, and you may never see him."[69]

By questioning white attitudes and beliefs concerning black Americans, these college students embodied the notion of the liberal "silent Southerner" who emerged from the experience of the Second World War with a different perspective on race relations.[70] They rejected the status quo of racial segregation in the light of the universal nature of Christianity. A religion that practiced racial intolerance was unacceptable. Herein lay the hope that these students, when they graduated from college, would assume the mantle of leadership within the secular as well as religious realms and thus change their world for the better.

These collegians not only wrote about racial tolerance but put it into practice by organizing "Interracial Sunday" in the winter of 1949. The NFCCS had been sponsoring these events since 1945 at various Catholic colleges around the country.[71] The commission decided its gathering would take place on 13 March 1949 at Ursuline College. Neither Loyola University nor Xavier University were chosen to host this inaugural event because the former was already sponsoring the NFCCS's "Inter-American Day" (publicity for the Interracial and Inter-American gatherings became a source of confusion and tension on Loyola's campus), and the latter venue, students believed, might limit participation and attendance. In other words, whites would not go to a black campus.[72]

The half-day program for Interracial Sunday would begin with Mass and breakfast. Two guest speakers, one black and one white, were to address the gathering, and a discussion period would follow. To foster interest among high school and college students, commission members decided to sponsor a speech contest for collegians and a poster contest for high school students; the respective winners would receive trophies for their efforts. In the latter part of the morning, the collegians would organize their own forum or discussion period, and the program would conclude with closing remarks and benediction by Archbishop Rummel. Seating at all events was to be integrated.[73]

Publicity would be the key to a successful gathering. In an effort to explain the purpose of Interracial Sunday and to encourage high school students to participate in the poster contest, the collegians established a speakers bureau. Integrated teams of two visited the Catholic high schools in New Orleans encouraging students to become involved in the poster contest and to attend the Interracial Sunday forum. Publicity for the speech contest would consist of circulars and posters announcing the contest; members distributed the advertisements around the member campuses. Local, archdiocesan, and collegiate newspapers were also given press releases announcing the upcoming event.[74] And the archbishop endorsed the event in his financial appeal letter for the "Indian and Negro Missions," in which he designated 13 March as Interracial Sunday, asking the faithful to "pray most sincerely for an increase of that Christlike spirit, which will prompt and enable us to exercise towards the Negro true justice and charity worthy of the Christian name."[75]

The addresses to the high school students emphasized Catholic social and interracial theology. Being a Christian, the students were told, meant practicing justice and charity toward all. Moreover, Christianity embraced all believers, blacks as well as whites. The high school students were encouraged to attend Interracial Sunday as an opportunity to put into practice what they believed. Black and white Catholics would attend a racially integrated Mass, discuss racial issues together, and hear prominent white and black speakers address the race issue from a Catholic perspective. More importantly for the white students, Interracial Sunday afforded them the opportunity to meet black students who were their peers, and in doing so, they would come to understand the "fallacy of racial myths." Besides attending the Sunday gathering, the students were encouraged to take a stand on the race question: "have courage to state your views when the race question arises," they were told. And when they recognized violations of justice and Christian charity toward blacks, they were told "to talk over the problem of race with others sympathetic to the problem," for in so doing they would participate in the building up of the Christian faith and ideals.[76]

On 13 March the first annual Interracial Sunday gathering began with Mass followed by breakfast. Black and white Catholics worshiped together and shared a common meal together at Ursuline College and Academy before adjourning to the auditorium to hear the guest speakers, Reverend Clarence Howard, S.V.D., and Commission on Human Rights member James Impastato,[77] address the crowd on the theme of "The Spiritual Price of Prejudice." The walls of racial separation within the Catholic Church in New Orleans began to crumble when black and white Catholics sat down together as equals that Sunday morning.

Howard began his talk by highlighting the contradictions between Christian teachings and Catholic practices in the world at that time. He noted that because of the accident of birth some people were denied equality in social, economic, and religious opportunities. The individuals practicing discrimination, he pointed out, were not pagans, but rather "persons bearing the name of Christ—going against the name and holy will [of God], while trying to justify their actions." Highlighting the problem of prejudice and discrimination in the archdiocese of New Orleans, Howard noted that none of the forty thousand black Catholics in the city could be admitted into any of the city's Catholic hospitals, Hotel-Dieu and Mercy Hospital. With this reality in mind, he suggested that the faithful "must heal ourselves first—and then try to heal others—as far as discrimination is concerned."[78]

Focusing on education, Howard praised the administration of the Catholic University of America for integrating its student body in the 1930s. He then noted that of the 216 Catholic colleges in the United States, 129 admitted blacks. Only four southern states (Florida, Tennessee, Kentucky, and Oklahoma), he pointed out, legally proscribed private educational institutions from having integrated student bodies. This being the case, he questioned why Catholic institutions of higher learning in Louisiana, which were not bound by any state segregation law, refused to accept black applicants, saying that "it makes Catholics look funny and ridiculous if they try to hide behind state laws which are not there."[79]

Howard concluded his remarks by presenting practical ways to further interracial justice. Through meetings, discussions, prayer, and missionary work, he believed much could be accomplished. Howard urged the students to become "missionaries" to their parents in order to break down any prejudices found in their homes. "Even if we do not destroy their prejudice," he told them, "perhaps through prayer and good example we can abolish their negative attitudes."[80]

James Impastato devoted the first portion of his talk to family life. It was from the family that one learned "this business of living peacefully and in harmony." He argued that the first principle parents should teach their children was the dignity of every human being. From this principle, he reasoned, one would learn how to value other human beings. And once this lesson was learned at home, an individual could then practice it in public.[81]

He noted that through daily contacts with others "we will be able to give public expression to our faith and our convictions." He realized that living out one's principles and beliefs would not be easy because it might lead to ridicule and the loss of friends and acquaintances; however, he believed action would have a leavening effect on society. Prayer, he noted, would be needed to sustain one in these efforts to change hearts and minds.[82]

Following their presentations, Howard and Impastato answered prescreened questions from the audience in order to avoid "trouble makers" asking questions in an open forum.[83] During the scheduled intermission, judges for the high school poster contest rendered their decisions on the artwork exhibited, with Ronald Rousseve of Xavier Prep taking top honors. The collegiate oratorical contest followed with Doris Walker of Xavier, Robert Drez of Loyola, Lucille Briou of Dominican, and Jeanne Schrewe of Ursuline representing their respective institutions.[84]

In her winning address, Doris Walker asked audience members to think of reasons anyone should think "ill of our fellow man." She answered this rhetorical question with additional questions: "Is it because my fellow man is a Catholic and I a Protestant? Is it because he is poor and I rich? Is it because he is of one race and I of another?" Walker replied, "Yes, it is all these, and more." This prejudice, she argued, was the result of Christians' forgetting the foundation of their faith: salvation in Christ. Prejudicial behavior and attitudes among whites, she noted, had allowed false ideologies to convert blacks. "[W]hile communism has painted many a black man red with its offers of justice and equality," she continued, "prejudice has stained many a soul once gifted with a purity of the state of grace, with sin." She contended prejudice had exacted too high a price. "The spiritual price of prejudice," she asserted, was "enslavement; enslavement of the mind, of the conscience, of the will. The spiritual price of prejudice is sin."[85]

According to Walker, prejudice was an opiate. It deadened and paralyzed the human intellect and destroyed human reason. Prejudice, she told her audience, was also a disease. She likened it to cancer, which destroyed the body by consuming the host. Prejudice, she said, "eats away the idea of human rights, it paralyzes the conception of justice, it undermines the very foundation of Christianity, for the individual infested with the malady of prejudice is, by necessity, opposed to Christian ideals, for in the teachings of Christ there is no place for hate, injustice or segregation, all of which are but an expression of prejudice." She concluded her remarks by contending that prejudice was sinful and that anyone who participated in prejudicial thought or behavior committed sin. Sin, she reminded her audience, resulted in the death of one's soul. The spiritual price of prejudice was death.[86]

A student forum followed the oratorical contest. At the end of the half-day affair, Archbishop Rummel handed out awards to contest winners Rousseve and Walker. The Archbishop then made a few concluding remarks and blessed the crowd, thus ending the proceedings. By all accounts, the first collegiate-sponsored interracial gathering in New Orleans was a success.[87]

OPPOSITION TO INTERRACIALISM

The Ursuline sisters, however, received a letter of protest after a newspaper article recounted the events of Interracial Sunday. The author of the letter, identified only as "A Mother," questioned why these religious women allowed whites and blacks to intermingle. "God forbade the mixing of white and black," the writer informed the sisters. "We know they have a soul," she wrote, but "this mixing up will not save their souls." The author argued that while blacks should have their churches and schools, whites did not want "to be mixed" with them. The author did not care for black and white speakers appearing together on stage at the Interracial Sunday event: "The idea to have a negro man to make a speech with the whites . . . why not go to Xavier and don't disgrace our white schools."[88]

Claiming "to [sic] much respect for myself and my family," this mother would not allow her child to attend Ursuline Academy if it were integrated: "If you Sisters wish to cater whit [sic] negros take only negros but my *child* will not be in your School with negros." The author of the letter believed the worst result from integrated activities would be miscegenation. "[A]re you Catholic try [sic] to wipe out the white race, *mixed blood* and who's fault[—]white priest." She believed the archbishop allowed these activities to take place in order to make money. In closing, this woman lamented the fact that the whites were "degrading themselves" by associating with blacks.[89]

Others shared the anonymous writer's views, and it seemed racial prejudice did hurt enrollment at Ursuline College. Writing to his Jesuit friend Louis Twomey concerning the interracial gathering, Edward Rapier argued that such activities at the women's college explained "why many leading Catholics do not send their children to Ursuline."[90] Promoting racial equality within the church came at a price.

Letters of protest notwithstanding, the college students were pleased with the Interracial Sunday. Members of the Loyola University board of directors were not. Two days before the gathering was held, a special meeting of the board was called to discuss the racial situation at Loyola. According to the minutes of that meeting, board members voiced concern that because of "excessive and imprudent publicity for the Inter-racial Day, unhealthy sentiment has been aroused among certain of our students towards the Negro race and thus those who would promote better race relations have actually caused them to suffer a setback here at Loyola." In particular, the letters "KKK" were scrawled over a poster advertising the event. The directors' fears about the situation on campus had worsened, as it was stated in their meeting that month that "this question of inter-racial relations has caused increasing difficulties at Loyola both on the part of the faculty and the student body. Jesuit members of the faculty are not teaching the same doctrine in regard to race relations and two in particular [i.e., Fichter and Burke] are teaching diametrically opposite doctrines. This has never happened before at Loyola and cannot be tolerated now."[91] The tension created by these two Jesuits' opposing positions was a major factor compelling the New Orleans Province of the Society of Jesus to reevaluate its position on race.

Concerning the student body, the board members believed that "some few favor abolition of segregation; the majority . . . do not believe the present time is propitious for such a move." How the Loyola board members came to this conclusion is not documented. Whether these Jesuits were actually speaking for the students or for themselves is unknown. Nevertheless, these men had decided that the time for challenging the racial practices in New Orleans was not ripe. Furthermore, university officials were alarmed by the "well substantiated accusations that the extremists in the matter of race relations have actually asked white girls, stenographers employed at Loyola University, to have dates with Negro men. Upon refusing, one girl was told: 'Why not, aren't you a Christian?'"[92] The possibility of interracial dating was greatly feared by most white southerners.[93]

While "all at Loyola are in full accord with Christian principles of morality and sympathetic with every effort to better the Negro race," board members stated, Loyola University needed to reexamine the efforts being made to improve race relations "both for the good of the university and for the good of inter-racial relations." Members of the board of directors were especially critical of the moderator of the interracial commission, Joseph Fichter, who, they perceived, was harming rather than improving race relations: "It is with regret that we note that after all this time [almost two full years] inter-racial relations are worse than they ever were." They pointed to the interracial commission of the NFCCS as the source of the trouble on campus. The board wanted the students to work for the betterment of blacks—not for desegregation. The directors believed "the Commission was starting at the wrong end, namely, with efforts to abolish segregation, whereas, the efforts of the Commission should be for the solution from the ground up, namely, anything that will benefit the economic, housing, educational condition of the Negro race." These Jesuits seemed to advocate maintaining the legal and social standard of "separate but equal," with emphasis on "equal." If blacks could rise to the same educational, economic, and social status as whites, they reasoned, then "the question of segregation will almost automatically solve itself."[94]

Relying on reasoning that had been used time and time again when the issue of integration confronted them, some of the Jesuits of Loyola University argued that "one cannot legislate morality." One reason they provided that integration could not be legislated was that "[w]e must take into account the feelings of the people among whom we live. This is not the time to agitate [for] the abolition of segregation."[95] Yet members of this religious order appeared to have dissociated themselves from their own upbringing. Even though most of the Jesuits were from the South, they acted as though they were missionaries in a foreign land where they had to respect the "traditions" of their newfound converts. For the time being, for these men, as for Archbishop Rummel, the issue remained a political and social one, not a moral one.

In order to restore peace and tranquility on campus and to maintain the status quo, the Loyola University board of directors decided that the *Christian*

Conscience should be distributed only to the members of the interracial commission and not to the general student body. The board prohibited the posting of fliers, placards, or any other advertisement regarding interracial matters. Black speakers on campus, already limited by the president of the university, were to be "few and far between."[96]

Attempting to silence debate regarding segregation, the board informed Jesuit professors of philosophy and the social sciences, particularly Burke and Fichter, that they were "to restrict themselves to the non-controversial lines of economic, moral [and] educational opportunities for the Negro and to avoid questions of segregation which is frought [*sic*] with so much danger for both races." Board members believed that "better progress is made towards the abolition of segregation when segregation itself is not talked about."[97]

Regarding socializing between blacks and whites, the university officials prohibited Jesuit faculty from promoting or fostering, "directly or indirectly, social activities involving Negroes and Whites. No Negroes [were] to be brought to the cafeteria on the campus of the university." The practice of the interracial commission, when it had morning meetings at Loyola, was to celebrate Mass with Fichter and then go to the student cafeteria for breakfast. Nowhere in the city of New Orleans could one find blacks and whites eating breakfast together in a public place. The admonition from the board was directed at Fichter for transgressing this social norm.[98]

In what seemed like the second death knell for SERINCO, the board banned any further meetings of the interracial commission on Loyola's campus. Within a week of this special meeting, a policy statement regarding interracial affairs at Loyola University was drafted. During his annual visit with the Loyola University community, the provincial of the New Orleans Province, Harry Crane, had recommended just such a document. Wanting "to foster harmony and to prevent discord, and to enable all to 'say the same thing according to the Apostle,'" Crane believed that it was "opportune that a University policy on the interracial issue should be drawn up by the Rector and his consultors; and all should adhere to this policy in public utterances on or off campus."[99]

INTERRACIAL POLICY

In March 1949, Provincial Harry Crane, S.J., writing to his Jesuit superior in Rome, John B. Janssens, S.J., again outlined the difficulties arising from the discussion of the race question at the university. The situation had become more serious in Crane's opinion. The provincial attributed the trouble on campus to a "small group" of students led by Joseph Fichter. These students and their professor had antagonized the student body at Loyola as well as some Jesuits with their attack on segregationist practices. Crane acknowledged that Fichter's intentions were above reproach but found the young Jesuit professor "imprudent in his methods" in challenging the social mores of the South. Because the race question was a source of division and acrimony, Crane explained, he had asked the president of the university and his advisors to draft a policy statement that he said "should be followed by all in pubic utterances."[100]

Loyola University's official policy statement concerning interracial relations was "for the guidance of Ours"; that is, the statement concerned faculty and staff of Loyola University who happened to be Jesuits.[101] The administration viewed the efforts of those Jesuits promoting improved race relations as hindering rather than helping the situation. And while there was nothing wrong with aiming for the ideal of better relations among the races, the administration warned, "all must be aware of being practical." *Being practical* meant taking into account the "framework of human society in this section of the country"; in other words, segregation was not to be confronted directly. The Jesuits drafting this document stated that the policies outlined therein were the result "of much prayer, study and consultation." Diversity of doctrine would not be tolerated, as the members of the Society of Jesus would teach "what is certain as certain, what is probable as probable." Dissent was not an option; the preamble stated, "Ours are to be guided by strict obedience and full loyalty to the directives of the Superior charged with the administration of Loyola University."[102]

There is no indication that the one member of the Society of Jesus, Joseph Fichter, who would be directly affected by this new policy statement, was part of the deliberative process; rather it was Martin Burke who, upon the recommendation of the provincial, drafted the "doctrines" section.[103] Burke's selection appeared to signal Jesuit and university desire to maintain the status quo. This section also reveals Burke's attitude concerning race relations in America.

Burke began the "Doctrine" section with general principles and worked toward specifics: "[A]ll men are equal . . . and hence [have] an *inalienable* right to the pursuit of happiness, which ultimately is the gaining of Heaven. Hence the colored man has equal rights with the white man as to liberty of conscience, freedom of worship, etc., and all requisite means thereto."[104] Notably, his understanding of a person's inalienable right to the pursuit of happiness was not derived from Jefferson or secular democracy but rather had religious bases.

While he did not agree with the Supreme Court's decision in the *Smith* v. *Allwright* case of 1944, which struck down the all-white primary, Burke did accept the Court's decision and even agreed that "the colored citizen has equal rights with the white citizen *politically.*" The implication, he noted, was that blacks had "the right to vote, to hold office, elective and appointive, etc." Even in the field of economic justice, Burke stated that "the colored man has equal rights economically in that he has a right to a fair opportunity to make a decent living wage, to be paid an equal salary for equal work, etc." He did take exception with the Fair Employment Practices Committee (FEPC), which required companies doing business with the United States government not to practice racial discrimination in their hiring: "[T]he F.E.P.C. seems to extend this [equality] too far by denying to an employer the right to hire a white man in preference to a colored."[105]

Burke's support of equality, however, did not extent to social situations. "It is by no means certain," he wrote, "that there is social equality between the races. As is obvious, different groups of men, even of the same race, tend to form their own social units." That being the case, he concluded, "laws of segregation in means of transportation, hotels, stores, places of amusement, schools, etc., if approved by the majority, probably are not unethical or un-Christian. The same holds with regard to zoning laws restricting white or colored residential districts." Appealing to the social tradition of his day and the Supreme Court approval of "separate but equal" policies and institutions, Burke clarified that social segregation was based on the presupposition that "equal service would be given for equal price, i.e., if the colored man is charged the same as the white for riding the streetcar, he be given equal convenience with the white."[106]

He concluded that "it would seem if each race were given equal opportunity to develop itself separated socially from the other, this system would work out to the greater advantage of both than a system which would attempt to impose *social* equality by a fiat of civil law."[107] Burke expressed the attitudes of many southerners in articulating the belief that blacks should have their own facilities, be they social or religious, and whites should have theirs; hence social equality, like morality, could not be legislated.

The "Practical Rules" section of the directive demonstrates that the university officials wanted to defuse the segregation issue as much as possible. This section was based on the recommendations made at the meeting of the board of directors held 11 March 1949. Among these recommendations were (a) that the matter of segregation be de-emphasized because "precipitate action" had delayed the objective of ending segregation; (b) that posting of publicity materials (e.g., posters, fliers, announcements, etc.) concerning interracial matters be prohibited; (c) that the *Christian Conscience* not be distributed on campus except to members of SERINCO; (d) that black lecturers or speakers "very rarely" be invited to appear on campus and only with permission; (e) that encouraging interracial "dating" cease; and (f) that "no meeting of the Inter-racial Committee may be held anywhere on the campus of Loyola."[108]

After reviewing the policy declaration, the New Orleans provincial informed the president of Loyola that statements that appeared to be directed at specific persons or claimed that interracial activities already undertaken had hurt racial understanding should be excised, for "[t]hose who have acted thus would probably not admit this [that they did any harm], and its statement would possibly make them martyrs and rally friends to their side." Regarding the prohibition of interracial meetings on Loyola's campus, the provincial believed that Loyola would "come in for undue criticism if we are the only Catholic college (university) which does not tolerate" such meetings. He would reconsider his position, however, if the board still wanted to ban the meetings.[109]

This policy statement was never enacted; had it been, it would have been unlikely to achieve the intended goal of the Jesuit superiors, which was harmony. The section drafted by Burke was a ringing endorsement of racial segregation. His conclusions, therefore, would not have settled any disputes among the Loyola faculty; rather they would only have exacerbated them.

While not wanting to appear uncharitable toward those advocating interracial harmony, Catholic religious officials tried to thwart the students' attempts to practice what they believed. If Catholic leaders could not suppress student activities, they would at least control them. In the process they had to justify their actions, thus highlighting the contradictions inherent in promoting interracial harmony on a theoretical level while blocking concrete methods of achieving it in practice.

CHAPTER III

Interracial Activism: Belief in Practice, 1948–1949

WHILE CATHOLIC INTEGRATIONISTS in New Orleans faced strong opposition on the local level inside and outside their church, they were heartened by the growing commitment of some political leaders to civil rights on the national level. President Harry S. Truman was not the Missouri senator Harry S. Truman selected as Franklin Roosevelt's running mate in 1944. At that time many southerners thought Senator Truman would represent their social and racial beliefs; they were mistaken. Establishing a presidential commission to investigate civil rights violations (1946), speaking to the National Association for the Advancement of Colored People (1948), desegregating the military (1948), and calling for civil rights legislation (1948), all represented an atypical southerner.[1]

The results of the 1948 presidential election, however, demonstrated that the people of Louisiana favored racial segregation as the States' Rights candidate, Governor Strom Thurmond, carried Louisiana with 49.1 percent of the vote (204,290), President Harry Truman came in second with 32.7 percent (136,344), and the Republican candidate, Governor Thomas Dewey of New York, was a weak third with 17.5 percent, or 72,657 votes. This election represented the world that members of the Southeastern Regional Interracial Commission (SERINCO) and the Commission on Human Rights (CHR) inhabited, and it was the world they were trying to change.[2]

CHR INEFFECTIVENESS

While Catholics in New Orleans had no legal power to challenge Jim Crow society through civil or ecclesiastical legislation, they could promote better race relations among their coreligionists. Try as they might, members of the CHR faced indifference and opposition to their cause. Their attempts to promote interracial activities were limited in scope and effectiveness. Nevertheless, this small determined group of adult Catholics manifested an alternative approach to the practice of southern race relations. Their example could have served as a model for reforming southern Catholic racial attitudes and behavior.

The one significant and visible manifestation of racial harmony CHR members attempted was attending Sunday Mass together on an integrated basis. Rather than desegregate the altar, these Catholic laymen and laywomen would desegregate the pews and thereby begin the dismantling process of Jim Crow society within the Catholic community from below; integrating sacred space would call into question the legitimacy of maintaining segregated secular space.[3]

Though they wanted to attend "white" parishes as an integrated body, commission members could not always obtain permissions from the pastors of these churches to do so. Even when they did, the parishioners of the host church saw their presence as an act of defiance. Given these difficulties, members wanted to obtain the approval and support of Archbishop Rummel for their efforts because his office and influence might encourage reluctant pastors to open their doors to the group. An alternative to appealing to Rummel was inviting pastors to the monthly CHR meetings in order to explain the organization, clarify its goals and objectives, and then solicit their support.[4]

Again, the inability of the CHR to infiltrate and challenge racial mores at the parish level demonstrates the degree to which racial prejudice had influenced Catholic society. White supremacy was a given in New Orleans Catholic society just as it was throughout the state and region. Catholic principles of unity, charity, and justice simply did not apply to the black community. For most white Catholics, racial segregation was a social practice or custom, not a moral issue.

The commission's inability to promote racial justice by attending Mass as integrated groups points to the larger issue of prejudice in the pews. Social acceptance of segregation by many New Orleans Catholics translated into religious discrimination in the church. This presented a dilemma: how to challenge the practice of Jim Crowism in church after having given tacit approval to it for decades. Making people aware of the moral dimension of segregation would prove to be the greatest challenge for CHR members. It would also be a challenge for the church at large because this contradiction between church teaching and historical practice would lead to open defiance by some and subtle defiance by many others at a time when Catholic leaders eventually called for the elimination of racial segregation within the church.

SERINCO, CHR, AND MINSTREL SHOWS

Consciousness-raising among Catholic college students was also difficult. When the student chapter of the Catholic fraternal organization Epsilon Kappa Sigma (Knights of Columbus) at Loyola University publicized its upcoming minstrel show in the fall of 1948, the faculty moderator of SERINCO, Joseph Fichter, S.J., sent letters of protest to the president and dean of men of the university. Fichter explained to these university officials that blacks objected to minstrel shows as demeaning to their race. He also contended that sponsoring such a show would harm relations between Loyola and Xavier, making it seem that the Jesuits were saying one thing and doing another. To the dean of men, Fichter argued that it was not enough to say that blacks should not be offended by these performances, because they were. He wondered if the dean could "persuade the boys of EKS to present a substitute for their blackface minstrel? Like many others, they probably do not understand the implications behind their proposed spectacle." Protestations notwithstanding, the show went on as planned.[5]

One of the two photographs submitted by Epsilon Kappa Sigma for the 1948 issue of the *Wolf,* Loyola University of the South's yearbook, featured their minstrel show participants. The other is of members of the fraternity presenting a check to the dean of students for the annual NFCCS European "Displaced Persons" fund-raising drive. In the 1949 *Wolf,* the text describing the work of the fraternity stated that the organization "shows itself as a genuine credit to Loyola with such activities as regular general communions, works of charity and the annual minstrel show. Covering spiritual, intellectual, and social fields, it has much to offer to members." Also included in this two-page spread were photos of the members, one of whom, Daniel Quinn, merits particular attention because he was also chairman of the interracial commission (1948–49); there are no indications, however, that he was a member of the minstrel ensemble.[6]

Like the rather ambiguous attitude some SERINCO members held regarding minstrel shows, members of the CHR provided a tepid response to the performances. While some CHR members viewed them as a blatant form of racism, not all objected to these productions. The suggestion to send a letter of protest to the Knights of Columbus led one member to ask "for reasons why minstrel shows were considered undesirable." In reply, CHR member John McCann explained that "as played in the South, they [minstrels] were vulgar, sly and underhanded and definitely mocked the Negro race." Robert S. Shea, a white faculty member at Xavier University, worried that in protesting minstrel shows, the CHR would be seen as opposing entertainment "which put the Negro in a bad light." He was not concerned with the morality of minstrel shows, but he saw the commission making a broader statement that he obviously did not want to support. When Loyola's Joseph Fichter recommended that the commission draft an open letter to the press regarding minstrel shows, he, too, faced opposition. One member felt that "we were definitely wrong in coming out with a policy against them" because the group was not in agreement.[7]

In a subsequent debate regarding the minstrel shows, CHR members questioned why the Knights of Columbus were being singled out; there were other

Catholic organizations, especially Mothers' Clubs, that produced the same shows. Clarence Laws, a black Catholic and staffer at the *Louisiana Weekly*, was of the opinion that the minstrels "helped to confirm popular [negative] impressions of the Negro." He favored approaching the archbishop directly on the issue. Other members suggested writing the pastors of the parishes where minstrel shows were held. A. P. Tureaud, a black attorney, suggested that the shows were not the real problem, that the Mardi Gras parade of the black Krewe (i.e., social club) of Zulu was more degrading and hence damaging to the black image.[8]

SERINCO AND THE PASSION OF CHRIST

While CHR members were trying to stop racial stereotyping, SERINCO members were trying to integrate a local city theater. The production of the 1949 passion play, sponsored by Archbishop Rummel and promoted by the New Orleans Sodality Union, was the occasion for college student activism.[9]

Jesuit Sam Hill Ray,[10] director of student counseling at Loyola University and executive secretary of the New Orleans Sodality Union, along with Alfred Bonomo, drama professor at Loyola, were overseeing the staging of the production at the Poche Theater in downtown New Orleans. The play was to be staged during Holy Week with matinee shows performed for students and evening performances for reserved seat holders. What was not advertised was the fact that only white patrons, whether young people or adults, could attend the performances at the Poche.[11]

At the April SERINCO meeting, Xavier commission member Frank Lapoleyrie first addressed the theater situation. "The purpose of the play," Lapoleyrie argued, was "to help all Catholics better know and understand the passion of Jesus Christ . . . [and] the leaders of the play were doing an injustice to the Negro by excluding him from the audience." Fellow Xavierite Mason Reddix agreed, observing that "the Negro cannot stand the publicity of this type of denial within the Catholic Church itself." He concluded sarcastically, "[T]he Negroes in New Orleans are not so gifted with grace and a strong will that they would not benefit from the Passion Play." The chairman of the interracial commission at Xavier, Charles Felton, stated, "Xavier students feel it an insult that they were excluded [because] the idea of it was to help all the Catholics of New Orleans."[12]

For those who knew Irwin Poche, owner of the theater, his policy on the passion play was nothing new; he had previously denied admission to Xavier students. SERINCO vice chairman Carmelo Graffagnini suggested giving Poche a chance to redeem himself by allowing anyone who wanted to see the play to attend on a particular day. If Poche rejected the idea, then, Graffagnini argued, the interracial commission should launch a boycott against the theater. Loyola's Ed Kammerer wanted to contact the archbishop, the local newspapers, college presidents, and sponsors of the play for their reaction to the situation. Any action against the Poche Theater, he argued, would be taken in light of the responses from those contacted. Finally, with the commission's approval, Robert Shea, faculty moderator of the Xavier interracial commission, volunteered to speak to Archbishop Rummel about the situation.[13]

The passion play situation gave the students an opportunity to take a stand against discrimination. Because Loyola University staff and faculty were directly involved with the production of the play, the commission members expected support in protesting this injustice. What these students did not know was that Sam Hill Ray, S.J., was unsympathetic to their cause. That very spring, in 1949, Ray vetoed a motion by the college sodalities to consolidate into one local unit because it would have meant integrating the organization.[14]

Over the signature of SERINCO chairman Daniel Quinn, the collegians sent letters of protest to the moderators of the college, high school, and parish sodalities; the presidents of Loyola University, Ursuline College, and Dominican College; the archbishop of New Orleans; and the chairman of the Commission on Human Rights of the Catholic Committee of the South. In his letter to Ray, Quinn stated that exclusion of blacks from the audience "was at best an oversight on the part of those in charge, and at worse [sic] a scandalous spectacle to Communists and non-Catholics who mock at our pretensions of universal charity." He noted that all blacks were deprived of the intellectual and spiritual benefits derived from attending such a performance and that exclusion only fueled resentment against the Catholic faith. Quinn assured Ray that the student group did not hold him personally responsible for the situation; they were sure he "did not know of the implications in this particular situation." The chairman did tell the sodality moderator that other church leaders were being informed in the hope that positive change might come in the future.[15]

Archbishop Rummel responded immediately to Quinn's letter. While the archbishop was in complete sympathy with the student's charge, he offered the explanation that perhaps there was no other theater available for staging the production. "The alternative," he noted, "might have been no production at all, which would imply depriving the white population of the opportunity of seeing this inspiring presentation and deriving from it many spiritual advantages." Rummel did suggest that in the future the students should try to influence the Poche Theater to make an exception to its admission policy. In the meantime, he recommended that the collegians investigate the legal statutes concerning segregation in public places. "Such an investigation might offer the basis for future action and even agitation in favor of a more liberal interpretation of the 'custom' of segregation."[16] When the collegians did investigate, they discovered that were no legal prohibitions in Louisiana against allowing blacks and whites to attend the theater together. They so informed the archbishop, stating that Poche's "discriminatory policy is the result of personal choice."[17]

A few days later, Ray responded to the commission's letter. Addressing his remarks to Chairman Quinn, Ray was "thoroughly surprised and offended by [his] . . . lack of good taste and good judgement." The director of student counseling found that Quinn and his associates had "caused more dissension than I have seen through my long years of student adviser here on this campus." Continuing his reprimand, he noted that SERINCO's boldness, misplaced zeal, hasty conclusion, and warped views were "calculated to do a great deal of harm to a cause that I have spent more time in than you can count in years." Furthermore, this Jesuit would have preferred seeing the students in person rather than receiving a letter of protest. Ray informed the undergraduates that the faculty were "not accustomed to these unwarranted and misinformed reprehensions from the student body as a whole nor from the individual student."[18]

Thomas Shields, S.J., the president of Loyola University, claimed that the students' letter was the first indication he had that blacks were not allowed to attend the performance. Unaware of the details of this university-sponsored performance, he subsequently discussed the matter with the moderator of the sodality. Ray informed Shields that, while regrettable, the exclusionary policy at the Poche Theater was discovered only after arrangements for the play had already been made.[19] The play proceeded as planned on a racially segregated basis.

As he was not a supporter of integration or activities to promote interracial harmony, Sam Hill Ray's failure to challenge segregation is not surprising. So incensed was he over the behavior of the interracial commission that he wrote his provincial, Harry Crane, S.J., regarding the group's activities in order that the provincial "may know the type of 'agitation' which is bringing more and more dissension to Loyola campus." Ray took exception to the fact that SERINCO chairman, Dan Quinn, was a student of sociology and originally from Massachusetts; the implication was that not only was this undergraduate under the influence of sociology professor Joseph H. Fichter but he was also a northerner—an outside agitator. Ray explained to Crane that blacks were excluded from the theater "not because we deliberately wanted to exclude negroes [sic] and thus promote communism, but because the Poche Theatre never had any place for negroes." The sodality leaders had discussed the situation with the theater owner at the outset, he noted, with Poche explaining that he did not find it profitable to cater to a black clientele. Furthermore, he argued, the Xavier students were not deprived of seeing this production, as their own theater department had performed this work several times in the recent past. He concluded by noting, "In spite of no appeal to children, Jews and negroes, the Passion Play was a great success."[20]

CATHOLIC INTERRACIALISM: PRAYER, THOUGHT, ACTION

The opportunity for the interracial commission to challenge segregationist practices in New Orleans, such as the passion play incident, arose infrequently and did not occupy a great deal of the students' time. Presentations by guest speakers at their monthly meetings did. The members heard from a variety of speakers: women and men, clergy and lay—all Catholic. Most were from New Orleans; some had connections with one of the member institutions, while others were known to the commission moderator. What these speakers had to say to the college students offers insight into the Catholic perspective on race relations in the 1940s and 1950s.

In her talk, "Catholic Action: Its Meaning, Its Implications, and Its Significance,"[21] Xavier alumna and instructor of history Leona M. Williams, a black Catholic, presented a three-part reform plan for challenging racial practices within the church. First, parish priests, she argued, should instruct their congregants in Catholic principles regarding race relations and then "instruct ushers to carry out these principles in church," which would eliminate the practice of ushers forcing blacks to sit in the back of the church. In order to break down racial stereotypes, she recommended that Catholic school teachers "inform pupils of the reality of the Brotherhood of Man under the Fatherhood of God." And third, she believed that "Catholic Universities should be open to students of required moral and educational qualities, without discriminatory practices concerning racial differences."[22] If implemented, Williams's three-part program would have integrated the key facilities in the archdiocese of New Orleans.

Guy Lemieux, S.J., philosophy professor at Loyola University of the South, spoke to the commission members as a Catholic priest speaking to Catholic college students.[23] Love, he told his audience, was the sign left by Christ in order that all could come to know him and his church. The "goal as Catholic students," he stated, "must be to take away injustices from Negroes and other minorities, thus sharing the Divine love of Christ with others." Lemieux said that "the Negro is Christ's chosen one to carry His cross at this time." However, he was not suggesting that blacks should endure the pain and suffering of such a burden alone; rather, he encouraged his listeners to help carry this cross.[24] Contrary to the thinking of his day, Lemieux did not present the standard pious answer of "offering up" one's suffering for a greater good in expectation of a heavenly reward. Instead, he wanted the students to help lift the burden of injustice from the shoulders of black Americans in this world.

CHR AND THE ARCHDIOCESAN HOLY HOUR

While the college students of SERINCO met to organize their own protests against racial prejudice and to listen to Catholic speakers address various aspects of the race question, their older counterparts of CHR undertook their own challenges to racial segregation within the archdiocese of New Orleans. Their efforts, in part, resulted in the cancellation of a major church affair in the fall of 1949. Here Catholic interracialism did make a difference.

In the spring of 1949 CHR members approached Archbishop Rummel to express their displeasure with the segregated seating policy enforced during the Holy Hour service held in New Orleans City Park. Held during the month of May and again in October, this religious ceremony was sponsored by the white Catholic members of the Metropolitan Council of Holy Name Societies and the black Catholic men of the Archdiocesan Union of Holy Name Societies. Even though this affair was religious in nature, Catholic participants had to abide by park policy, which required segregated seating in the stadium. In response to the CHR's complaint, Rummel was of the opinion that the group had waited too long to raise its objections; furthermore, he was unaware of the segregated conditions at the stadium. He did, however, promise to write the mayor as well as the superintendent of the park concerning the situation. While the spring service was held as planned and on a segregated basis, there were no guarantees that the fall celebration would proceed as usual.[25]

During the summer of 1949 Archbishop Rummel raised the issue of racial segregation with New Orleans City Park officials, asking permission to host an upcoming religious function on a nonsegregated basis. Presenting several objections to Rummel's request, park officials denied the archdiocese an exception to the segregation policy. The archbishop responded to the objections in a follow-up letter and again requested approval to host a desegregated event. Park officials again denied the request.[26]

After the archbishop left on a European pilgrimage in September, his assistant, Monsignor Lucien J. Caillouet, writing on the archbishop's behalf, petitioned park officials yet again to reconsider their position. And for a third time, New Orleans City Park officials rejected the archdiocesan request, informing Caillouet, "It is regrettable that the Archbishop's views and the unanimous views of the board do not coincide." As far as park officials were concerned, their decision was "definite and final." They did not want to hear from the archdiocese again.[27]

While the archbishop and his representative fought to hold a desegregated service in City Park, members of the Archdiocesan Union of Holy Name Societies took matters into their own hands and voted to participate in the procession regardless of City Park statutes. These black Catholics would defy city policy in the name of religious unity, and in doing so they had the support of the New Orleans Archdiocesan Holy Name Interracial Liaison committee, which approved the initiative and encouraged these black Catholics to "[g]o ahead and we will back you up."[28]

At a meeting of the Commission on Human Rights, A. P. Tureaud informed commission members that he expected to file suit against the New Orleans City Park Improvement Association in the name of one or more members of the Archdiocesan Union of Holy Name Societies to bring an end to this Jim Crow practice. Legal fees, he noted, would be furnished by the Knights of Peter Claver, the black Catholic fraternal organization for men.[29] City Park officials and their policy would be challenged on legal as well as religious grounds.[30]

When Rummel returned from Europe, he was faced with several choices: host a segregated Holy Hour program, allowing civil officials to dictate ecclesiastical policy; proceed with the program on an integrated basis and suffer the legal consequences for doing so; or cancel the whole affair, thereby offending some Catholics while gaining the approval of others. Rather than allowing public officials to dictate how a religious service would be conducted or participating in an act of civil disobedience, the archbishop chose instead to cancel the program.[31]

In explaining his decision to cancel the October Holy Hour, Rummel stated that segregating the races for a religious service was out of harmony with church doctrine. The archbishop had anticipated city approval for this function, since it would have been carried out "on a strictly religious basis under conditions that guaranteed perfect order and a genuine atmosphere of reverence, Christian charity and goodwill." As far as Rummel was concerned, this observance could "in no way be compared with certain incidents that have occurred elsewhere as demonstrations emphasizing segregation in the use of recreational and social facilities or in protest against certain unfortunate incidents or transgressions." And while certain forms of segregation might be justified, Rummel could not understand the park officials' stance, as this function was a "purely religious observance under circumstances which offer[ed] every guarantee of orderliness and disciplinary control, not to speak of the respect and reverence which all members of our Church have for religious functions."[32]

The CHR commended Archbishop Rummel, the Metropolitan Council of Holy Name Societies, and the Archdiocesan Union of Holy Name Societies for their courageous stances.[33] While the archbishop appreciated the commission's words of praise, he indicated that the issue was far from over: "this problem is not finally settled, for it has many complications which it will be necessary to meet and adjust."[34] Writing on behalf of his organization, Clarence Thomas, president of the Archdiocesan Union, informed CHR members, "There never was a time when it was more important for the Catholics to show a spirit of solidarity, to allow a small group of men, heading this public facility to rent this stadium, and dictate the terms of the porgram [sic] to the point where they would select what element of the membership that will be privileged to participate, is much more that an ordinary insult." He concluded by asking for God's blessing on CHR members and on their "endeavor[s] to bring Christian thinking to so many who only go to Church."[35]

The CHR was not the only organization that publicly praised the archbishop for canceling the Holy Hour event; the black newspaper the *Louisiana Weekly* also noted the significance of the decision. In commending the archbishop for his stance, however, the editors of the *Louisiana Weekly* questioned whether this was an isolated episode or the beginning of the end to racial segregation within the Catholic Church. The editors wondered if Rummel's decision was an "expedient" one, determined by the actions of park officials, or one meant to advance the Christian belief that all people, regardless of race, "are members of Christ's Mystical Body."[36] Only future actions by the archbishop would answer this question.

This conflict between City Park officials and the archbishop of New Orleans highlighted the reality of segregated life in New Orleans. Black New Orleanians were not only denied use of City Park but they were also excluded from using Audubon Park, located directly across from Tulane and Loyola universities. Allowing blacks to participate in an integrated service in City Park would challenge the societal norms and raise the possibility that other events at other venues might take place on an integrated basis. While the Holy Hour was a minor affair, much was at stake for the cause of racial justice. Rummel's challenge to the status quo questioned the legitimacy of the segregated way of life. The first efforts of the CHR to challenge racial discrimination had produced results—even beyond the cancellation of a church event. In part because of CHR pressure, the archdiocese finally merged the Archdiocesan Union and the Metropolitan Council of Holy Name Societies in 1952, thus ending the segregated system.[37]

Joseph Fichter used the Holy Hour incident to preach on the destructive force racial segregation was having on New Orleans. On Sunday morning, 2 October 1949, at Mater Dolorosa Church, Fichter addressed a white audience describing the efforts undertaken by men of the Holy Name societies to plan this public display of religious devotion. "The Catholic men from all of the parishes," Fichter noted, "wanted to demonstrate that the Mystical Body of Christ is one, that Catholics are united in their faith and in their love of God. They wanted to show that banker and bricklayer, educated and uneducated, rich and poor, white and colored, can walk shoulder to shoulder in common in worship of God."[38]

Fichter excoriated the park officials who interfered with this religious worship, calling them "irreligious people." While expressing sympathy for those living behind the Iron Curtain who suffered for their faith, he drew attention to the fact that this incident occurred in New Orleans, not in Russia, Hungary, or Yugoslavia. And he wanted to know how long the people of New Orleans would allow public officials to interfere with social and religious affairs. For Fichter, "every self-respecting Catholic ought to raise up and shout: Put an end to this mockery of Christian disintegration, this blasphemy against the Mystical Body of Christ. This separation and discrimination among Catholics and by Catholics."[39]

But were there members of the congregation who agreed with the City Park decision, he wondered. If there were, Fichter wanted them to make that very day a day of decision—deciding whether an individual was with Christ or against him. "If you are in favor of a separated and segregated Church," he told his listeners, then "stop pretending that you are a Catholic and a follower of Christ." If they were believers, he wanted them to "come out in the open and say so. . . . Stand up and be counted, either among the enemies of Christ or among His friends." He encouraged those present for this Mass to demonstrate their love for their fellow Catholics, especially black Catholics. And, in what many would consider the mixing of religion and politics, Fichter called upon the congregation to let their "voice be heard in protest against this injustice. . . . let your vote be felt in the next election against public officials who dare to interfere with the true Church of Christ and who refuse to us Catholics our inalienable right to worship in public as we please."[40]

Reaction to Fichter's impassioned sermon was negative. News of his open challenge to segregation circulated throughout the city and beyond; it was even reported to the superior general of the Jesuit order, John B. Janssens. Loyola's William Crandell, soon to be appointed provincial of the New Orleans province, recounted the incident to Janssens, noting, "About two months ago, he [Fichter] gave a very strong sermon about segregation. The parishioners were so incensed that word of it spread quickly through the city. Fr. Fichter has not been back to that parish since."[41]

CATHOLIC INTERRACIALISTS

The clergy were not the only people inviting the Catholic laity to reexamine their racial attitudes. At the June 1949 SERINCO meeting, CHR members Bertha Mugrauer and Alexander P. Tureaud, Sr., addressed the college students regarding race relations within the church. Mugrauer was an instructor of sociology at Xavier University. After receiving her bachelor's degree from Loyola University in 1945, she continued her education at the Catholic University of America, where she earned her master's degree in 1947 and her doctorate in 1949, both in sociology (the title of her dissertation was "Cultural Study of Ten Negro Girls in an Alley").[42] As the only black lawyer in New Orleans at the time, Tureaud was active in National Association for the Advancement of Colored People's legal cases.[43] He was also an officer of the Knights of Peter Claver.

In her address "The Lay Apostolate in Interracial Activities," Mugrauer explained that the lay apostolate was living a life of Catholic-Christian piety regardless of occupation. The lay apostle meant practicing a life of faith, humility, charity, voluntary poverty, and religious observance. Through charity one demonstrated concern for others by not judging others "who apparently do not agree with us." Through humility, that is, realizing that one is nothing compared to God and the saints, one gained "real courage to rely on God and stick to our principles." For Mugrauer voluntary poverty was "a means and not an end in itself." By voluntarily embracing poverty, the lay apostle would give witness to a higher good and demonstrate to others the fallacy of acquiring material goods; one might even come to understand what it means to be poor. One would come to see society's poor, including poor blacks, in a different light.[44]

"The interracial apostolate," she told the students, "demands the following . . . a fresh and vigorous charity, a contemplative life of prayer, saving souls from hell who are opposed to being saved, and lastly, an undying faith in God." She coupled these spiritual virtues with temporal capabilities: "In this world there is a great need for intelligent people who know and use well the answers found in sociology, anthropology and philosophy. We must know the answers based on solid fact, and be able to apply our Catholic principles to situations as we meet them." Religion and science, she argued, would work together to overcome racism in the United States and the world.[45]

As national secretary of the Knights of St. Peter Claver, Tureaud focused on the work of the organization in his talk. Founded in Mobile, Alabama, in 1909, the Knights were established to provide black Catholic men with their own fraternal organization because the Knights of Columbus rarely, if ever, accepted black members.[46] Between 1909 and 1949, Knights of St. Peter Claver membership had grown to almost 11,000 individuals; half that number were members of the women's auxiliary. Members were expected to be practicing Catholics; to fulfill their Easter duties, that is, go to confession and receive Communion during the Easter season; and to engage in charitable programs sponsored by the group. Involvement in charitable works, Tureaud explained, demonstrated "to others that they [the men and women of St. Peter Claver] actually live the principles of their Catholic faith."[47]

At the parochial level, Tureaud explained, members of the fraternal order were gaining experience in leadership, particularly in the field of social justice. "The Knights," he explained, "are trying to remove segregation and discrimination in the Catholic Church by educating people and showing them the harm that is being done to the Church because of the existing injustices." Another way the Knights were working toward removing discriminatory practices from within the church, he noted, was by providing financial help for the education of black seminarians at St. Augustine's Seminary in Bay St. Louis, Mississippi.[48] Tureaud would return in 1953 to speak to SERINCO members regarding his personal and professional efforts to desegregate Louisiana State University.[49]

Of the various speakers who addressed southern Catholics regarding the race question in 1949, none was more prominent than John LaFarge, S.J., founder of the Catholic interracial movement, who addressed a joint meeting of SERINCO and CHR members. For LaFarge, the race question was not a complicated one; it involved a few simple principles concerning education and religion. Prejudice, he believed, could be overcome through education and the practice of one's "deepest religious convictions." The power of love must not be underestimated, he told the gathering, for "love is stronger than death, and 'tis true where hate and love are given a chance, love will win." In order for the love of humanity to prevail over the "death" of intolerance and prejudice in the South, "[t]he bridge to be crossed is relinquishing the idea that white supremacy is a good thing, a necessary thing." A practical plan to promote interracial justice, based on Christian love and charity, could be established, he posited, once the idea of white supremacy was vanquished.[50]

Presentations by Mugrauer, Tureaud, and LaFarge as well as those by Lemieux and Williams reinforced the basic message of Catholic interracialism: unity through faith. Belief in God, belief in the teachings of Jesus Christ and His church, and belief in the perfectibility of men and women would unify the human race and eliminate discrimination. But talking was not the same as acting. Belief without works was fruitless. The commission members knew this and tried to put their faith into action. Their first opportunity to fight racial discrimination in the field of graduate education came in 1949.

CATHOLIC DESEGREGATION

The first serious attempt at desegregating a Catholic institution of higher learning in New Orleans occurred in 1949 when SERINCO member Harry Alexander of Xavier University applied for admission to Loyola University's School of Law. His was the first serious attempt at desegregating the law school. While he would ultimately be turned down, Alexander's application served notice that the challenge to racial segregation in Catholic educational institutions was just beginning.

This was not the first time Loyola had to face the issue of desegregating the law school; earlier in the decade rumors abounded that the National Association for the Advancement of Colored People (NAACP) was going to force Loyola into accepting a black applicant. So real was the perceived threat of such action in 1942 that the president of the university at that time, Percy A. Roy, S.J., convened a special meeting of the board of directors to discuss the situation.[51] At that meeting Roy "called the attention of the Board to what he thought was a very persistent movement fostered by the American Association for the Advancement of the Colored Race to foster negro [sic] students into white schools, and he cited an instance in which considerable pressure was exercised in regard to the Law School of Loyola." The sense of the board was that they "should be on guard at the University, and at the same time be very careful not to give offense." The Loyola board members agreed that "it would be the ruination of our University to admit colored students, as long as the laws and customs of the South are what they are."[52]

Harry Alexander gave a name and a face to the question of integrating Loyola University. He was an ideal candidate for admission because he was a Catholic, a veteran of the Second World War, and a graduate of Xavier University, where he was a member of the collegians' interracial commission as well as a student leader.[53] At the end of his college career, Alexander was awarded the Dr. Percy Creuzot award for general excellence and the Frederick Walter Shea award for outstanding service in student activities at the national level; he had been the president of the NAACP's Youth Council at Xavier and vice president of the Louisiana-Arkansas-Mississippi region of the United States National Students Association.[54]

The Jesuit regent of Loyola's law school, Louis J. Twomey, personally favored Alexander's admission.[55] He believed that the acceptance of one or more highly screened black students to the law school could pave the way for the admission of qualified black students to all departments of the university, and he said so to Vincent McCormick, the American Jesuit representative in Rome.[56] By accepting a black applicant into the law school, Twomey informed McCormick, "Loyola could have a magnificent example of Catholic leadership, which would certainly have redounded generously to the Glory of God, of the Catholic Church in the United States, of the American Assistancy, and of Loyola itself." Twomey recognized that the university might suffer a decline in enrollment by integrating, but he "doubted that any notable dropping off of white students would follow." He argued that "even though the student body might conceivably be severely curtailed, the resulting gain for Christ, the Church and the American Assistancy would far outweigh whatever loss Loyola would sustain." He saw a greater good coming from the admission of black students than from maintaining a prudent posture of continuing the status quo.[57]

But despite Twomey's endorsement, Alexander's application was denied, an action Twomey blamed on the shortsightedness of the Jesuit consultors.[58] He did not question their sincerity but did question their judgment. "It seems to me," he wrote, "that they are considering the problem only within the perspective of Loyola or at widest within the perspective of the New Orleans Province." He explained, "Apparently they fail to recognize that the problem is primarily not one of a single unit in the Jesuit educational system, but of the whole system, primarily not one of the South, but of the United States and even of the world. They seem to forget that what Loyola and the New Orleans Province do in race relations will have for good or evil repercussions far transcending the limits of either."[59]

Twomey questioned the consultors' ability to evaluate the situation properly. One of the consultors' contentions was that, as southerners, they knew the problems in the South as no one from outside the region could, and they knew what was best for Loyola, the city, and the South. As a native of Tampa, Florida, and therefore a fellow southerner, Twomey found that argument wanting: "There are other Southern Jesuits, whose number is rapidly increasing, who likewise feel they know the problem, and that while maintaining loyalty to the many fine things which are southern, they can be constructively critical of our racial policies." The regent of the law school contended that "it is the exception among our younger priests to find one who does not think that we must assume a calm, but forthright position relative to this issue." Here he was referring to such men as Joseph Fichter, Henry Montecino, and Guy Lemieux. The attitude of the consultors, Twomey believed, was representative of "many other Jesuits in the South and elsewhere for that matter." Such an outlook, he concluded, could "be accurately if bluntly described as one which upholds the theory of 'white supremacy.'"[60]

Frustrated by what he considered Loyola's timidity, Twomey petitioned Francis E. Lucey, the Jesuit regent of Georgetown University Law School, to accept Alexander. Just the previous year, the archbishop of Washington, Patrick A. O'Boyle, had integrated the archdiocesan parochial school system, so there were no apparent obstacles keeping Georgetown University from accepting a black applicant. Twomey explained to Lucey that "under prevailing conditions it is not possible for us to consider his [Alexander's] application." Twomey assured Lucey that Alexander was an outstanding applicant: "he is a Catholic boy, a good Catholic, well mannered and splendidly poised. A man who knows how to move gracefully in racial circles, and I am sure he would cause you no embarrassment because of his personal conduct."[61]

Twomey knew that Georgetown would be taking him "off the hook" by accepting Alexander, but this Jesuit also viewed the acceptance in another light. He believed that Georgetown would be "helping to build up the esteem of the Church in the minds of our Southern Negro population" if they accepted this qualified Xavier graduate.[62] Twomey was concerned that the church would be perceived as a racist institution because Loyola would not accept a black applicant. Georgetown accepted Harry Alexander, who began his law studies there in the fall of 1949.[63]

The theoretical question of integrating Loyola law school, raised in the summer of 1948 by Catholic college students, became a practical matter in the summer of 1949. In order for the only Catholic law school in the South not to appear prejudiced, officials of the institution made arrangements to have a black

Catholic applicant accepted elsewhere. The issue of integration was no longer theoretical but practical. The question now facing the law school was how long could it continue to refuse to integrate. And once that educational front was breached, one wondered how much longer other church-sponsored institutions, or even the church itself, could maintain racial segregation. Forces from within and without the church would help bring the issue to a head.

Joseph H. Fichter, S.J. (1908–1994), Professor of Sociology, Loyola University, New Orleans. Fichter was the faculty moderator and chaplain of the Southeastern Regional Interracial Commission (SERINCO), which was comprised of Catholic college students in New Orleans, and a founding member of the Commission on Human Rights (CHR), a sub-unit of the Catholic lay organization, the Catholic Committee of the South. (Photo courtesy of Special Collections & Archives, Monroe Library, Loyola University, New Orleans.)

Officers of the southeastern region of the National Federation of Catholic College Students (NFCCS), the parent organization of SERINCO. (Left to Right) Claire Brechtel (Ursuline College), Anna May Kingsmill (St. Mary's Dominican College), Daniel Quinn (Loyola University), Peter Duffy (Loyola University) c. 1948–1949. Daniel Quinn was the first chairperson of SERINCO. (Photo courtesy of Claire Brechtel.)

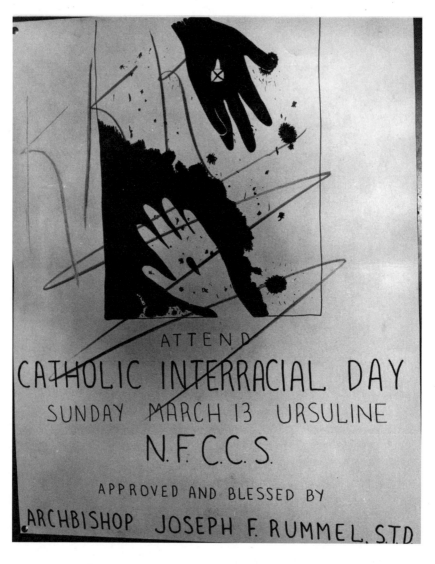

Opposition to the Interracial Commission was evident by the defacing of a poster announcing the 1st Interracial Sunday gathering in 1949, Archbishop Rummel's approval notwithstanding. (Photo courtesy of Special Collections & Archives, Monroe Library, Loyola University, New Orleans.)

Black, White, and Catholic. The fear of many white southern Americans was that interracial activities would ultimately lead to interracial marriages. This 1950 Interracial Sunday blessing given by Rev. Leander Martin, S.V.D., to Larry Brown of Xavier University and Joan Forshag of Loyola University, while purely a spiritual action, embodies that anxiety. (Photo courtesy of Special Collections & Archives, Monroe Library, Loyola University, New Orleans.)

ABOVE AND FACING PAGE: To advance the cause of interracialism, SERINCO members organized intercollegiate basketball games in the winter of 1952–1953 between member institutions. Xavier men played the men from Loyola, while Xavier women played a team comprised of Ursuline and Dominican students. The first integrated NCAA basketball game was played at Loyola University in December of 1954. (Photo courtesy of Special Collections & Archives, Monroe Library, Loyola University, New Orleans.)

CHAPTER IV

Catholic Choice: Jim Crowism
or Jesus Christ, 1949–1952

IN ADDITION TO PRESIDENT TRUMAN'S and the Democratic Party's call for civil rights reform in the post–World War II period, the major civil rights developments during Truman's term in office occurred at the judicial level. The Supreme Court decisions in *Shelley* v. *Kraemer* (1948) and *Hurd* v. *Hodge* (1948) on discrimination in housing practices, *Henderson* v. *United States* (1950) on discrimination in interstate travel, and *Sweatt* v. *Painter* (1950) and *McLaurin* v. *Oklahoma State Regents for Higher Education* (1950) on racial segregation at the graduate school level all indicated a court ever so slowly dismantling Jim Crow society. In 1952 the court heard the first arguments of *Brown* v. *Board of Education of Topeka et al.*[1]

As the United States came to terms with its racial policies, the country also had to deal with challenges abroad. The United States entered into a cold war against Communism and the Soviet Union with its involvement in the Berlin Airlift and the creation of the North Atlantic Treaty Organization and its reaction to the Soviet development of the atomic bomb and expansion of Communism in Asia. The Alger Hiss spy case, the Rosenbergs' trial, and Senator Joseph McCarthy's charge of Communist influence in the federal government caused many Americans to question the nation's domestic security. It was a period of unease.[2]

For the universal Roman Catholic Church, the post–World War II period was a time of trial and tribulation. In Eastern Europe and mainland China, the church endured oppression at the hands of Communist regimes, with Cardinal Jozsef Mindszenty of Hungary, convicted of treason in 1948 and serving a life sentence, among the most celebrated of persecuted Catholics. The church's strong stand against Communism along with American Catholics' desire to be accepted by the Protestant majority created a fervent anti-Communist, almost superpatriotic, culture among Roman Catholics of the United States. For most, Christian beliefs and democratic virtues were superior to atheistic Communism. Aware that the practice of Christianity and democracy was wanting, American Roman Catholics were forced to address racial policies and practices. Catholic interracial activities of this period highlighted the incongruities between belief and practice and forced church leaders to address the issue.[3]

INTERRACIAL ACTIVISM

As the nation dealt with issues of war and peace, members of the Southeastern Regional Interracial Commission (SERINCO) and the Commission on Human Rights (CHR) continued their efforts to effect change within the church. Both groups held monthly meetings, published newsletters, hosted guest speakers, organized annual interracial gatherings, and put on social affairs. Compared to the campaigns against segregation a decade or so later undertaken by the major southern civil rights organizations such as the Southern Christian Leadership Conference and the Student Non-Violent Coordinating Committee, the activities of SERINCO and the CHR pale in comparison. And yet these New Orleans Catholics fought for civil rights years before these other organizations even existed. Holding meetings, working together to publish a newsletter, planning an annual day of prayer, or gathering for a social affair, all on an integrated basis, undermined the racial customs and standards of the day.

Innocuous as some of these activities may appear a half-century later, they were unprecedented at the time and challenged the religious and social landscape of Catholic New Orleans. Participation in SERINCO and CHR activities prepared individuals for the eventual transition from a segregated to an integrated society. Unfortunately, these organizations were short-lived and did not fully implement their objectives. Had these organizations survived into the 1960s, however, Catholics interracialism would have provided the leadership and example necessary to produce a new social order.

Nevertheless, during the organizations' existence, SERINCO and CHR members heard guest speakers address the inconsistency between the ideals of Christianity and the practice of segregation by Catholic institutions. Christian principles and ideals called for unity rather than division, inclusion rather than exclusion. One could not be a Christian and discriminate against others. For some Catholics there was a choice: follow Jesus Christ or Jim Crow.

In his 1949 SERINCO address concerning Catholic social teachings and American society, Louis Twomey, S.J., regent of Loyola's law school, focused on the Christian ideal of love. He saw this as a way that church teachings could effect change in American society, especially when applied to the race question. Catholics say that they love one another, he pointed out, but then they contradict themselves with their lack of charity. He asked his audience to apply the golden rule to people of color: "How would you like to be done by as you do to the Negro?" The time had come, Twomey emphasized, to stop circumventing the Christian principle of loving one another. Racial segregation was contrary to Christian teachings and so had to end. "Either the law of love is the law of Christianity or it is not," he concluded; "if it is, then we are bound to love all in our practice."[4]

Reinforcing Twomey's ideas was Jonas Mason's address in October 1949 concerning the archdiocesan Holy Name societies.[5] Mason, a black Catholic, was an officer of the Archdiocesan Union of Holy Name Societies (the black branch of the archdiocesan Holy Name societies), a past national treasurer of the Knights of Peter Claver, and a past president of the Holy Name Society at St. Katherine's Church.[6] From its establishment in the archdiocese until the turn of the twentieth century, the organization, he informed his audience, had been integrated. "It was not until around 1908 and 1910," he noted, "that prejudice crept into the society and the trouble about segregation in the Church arose." The rise of race-based parishes precipitated the call for segregated Holy Name societies.[7]

Furthermore, the development and practice of racial segregation within the church had not been lost on non-Catholics, Mason noted; black Protestants often told black Catholics, "[A]fter all the love and charity you preach, you [Catholics] still cannot be part of the whole" because of the church's segregationist policies. An example of this division within the church was the presence of "signs which reserve the last two or three pews for Negroes who dare to go to that [white] Church." While he was under the impression that Archbishop Rummel was against segregation and that the archbishop had called for the removal of segregation signs in church, Mason also knew that, the admonitions notwithstanding, this form of discrimination would not disappear in the near future.[8]

Racial segregation at the parish level and within the various parish and archdiocesan organizations highlights the culpability of New Orleans Catholics, clergy and laity alike, in committing an injustice. What percentage of parishes discriminated against blacks? All the white ones did, and the evidence suggests that the vast majority of white Catholics endorsed or at least accepted the practice. Otherwise there would have been no need to establish a separate Holy Name organization for black Catholics, the Knights of Peter Claver for black Catholics, or St. Katherine's parish, among others, for black Catholics.

Encouraged by their guest speakers and eager to take a principled stand against racial segregation, SERINCO members called for the passage of an anti-segregation resolution at the first annual congress of the New Orleans region of the National Federation of Catholic College Students (NFCCS) in November 1949. Formulating such a resolution, however, proved contentious because not all those attending the gathering were members of the interracial commission, and not all NFCCS members favored integration.[9]

Based on the resolution passed at the national convention in Philadelphia that spring, the regional congress resolution called for an end to discriminatory practices within the church, especially at the college level. This document began by chastising those Catholic organizations that discriminated against black Catholics. The authors of the resolution then called for implementing NFCCS programs and policies that presented true Catholic doctrine regarding the immorality of racial discrimination. The students also endorsed any effort that would "lead to the abolition of segregation in the Catholic Colleges of the New Orleans Region and to the admission of qualified students without racial discrimination." Finally, the resolution called for students to undertake practical efforts to develop a spirit of Christian integration through work and recreation.[10]

As the minutes of the meeting reflect, members of the congress disagreed over the wording of the resolution. Various participants, not identified by name, rationalized their position by stating that "those people [delegates to the national convention] can't come down here with their resolutions to their problems and apply them to us[;] it's silly and poorly worded[;] it says a lot of stupid words that if we do not do it we'll be uncharitable." Two members voted against the section that called for the admission of blacks into Catholic colleges. One dissenter claimed that "on Loyola's campus and I'm sure on others it [desegregation] would really do more harm than good." Others questioned the wording of a section that called for promoting integrated group work and recreation, with the word "recreation" being the source of dissension. For these students, the implication was that blacks wanted social equality with whites. Xavier student and NFCCS regional treasurer Richard Gumbel assured the delegates that blacks did not want social equality; rather, their objectives were economic equality and political rights.[11]

After much debate and several revisions, the collegians passed a resolution concerning the race question. The statement began by presenting a positive interpretation of the work initiated by the interracial commission of the NFCCS rather than chastising their coreligionists. As in the drafts, the document called upon member schools to adopt NFCCS programs and policies in order that Catholic doctrine might be presented without compromise and ambiguity. Again, the resolution advocated the admission of all qualified students to any member college regardless of race. The resolution also expressed the hope that students would inculcate a spirit of Christian integration through work and recreation.[12]

Archbishop Joseph Francis Rummel, present at the conclusion of the congress, addressed the delegates. He commended the undergraduates for their efforts and encouraged them to continue their Catholic involvement after graduation. Participation now, he argued, prepared them for leadership roles in the future. Rummel saw this trained laity as a helping hand that would cooperate with the hierarchy. "Intelligent Catholic lay people," he commented, "must practice what the hierarchy put forth. It is one thing for the hierarchy to give a solution to these problems and another thing for the intelligent educated Catholic laity to put these things into practice."[13] The archbishop, however, would soon find out that the laity was of a different mind regarding the race question. While some Catholics would support the archbishop when he began to push for integration, others resisted, often vehemently and publicly, creating major problems for Rummel and the church as a whole.

SECOND ANNUAL INTERRACIAL SUNDAY GATHERING, 1950

Following the regional congress, SERINCO's next major undertaking was planning the second annual Interracial Sunday gathering, which was also supported by the CHR. SERINCO members had trouble finding a host institution for the affair; none of the New Orleans-area schools volunteered. Interracial commission chairman George Saporito, writing to the NFCCS national office, explained that "we are again looking for a suitable place to hold Catholic Interracial Day on the second Sunday of Lent, 1950. As yet we cannot find a 'white' Catholic College which will be willing to have the program." Neither Loyola University nor Dominican College offered to sponsor the event, and because it had hosted the previous year, Ursuline College was not an option. Finally the College of the Sacred Heart in Grand Coteau, Louisiana, volunteered.[14] In an effort to generate interest in and support for the gathering and to encourage high school students to submit entries for the poster contest, Richard Gumbel, Aaron Henry, Carmelo Graffagnini, and Daniel Quinn, among others, visited area Catholic high schools to promote the affair and the poster contest.[15]

The second annual Interracial Sunday gathering took place on 12 March 1950 with some three hundred persons in attendance. The program of the day followed that of the previous year: Mass, breakfast, guest speakers, collegians' speeches, discussion period, and an awards presentation. A black priest, Leander Martin, S.V.D., celebrated Mass for an integrated congregation. The guest speakers were CHR members: John McCann, attorney, and Clarence Laws, public relations director of the black newspaper the *Louisiana Weekly.* Following the guest speakers, Aaron Henry of Xavier University presided over the college forum, which consisted of speeches and a discussion period. At the end of the day, Bishop Jules B. Jeanmard of the diocese of Lafayette presented trophies to Carol Woods of Xavier Prep, winner of the poster contest, and Norman Francis of Xavier University, winner of the speech contest.[16]

The *Louisiana Weekly* praised Bishop Jeanmard and the students for their efforts in furthering better race relations. "As we reflect upon the moral dishonesty and outright race baiting of many of our leaders in the state," the editors wrote, "it is indeed refreshing and heartening to have that [a call for racial unity] expressed from the Bishop of Lafayette." The *Weekly* editorial expressed appreciation for the attitude of the college students involved in interracial activities, stating, "It is exceedingly gratifying . . . to note that the students of both races are no longer satisfied to accept the questionable theories and evaluations of individuals based upon their race, color or creed."[17]

ARCHDIOCESE OF NEW ORLEANS AND THE RACE QUESTION

By the spring of 1950, SERINCO and CHR members had another successful Interracial Sunday to show for their efforts. However, more importantly, earlier that year, the archdiocese of New Orleans produced a policy statement concerning the evangelization of blacks. In this document church officials decreed that Catholics seeking black converts "bind themselves in conscience to the following laws and constantly observe them." One of the laws concerned the practice of segregated seating and communion lines in the church; this practice was to end, and the individuals "who carry out the work of keeping order in the church (*the ushers*)" were to be "thoroughly informed about this law." Priests could not "refuse the sacraments nor the sacramentals to the faithful of the Negro race." If a black parish was nearby, however, members of the clergy might advise blacks to frequent that particular church. All Catholics were admonished not to make "the practice of their religion difficult for Negroes who are actually their brothers and sisters in Christ." The faithful were asked to desist in practicing racial segregation and to abide instead "by the principles which are in conformity with the Divine precepts and the teachings of the Church."[18]

This archdiocesan document, which the CHR translated from Latin, reproduced, and distributed to fellow Catholics, also called on archdiocesan organizations such as the Holy Name societies, Marian sodalities, and other devotional and pious groups, to examine the race question by forming study groups in order to discover ways to end racial tension and friction in American Catholic society and assist evangelization efforts among blacks.[19]

The 1950 archdiocesan document, produced by members of the hierarchy and clergy, represented a shift in the thinking among members of this body. While the clerics did not call for the dismantling of segregated parishes, their recommendations called for an end to the practice of racial segregation within parish churches. The archdiocese was now on record stating that segregation was neither desirable nor permissible; however, implementation of this directive would be slow and sporadic. A major crisis within the archdiocese would occur before the Catholic faithful embraced, at least outwardly, racial integration.

INTERRACIAL GOVERNANCE

While Archbishop Rummel and members of the clergy struggled to implement the new order within the archdiocese, the Catholic college students attempted to do the same within their interracial organization. The elections for SERINCO officers in 1950 was one such occasion. From its inception, the chair of the interracial commission had been held by (white) Loyola students. SERINCO members now wondered whether the time had come for another institution to assume responsibility for the chairmanship. New ideas and leaders, members believed, would bring a fresh perspective to their work; therefore, members turned to Xavier. Loyola delegates Ted Craft and Joan Forshag argued for Xavier leadership; "the psychological effect of a Negro chairman would be good on the white campuses." They believed that "Negroes must take steps to help their own people if they expect the white people to cooperate." These students found that all too often the white population used the lack of black involvement and participation as an excuse for not becoming involved in interracial movements. Xavier representatives Norman Francis and James Mundy countered; they "did not want the regional chairmanship because they did not have sufficiently outstanding leadership ability." Furthermore, they noted, the Xavier University administration preferred Loyola's retaining the position because "white leadership made the commission more favorable in the eyes of the [white] people." The members resolved the issue by awarding the chairmanship to Ted Craft of Loyola and naming Norman Francis of Xavier vice chairman.[20]

This reliance on Loyola University to provide the leadership for the interracial commission proved to be a major weakness in the organization. Xavier University's reluctance to take a leadership role in SERINCO meant the success or failure of the organization rested with Loyola University—its students and faculty. With Loyola's Joseph Fichter as moderator and Loyola students assuming the interracial chairmanship on a regular basis, SERINCO was dominated by one white Catholic university. Given the degree of antipathy shown by the Loyola University's board of directors toward the organization, the interracial commission would have been better served by choosing officers from various schools; if the organization had found itself prohibited from operating on one campus, the students could shift the operation to another institution.

While most of their energy was devoted to local issues, these New Orleans Catholic college students saw themselves as part of the broader world of American Catholicism. In the spring of 1950, representatives from the New Orleans area institutions attended the seventh national congress of the NFCCS held in Pittsburgh, Pennsylvania.[21] However, getting to these gatherings reminded students that the quest for racial equality was far from won. Dominican College delegate Betty Prillmayer remembered how odd it was for her and her classmates to be standing on the train platform in New Orleans talking to Xavier delegates Norman Francis and Richard Gumbel prior to boarding the train but then not seeing them during the trip. "We were standing on the platform having the best time talking to one another, college students, and having a really nice conversation; and then we got on the train and they got on the train. We never laid eyes on them until we got to Pittsburgh." The Dominican student knew that "they had to sit in another car, that was the norm; they went to their car and we went to our car. We never saw one another, but then when we got to Pittsburgh we were in the hotel together and we were going to meetings together." Prillmayer knew that the situation "was not right, there was something wrong," but there was nothing she could do to change the transportation laws.[22] At the convention Gumbel was elected national treasurer of the NFCCS.[23]

RACIAL INTRANSIGENCE AND CATHOLIC DESEGREGATION

While the members of the NFCCS strove to implement interracial justice, segregation was still practiced in the archdiocese of New Orleans in the summer of 1950, church decrees notwithstanding. Surveying New Orleans parishes that summer, members of the CHR reported that segregation signs were still posted.[24] CHR members saw the continued presence of these signs in churches as an indication of a lack of Catholic leadership regarding the race question. The decrees of the 1950 synod explicitly called for the clergy and the laity to end the practice of segregated seating within the church. While blacks and whites might have to sit in separate areas while using public transportation or frequenting public establishments such as theaters, the Roman Catholic Church would not tolerate such discrimination in its churches. It was the duty and responsibility of the clergy to see to it that the faithful understood and embraced this new way of life, however painful it might be. The fact that signs had not been removed by the summer of 1950 indicated that the clergy either supported segregated seating in their parishes or that they feared the reaction of their congregation should they end it.

However, some progress, albeit limited, was being made in the area of race relations at the level of Catholic higher education in New Orleans, specifically at Loyola University of the South. The outbreak of the Korean conflict in the summer of 1950 provided coverage for the president of the university, Thomas J. Shields, S.J., to admit several blacks into select educational programs. Echoing the thinking of many American black leaders, W. E. B. Du Bois for one, Shields reasoned that if blacks were fighting for democracy abroad, then they deserved the same rights as any other American at home. Also influencing Shields was the September decision of the Fifth Circuit Federal Court of Appeals, whose jurisdiction encompassed Louisiana, which called for the desegregation of Louisiana State University's School of Law. In light of these developments, Shields decided to integrate part of Loyola University.[25]

Earlier that summer, however, Shields had presented a different view of the race question to his Jesuit superior in Rome, John B. Janssens. "Unfortunately, and admitting with shame that racial prejudice is still too strong in this area," Shields informed Janssens, "[T]he time has not yet come when it would be advisable to accept Negro students at Loyola. However, in view of the truly remarkable progress in better race relations in the Southern states during the past fifteen years or twenty years, and provided no precipitate or imprudent action retards the constantly improving relations, I am of the opinion that it will not be too many years before it will be possible to admit Negroes."[26]

But by September 1950 the president of Loyola had changed his mind. As he explained to Janssens, Shields decided to accept blacks into select programs at the university because of "the outstanding work done by a Negro regiment in the Korean War, with certain legal questions arising in the state regarding segregation, and with the minds of our people occupied with the possibility of military mobilization." Considering these factors, Shields felt that the university "had at last arrived at the point where we might admit without any public announcement or demonstration a few Negroes." By allowing three religious black women, members of the Sisters of the Holy Family, to attend Saturday classes, one black man to attend the evening school, and twelve black men to participate in the Institute of Industrial Relations (a noncredit program), token integration at Loyola took place in the fall of 1950.[27]

The president of Loyola reported to his Roman superior that the acceptance of the sisters and the laymen was "accomplished without any difficulty or adverse comment except a few remarks on the part of two or three of Ours and on the part of one lay teacher." He did not consider their remarks as being of any significance. Shields tended to downplay the divisive nature of the community's disagreements and to stress the positive whenever possible. So optimistic was he about the progress made in admitting a handful of black nuns and laymen to Loyola that he predicted, "If conditions continue well during the year, then it should be possible to make a further advance next year."[28] What Shields failed to report, however, was that there were troubles at the Institute of Industrial Relations (IIR) because of desegregation; white attendance in the program dropped significantly once blacks were allowed to attend IIR sessions. By December 1950 it appeared that, in order to survive, the IIR would either have to exclude blacks from attending programs or allow the organization to become a black-only group. The other possibility, albeit a rather drastic one, was discontinuing the institute altogether.[29]

While Shields reported that only a few caustic remarks were made regarding the admission of black students to various Loyola programs, Andrew Smith, S.J., dean of men at Spring Hill College and a province consultor,[30] presented Janssens with a different impression. Smith noted that the admission of black students did not pass "without unfavorable comment from certain members of the Jesuit [Loyola] faculty." Because of this reaction and several other factors, he explained to Janssens, "the Provincial is now studying with his consultors some statement of policy that might be issued to the province." According to Smith, the source of division among fellow Jesuits concerning the race question was with regard to "*timing* in the matter of eliminating segregation." Because Harry Crane's term as provincial was drawing to an end, the drafting of a policy statement would be left to his successor.[31]

WILLIAM CRANDELL, S.J., SOUTHERN JESUITS, AND CATHOLIC INTERRACIALISM

In September 1950, forty-one-year-old William Crandell succeeded Harry L. Crane as provincial of the New Orleans Province of the Society of Jesus. Born in 1909, Crandell entered the Jesuits in 1926; he was ordained in 1939. Coming from a northern Louisiana plantation family, Crandell was a traditional southerner with the usual paternalistic attitudes towards blacks. He was poised and articulate and, as such, made a good public representative for the church and his religious order. Crandell inherited a Jesuit province divided over the race question, an issue that needed to be addressed in a judicious manner. As provincial he was in a position either to further or hinder the cause of racial justice within the local church and southern society at large.[32]

Prior to becoming provincial, Crandell had spent nine years working at Loyola University of the South, first as dean of men, then as the dean of arts and sciences, and finally as the academic vice president of the university. In addition to his work at Loyola, he was selected as a province consultor in 1945, which gave him a broader view of the works undertaken by his fellow Jesuits throughout the southern United States. The consultor's position also afforded him the opportunity to discuss and listen to what other Jesuits had to say about the pressing issues of the day, especially the issue of segregation. When the interracial activities of the collegians produced consternation among the Loyola University Jesuits, William Crandell was well aware of the situation. Indeed, his last letter as a province consultor provides insight into his thinking on the race question at the time.

Crandell was sympathetic to the plight of the black American: low wages, substandard housing, inferior educational opportunities, lack of recreational facilities, etc. He informed his superior in Rome, John B. Janssens, that because of public opinion, segregationist practices were followed even when the law did not require it. He noted, however, that individually and collectively Americans were working to remedy the situation.[33]

Regarding the difficulties at Loyola, Crandell identified for Janssens the various "race camps" found among the Jesuits at the university. He noted that the first group, which he designated "men of action," favored a direct attack on segregation: Joseph Fichter, Louis Twomey, Jacques Yenni, Guy Lemieux, and

Franklin Lynette; those "[v]iolently opposed to them are Fr. Burke, Fr. S. Ray, Fr. Mulherin, and Fr. Rogero," the prosegregation group; and a "middle-of-the-road" majority—racial gradualists, among whom he placed himself. "The majority of the Community," he wrote, "including myself, feels that segregation is an explosive issue that can best be broken by indirect methods aimed at remedying the present economic inequality of the Negro, bettering his housing, recreational and educational facilities within the framework of existing segregation laws." The majority faction believed that if blacks were first elevated from a position of inequality to that of equality, albeit still separated racially but now acceptable to whites, then public opinion (i.e., white public opinion) would shift in favor of the dismantling of segregation laws. Resolving the differences between the various factions, Crandell observed, would be difficult because the "men of action" were "unwilling to restrict their activities to the methods proposed by the . . . [gradualists] and scorn these methods as a 'do nothing attitude.'"[34] Crandell's endorsement of a gradualist position regarding desegregation reflected the thinking of many in the South.

He also addressed the specific problems facing Loyola University: "Pressure is being brought to bear upon us to admit Negroes to certain departments of the University (Dentistry and Law) in which Catholic Negroes have no other facilities in the city. Word of this pressure has reached some students and professors who claim that they will leave Loyola the day a Negro is accepted." Crandell admitted to Janssens that he did not know if this was the sentiment of a majority of students and faculty, and he did not know what should be done for the "Greater Glory of God."[35]

On the basis of this letter, it can be argued that Janssens knew what kind of man he was appointing to become the next provincial of the New Orleans Province. He had some idea what direction Crandell would follow regarding the race question once in office. Here was a man who would favor attempts to ameliorate the effects of segregation and eventually see its dismantling; however, Crandell was a gradualist, which meant he would not advocate a direct attack on Jim Crow society. He could be counted on, therefore, not to place the province in direct conflict with the social attitudes and practices of a majority of Catholics in the region. It appeared that the new provincial did not regard segregation as a grave moral issue but one that needed to be addressed in due time.

RESISTING RACISM AND SAM HILL RAY, S.J., PART ONE

The appointment of William Crandell had no immediate impact on the practice of racial segregation within the church or on the activities of the interracial groups in New Orleans. SERINCO and the CHR continued their efforts to promote racial equality. A notable achievement was the publication of SERINCO's article "Southern Collegians Resist Racism" in the *Catholic World.* Written by the white members of the interracial commission, who claimed to speak for most southerners, the authors addressed the issue of desegregation. These young Catholics informed their readers that they looked forward to the day when black and white students would study together. To prepare everyone for the impending change, the authors recommended a four-point plan of action within the university calling for (a) informed and unbiased lectures on the race question, (b) well-rounded and factual courses in various fields addressing racial issues, (c) intelligent class discussions, and (d) supplementary readings on the topic. Instructors, courses, and conversations would educate and inform Catholic college students of the teachings of the church regarding race relations, and so ignorance and prejudice would give way to enlightenment and acceptance.[36]

Through courses in religion, philosophy, history, biology, sociology, and economics, the authors believed, the race question could be addressed directly. In religion and philosophy courses, which formed "the bases of our Christian lives," the students expected to learn "how to deal with current social sins like segregation and discrimination." From courses in ethics, they wanted to learn about "the morality of restrictive covenants, segregated education, underpayment of Negro servants, exclusion of Negroes from public facilities." In calling for history courses that would "clarify the numerous misconceptions about the 'dark continent' [and] supply omissions concerning the part Negroes played in the building of the United States," these mid-century collegians were presaging the introduction of Black Studies by some twenty years. Through discussions in classes and supplemental reading on the topic of race relations, the students believed individuals could prepare themselves for entering an integrated world.[37]

The students concluded their article by challenging and refuting three of the most frequently repeated counsels used against interracial work: "don't be radical like the Communists, . . . the time is not ripe for change, . . . and you'll do more harm than good." Puzzled by the admonition not to be "radical," the student authors could not understand how being in favor of Christianity was akin to being a "Red." "If the removal of pride and the practice of love and justice are the actions of radicals," they reasoned, "then we shall have to follow Christ." The position that "the time is not ripe for change," argued the students, showed a lack of understanding. Society was changing, and Catholics needed to be aware of that change, especially in the area of race relations. "Are we going to say 'me too' after all the non-Catholic colleges and universities have opened their doors to Negroes, and it is safe for us to do so?" they asked. The writers believed that the time to change had come and was long overdue. And finally, the counsel "you'll do more harm than good" was the hardest for these collegians to comprehend.

They wondered what the harm was when blacks and whites went to college together. The experience of integrated colleges and universities in the South demonstrated that a great deal of good came from their interracial experiences, not harm. Hence, these students wanted the harm done by maintaining segregation addressed forthrightly.[38]

As expected, not everyone was pleased with the collegians' article and the positions the students presented. Sam Hill Ray, Jesuit director of student counseling at Loyola, took exception and so informed William Crandell, S.J., the provincial of the New Orleans Province. The students' claim that the opinion expressed in the article was that of most southerners, Ray noted, was "just . . . not true. It is not the opinion of 'most.'" After attacking the article, Ray called for the severing of relations with the NFCCS. "I still insist on withdrawing from the NFCCS," he informed the provincial. And if Loyola would not withdraw from the organization, he suggested that a southerner be appointed moderator in order to "tone down this interracial threat." For Ray, there was "too much inexperience and non-Southern opinion influencing Loyola."[39]

Ray's letter of protest against integration was nothing new; the director of student counseling had expressed similar sentiments to the provincial just weeks before. "If the policy of Loyola," he wrote, "is to admit negroes [sic] to eat with the whites in the cafeteria (October 15th); to sit with the whites in the class rooms (Sept. 26th); to mingle in the auditorium together (Oct. 15th); to ride together in the Loyola bus to Bay St. Louis for the negro ordination [of Joseph Francis, S.V.D., brother of SERINCO member Norman Francis]; then I think we should remove segregation at Loyola and admit the negroes all the way now."[40] Ray was prone to hyperbole.

This traditional southerner was concerned about the impact the interracial commission was having on the campus community. The Jesuits at the university were already divided on the race question, and the student interracial commission, he believed, was adding to the division on campus. Ray presented himself to the provincial as a Jesuit who possessed the broader experience necessary to deal with the race question rather than those Jesuits associated with the student interracial organization; his approach was more practical, theirs theoretical. This group of Jesuits, Ray argued, "has had racial equality pumped into them" throughout their religious formation, and while he wanted to give those men the benefit of the doubt regarding the sincerity of their actions, their policy was "harmful to Loyola." He wondered if the other Jesuits took into account where the university was located and against whom the institution competed for students. Ray understood the interracial question as a "Communist trap" leading to disunity, and he hoped that Loyola would not follow that path. A few weeks later, he would again be writing the provincial with concerns about the NFCCS and the interracial commission.[41]

FAULT LINES DEVELOPING

As the interracial commission gained national exposure, Dominican College student interest diminished. By early 1951 representatives of the college had stopped attending meetings.[42] SERINCO chairman Edward Kammerer expressed concern to an NFCCS official, stating that "[t]he loss of one of our member colleges from the commission is another problem facing us constantly."[43] Dominican attendance was intermittent, at best, after the fall of 1952.[44]

In the spring of 1953 a layman criticized the Dominican order for its lack of resolve on the race issue. James A. McInerney, O.P., a former chaplain and teacher at St. Mary's Dominican College, in a letter to Mother Mary Dominic, O.P., president of the college, defended not only the order's work among black Catholics but also the college's commitment to bettering race relations in New Orleans. "As for Dominican College's participation in interracial endeavors," he said,

> I cannot see how anyone can criticize your wholehearted cooperation. I have been present at many of these functions. I know how enthusiastically Xavier students have spoken of their cordial treatment at Dominican. The fact that neither Xavier nor Dominican wish to have the reputation of being silly radicals of a very impractical order cannot be held against these schools. I know that on a few occasions we blocked what we considered ill advised pronouncements which would serve no genuine purpose nor advance the cause of racial harmony.[45]

Sporadic attendance by St. Mary's Dominican College continued throughout the rest of SERINCO's existence. This women's college would, however, continue to be listed as a participating member at every Interracial Sunday gathering, but that was the extent of the school's involvement. There were no apparent reasons for this drifting away, and Dominican's absence did not hinder day-to-day operations, but it did hinder SERINCO efforts to reach and influence as many Catholic students as possible. Hence, because neither Xavier University nor Ursuline College readily assumed a leadership position, Sacred Heart College in Grand Coteau was too far away to participate fully in the commission, and Dominican College rarely attended meetings, the interracial commission regularly depended on the leadership of Loyola students and its existence on the good will of the Jesuits of Loyola University of the South.

At Loyola, SERINCO and the race question continued to be a source of conflict for the Jesuits. William O'Leary, regent of the dental school and consultor of the community, expressed his opposition to desegregation to the provincial.[46] "If it comes in the south," he stated "it will be time enough for us to act but I do not think we should be the first—or even among the first—to try it." Economics influenced his position. Concerning the finances required to run a university, O'Leary argued that Loyola was "dependent on public sentiment to a large extent for the success of that investment. We cannot afford to take undue chances." If the Jesuits were more independent financially, he posited, they could be "more vocal in the matter of changing existing customs and traditions." O'Leary believed that Communists were fomenting trouble in the area of race relations. "It seems to me that a lot of our Jesuits and other good people have been taken in by the Communists who are anxious to destroy the capitalistic form of life but who hold up the idea of 'complete Christianity' or some such thing as a bait for the holy ones." While he complimented the work of fellow Jesuits George Bergen, assistant dean of arts and sciences, and Anthony O'Flynn, dean of men, he also criticized them as "too eager to be pioneers in this crusade against segregation." O'Leary held to a gradualist position and would continue to express his opposition to desegregation on economic grounds.[47]

The assistant dean at Loyola and community consultor, George Bergen, S.J., presented a different viewpoint to Crandell. He saw the Jesuits becoming more and more divided over the race question. "This division," he believed, was "not simply between older and younger members." It was much greater than that and more problematic, as "some members of the community are now expressing their opinions violently and—on at least one occasion—viciously at table and at recreation." Rumors abounded that one member of the Loyola Jesuit community was writing letters to friends and alumni to counter the interracial work undertaken by other Jesuits on campus.[48] The Jesuit most likely to undertake such a letter-writing campaign was Sam Hill Ray, given his propensity to write the provincial concerning activities of the interracial commission. Philosophy instructor Martin Burke was another possibility.

Parents of Loyola students also took an interest in the interracial activities on campus. When the parent of one of the women students forbade her daughter to attend an interracial function, the student asked Joseph Fichter if she had to obey her parent. Fichter explained that since the matter concerned a question of justice, the student did not have to obey her parent. Upon learning of Fichter's advice, the parent in question went to see the president of the university. There is no indication how this incident was resolved, but the assistant dean of arts and sciences expressed concern that Fichter's action was not "helping the relations in the community, or helping the University as a whole."[49]

Less than two weeks prior to the staging of the third Interracial Sunday gathering in February 1951, Loyola's Sam Hill Ray sent yet another letter of protest to the Jesuit provincial concerning the upcoming affair. Ray believed that the theme of the annual event, "Jim Crowism or Jesus Christ," was insulting to the Society of Jesus, as it condemned the order, the Jesuits who had labored in the

South, and those who continued to work in a racially segregated environment. Ray sought to justify segregation, explaining that it "had to be enforced in the South against whites and blacks when the carpetbaggers from the north brought to the South a condition so serious that police power, granted by the federal constitution, had to be invoked to keep the peace." For Ray, such action was "not unchristian nor unjust." Loyola's director of student counseling judged that the individuals advocating integration were sincere, and he surmised that Abraham Lincoln was too, but "he caused so much blood to be spilt that might have been averted." The danger in the mid-twentieth century, as far as Ray was concerned, was further bloodshed over the race question. "Such is the temper of the people of the south that if the effect of this meeting is carried out, another meeting may be necessary years hence to beg the whites and blacks to desist from riots."[50]

The interracial commission, Ray informed the provincial, was doing much harm at Loyola. He understood those favoring integration as belonging to a "click" which was "destructive of Ignatian charity" and "destroying respect for the Society and for priests." For Ray, the Jesuit faculty and staff, rather than collegians, were the leaders of this circle. He wondered why the interracial activities had to be continually suppressed and observed that the *Christian Conscience* had been proscribed. These activities and those sponsored by other interracial organizations, Ray predicted, would "bring such division and dissention in our christian ranks that the communists can rejoice in making us their tools." In closing he informed the provincial that he was too busy to object continually to the activities of the interracial group, but he did have other means at his disposal to act. "I can very easily force the issue on my side," he stated, "and publicly dismiss from the Sodality any student who belongs to this interracial group."[51] This was no idle threat; one month later Ray did exactly that.

THIRD ANNUAL INTERRACIAL SUNDAY GATHERING, 1951

On 18 February 1951, Loyola University of the South hosted SERINCO's third annual Interracial Sunday gathering. "Christian Youth at the Crossroads: Jim Crowism or Jesus Christ" was the theme of the meeting, with Benjamin J. Johnson, secretary of the People's Industrial Insurance Company and Xavier graduate of the class of 1939, and Philip S. Ogilvie, executive secretary of the Catholic Committee of the South, as the guest speakers. A black priest, Maurice Rousseve, S.V.D., presided at the morning Mass.[52] All five Catholic colleges had speakers participating in the oratorical contest, with Norman Francis presiding over the student forum.[53]

As usual, members of the interracial commission spoke at area Catholic high schools in an effort to encourage students to attend Interracial Sunday and to participate in the poster contest. In his prepared remarks to a white student body,

Norman Francis explained that Interracial Sunday was the most important work of the interracial commission because it afforded Catholics the opportunity "to put into practice the theories and philosophy of our Catholic education. As Catholic college students, we of the Interracial Commission, are striving to foster better race relations in building a Christian atmosphere which is truly part of the Mystical Body of Christ." Furthermore, he noted, the gathering allowed blacks and whites to come together in an integrated setting to hear and learn what prominent Catholics were saying about race relations. He also encouraged the high school students to attend the affair because it was "an excellent opportunity to meet Negroes of your own educational level and see the fallacy of racial myths." Francis closed by telling the students that he hoped and prayed that one's Catholic education meant "more than merely learning how to make a living but rather how to live in the service of God."[54]

To those attending Interracial Sunday, Benjamin Johnson explained that one could title his address "Negro Catholic layman looks at this business of segregation and discrimination within the Catholic Church." Johnson first recounted those factors influencing the development of segregation within American society, especially the impact of slavery. He then addressed the evolution of segregation practices within the church over the previous fifty years, specifically drawing attention to the establishment of St. Katherine's parish by Archbishop Janssens in the latter part of the nineteenth century. He questioned why the church had not invested as much energy in converting the newly freed people of the South as she had in other lands. He wondered why the church, which "had been militant and firm in other countries" when defending the faith, was a practitioner of practicality in the United States. He attributed the lack of interest in black conversions to the fact that European immigrants had consumed much of the church's resources, both money and personnel, but that did not satisfactorily explain the current situation. To Johnson, there seemed no good reason for maintaining segregation within the church, or society as a whole, for that matter.[55]

"To me it is high time that Catholics push aside conventions and customs which are merely subterfuges employed to escape our real obligations," he told his listeners. There was no middle ground and no alternative for Johnson: the church had to integrate. He placed his trust in the younger generation present at the interracial gathering and believed that those who favored the maintenance of segregation would find themselves in the minority.[56]

Philip Ogilvie prefaced his remarks by stating that he was firmly convinced that "the Negro is all right in his place and that he should strive diligently to take his place and to stay in it." The "Negro's place," he explained, was not the "place" most people presumed: in the back of streetcars and buses, in the rear pews at church, or as "Uncle Toms" and domestic servants. No, "God Himself has designated the place of the Negro in human society," and that place, he stated, was with all other human beings and not separated from them. This white speaker asked the white audience members to examine their past treatment of blacks. He asked if they had taken concrete steps to speak out against the injustices visited upon their brothers and sisters, and he encouraged the audience to work toward removing those barriers that kept blacks from assuming their rightful place in American society and the church. Acknowledging that the world was "fouled up," Ogilvie believed that his fellow Catholics could change things for the better. "We owe it to God, to ourselves, to our country, and to the South that we love to change them."[57]

Again, by all accounts, the Interracial Sunday gathering was a success. Catholics gathered on an integrated basis to put their religious beliefs into practice. While hundreds rather than thousands attended, those southern Catholics present were dismantling Jim Crow society. Law and custom might dictate separation, religious conviction and practice called for integration. These Catholics, black and white, were challenging southern society.

RESISTING RACISM AND SAM HILL RAY, PART TWO

Changing southern society was not what Sam Hill Ray had in mind when he attempted to crush SERINCO in March 1951. Acting under the authority of the president of Loyola, Ray issued a public statement prohibiting sodality members from participating in NFCCS activities or belonging to any organization (e.g., Catholic Action, Young Christian Students) not approved by the spiritual director of students. The memo read: "From now on, no Sodalist is to take part in any activity of the NFCCS or the group which arrogated to itself the name of Catholic Action, or the other group which calls itself the Young Christian Students but is not authorized by Loyola University, or any other spiritual activity or organization not approved by the Spiritual Director of Students, Fr. S. H. Ray, S.J. By Direction of Rev. Fr. President [Shields]."[58] Ostensibly, organizational integrity of the sodalities was the reason given for removing students involved in these other Catholic organizations, but the fact that these other groups were interracial in composition cannot be overlooked.[59] The sodalities were influential campus organizations both religiously and politically. Membership afforded prestige as well as spiritual sustenance, and many of the campus leaders belonged to these devotional groups. Expulsion from such an organization would result in the loss of campus political influence as well as spiritual graces.

This was not the first time Ray had threatened to purge the ranks of the Marian organizations of NFCCS interracialists, but this time he had the authority to do so.[60] Previously, Ray had threatened to expel students from their sodality if they attended an NFCCS-sponsored Marian devotion at Dominican College, which also happened to be an interracial affair. If Ray could purge the sodalities of NFCCS members, SERINCO could be eliminated. In reaction to Ray's efforts to punish students who were involved in interracial activities, Joseph Fichter lodged an official complaint with the provincial, William Crandell, calling for Ray's removal as unsuited to be a university student counselor and teacher. Fichter found Ray's behavior to be not only "childish" but also biased. "The fanaticism of this man," Fichter informed Crandell, "is indicated . . . in his blind anti-Negro prejudice."[61]

When the president of Loyola learned that Ray had made a public statement concerning student participation in the NFCCS and the sodalities, the president revoked the terms of his understanding with Ray. It was never Shields's intention to disclose publicly the arrangement he had made with the director of student counseling—namely, the removal of NFCCS members from the sodalities. Shields informed Ray that if he were ever asked about the statement, he would "deny such publication because I did not authorize it." As far as Shields was concerned, Ray was "simply making trouble at Loyola by such actions,"[62] trouble that Shields had to undo. Using his powers as president of Loyola University "to suspend or abrogate all or any part of the official duties of officials in the university," Shields rescinded and nullified "any authority you [Ray] may possess as Spiritual Director of the students to suspend from the Sodality or otherwise molest any student who is a member of the N.F.C.C.S."[63] The NFCCS member purge from the sodalities never took place.

Later that spring and again that summer, Ray complained to the Jesuit provincial about the activities of the collegians' interracial commission and the Jesuits advocating interracial justice. Concerning the collegians, he informed Crandell that he had in his possession "the latest copy of the notorious 'Christian Conscience' all about the downtrodden jigaboos."[64] Ray commented that he knew many New Orleanians and their views on the race question and wished that "our men from the North could grasp their views." If individuals continued to agitate for racial equality, Ray feared there would be "hatred between the races in the South as we have never known before." He told the provincial that he advocated "a parallel civilization with equality but not identity." If individuals continued to discuss the race question, Ray feared that the resulting dissension would have everyone falling into a Communist trap.[65]

As the director of student counseling was lodging complaints against the interracial commission, Loyola students were also raising questions about the NFCCS. In a signed editorial of 2 March 1951, *Maroon* editor Blanche Mouledoux encouraged NFCCS officials to explain the goals and purpose of their organization in order to remove any confusion existing in the student body. Whereas the NFCCS had previously been heavily involved with overseas relief work, now there was a sense on campus that it was only interested in interracial affairs. Mouledoux worried that with this apparent shift in emphasis and direction the Loyola campus was being polarized between pro-NFCCS and anti-NFCCS camps. In November 1952, Norris Fitzmorris, chairman of the Southeastern Region of the NFCCS, penned an editorial dealing with this same issue. He claimed that most students had made no attempt to learn about the national federation or had "been content to listen to a few entirely MISINFORMED students. These know-it-all experts have distorted the true nature of NFCCS into a lop-sided picture of the Interracial Commission." He feared that too many students were accepting as fact "the 'quack' opinion" of others, thus harming the work of the NFCCS. He acknowledged that the interracial commission was part of the national federation, but he also pointed out that "it is only one of a total of 16 active commissions."[66]

Whereas Sam Hill Ray's attempt to neutralize the interracial commission failed, the president of Loyola, Thomas Shields, tried to silence the organization in the fall of 1951 by proscribing its publication, the *Christian Conscience.* In his instructions to Loyola's dean of men, Anthony O'Flynn, Shields stated that the "'Christian Conscience' was not to be printed, prepared, distributed, or circulated on the Loyola campus."[67] Shields's directive meant complete censorship, and if it were enforced, those advocating integration would be silenced.

O'Flynn communicated this directive to the moderator of the interracial commission with the proviso that if the newsletter was prepared elsewhere it was "to be submitted to me for censorship before being placed in circulation."[68] SERINCO moderator Joseph Fichter and the collegians ignored the conditions for publication. The students continued to prepare the newsletter on Loyola's campus but printed it elsewhere.[69] In 1953 Ursuline College assisted in publishing the newsletter; the chairman of the interracial commission thanked Sister Mary Columba, O.S.U., a professor of English at the college, for helping with the group's activities, "especially in regard to the *Christian Conscience.*"[70]

RICHARD GUMBEL AND RACIAL JUSTICE

As the administration at Loyola University of the South dealt with internal dissent concerning interracial activities on its campus and Catholic college students of New Orleans debated the purpose of the NFCCS, another black Catholic applied for admission to the school of law at Loyola. A Roman Catholic, native of New Orleans, veteran of the Second World War, married and father of two, a Xavier member of SERINCO, and a national officer of the NFCCS, Richard Gumbel seemed the ideal candidate to integrate the law school. The president of Xavier University, Mother Mary Agatha, S.B.S., found him so promising that she wrote a personal letter of recommendation to the president of Loyola University, Thomas Shields, S.J.

Gumbel, she declared, was "probably the most outstanding student on our campus." After recounting some of his accomplishments at Xavier, Mother Agatha stated: "I sincerely hope that this time you won't refuse to accept him into the Law School. . . . If you accept him I think he will be a credit to Loyola and Xavier; and I know of no more acceptable person as your first Negro law student. I hardly think you can realize what it will mean if you give him the opportunity."[71] Continuing, she stressed the personal, professional, and moral dimensions of the situation:

> Probably, dear Father, you will think me very bold and believe that I don't understand. I may truly say to you that I think I understand but I also feel this is the opportune time in which it would be most wonderful thing for Loyola, for the Colored people of New Orleans, for the cause of interracial justice in general, and above all for the cause of God if you agree to accept this young man. From my own position I know that if *you* say the word that is all there will be to it.[72]

In her closing sentence to Shields, this religious woman, who had given her life to the education and betterment of black Catholics in the United States, implored the authorities at Loyola University to do the right thing: "I have never asked you for a favor but I do beg you for this one—not so much for the young man in particular as for the cause, as I know what it will mean." [73] Gumbel received a letter of rejection from Loyola law school. He appealed the decision.[74]

Basing his appeal on "Christian rights," Gumbel asked the president of Loyola to reconsider the university's decision. In the letter of rejection, the dean of the law school, Antonio E. Papale, had written that "conditions for men in your position seem to be improving." Dean Papale's statement led the Xavier graduate to believe "that the reason for the rejection of my application was solely on the basis of racial discrimination," hence the appeal to the president.[75]

Gumbel had expected more from Loyola. Given that state and even private institutions were opening their doors to qualified blacks, he "was hoping that Loyola University of the South would join with those institutions in helping bring about true Christian justice and charity." In a stinging commentary on the religious foundations on which Loyola University was established, the Xavier graduate reasoned that "if the courts of the land could force those state universities to admit men of all color, then most certainly an institution founded upon the philosophy of Jesus Christ, administered by men dedicated to the upholding of those principles, and in whose care Mother Church had entrusted the continuance of those teachings, would do so."[76]

Gumbel's reference to "the courts of the land" concerned the United States Supreme Court decisions of June 1950 in *Sweatt* v. *Painter et al.* (1950), and *McLaurin* v. *Oklahoma State Regents for Higher Education* (1950), in which the Jim Crow practices of the University of Texas and the University of Oklahoma, which kept black Americans out of their graduate schools, were ruled unconstitutional. These decisions followed earlier cases: *Missouri ex rel. Gaines* v. *Canada* (1938), and *Sipuel* v. *Board of Regents of University of Oklahoma* (1948), which dealt with law school admissions at the University of Missouri and the University of Oklahoma, respectively. Gumbel was also referring to the decision of a special panel of the Fifth Circuit Court of Appeals in New Orleans, which ruled that Louisiana State University's law school proscription against black applicants was unconstitutional.[77]

Foreshadowing the difficulties that would befall New Orleans and the church as integration became the law of the land, Gumbel commented on the possible student and alumni reaction to integrating the university. "Any objection that students or Alumni may have to a university committed to a policy of admitting all who qualify," he wrote, "stems from the fact that institutions foster such feelings by permitting the continuance of separate education." He thought that the administrators of such an institution would be shocked that the "objectors are the products of said institution, reflecting a philosophy detrimental to their Alma Mater."[78] Gumbel was politely intimating that Loyola encouraged and sanctioned Jim Crow practices.

Gumbel was not looking to invade white society through attendance at Loyola law; rather, he desired "to secure the education which . . . Loyola [was] capable of affording . . . and the opportunity of giving service, service based on Catholic principle, to this community which sorely lacks servants in Christian principles." If Loyola would not afford him that opportunity, he, like Harry Alexander, would be forced to apply to Georgetown. Gumbel did not relish the thought of leaving his hometown, for it would be a hardship on him and his family. He and his wife owned a home in New Orleans; they wanted to raise their children in Louisiana, and their extended families were in the city. Gumbel also knew that the community would lose if he left. "I, like many other able Negroes who could have and would have helped the community," he wrote, "have been forced North for their education, and other communities have all received the benefits of their efforts." And as a Catholic, Gumbel wanted to attend Loyola because it was "the only place in the area where . . . [he] might secure a Catholic Law Education."[79]

In responding to Gumbel's plea, President Shields began by sympathizing with his anguish: "I fully understand your feelings in this matter, totally agree with much that you have written. . . . I am determined to do all I can to rectify these prejudices and even unjust attitudes." After expressing personal concern, however, Shields then began to berate Gumbel for his impetuousness. Shields informed Gumbel that he was "in error" for stating in his letter "that the reason for the rejection of my application was *solely* on the basis of racial discrimination." Gumbel's assertion, the president stated, was an "implied insult to Loyola University and the Jesuit Fathers [and] should be withdrawn with proper apologies." Taking Gumbel to task for his effrontery, Shields informed this black veteran and father of two, "Christian charity and social justice are not one way streets. If one party has rights and duties in the social order, so has the other. If it is wrong for the white to discriminate against the Negro, it is equally wrong for the Negro to be prejudiced, precipitate, impatient and intolerant."[80]

The president continued, stating that "it should be clearer than light to the unprejudiced mind that at present Loyola University and the Jesuit Fathers are making great progress despite opposition and a degree of danger to the whole university in the overcoming of racial prejudice." The president was discouraged that Jesuit efforts were "so little appreciated by the very people who should be the first to recognize the tremendous problem we face and the most ready to approve the progress we have made." To enlighten Gumbel on the situation at Loyola, Shields then outlined the efforts he had undertaken to desegregate the university: black nuns, members of the Sisters of the Holy Family, admitted into the summer school program; one black man admitted to the Evening Division; and sixteen blacks admitted to the Institute of Industrial Relations. The president was quick to point out that these admissions "were not forced upon us by pressure of court decisions of the State or by ecclesiastical authorities of the Church."[81]

Continuing to justify his actions, Shields also called attention to the efforts made by faculty and staff, Jesuit and lay, in promoting racial integration. He pointed to the numerous integrated meetings on campus, sponsorship of Interracial Sunday, and integrated meals in the cafeteria and refectory as signs of progress. Given his role in attempting to control, if not abolish, SERINCO in 1948, 1949, and 1951, Shields's comments appear to be disingenuous.

Striking a note of conciliation, the president expressed regret that the university could not accept Gumbel into the law school

> because of conditions over which we have no control. Would that many white Catholics who for the sake of social prestige or business connections are attending non-Catholic universities, might measure up to the stature of your zealous and active Catholic faith and your determination to carry on your professional education in a Catholic university even if it means the personal sacrifices attendant upon moving from your home town so that you may get your legal education at Georgetown University. May these sacrifices joined with the

prayers of all who are interested in social justice hasten the day both of us look forward to and for which both of us must continue to work prudently, courageously and effectively.[82]

Using gender as an argument, Shields then attempted to deflect Gumbel's accusation of discrimination based on race. He noted, "[Y]ou are not the only one who has had to go elsewhere for a Catholic education because of a policy of 'segregation' which might be said to 'discriminate' against certain persons. Because of the efforts of a well organized and soundly financed group the emphasis today is on race."[83] In the former reference, Shields was referring to women, in the latter, the National Association for the Advancement of Colored People.

Loyola University was prohibited by the Jesuit authorities in Rome from admitting women into the College of Arts and Sciences; however, they could be admitted to the professional schools or departments (e.g., medical technology or education).[84] The president informed Gumbel that as late as 1948 Loyola University and Xavier University were the only two accredited Catholic institutions of higher learning in New Orleans, which meant that "all Catholic white girls who wanted a college course in Arts and Science had to go to another city (unless she wanted to attend Xavier) in order to get a course fully accredited by a standardizing agency." Given this reality, Shields wondered why "there is such agitation about racial discrimination and so little protest about sexual discrimination." The president closed by admonishing Gumbel not to be "too quick in branding selectivity by any group as necessarily un-Christian or intrinsically evil, particularly at the very time when we have broken down the barriers of racial segregation and are progressing to better race relations."[85]

Shields's response to Gumbel's letter was less than forthright. Desegregating the law school had been an issue for several years. The president of Loyola University had already turned down one black applicant in 1949, and in 1950 the superior general of the Society of Jesus himself had inquired about desegregating the law school. In March of that year John B. Janssens asked Shields, "Is it not the acceptable time to admit select Negroes into this school?"[86] Jesuit officials in Rome were aware of the situation in New Orleans and were prodding southern Jesuits to act, but the president was looking for a way to rationalize not accepting a black applicant.

As in Harry Alexander's situation, the best Loyola could do for Richard Gumbel was to recommend him to Georgetown University's School of Law, which did accept him.[87] While attending law school, Gumbel supported his family by working for the United States Post Office. After passing the bar, he practiced law in Chicago, eventually becoming a probate judge in Cook County, Illinois.[88]

FOURTH ANNUAL INTERRACIAL SUNDAY GATHERING, 1952

While disappointing for SERINCO and CHR members, Richard Gumbel's misfortunes did not hamper interracial activities in Louisiana. During the fall of 1951, SERINCO and the CHR continued their usual activities, including planning for the fourth annual Interracial Sunday gathering, scheduled for 9 March 1952. The year 1952 would also turn out to be a pivotal year in southern Catholic interracial history, as the efforts of SERINCO and the CHR would influence race policy within the church.

As Ursuline and Sacred Heart Colleges as well as Loyola University had all played host for the annual interracial affair, Xavier University now was called upon to sponsor the event. The theme for that year's gathering was "All the Same in Christ." James Jones of the United Steelworkers Union and Morton Elder of the Catholic Committee of the South were the guest speakers. Joyce LaBorde of Ursuline College won the collegians' speech contest.[89]

In her winning address, LaBorde focused on the theological and scriptural presuppositions that supported an all-inclusive view of the human race. Because "God sees only the souls made to His own image and likeness," she declared, "[a]ll else in man is accidental." In Jesus, the Christ, a new way of life was established: "the way of Christian democracy." The essence of this new way, she explained, was "respect for the individual based upon equality before God." She lamented the fact that even though Catholic Christians believed in Jesus, they did not practice what they professed: "[W]e see history repeating itself—selfishness again enslaving men by the bonds of prejudice everywhere; segregating so-called undesirable minorities in schools, hotels, and worst of all in Churches, in the presence of that very Savior Jesus Christ Who gave us the Christian way of life." So convinced was LaBorde of her position regarding Christian unity and the necessity of good interracial relations, that she told her listeners anyone who would undermine Christian doctrine and avoid promoting good interracial relations could not "be called Catholic in any strict sense."[90]

Archbishop Joseph Francis Rummel reinforced LaBorde's views in his closing remarks at the 1952 gathering. Evoking the image of the Communist "iron curtain" in Eastern Europe, Rummel told his listeners, "Truth and love demand that there can be no curtain between the races—no iron curtain, no social curtain, no curtain of hatred and prejudice." Prudence, patience, and tact, he noted, would be needed to win over those who harbor racial prejudice, especially since the form of race prejudice in the region had the force of custom to support it.[91] In the not-so-distant future, the archbishop and others would discover that the force of custom would seem as impregnable as the "iron curtain" of Eastern Europe.

SERINCO's Interracial Sunday gathering again received attention from the *Louisiana Weekly;* the editorial "A Heart Warming Occasion" praised the efforts of the college students. "The students of the various schools that participated in the observance of Interracial Sunday are to be commended for trying to show the world that God created all men equal, and with love for all," the editors stated. Through the activities of the college students, the *Weekly* judged that the day was fast approaching when every day in the United States would be an interracial day, not just one Sunday a year.[92]

The opportunity to practice interracial justice among the member institutions of the NFCCS and SERINCO was soon approaching. Members of the CHR of the Catholic Committee of the South would also support this interracial effort. Catholic desegregation was coming of age.

CHAPTER V

"Norman Francis Is a Negro": Desegregating Catholic Colleges, 1952–1953

IN JUNE 1952, NORMAN FRANCIS APPLIED to Loyola University's School of Law. A senior at Xavier University, he was president of the student body, chairman of the collegians' interracial commission, an honor graduate of his class, an exemplary Catholic, and brother of a priest. Writing to Patrick Donnelly, S.J., the president of Loyola University of the South and Thomas Shields's successor, Louis Twomey, S.J., regent of the law school, stated, "In many ways . . . [Norman Francis] represents the type of law-school applicant whom we rejoice to welcome into our student body. Ordinarily we would not hesitate to accord him unqualified acceptance." However, Twomey continued, "despite Francis' excellent record as a student, a leader and a gentleman, we cannot act affirmatively on his application without prior clearance from higher authority. For it happens that Norman Francis is a Negro."[1]

Unlike black applicants Harry Alexander and Richard Gumbel a few years earlier, Norman Francis would, however, be admitted to classes that fall. Pressures from above and pressures from below influenced the decision to desegregate Loyola University's School of Law in 1952. From above, academic accreditation, tax-exempt status, and university leadership all contributed to Francis's acceptance. From below, interracial activities forced southern Jesuits to confront the race question and, in doing so, end the practice of racial segregation in the province.

PRESSURES FROM ABOVE: ACCREDITATION, TAX EXEMPTION, UNIVERSITY LEADERSHIP

At the 1950 Annual Meeting of the Association of American Law Schools (AALS), delegates to the convention had passed a resolution calling for the revocation of membership of those law schools practicing discrimination based on

race or color: "No school which follows a policy of exclusion or segregating qualified applicants or students on the basis of race or color shall be qualified to be
admitted to or to remain a member of the Association."[2] The following year the
Special Committee on Racial Discrimination of the AALS reported that a new
legal strategy to end segregation in private law schools was being considered. It
called for challenging a law school's right to tax exemption and other privileges
as long as the institution discriminated on the basis or race or color. If these initiatives were successful, the Loyola University School of Law, a member of the
AALS since 1934, would be in grave jeopardy unless it integrated.

Loyola also had a new president, Patrick Donnelly, S.J., who was far more
open to change than his predecessor, Thomas Shields, S.J., who left office at the
end of the 1951–1952 academic year. Cautious by temperament, Shields had not
been able to shed completely the traditional white southern attitudes regarding
race relations. Furthermore, he was loath under any circumstances to take action
unless forced to do so, and so despite growing pressures, he had not acted deci-
sively on integration.[3]

It is not known to what extent the racial question figured in the appointment
of Patrick Donnelly, but there can be no doubt that the Jesuit hierarchy was aware
of his position on the matter. Chosen to lead Spring Hill College in Mobile,
Alabama, in 1946, Donnelly had been as forthright on civil rights as Shields had
been equivocal and temporizing. In his 1948 commencement address at Spring
Hill, for example, titled "World Citizenship and the Unfinished Business of
Democracy," Donnelly called on individuals to improve world relations by
becoming "Citizens of the World," willing to help each other in times of need
and being good neighbors at all times. He made this plea as he saw democracy on
trial throughout the world as well as at home in 1948. The time had come, he
argued, for the United States to give every man and woman the rights granted by
God, especially in a country which professed to be Christian and democratic.[4]

In June 1952, Louis Twomey pleaded with the new president of Loyola that he
break with the past and authorize the dean of the law school to accept Norman
Francis. The law school regent was convinced that the faculty and students were
prepared to accept blacks as students and classmates. With the AALS taking a stance
against segregation and the federal courts ruling in favor of integration, Twomey
believed the time had come to act. He explained to Donnelly that "it would be
nothing short of a calamity—such a strong word is in order, I believe—were Loyola
to open its doors to Negroes only after court action or even the threat thereof."[5]

Nine months earlier, Twomey had written Vincent McCormick, S.J., the
United States assistant to the superior general of the order, concerning the law
school situation asking him to take action: "The fact of the matter is that there
are Negroes now enrolled in the Law School of Louisiana State University, at least

one of whom is among our rejectees. . . . And yet despite the fact that L.S.U. has received Negroes, Loyola is still holding back." Loyola's failure to take a leadership role in desegregating an institution of higher learning troubled Twomey, for he saw the initiative in race relations being "taken away from us to a considerable degree." He pointed out that the University of North Carolina, the University of Oklahoma, the University of Texas, Southern Methodist University, Texas Christian University, Our Lady of the Lake College (San Antonio), and three Catholic colleges in Kentucky were accepting black students. Twomey continued,

> [H]ow much longer must Loyola preserve its present admission policies[?] The time for us to have become genuine pioneers in setting an example of dynamic leadership for Christ in race relations is passed. That opportunity will not return. But there is still time for Loyola and the New Orleans Province to recapture something of the initiative we have lost. We can yet bring to bear on these critical problems of human relations such well-conceived and well-executed applications of the eternal principles of Justice and Charity as to place Loyola and the New Orleans Province in the front ranks of those willing to fight for Christ without counting the cost.[6]

Norman Francis's application to Loyola's School of Law was held in abeyance as members of the Jesuits New Orleans province prepared to gather at Grand Coteau, Louisiana, in the summer of 1952 to develop a race policy.

BLACK, WHITE, AND CATHOLIC: SOUTHERN JESUITS CONFRONT THE RACE ISSUE, 1952

Activities of the college students' interracial commission helped provide the impetus for forcing members of the New Orleans Province of the Society of Jesus to examine the race question. The Southeastern Regional Interracial Commission (SERINCO) was causing bitter conflict among Loyola University Jesuits. Interracial thought and action compelled Catholics to reexamine their racial attitudes and practices, and once they did so, they found them wanting. Now Jesuit leadership had to act.[7]

New Orleans provincial William Crandell, after visiting the Loyola campus in the winter of 1951, wrote members of the Society of Jesus at the university expressing his disappointment that "the spirit of charity and fraternal union which should exist in the Community has been harmed considerably by the personal animosity and bitterness which has arisen as a result of differing opinions concerning the best practical solution of present-day social problems." He wanted

Loyola Jesuits to reach a unified position regarding social issues in order to reduce the level of conflict; given the structure of the Society of Jesus, however, such a position would have to apply to the province as a whole.[8]

In writing to his Jesuit superior in Rome, John B. Janssens, on the attitudes of the southern Jesuits and the race question, Crandell informed Janssens that

> our minds are divided, our teachings are different, our approaches various. We are confused, and so are our students. I fear that we are wasting much time and losing many advantages while we constantly bicker, engage in plot and counterplot, and fail in obedience and charity while each justifies the stand that he takes. It seems to me that it is time for us to formulate a definite Province policy in this matter, concentrate our efforts along these lines, and vigorously resist any departure from them.[9]

Hence Crandell informed Janssens of the plan to hold a province meeting to formulate a policy regarding the race issue. Province superiors, that is, rectors and superiors of Jesuit communities, as well as individuals who could present various perspectives in promoting better race relations, would be invited to attend the gathering, which he planned for the summer of 1952.[10] In January 1952, Crandell decided to convene "a meeting of the Superiors and other interested parties in the Province to discuss thoroughly the matter of interracial relations in the Southern [New Orleans] Province."[11] This gathering would be held in August in Grand Coteau, Louisiana, site of the province novitiate.[12] From January to July an interracial planning committee, chosen by the provincial, would meet to draft position papers regarding race matters. These documents then would become the basis for discussing racial issues at the summer assembly. All the necessary planning for the Grand Coteau meeting was to be completed by July.

On 28–29 August 1952, some fifty members of the New Orleans Province of the Society of Jesus met at Saint Charles College in Grand Coteau, Louisiana, to hammer out a policy statement on racial matters. Building on the work of the planning committee, the Jesuits gathered in Grand Coteau began by addressing the moral aspects of the interracial question. Once they had formulated a position regarding the morality of segregation, the delegates spent the bulk of the meeting developing strategies for implementing change.[13]

In principle, racial segregation was immoral, the attendees decided. They concluded that it was "morally evil because it violates commutative justice [i.e., fairness in agreements and exchanges between people] since it implicitly denied the unity of the human family and the equal rights of all men." Hence, racial segregation was deemed to be "*in itself*, unjust and intrinsically evil."[14]

While the Grand Coteau members forthrightly and unequivocally rejected racial segregation in principle, they also concluded that it could be tolerated, for a limited time and under special circumstances. Nevertheless, they decided to integrate all Jesuit apostolic endeavors; that is, their retreat houses, high schools, college and university, parishes, and the order itself. In the province's two institutions of higher education, they endorsed complete equality, with no distinction between whites and blacks. This meant that Spring Hill College in Mobile, Alabama, and Loyola University of the South in New Orleans would desegregate, and, in particular, qualified blacks would be admitted to Loyola University's School of Law School.[15]

As far as implementation was concerned, the provincial informed members that the local superior and his advisors would have discretionary powers in carrying out the new province policy. But he emphasized the fact that once a policy statement was promulgated, "it was not to be lightly departed from, although local situations would be worked out by the Rector and consultors of the house affected." Crandell also informed the attendees that this new policy was not to be made public. Jesuits were instructed not to give statements to the local press, journals or magazines, nor were student newspapers to be informed or allowed to publish the fact that the Jesuits had decided to integrate. Crandell believed that these proceedings should be considered confidential, and could be kept private if Jesuits "would exercise prudence in such matters." He did acknowledge that eventually the public would learn of the policy change, but none of the Jesuits knew what the reaction would be. "For that very reason," Crandell explained, "it would be very imprudent to publicize the matter or engage in any propaganda campaign advertising the fact [at the present time]."[16] Within one week of the meeting, the president of Loyola was given permission by the provincial, "viva voce," to desegregate the law school.[17]

NORMAN FRANCIS: DEFYING RACE PERCEPTIONS

Norman Francis and Benjamin Johnson, another black applicant, would begin classes in October 1952. Though token blacks in a white professional school, they challenged preconceived notions concerning the abilities, talents, and intellect of blacks and in doing so contributed to the dismantling of the segregated South. Unlike G. W. McLaurin, who was admitted to the graduate school of education at the University of Oklahoma but was forced to sit at a desk in an anteroom adjoining the classroom, to sit in a designated area of the library away from the main reading area, and to sit at a separate table in the cafeteria, Norman Francis and Benjamin Johnson were afforded the same courtesies and privileges granted other law school students.[18]

Relying on the findings of a survey conducted by Robert A. Leflar, dean of the University of Arkansas School of Law, the dean and faculty of Loyola Law decided to maintain a "business as usual" attitude when Ben Johnson and Norman Francis arrived for classes. Leflar's survey had covered over a dozen southern law schools that had recently and successfully integrated their institutions. In his letter to the dean of the Loyola law school, Leflar recommended that Loyola University do nothing in the way of advance publicity regarding its new policy: "It is better to let folks find out about it [integration] after it occurs. . . . The less publicity that accompanies the event the better."[19] Loyola followed his advice, for in addition to the "business-like attitude" at the law school, there was no mention in the local papers, black or white, of the historic step being taken at Loyola University. How Francis and Johnson would be received by their white classmates remained to be seen.

As fellow classmate Michael O'Keefe recalled, the faculty "acted as though there was nothing unusual about having blacks in the classroom that fall. They acted like 'What's the difference? We don't notice anything different this year than last year.' They didn't make a fuss, there wasn't an orientation of saying, 'Look, we've got this situation. . . .' We showed up for class and there were two blacks in it and that was it—no big fanfare about it." The new students were accepted without incident, but that did not mean everyone was pleased with their presence. In the law school student lounge, O'Keefe recalls, one of his classmates stated that "he was going to throw them [Johnson and Francis] out of the window." O'Keefe observed that "after several months" the same classmate "started to go to the cafeteria with Ben Johnson, and he would bum cigarettes off Ben Johnson and eat lunch with Ben Johnson—all the things which a real segregationist would never have done. They would [even] exchange school notes and such." O'Keefe finally inquired of his classmate the basis for his conversion regarding blacks. There was no change in attitude, O'Keefe discovered; his classmate still thought that integration was wrong. When he asked him why he associated with Ben Johnson, the response was "Ben Johnson is different."[20]

In late September 1952 an article concerning Loyola University's registration and orientation dates for the coming academic year, including the law school, appeared in the local paper; no mention was made of Norman Francis or Ben Johnson.[21] On the first of October, the university announced that the law school's commencement exercises would be held three days hence; again no mention of the new policy regarding integration was made.[22] The day before graduation an article appeared in the local paper announcing the law school's commencement speaker and the honors to be awarded the graduates, but still there was no reference to the desegregation decision.[23] Quotes from the commencement speaker, Rev. Maurice B. Sheen, were reported in the paper the day after law degrees were conferred. Again there was no mention of the fact that Norman Francis or Ben Johnson had begun law classes that very week.[24] Even the student newspaper, the *Maroon*, failed to report on the policy change.

Not publicizing the integration of Loyola law school was a calculated decision on the part of both the university officials and the Jesuits. The Jesuits who attended the August 1952 interracial meeting had decided not to publicize any steps taken to improve race relations; they did not want the attention. This prohibition against public pronouncements affected every apostolic endeavor, whether high schools, parishes, retreat houses, the novitiate, the university, or the college. Jesuit policy was one of prudence. The Jesuits could bring about social change, but they did not want to jeopardize their various works. To proclaim their change in policy publicly, they feared, would court possible reprisal, recrimination, and destruction.

Norman Francis credits the ease of transition that year to the professional behavior of the staff and faculty of Loyola as well as his own interracial experience as a Catholic collegian. As a member of SERINCO, he had spent more than three years getting to know Loyola undergraduates. As Francis recalled:

> I had gone over [to Loyola]. They had come over [to Xavier]. We traveled together. I first met [Maurice] "Moon" Landrieu [a law school classmate] when Moon was at Loyola as an undergraduate and we traveled on buses to Grand Coteau to Sacred Heart for [SERINCO] conferences and the like. I laugh because Moon learned for the first time why blacks planned, wherever they traveled, very minutely, and he always wondered about that. We knew where the bus could go and where the bus could stop because we knew where we were going to be served and where we could use the restrooms, and there were cities where we knew the bus couldn't stop in. Now, for Moon, he never thought of this because he could always, as he said, 'Drive to Lafayette or Grand Coteau [and] stop wherever [he wanted],' but we couldn't in 1949, '50, or '51. . . . [I]t was impossible.[25]

Cooperation between black and white students involved in an interracial organization that had laid the groundwork for eventual acceptance of integrated classes at Loyola. Norman Francis's membership in SERINCO made his acceptance at Loyola law easier because he already knew some of his classmates from this organization.

For those white students who did not feel that blacks should be at Loyola, the first semester of law school was crucial. Norman Francis presented himself very well; he was likeable, capable, and hardworking, and in general he made a favorable impression on skeptical white students. The older, married professional businessman Ben Johnson did likewise. Norman Francis and Ben Johnson dispelled the notions some whites had that blacks were intellectually inferior, unhygienic, or morally depraved.[26]

While Ben Johnson had the independent financial means to attend law school, Norman Francis did not. He had already worked his way through undergraduate school on a work-study scholarship and would again need financial aid to attend Loyola law.[27] His father's salary as a barber did not afford the family the luxury of higher education without outside help.[28] In exchange for room and board, Francis served as a residence hall moderator at his alma mater, Xavier University. Robert Smith Shea, a member of the United States consulate in Tangier, Morocco, and a former member of the Xavier University administration and the Commission on Human Rights, provided funding to cover the cost of Francis's first year's tuition, books, and other incidentals. Shea did not want to see the opportunity to integrate the law school missed because of monetary problems.[29]

HARRY ALEXANDER AND RICHARD GUMBEL:
GEORGETOWN OR LOYOLA LAW?

Louis Twomey tried to get both Harry Alexander and Richard Gumbel to return to New Orleans to attend Loyola law in the fall of 1952 but to no avail. In a thoughtful and painfully honest letter, Gumbel explained to the regent of Loyola law that moving back to New Orleans was impossible. Financially he could not afford to move. He had to work while studying law, but returning to New Orleans would mean returning without a job in hand. "I can assure you," he explained to Twomey, "I cannot live for one week without work—last year took care of that. Two months without work wrecked me." The Gumbels had rented their New Orleans home to relatives, so housing was also an issue. He did not feel he could ask his aunt and uncle to vacate his property and "still consider [himself] a child of God." The hardship on his relatives would be too great, as they would have to find a new place to live; he did not want to force them out of his home.[30]

During his first year of law school, Gumbel lived in Washington, D.C., while his wife and children remained in New Orleans, because their eldest son, Gregory, was in school. During that time, Gumbel explained, "I became but an affectionate name 'daddy' to my sons; my wife had to be both mother and daddy to them and things were not easy for her financially." The separation put a strain on both him and his wife. "Many times in the past," he wrote Twomey, "I have looked into a mirror and wondered if I have my sane mind. I can attribute my survival to prayer—nothing else. Many times I have cried on my knees—I am not ashamed to tell you, although I have not told others. And many have been the times that my wife has cried on the phone and before me when I was home for Christmas." He could not bear to experience all that again; he would not ask his wife to go through all that again.[31]

Gumbel wanted to assure Twomey that he appreciated everything he had done for him and hoped that the Jesuit was not hurt by his decision. Twomey was one of the few people Gumbel believed was sincere in trying to help him, and he did not want him to think that his efforts had been in vain. "Please believe me," he concluded, "when I say that deep down in my heart I wish that I were at home, but when I think of all I have stated to you I cannot follow my heart—I must follow my head."[32]

If Richard Gumbel would not return to New Orleans, perhaps the other Xavier graduate at Georgetown, Harry Alexander, would. Both the regent of Loyola law and the president of Xavier University believed that Harry Alexander should come back to New Orleans to study law at Loyola. Unmarried at the time and without the responsibility of a family, Alexander still shared Gumbel's concern about getting a job. Because the opportunities for work as a government lawyer appeared most promising in Washington, Baltimore, and New York, Alexander decided to stay at Georgetown.[33]

Despite the acceptance of Norman Francis and Ben Johnson, the Jesuits had been right to fear there would be at least some protest. Five weeks after Francis and Johnson began law school, a letter of protest from Hugh St. Paul, a Loyola graduate, was sent to the provincial. St. Paul and his family had longstanding ties to Loyola University; his father had helped establish Loyola law night school in 1914. The letter claimed to represent the thinking of the average Catholic in New Orleans. Condemning the admission of blacks to Loyola, St. Paul reviewed the State of Louisiana's policy regarding segregation as well as Roman Catholic tradition concerning integration. He noted that the church and the Society of Jesus had "long recognized the purposes and accepted the fact of segregation." He argued that blacks should go to "their" law school at Southern University in Baton Rouge rather than attend Loyola.[34]

St. Paul feared that the long-range effect of the Jesuits' change in racial policies would be intermarriage, which he believed would result in great harm to society. "If the whites and the Negroes can rise side by side and not arm in arm," he argued, "much unhappiness can be averted." He lamented the fact that in New Orleans "we no longer have a white Catholic University where the children of 'misguided' southern parents [himself and others] can send their children." He concluded by warning the provincial of the New Orleans Province, "The consensus of opinion among the graduates of Loyola Law School is that Loyola will have no *future*, if the 'policy' be continued."[35] St. Paul's was the only protest from among the alumni, and there were none from the community or university. There are no indications that Jesuit officials responded to St. Paul's letter.

LEGAL BUT NOT DENTAL: THE POLITICS
OF PHYSICAL INTEGRATION

The successful admission of Norman Francis and Ben Johnson into the School of Law prompted the president of Loyola to suggest to his consultors in February 1953 that blacks be admitted to Loyola's School of Dentistry.[36] This issue was discussed during the provincial's annual visit the following month. Fear of unfavorable reactions from students and alumni caused the consultors to respond negatively to the idea; however, the provincial suggested that the dean of the dental school, Frank J. Houghton, be consulted regarding a possible change in policy. Dr. Houghton was asked to consult, informally, with the faculty on the advisability of accepting Negro applicants, but he was not to consult the students. His findings would be presented at a subsequent meeting. If at least one of the consultors voted with the president, the provincial declared, he would allow integration of this school also.[37]

As Houghton began querying the faculty, an application to the dental school arrived from Ernest Boykins, a senior at Xavier University. A native of Vicksburg, Mississippi, he had been educated by the Missionary Sisters of the Holy Ghost and the Fathers of the Society of the Divine Word, graduating from St. Mary's High School in 1949 with a class of seventeen, three of whom went on to college, two attending Xavier. Boykins majored in biology, planning to become a dentist. During his senior year, he consulted with Dr. Philip Hornung, chairman of the department, about his options, and it was Hornung who encouraged him to apply to Loyola.[38] As a member of the Committee for Human Relations of the Catholic Committee of the South and a friend of Joseph Fichter's, Hornung undoubtedly knew about the new Jesuit policy on integration.

Without waiting to receive the dean's report regarding integration, William O'Leary, S.J., the regent of the school, sent Boykins a rejection letter, stating: "Under the present policy of this dental school we are not in a position to accept applications from negro [sic] students." There are no indications that O'Leary consulted with the dean or president regarding Boykin's application, and given that he was against taking the lead in desegregating Jesuit institutions, his negative response was not surprising.[39] Boykins did not appeal the decision.[40]

In early May 1953, Dr. Houghton reported his findings to the president and board of directors of Loyola. The dean explained that he had broached the subject of black admissions with the faculty on a hypothetical basis. One or two faculty members felt the time had come to admit blacks but counseled delaying as long as possible. The experience of the Temple University Dental Clinic in Philadelphia gave the dean and faculty reason to pause. When blacks were admitted to the Temple clinic, the patient ratio became 75 percent black to 25 percent white. Loyola did not want the same outcome. Nor did it want to deal with possible black student failure. According to the dean, New York University Dental School had admitted two blacks who ultimately withdrew from the school citing racial difficulties. Dr. Houghton, convinced they were not prepared for the rigors of dental school, believed the reason for their departure was poor academic training, not discrimination. Furthermore, the dean explained, Loyola alumni were opposed to integrating the school.[41]

Frank Houghton pointed out that Loyola's dental school had been financially sound, but he was not sure the same would be true once blacks were accepted. He was afraid that upperclassmen would transfer and prospective students would not matriculate if integration took place. In addition, separate clinics would have to be established to serve white and black clients because, he believed, "there would be many difficulties if a negro [sic] served a white patient."[42] A black man touching a white person was a social taboo few were ready to transgress. O'Leary resented the way in which President Donnelly questioned Houghton regarding integration; the president had made every effort to prompt the dean to say what he wanted to hear. According to O'Leary, a frustrated Houghton eventually told Donnelly that "it was his school and he could ruin it if he wanted to" by admitting blacks.[43]

While the Donnelly administration favored desegregating the dental school, the faculty and alumni of Loyola University did not. There was no outside pressure from either the courts or professional organizations to support Donnelly's cause. None of the southern regional dental schools accepted blacks, and, unlike the American Bar Association, the American Dental Association had not yet adopted a nondiscriminatory admissions policy. Loyola's school of dentistry, unlike its school of law, would have had to go it alone in breaking down the color barrier. When the issue was put to a vote, not surprisingly, the four Jesuit consultors voted against admitting blacks; the president alone voted in favor. As the provincial had indicated that he would only support a change in the admissions' policy if at least one consultor voted with the president, the result of the balloting meant that Loyola University's School of Dentistry would remain segregated.[44]

WOMEN RELIGIOUS AND THE RACE QUESTION

As the Jesuits moved cautiously to desegregate their graduate programs at Loyola University, the Religious of the Sacred Heart, the religious women who administered the College of the Sacred Heart in Grand Coteau, Louisiana, decided in September 1953 to integrate their institution of higher learning, thus becoming the first white Catholic college in Louisiana to desegregate its undergraduate program. The sisters accepted a young black woman who had successfully completed the summer school program, thereby proving her ability to meet the academic requirements of the college. A few weeks after accepting its first black student, the College of the Sacred Heart College accepted its second black applicant.[45]

On Alumnae Day, 10 October 1953, the superior of the religious community, Reverend Mother O. Lapeyre, R.S.C.J., defused a potentially contentious encounter with the alumnae by making a forthright statement defending the college's decision to admit black students. She informed the graduates that white Catholics could not be considered "loyal" to the church if they continued to deny their coreligionists the right to a Catholic education solely on the basis of skin color. While some of the alumnae were upset by this decision, the current college students were not.[46] At the business meeting of the alumnae association held a few days later, Lapeyre was asked if the college would not lose white students because of integration. The reverend mother replied that she did not believe enrollment would be affected and again reiterated the necessity of opening Catholic education to all. Most of the members present accepted the new situation without much disagreement, but a few did express their displeasure with the notion of the "mingling of the races."[47]

In public the sisters stated that their decision to integrate the college was based on church teachings, but economic considerations also may have played a role in their decision-making process. Beginning in the winter of 1948–1949, community records paint a dire financial picture. At that time the sisters were implored by their superior to be "very faithful to our Vow of Poverty," since funds were very low. The subsequent years were not much better.[48] At the end of the fall semester of academic year 1949–1950, the financial situation again appeared to be ominous. The sisters were reminded to be "very careful with regard to poverty, so that we can 'tide over' until February, when the second semester tuition will be coming in."[49] By the end of the academic year, the treasurer reported that funds were so low that members of the community "must all take great care and not ask for things which are not really necessary."[50] While the finances for the following academic year (1950–1951) appeared to be less dire than before, the treasurer still commented that the balance in the bank "would be much greater if it were not for the extremely high cost of food, and the salaries for so many secular teachers."[51]

In the fall semester of 1953, Sacred Heart College had sixty-eight students enrolled for courses, which was not enough to offset their institutional debt of $22,000. The sisters did not have enough money to cover expenses, and they expected to go further into debt until all tuition bills were paid that semester. The college continued to experience financial difficulties, as the sisters had to pay their faculty no matter the size of the student body. Tuition would have to be increased to cover expenses.[52] And in an effort to generate interest in the college and to raise their enrollment, the sisters asked Auxiliary Bishop Maurice Schexnayder of the diocese of Lafayette to send a letter to every pastor of the diocese regarding Catholic education. They emphasized that young women were attending secular colleges and receiving no Catholic education. The sisters hoped that the pastors would encourage their parishioners to consider Sacred Heart, and to ensure that they would, the sisters sent out college brochures to all the parishes in the diocese.[53]

The religious women of Sacred Heart College integrated their undergraduate student body while struggling to maintain a viable academic program. By the fall of 1953, then, the first steps to integrate Catholic higher education in Louisiana had been taken, but most Catholic entities were still segregated, and public institutions were only minimally integrated. The United States of America was about to undergo its own transformation in the area of race and education. How the country, especially its southern citizens, would react to the change remained to be seen. For southern Catholics, the change would be viewed as a vindication of their convictions.

CHAPTER VI

Bearing Fruit: Catholic Interracialism in the Age of *Brown*, 1952–1956

C ATHOLIC INTERRACIAL ORGANIZATIONS continued their activities in New Orleans between Dwight Eisenhower's two successful presidential campaigns in 1952 and 1956. This was a time of civil rights progress, with the Supreme Court rendering landmark decisions on race, the Montgomery bus boycott, and the dawn of the modern Civil Rights Movement. This progress unleashed strong reaction in American society that reflected the changes initiated from the government, the courts, and the church.[1]

In 1952 the Republicans nominated General Dwight D. Eisenhower for president with Senator Richard M. Nixon of California as his running mate; the Democrats chose Governor Adlai E. Stevenson of Illinois to head the ticket and Senator John Sparkman of Alabama as the vice presidential nominee, thus acknowledging the party's need for southern Democratic votes. Unlike their 1948 platform, the Democrats' 1952 platform contained a muted civil rights plank, thus avoiding a possible split between the northern/midwestern and liberal wing of the party and the southern conservative (prosegregation) wing. While the popular Eisenhower won the presidency, he did not carry Louisiana. The Stevenson-Sparkman ticket carried the state with 52.9 percent of the vote (345,027 votes) to Eisenhower's 47.1 percent (306,925 votes).[2]

In December 1952 the U.S. Supreme Court, under the leadership of Chief Justice Frederick M. Vinson, heard the first arguments of the *Brown v. Board of Education, Topeka, Kansas* school desegregation case. With the death of Vinson the following year, President Eisenhower appointed California governor Earl Warren to the Court as the new chief justice. Warren obtained a unanimous vote of the justices in the *Brown* decision (1954), overturning racial segregation within the American educational system and rendering the "separate but equal" clause of *Plessy* null and void. The following year, 1955, the death of Emmett Till, a young black teenager from Chicago killed for whistling at a white women when visiting relatives in Mississippi, and the Montgomery bus boycott signaled the

111

beginning of the modern Civil Rights Movement; black Americans, tired of being harassed, intimidated, and assaulted, fought back through nonviolent protest.[3]

In Louisiana and New Orleans, the Eisenhower years were a progressive period. Historian Edward Haas notes that these were the "glory years" for Mayor DeLesseps Morrison as his administration promoted international trade, municipal improvements, and urban reform in the Crescent City. Buoyed by his success in city governance, Morrison ran for governor in 1956, losing to Earl Long, brother of former senator Huey Long. At the state and local level, the race question was constantly in the forefront. In 1953 blacks residing in Baton Rouge staged a week-long boycott of the city bus system challenging its segregated seating practices. The following year in New Orleans, black children, their parents, and teachers boycotted the annual McDonogh Day parade, which honored a public school benefactor, rather than march at the end of the parade, behind all the white students. And the archbishop of the archdiocese of New Orleans, in 1953 and again in 1956, addressed the race question, calling for an end to the practice of racial segregation within the church.[4]

PRACTICING INTERRACIALISM

The histories of the Commission on Human Rights (CHR) and the Southeastern Regional Interracial Commission (SERINCO) between 1952 and 1956 were similar to the organizations' earlier years: attending monthly meetings, publishing newsletters, sponsoring and planning annual Interracial Sunday gatherings, and organizing social affairs. All these activities, considered radical in their day, continued to confront racial injustices. Like other liberal organizations of the era, these Catholic interracial groups would be accused of un-American and pro-Communist views during the McCarthy era.[5]

The interracial commissions continued to inform and challenge Catholics to practice their faith more authentically. Members, however, wanted to do more than just attend meetings and listen to speakers talk about the importance of racial justice. These southern Catholics wanted to *do* something that manifested their belief in interracial harmony. Attending religious functions on a nonsegregated basis was one way; holding social affairs was another. However, there were obstacles to holding interracial gatherings in public places in New Orleans. Because tradition, custom, and law prohibited blacks and whites from associating in public, commission members turned to the church for assistance. St. Joseph's Seminary, located on the northern shore of Lake Pontchartrain in Covington, Louisiana, provided a safe haven for racial "mixing." On the west bank of the Mississippi River, Madonna Manor, an orphanage, was another locale where black and white Catholics could intermingle. Throughout the history of these commissions, both institutions hosted picnics for commission members.[6]

Intramural basketball games between black and white teams provided another interracial forum. In the fall of 1952, SERINCO members arranged for basketball games between the men of Xavier and Loyola as well as the women of Ursuline, Dominican, Loyola, and Xavier. Held at Xavier University, the games were well attended, drawing as many as two hundred spectators. Given the success of the Xavier-hosted matches, members decided to continue the competitions at other institutions.[7] The significance of these interracial athletic events, albeit at the intramural level, cannot be underestimated. These Catholic college students were violating the racial norms of their day openly, consciously, and deliberately. As far as they were concerned, Jim Crow was a thing of the past.

Preparing for the future, the collegians planned for their annual Interracial Sunday gathering. In March 1953, Ursuline was once again chosen to host the affair. This would be the last NFCCS function sponsored by Ursuline College; the institution closed its doors three months later because of accreditation and enrollment issues, though there were no indications that the college was on the verge of collapse at the time of the interracial gathering. And while Ursuline grammar school and academy (i.e., high school) remained open, the college closing meant that the interracial commission was reduced to Loyola, Xavier, Dominican, and Sacred Heart, with Loyola and Xavier the most active interracial chapters of the four.

Addressing the crowd at the fifth annual gathering were Leo Blessings, a municipal judge in the juvenile court system of New Orleans and member of the Urban League, and Elliot Keyes, CHR member and an official of the Federal Housing Authority. Both men focused on improvements in race relations.[8] Keyes told those gathered, "Cooperation between Whites and Negroes is . . . paying off in a better society." He argued that when the values of American society, which he defined as respect, opportunity, and responsibility, were enjoyed by all, then all of society benefited. Blessings advocated "a continued revision of legal procedures" to bring about an orderly transition in American race relations. He proposed a step-by-step program for implementing racial justice and integration to avoid any "sudden violent upheavals." "Gradual, positive integration," he argued, "is more effective than intermittent aggressive action."[9] The Interracial Sunday gathering was one such positive and gradual effort recommended by Blessings.

This fifth annual gathering was deemed a success. There were no letters of protest regarding the function. No action was taken against SERINCO by university officials.

ARCHBISHOP RUMMEL AND RACE

Two weeks after the 1953 interracial gathering, Archbishop Rummel officially ended racial segregation within the archdiocesan churches with the promulgation of his pastoral letter "Blessed Are the Peacemakers."[10] After recounting the ways individuals and society as a whole could create peaceful relations, he called on New Orleans Catholics "to exercise the role of peacemakers in our intercourse with those who may differ from us by characteristics of race, nationality, color of skin, habits or creed." Rummel reminded the faithful that every human being deserved dignity and respect because all persons were created in the image and likeness of God: "In all, we must respect the common bond that stems from the fatherhood of God and the brotherhood of man."[11]

This pastoral letter was the third time the archdiocese had called for an end to segregation within the church. The 1950 archdiocesan synod had stipulated it. In his 1951 appeal letter for the "Indian and Negro Missions," Archbishop Rummel called upon New Orleans Catholics "to cooperate in breaking down painful lines of segregation in the ordinary relations of human life and in the fields of education, industry and opportunity." In the church, he stated, "the lines of segregation must disappear . . . not only physically but in the true spirit of Christian brotherhood, in the seating accommodations, at the confessional, at the Communion rail and in general in the reception of the Sacraments and sacramentals of the Church." Those 1951 comments, however, were only an exhortation and not a directive.[12]

The *Louisiana Weekly,* believing the archbishop had set new policy in his 1951 appeal letter, ran a two-tiered banner headline announcing the end of segregation in the archdiocese: "Archbishop Rummel Calls on Orleans to End Segregation in Catholic Church." The black weekly ran the archdiocesan letter in its entirety. Editorials in two subsequent issues made reference to the archbishop's letter and praised the church for taking a positive stand in promoting better race relations.[13]

The official archdiocesan paper, *Catholic Action of the South,* however, did not emphasize Rummel's call for desegregation. The article "Better Opportunity for Colored Urged" focused on the support of the missions rather than the challenge to segregation. Only by reading the whole letter did one discover that in 1951 the archbishop had urged an end to the segregationist practices within the church.[14]

The 1953 letter was different. It clearly stated Rummel's and the church's position regarding racial practices. In his missive, the archbishop presented the same rationale for ending discrimination within the church as he had two years prior, but this letter was devoted solely to the issue of segregation, which the archbishop now was determined to end. It was a clear directive meant to set official policy. Since black Catholics shared in the same spiritual life and destiny as any other Catholics, especially in reception of the sacraments, Rummel ordered that there was to be "no further discrimination or segregation in the pews, at the Communion rail, at the confessional and in parish meetings." While he encouraged blacks to remain as members of their separate "Colored" parishes, he instructed white Catholics not to harass black Catholics if they decided to attend services at a white parish or wanted to join a parish organization. Rummel foresaw the day when segregation would disappear from public life. "Undoubtedly," he wrote, "the Federal and State Courts, supported by wholesome public opinion, will in due time define where such [segregation] laws and customs are in conflict with the American Constitution and way of life, but we can help hasten the day of complete peaceful adjustment by an ever increasing spirit, in word and action, of good will, respect and sympathy towards the Colored people." He noted that long-standing customs, laws, and regulations supporting and enforcing segregation were obstacles that would not be easily overcome, but he believed that Catholics could do much "to aid this cause of justice and charity by making segregation disappear in our Catholic church life."[15]

As teacher and pastor of the archdiocese, Rummel was well within his duties and responsibilities to speak to this issue. He was ending discriminatory practices within the church and encouraging the faithful to prepare for eventual desegregation in American society. Later protests by Catholic New Orleanians would be contrary to church teachings and lead to church sanctions.[16]

SAM HILL RAY, S.J., AND THE RACE QUESTION, PART THREE

While Archbishop Rummel called for an end to segregation in the church, Sam Hill Ray, S.J., in the same spring of 1953, distributed a letter to his fellow Jesuits arguing for the maintenance of racial segregation. Ray was countering the August 1952 New Orleans Province decision to desegregate. The philosophical position he advanced, titled "Equality but not Identity," argued that black Americans should be provided opportunities equal to whites but that the two races should not be made equal. Ray reasoned that while men and women have natural rights originating in natural law, for the common good of society the exercise of those rights could be denied. Such was the case, he claimed, for the separation of the races after the Civil War. Segregation, "not wrong in theory," he claimed, "was required by the State to keep the peace and justified as a state right and duty by the police power given the state." According to Ray, segregation was practiced for the "good of the blacks." He worried that unless the New Orleans Province Jesuits followed a gradualist approach to the race issue, "the attempted transition will create riots and bloodshed." He cited the Holy Name Rally of 1949 as an example of a "near miss" of such chaos.[17]

He also raised the specter of miscegenation. The Grand Coteau meeting of August 1952, he noted, was "stacked . . . in favor of the new [racial] policy from a count of the larger number present for miscegenation than against it." Given the unfavorable composition of the Grand Coteau members, Ray called for another meeting to discuss and draft another statement on race. Composed of the older, more mature and seasoned members of the province, this group, Ray believed, would be better prepared to address the issue because "[i]t is well known that impulsive youth can be swayed by emotion more easily than matured men— stamped by experience and the Society as such."[18]

Through this act, Ray was not only attacking the members of the New Orleans Province of the Society of Jesus who had decided to change racial policy, but he was also challenging religious superiors and church officials who had also decided that the time had come to reorder society. If there was a response or reaction to Ray's circular, none has survived. Nor is there evidence that he received a letter of warning or admonition from his superior. If there was a verbal admonition, again, there is no record of one.

The following year, Sam Hill Ray again addressed the race question in a talk he gave before members of the Exchange Club in New Orleans.[19] While his formal presentation focused on the need to ban the sale of licentious literature, he took the opportunity to comment on the issue of racial segregation. Given that the province policy statement had not yet been promulgated (that took place in 1954), this Loyola University staff member was not directly disobeying any instructions not to speak contrary to Jesuit policy by commenting on the topic. Ray's remarks signaled to his audience that some clergy, at least, agreed with the established social structure. He informed his listeners that he did not believe integration would bring any improvement because "in cities where there is no segregation no one has benefitted."[20] While his views were published in the local newspaper, there are no indications that Ray was reprimanded for publicly voicing his support for segregation.

AGITATION AND SUPPLICATION

Nevertheless, the students continued to agitate for change through formal venues. Preparing to attend the 1953 annual national convention of the NFCCS to be held in Cincinnati, Ohio, the Louisiana delegates met to draft resolutions that they would present for adoption at the meeting. The most far-reaching resolution formulated by the student delegates called for the removal from the NFCCS of member institutions that practiced racial segregation. If adopted at the Cincinnati convention, the resolution would force Loyola University of the South and St. Mary's Dominican College to resign from the national organization. Not all the delegates agreed with the proposal. Loyola's representative, Maurice "Moon" Landrieu, objected, arguing, "[W]e would be excluding the very schools which needed conversion and hence defeating our own purpose." Wilbert Sykes of Xavier did not believe it was "in the power of the students to regulate the enrollment policies of their schools." The students compromised on a resolution

that granted a five-year grace period for member schools to comply with the resolution to integrate. If, after five years, an institution still had not opened its
doors to blacks, then it would be expelled from the NFCCS.[21]

There are no indications that the resolution was ever presented at the national
congress. Delegates from the New York–New Jersey Region did, however, introduce a resolution that opposed "racial discrimination in all its forms and . . . segregation in employment, housing, education, and church." Furthermore, the
collegians called upon all Catholic college youth "to do everything in . . . [their]
power to end discrimination in all forms in campus student life."[22] In New
Orleans, the resolution had no effect on member institutions. For the time being,
the interracial commission had to settle for continuing a campaign of information and education.

SERINCO members did this by producing a pamphlet titled "The Best of
the *Christian Conscience* for Five Years." A collection of the journal's most representative articles from 1948 through 1953, the pamphlet allowed the collegians
to explain the history and purpose of the organization and to present arguments
against segregation and for integration. In six sections, the editors emphasized
four topics: education, morality, action, and good will.[23]

"Blackface Minstrels," an editorial from June 1952, challenged the staging of
such productions. According to white Catholics, minstrel shows were performed
in fun with no harm intended. Besides, they argued, parish organizations had
sponsored such entertainment as fund-raising activities for years. But even though
in these performances "the white man hides himself in grease paint, doing his little dance, cracking his coarse jokes, singing his suggestive songs, and *pretending*
that he is acting like a Negro," the editor wrote, his understanding of Christian
charity should "prevent him from insulting his colored brothers in Christ."[24]
Lacking Christian charity was deemed inappropriate and an occasion of sin for
most Catholics, and therefore the minstrel shows should cease.

Regarding the race question and Communism, the editors argued that, contrary to earlier arguments, segregation encouraged infiltration of subversive elements into American society. Racial myths of white superiority and black in-
feriority, they argued in "Christ or Kremlin," April 1951, provided openings for
Communists to exploit. Prejudice and discrimination against minorities led to
internal strife and upheavals, which the Kremlin manipulated. "National sores
become gaping wounds which bleed countries until they are weak prey for
Communism," the editorial maintained. SERINCO members hoped that
America's racial problems would be corrected lest the United States remain "sus-
ceptible to Red Attack."[25]

In "Amateur vs. Professional," published in May 1950, the editors saw
Christianity as the most dangerous weapon in the world at that time, even more
dangerous than "the contemplated Hydrogen bomb or Germ Warfare." The type

of Christianity they meant was "Christianity in the hands of amateurs and dem-agogues who distort it, rationalize it, and employ the perverted result to seduce their own intellects and those of their fellow men." SERINCO writers took the "amateur" Christian to task for limiting his or her practice of the faith to occa-sional acts of charity and to the emotional appeal of hearing a High Mass sung on Sunday. Amateur Christians were unwilling, the writers noted, to "turn Pro" when asked to put into practice God's difficult command to love one's neighbor. As far as the writers of this editorial were concerned, this hesitancy to love others was the result of not wanting to endanger one's status "with fellow lukewarm Christians." Christianity, the collegians argued, could be a weapon that could be used for repulsing evil, or it could be misused, they feared, and "twisted around to annihilate a whole nation."[26]

The CHR, for its part, promoted a spiritual means to ending segregation: a monthly Hour of Reparation to acknowledge the sinfulness of the racial practices within the church and to pray for their end.[27] The notion of spiritual reparations for sinful, or at least uncharitable, behavior has a long history within the Judeo-Christian tradition. For Christians, admitting one's faults and failures, as well as seeking forgiveness, brings about a change of heart and a change in behavior. CHR member Edmund Vales, originator of the reparations idea, felt the need for public atonement for the "many violations of the Laws of Justice and Charity that take place daily in our community."[28] Commission members would, therefore, pray for a change of heart within the Christian community regarding the prac-tice of racial discrimination, confident that prayer would effect change. Vales wanted the group to atone for its collective sin. With its focus on the communal (social) aspect of behavior, this Hour of Reparation was a departure from the usual approach to sinful acts.

The first Hour of Reparation was held in the fall of 1953 at Xavier University with thirty-four in attendance.[29] With this success, the CHR sought official per-mission and endorsement from Archbishop Rummel to continue the practice on a monthly basis,[30] which Rummel granted with the proviso that the intention of the hour be to advance social justice in general, rather than to focus exclusively on the race question.[31] Prayer was an important element of the interracial move-ment, but so, too, was education and information. By educating and informing Catholics of the errors of racial segregation, interracialists believed that they could effect change within the church. The power of prayer and the power of ideas, they contended, could and would change the world.[32]

THOUGHTS, IDEAS, ACTIONS

In the pre-*Brown* era, the college students invited guest speakers to their monthly meetings to discuss the obstacles thwarting efforts to end racial segregation in

American society. Hap Glaudi, a white sports editor of the *New Orleans Item,* spoke on race and sports, and black lawyer and CHR member A. P. Tureaud, Sr., reported on his legal case to desegregate Louisiana State University.[33]

Glaudi spoke of the importance sports was playing in removing racial barriers. Interracial sporting events were changing attitudes among white southerners as televised games were being brought into peoples' homes and living rooms. He noted that the performances of "Negro athletes have done much to change" impressions and attitudes among whites.[34]

When the *Item* became the first white newspaper in New Orleans to print photos of black athletes in its sports section, Glaudi reported that 3,500 additional copies were sold. But when he published an article concerning an integrated baseball game played in New Orleans between the Chicago White Sox and the Cleveland Indians, the newspaper management complained, and two major advertisers canceled their ads in protest. Glaudi mentioned that he was not the only sports writer who had encountered difficulties with management, as an editorial by Harry Martinez of the *New Orleans States* concerning the same game had been suppressed. Highlighting a situation that would turn into a controversy in the near future, Glaudi complained that the Sugar Bowl was becoming "second rate" because promoters would not invite integrated football teams to participate in this sporting classic. This stronghold of white supremacy, he predicted, would not last much longer.[35]

On 19 October 1953, nine days before the Fifth Circuit Federal Court of Appeals reversed Judge Skelly Wright's decision ordering the integration of Louisiana State University's undergraduate program, Alexander P. Tureaud, Sr., once again spoke at the monthly SERINCO meeting. He began his presentation by recounting the lawsuit he had won in 1950 desegregating LSU's school of law and the subsequent integration of the graduate school as well as the integration of the school of nursing. Tureaud then turned his attention to the LSU undergraduate desegregation case.[36]

Tureaud had filed suit against Louisiana State University in August 1953 with his son, A. P. Tureaud, Jr., as the plaintiff: *Tureaud* v. *Board of Supervisors.*[37] Because the Tureauds were both counsel and plaintiff, the senior Tureaud asked Robert Carter of the New York branch of the National Association for the Advancement of Colored People (NAACP) to handle the trial. Arguing before Judge Skelly Wright, a Loyola University School of Law graduate, Carter pointed out that Southern University, the black public institution of higher learning in Baton Rouge, was not equal to LSU. He cited student expenditures as the most glaring example of inequity: LSU spent approximately $1,800 on each student from an annual budget of $12 million dollars, while Southern University operated on a budget of $2 million a year, with less than $700 to spend on each student. Given the evident inequalities between all-white LSU and all-black Southern, the

Supreme Court rulings in *McLaurin* and *Sweatt,* and Judge Wright's earlier decision integrating LSU law school, Carter expected to win this case.[38] However, eighteen lawyers, all alumni and working gratis, represented LSU; among them was Leander Perez, one of the leading prosegregation voices in Louisiana and the South.[39] LSU's legal team argued that the case should be dismissed because segregation was "necessary in this state to preserve and promote more friendly relations and mutual understanding between white and colored persons." Judge Wright found the reasoning unpersuasive, and on 11 September ordered LSU to accept the younger Tureaud.[40]

Once enrolled, however, A. P. Tureaud, Jr., did not have a pleasant experience at Louisiana State University. Part of the problem, the elder Tureaud explained to SERINCO members, was the fact that his son "rooms alone in the stadium dormitory. No overtures are made upon the part of his neighboring students." Due to this feeling of isolation, the younger Tureaud returned to New Orleans every weekend. The one area where he had not been shunned, his father noted, was in the Reserve Officer Training Corps (ROTC) program, where "there has been no distinction made among R.O.T.C. instructors."[41] In late October, the Fifth Circuit Court of Appeals overturned Wright's decision on the grounds that a three-member judicial panel should have decided the case, not just one judge. A. P. Tureaud, Jr., left LSU in early November 1953 and enrolled at Xavier University, where he became involved in the interracial commission. One month after the younger Tureaud left LSU, the United States Supreme Court reheard arguments in the *Brown* case.[42]

As the struggle to integrate the schools continued, the collegians in New Orleans decided to stage a talent show for the Catholic high school students as a way of promoting better race relations. SERINCO members approached the planning and execution of the program much as they had organized Interracial Sunday gatherings. The event itself would be hosted by two masters of ceremonies, one from Xavier and one from Loyola.[43] The idea of a talent show came from Jesuit High School of New Orleans. As the 1953–1954 SERINCO chairman, Gene Murret, recalled:

> I think we got the idea from the fact that we had heard that there had been one put on the year before by Fr. Levet [of Jesuit high]. . . . [W]e picked up on the idea and decided to hold an interracial talent night, and we booked the Jesuit High School auditorium and set about recruiting people in the high schools to participate, and so we would send speakers, just like we did for Interracial Sunday. We sent speakers to various schools in the city inviting them to compete for this talent show, auditions, and so forth.[44]

Among the judges were columnist Charles "Pie" Dufour of the New Orleans *Times-Picayune* and Charles Anthony Caruso, graduate of Loyola and a member of the Metropolitan Opera. While the students knew the talent contest would be interracial, the judges did not. "We never told any of them [the judges] that this was an interracial talent night," Murret stated. SERINCO members were afraid, he explained, that prospective judges "would turn . . . down [the request] if they knew that's what it was going to be." He believed the judges had to be surprised because "there hadn't been something like this [before] and certainly Pie Dufour was surprised, almost physically." Murret remembers, "There was a large turnout for the affair" and a "good mix of black and white students. . . . [I]t was a full house, every seat in the place was taken."[45] According to press accounts, over seven hundred people attended the affair.[46]

The following year another interracial talent show was sponsored for the high school students. Because of the loss of revenue in 1954, however, the interracial commission decided not to sponsor any future events.[47] By all accounts these were among the first interracial events of their kind at the high school level in Catholic New Orleans and generated no appreciable protest. The lack of objections indicated that there was either a limited amount of publicity concerning the event or there was tacit approval of such gatherings among high school teachers and administrators.

RED, BLACK, AND CATHOLIC

The sixth annual Interracial Sunday gathering was held at Loyola University on 14 March 1954. This was the first interracial gathering since Archbishop Rummel had issued his pastoral letter banning segregation within the church and the last before the Supreme Court rendered its historic *Brown* v. *Board of Education* decision two months later. The main speaker was CHR member Clarence Laws, public relations officer for the *Louisiana Weekly*, who had been a main speaker at the third (1951) Interracial Sunday function. Also participating in the affair as members of a panel discussion were A. P. Tureaud, Sr., Ernest Morial, Sr., Janet Riley, and John P. Nelson, Jr. Tureaud was the NAACP's legal counsel in the city, Ernest Morial became the first black mayor of New Orleans in 1978, Janet Riley was the first woman faculty member at Loyola University School of Law, and John P. Nelson would successfully sue Tulane University in the mid-1960s to open its doors to black students.[48]

In his address, Laws told his audience that brotherhood "must be practiced daily, it must be kept actively alive or it dies." The home, school, and church, he declared, had to become "centers for open and mutual friendships between the races" in order to make the transition from a segregated world to an integrated one. The guest speaker was certain that the Supreme Court would soon outlaw segregation in the United States not only because it was the right thing to do but also because of geopolitical considerations. Continuing the practice of segregation in America, he argued, "raises grave doubts in the minds of peoples abroad concerning our rights and qualifications to give spiritual and moral leadership to the free world when we continue to reject the concept of the unity, equality and dignity of man."[49] In calling into question America's ability to lead effectively abroad while maintaining segregation at home, Laws was echoing the concerns of civic, business, and government officials at the time. How could the United States be the leader of the free world and a beacon of hope to oppressed people around the world if the country failed to practice what it preached? These international concerns influenced domestic policy decisions and were considerations mentioned in court briefs dealing with segregation.

His experience with the United States Army had made Laws keenly aware of the connection between domestic and international policies and politics. Through the efforts of Leander Perez, Laws, a reserve officer, was called before an army investigative board in 1951 under suspicion that he was a subversive or had subversive connections because he had spoken before pro-integration groups.[50] Exonerated by the army, only to be discharged as a security risk in 1955, Clarence Laws was targeted for promoting racial equality.[51] Linking civil rights activities with subversive causes in order to discredit participants would become more prevalent as the decade progressed, especially after the rendering of the *Brown* decision.[52]

The citizens of New Orleans experienced this "linking," the negative association between interracialism and Communism, when Senator James Eastland of Mississippi, chairman of the Senate Internal Security Subcommittee, conducted a series of hearings, 18–20 March 1954, concerning subversive activities in the region. Begun four days after the sixth Interracial Sunday gathering, the Eastland Committee had come to Louisiana to investigate the Southern Conference Educational Fund (SCEF), the auxiliary branch of the then defunct Southern Conference for Human Welfare (SCHW), itself an interracial body established in 1938 to promote social reform in the South, especially regarding labor and race issues. Headquartered in New Orleans and under the direction of James Dombrowski, the SCEF continued the interracial and civil rights work of the parent organization with limited success, due in part to accusations that the conference and Dombrowski had subversive ties.[53]

Ostensibly looking for subversive influences in the organization, Senator Eastland called for testimony from Dombrowski as well as Aubry Williams, the current SCEF president; Myles Horton, an SCEF supporter and founder of Highlander Folk School located in Monteagle, Tennessee; and Virginia Durr, past president of the SCEF. For all practical purposes, however, Eastland was attacking the interracial nature of the SCEF and those who promoted integration. By associating the conference with "Communist influences," Eastland would be able to destroy the SCEF, just as similar charges (some verified) had been the demise of the SCHW in 1948. Even though he was unable to uncover any subversive activities, Senator Eastland's investigation did irreparable damaged to the work of the SCEF in Louisiana. As historian Adam Fairclough notes, "SCEF's influence would henceforth be felt mainly *outside* Louisiana."[54]

CATHOLICS IN THE AGE OF BROWN

Even as the collegians strove to advance the cause of interracial justice, the Jesuits at Loyola University were still arguing the merits of segregation. The Grand Coteau meeting of 1952 and the integration of the law school notwithstanding, these men found themselves still in disagreement over the course of action to take regarding race relations. One week before the Supreme Court rendered the *Brown* decision on 17 May 1954, Jesuit provincial William Crandell concluded his annual visit to the university community. His follow-up letter to the Jesuits at Loyola showed the depth of personal animosity and dissension of the order.

The provincial admonished the Jesuits at Loyola for disregarding proper seating arrangements in the dining room. While both the rule and the breaking of it appear archaic and trivial in today's world, closer examination of this breach of etiquette reveals a visible and physical manifestation of the division among Jesuits regarding the race question. No one except the local superior was to have a fixed seat in the refectory in order to avoid an inordinate attachment to a particular place. The norm and standard for Jesuits sitting in the dining room was for an individual to take the first available seat available nearest the superior, either on the right or left hand side, between the table and wall. After these places were filled, members were to sit on the other side of the table, filling in the seats left to right from the middle to the end of the table. At dinner the differences of opinions regarding the race question and labor issues arose. So contentious had the discussions become that individuals began "picking and choosing" where they would sit to avoid sitting next to an individual who held opposing views and having to listen to him during the course of the meal. The provincial wanted this violation of the rules to stop because such behavior violated "a spirit of true charity."[55] Crandell, in his annual letter to the superior general of the order, John Janssens, repeated what he had stated in previous years: there was "still too much argumentation and contentiousness in the community at Loyola" concerning the race question, leading "individuals to sit at definite places in the refectory so that the proper grouping would result when talking at table is allowed." Crandell hoped that the superior of the Loyola community would "use his best efforts to correct these abuses."[56]

One can imagine the table conversations in May 1954 when the United States Supreme Court struck down segregation in public schools by ruling in *Brown v. Board of Education* that the "separate but equal" clause of the *Plessy* case was unconstitutional. For some Jesuits and Catholic college students, the effort they had put into improving race relations appeared to be bearing fruit. Their dream of a truly integrated church, they hoped, would soon be fulfilled. For other Catholics, their worst fears were being realized. First the church and now the courts were "ramming" integration down their throats.[57]

While not dismissing the ruling outright, the editors of the *Times-Picayune* questioned the Court's decision, stating that it would "do no service either to education or racial accommodation" and predicting "considerable turmoil for some time to come." They argued that the equality test of *Plessy* was being met because school facilities were "now in fact approximately equal," and therefore there was no reason to overturn the 1896 court ruling. These editors were, however, resigned to the fact that change was coming, pointing out, "All the South can do—all the states and localities can do—is shoulder the burden the court has placed upon them and work soberly to redirect their educational effort along lines that will be acceptable to all and at the same time will preserve its vitality."[58]

The editorial board of the black newspaper the *Louisiana Weekly* had a different response. "Naturally we who have been the victims of segregation are happy and jubilant over the sweeping and far reaching ruling of the highest court in the land in this matter of segregation," the paper's editorial stated. "Our long years of hope and faith in democracy have been justified with this truly great decision." But the author wondered if southerners would feel free to express their approval of the Court decision: "[A]fter the majority of the legislators and politicians denounce to [*sic*] the decision, few, if any, private citizens, businessmen, clergymen, etc. will have the courage to publicly state they accept what the High Court has ruled." That was "understandable, to a degree, for Southerners generally are about as free as Russians to air opinions contrary to what is allegedly accepted as Southern custom. Their fear of repercussions is probably similar to that the Russian people have of the Communist Party bigwigs." The *Weekly* editor hoped that in the future, voters would elect leaders who would support the rule of law rather than subvert it.[59]

Within days of the announcement of the Court's decision, the Louisiana House of Representatives passed a resolution, by a vote of 84–3, favoring continuance of segregated schools in the state. Representative E. W. Gravolet, Jr., one of the cosponsors, argued that it was not the "time for compromise—no time to talk mealymouthed. I think the legislature should take further steps after the passage of this resolution to make sure that the rights of the state and the Legislature are not usurped by nine men in Washington." In the final version of the house resolution, members deplored the "unwarranted and unprecedented abuse of power by the Supreme Court in the antisegregation decision." The legislators believed that the *Brown* decision could only "result in racial turmoil, strife, and confusion to the irreparable harm and injury of the people of the state of Louisiana and of most of the states of the Union."[60]

One of the three representatives voting against the measure—that is, voting to allow schools to integrate—Representative Bernard Engert of New Orleans informed his house colleagues that his decision to oppose the legislation was based on the fact that he was a Catholic. Speaking to members of the CHR, Engert told his listeners that he had "acted not as a politician but as a Catholic" when casting his vote. He rejected political expediency to support the Supreme Court and democracy, noting that only the Communists would benefit from racial disturbances in the United States. "Communists would like to see Negroes against whites and farmers against organized labor. This must not be," he concluded. The state senate considered the resolution a few days later and passed it by a vote of 32 to 1.[61]

However, many New Orleanians agreed with the prosegregation stance of their elected officials. "I agree," wrote *Times-Picayune* reader Tom Brenan, "that the Negro question in America is a matter of evolution and environment." As far as he was concerned, the black man in America had "not yet evolved to a point where he is entitled to some of the considerations that some of their aggressive agitators are trying to make them believe." Citing the population statistics of blacks in the United States and invoking the democratic notion of majority rule, the author wanted to know how the Supreme Court could rule "that less than 10 per cent of our population should tell us what to do." For this writer, the race question was a southern issue, which he believed could be handled by reasonable southerners.[62] Another reader considered the ruling "as deadly a blow to statehood and individual liberty as could have been devised by the Communists." For him, the "politicized" court was practicing authoritarianism and contradicting the ideals of life, liberty, and the pursuit of happiness. This writer hoped that the federal government did "not try to carry out by force the unnatural, deplorable, implications in this decision."[63]

Responding to Brenan's letter, Mr. and Mrs. J. M. Dudley, who identified themselves as black, wrote in defense of the Supreme Court ruling. Citing a recent educational study, they noted that black education was not equal to that of whites, as black students and faculty were "forced to use 7000 of some 8500 one-room school houses in eight southern states." The situation was deplorable, and although the Dudleys were quite pleased that black children would no longer be forced to attend inferior schools, they did not want the white readership to misinterpret their comments. "Please don't get the wrong conception of us. We're not fighting to mingle or associate with whites. It's just that we are fighting for equal rights. I'm sure none of us care to associate with anyone who doesn't care to associate with us."[64]

One reader believed that the court decision went against the will of God. The only logical result of desegregation, Mabel Sheldon stated, would be "misery and heartache of mongrelization." She did not believe that "God himself intended it that way." Citing Old and New Testament prohibitions against intermarriage, Sheldon could only conclude that it was "man who has messed up things."[65] Still another reader counseled against writing letters to the editor, arguing that denouncing "Nine angry men" would be engaging in an act of futility. He wanted others to be practical and pragmatic regarding the decision because there was really no other option. "It [Brown] will soon be the law of the land, and like all good Americans we should and will abide by it and take it in good grace and make it work. I don't see how any other decision is possible—not in the Land of the Free and Home of the Brave."[66]

In an effort to promote adherence to the Supreme Court's ruling among young Catholics, the CHR sponsored an essay contest. Seventy-two high school students from fifteen schools submitted entries titled "My views as a Catholic on the United States Supreme Court Decision of May 17, 1954," with nine individuals meriting recognition. Anne Schekeler of St. Mary's Dominican High School was the first-place winner.[67]

In her noteworthy essay, Schekeler invited her audience to consider what America meant to them in theory and in practice, to examine what America stood for both at home and abroad, and to contemplate, if they were white, what it would be like to be born black—what that would have meant. She challenged white Americans to reconsider the notion that somehow, because of the accident of birth, they are "'superior' for something which was entirely the will of God!" Only if white Americans could experience life as black Americans did, she believed, "would they realize what it is to be an oppressed people in a free nation which is such a strong defender of democracy abroad." Finding irony in American opposition to the oppression of European peoples, Schekeler pointed out, "within our own country, Americans have been guilty of oppressing the Negro!" Though many African Americans had sacrificed their lives in battle for America, blacks were still denied their democratic rights. In order to rectify these injustices, she called on "tolerant Christians" to open their hearts and minds "to these children of God by acting in a spirit of brotherly love, which makes no discrimination on the mere basis of skin color."[68]

While archdiocesan students hailed the Court's Brown decision, there was no indication when the Catholic school system would be integrated. When asked for his reaction to the court decision, the superintendent of the Catholic parochial school system, Monsignor Henry C. Bezou, replied that "the decision is in accordance with what has been expected on the basis of natural justice and with the clear intent and purpose of the Constitution of the United States. For further comment and action we naturally await the supplementary directives of the United States Supreme Court and also await the reaction of our own legislators."[69] Millard F. Everett, the editor of the archdiocesan newspaper, *Catholic Action of the South,* chastened those who would circumvent the court ruling, especially government officials. Any appeal to states' rights in an effort to circumvent the law, he declared, was "political piffle." Failure to grant all American citizens their basic civil rights, he believed, meant that the United States was not a democracy.[70]

Two weeks after the Court announced its decision, Monsignor Bezou, representing the New Orleans archdiocesan school board, issued a statement supporting *Brown.* "We consider the statement of the court," he began, "fully in accord with Christian social principles affirming the equality of all men and the rights of all men to share equally in the blessings of the beatific vision in heaven." The board also viewed the decision as a way to increasing the prestige of the United States throughout the world, in full accord with the principles of democracy and as a means for promoting unity and peace among the people of the United States. New Orleans archdiocesan board members recognized that the process of desegregation would be difficult, but they urged that "all should work earnestly and sympathetically to the end that a practical implementation of the decision may be successfully and charitably affected." Bezou cited the archdiocese's successful integration of several religious organizations as a model worthy of emulation in future desegregation efforts.[71]

In the wake of the Supreme Court ruling, the Louisiana legislature passed house bills 1136, 1137, and 1138 on 28 June 1954. All three bills were designed to maintain segregation in the school systems. Without discussion of race, the legislators justified their actions by invoking the state police power to promote the health, peace, and good order of society. Bill 1137 mandated segregated schools for black and white students, forbade the state board of education from accrediting any school that violated the act, forbade any state college or university from accepting a student from an integrated school, and called for the revocation of state funds and supplies for any school that violated the act. Bill 1138 called for the superintendent of schools in each district to assign pupils to their respective public school (i.e., pupil placement), thus allowing segregated schools to survive. Bill 1136 was a state constitutional amendment, which needed public approval in order to become law. This measure would enable the Louisiana legislature to control the school system in each district and to enact laws regarding admissions standards and to provide alternative plans for educating the youth of the state. Once the amendment was passed, no further vote of the people would be necessary for the legislature to act.[72]

Catholic Action editor M. F. Everett wrote an editorial deploring the measures that would affect private schools as well as public ones. In these bills he found the worst forms of totalitarianism and statism at work. Parents would be denied the right to decide how and by whom their children would be educated. An individual could be fined and/or imprisoned for encouraging or assisting anyone attempting to integrate elementary or high schools. For lawyers, the penalty would be disbarment. According to the Catholic editor, the three bills "are not the way of justice and concord. They are the tactics of Hitler and Stalin. For heaven's sake, don't let the disgrace of totalitarianism be foisted upon Louisiana!"[73]

In light of the archdiocesan school board's statement supporting the Supreme Court ruling, rumors began to circulate throughout the city that the parochial schools would integrate that fall. In July 1954, Archbishop Rummel released a public statement to put a halt to the rumors, stating that it was impossible to act then, given the overcrowded conditions in both the white and black parochial schools, and adding, "For this precipitous action there is absolutely no evidence in the form of an official statement." He reiterated the position taken by his school board, that the archdiocese would "await further instruction from the Supreme Court."[74]

The archbishop's statement also condemned Louisiana State House of Representatives Bills 1136, 1137, and 1138. Even though the proposed legislation had been rewritten to exclude parochial and private schools from state control, the archbishop still found the bills objectionable. "Because they place education under the state police power, were conceived in an atmosphere of haste, prejudice and controversy and conflict with the federal constitution as interpreted by the supreme court," Rummel stated, the bills were unacceptable.[75]

Leander Perez, district attorney for Plaquemines and St. Bernard Parishes and a vocal proponent of the legislature's efforts to maintain segregation, believed that the archbishop's statement regarding the house bills was fallacious because of a misunderstanding of the term "police power." The Supreme Court, he pointed out, had ruled on numerous occasions in favor of a state's right to invoke "police power"—all for the "promotion and protection of public health, morals, education, peace and good order." According to Perez, the *Times-Picayune* reported, "'right-thinking Catholic citizens' of New Orleans and Louisiana will 'see to it that segregation will be maintained in the parochial schools not only next year but long after.'"[76]

While the legislature revised bills 1137 and 1138 to exclude control over private schools, bill 1136, a proposed state constitutional amendment, was placed on the ballot for the November elections. In response, Everett penned a series of eight articles deploring the legislation and urging his readers to vote against the amendment.[77] He highlighted the tragic effects resulting from practicing various forms of prejudice and racism; explained the heavy cost segregation exacted from people, both spiritual and economic; noted the grave damage done to American credibility throughout the world; reviewed the contradictions present in the practice of segregation, finding them contrary to God's law of love and to true democracy; recalled the opposition of non-Catholics to racial injustice; and finally asserted that the proposed Louisiana law was contrary to federal constitutional law. The state constitutional amendment, bill 1136, passed in November by a vote of 217,992 to 46,929.[78]

DESEGREGATING LOYOLA UNIVERSITY AND SPRING HILL COLLEGE

As members of the Louisiana state legislature devised ways of circumventing the *Brown* decision, members of the board of directors of Loyola University of the South debated the advisability of opening the department of education and the evening division to black students during the spring and fall of 1954.[79] The Jesuit integration policy required Loyola University officials to consult with Xavier officials before admitting black students into its degree programs if the same program was offered at Xavier University. Such a situation arose involving the master's degree program in education. Edward Doyle, S.J., director of the department of education, reported to the board that he had consulted with the president of Xavier, Mother Mary Agatha, S.B.S., on the issue. According to Doyle, Xavier's president "would be glad if Loyola took the few candidates that she felt would want to come over to Loyola or need to come to Loyola for their graduate work in education."[80] The evening division was less problematic because Xavier did not offer similar courses; the one question that needed to be resolved concerned evening division students registering for day classes. While black students were allowed to sign up for evening classes, board members decided, "Negroes admitted to the Evening Division would not be allowed to take courses in the day school."[81] Desegregation of Loyola University's undergraduate program would be delayed for several more years.

In Alabama, the situation was different; the New Orleans Province of the Society of Jesus made civil rights history there in the fall of 1954 by integrating the undergraduate program at its Alabama institution of higher learning, Spring Hill College. This was the first college or university in the state to desegregate and would remain so for almost ten years, the attempt by Autherine Lucy to attend the University of Alabama in 1956 notwithstanding.[82] Spring Hill followed Loyola's example of gradual integration by first accepting religious women of color and then black laymen and laywomen. Black sisters attended classes in the summer of 1952. Reporting to John B. Janssens, Jesuit superior in Rome, on the reaction to this development, Andrew Smith, S.J., president of the college, noted, "Thus far there had been complaint from no quarter."[83] In early 1954 Smith reported that Spring Hill accepted "four well chosen colored men in the evening classes." The successful integration of these men into the college encouraged the president to accept black lay people into the summer session. The expectation was that full-time black undergraduates would be accepted that fall. With the approval of Provincial William Crandell, Smith and his consultors moved forward and desegregated the undergraduate program in September.[84]

The easy desegregation of the college, Smith explained to Janssens, rested in part with his 1954 commencement remarks "praising the recent decision of the U.S. Supreme Court against segregation in public education." Regarding this decision to end the custom of racial segregation, Smith mused, "Doubtless we stand to lose some students in protest, but I feel we can take the loss for the sake of the cause. I find the younger generation much more broad-minded on the matter than their elders."[85] Neither in 1952 nor in 1954 was there any publicity surrounding the change in Spring Hill's admissions practices, again, fully in accord with the Jesuit policy directive of 1952. After the first semester of full desegregation, Smith reported, "With one or two exceptions there has been no public outcry about it. . . . We have lost a few contributions to our college funds, but that is a small price to pay for a clear conscience."[86]

At the end of the first year of integration, Andrew Smith reported that "acceptance of colored students has provoked no serious opposition in this area and we expect to go on with the practice." While the college did not keep or give out statistics regarding racial composition of the student body, the president believed "the total of this past year was some 25 Colored out of the 1,000 students in attendance."[87] Of the twenty-eight Jesuit institutions of higher learning in 1954, Loyola University of the South now was the only one still practicing segregation at the undergraduate level. Problems within the Jesuit community at New Orleans played a role in this lag.

Nonetheless, Patrick Donnelly, S.J., president of Loyola University of the South, did advance interracial policy. In late 1954 the president announced that the newly completed Field House would be an integrated facility: there would be no segregated seating in the arena, and integrated teams would be invited to play against Loyola.[88] Donnelly's decision to integrate the Field House was criticized by the Jesuit consultors at Loyola. One in particular, Aloysius Goodspeed, S.J., was annoyed that the issue was not discussed beforehand. In his letter to the provincial, Goodspeed stated that insignificant matters were reviewed by the university consultors, but "matters of far-reaching importance . . . such as the integration of white and Negroes in the Field House" were not. "The first thing any consultor knew of this bombshell announcement," he remarked, "was when he read it in the daily newspaper."[89]

The editors of the *Louisiana Weekly* commended Loyola University for making this change in Jim Crow practices. In the editorial "The Human Race Gets a Chance," the editors noted: "Negro sports fans of this community and surrounding areas will for the first time be treated as normal, ordinary human beings. For the first time in the lives of many they will not have to face the humiliating experience of being segregated, 'going around the back,' 'up the alley' to sit up in buzzard's roost to see a sporting event. Self-respect and dignity will not have to be sacrificed in order to see a sporting event."[90]

The editors of Xavier University's *Herald* also congratulated the Loyola administration for operating the field house on an integrated basis. The decision to desegregate, the *Herald* stated, was "another giant step . . . toward true Christian brotherhood." The Xavier writers also congratulated Loyola for the manner in which university officials announced their decision without any fanfare: "The announcement came minus the usual amount of 'flag-waving,' in other words, Loyola officials meant that we are not doing this for glory, but because it is fair and it is what God wants."[91]

In December 1954 Loyola's basketball team played a very demanding schedule. Having won a national championship title in the previous decade, the Wolfpack wanted to return to those glory days. The coach arranged for the team to play crucial games at the beginning of the season, hoping that early victories would bring significant national media attention to the team. The student newspaper, the *Maroon*, reported that Coach Jim McCafferty favored a tough opening schedule. "Yep," McCafferty explained, "we might as well go after the big ones early. Our past schedules had mostly [been] warm-ups until January, but you've gotta beat the big ones to get somewhere. That's what we want to do." December, the sports editor continued, would be "the biggest month in Loyola athletic history. It's the month when Loyola, for the first time, can possibly crash the nation's top 10 basketball ratings. The stepping stones: Southwestern Louisiana Institute tonight, La Salle and Tom Gola Sunday night, then St. Mary, the Sugar Bowl tournament and Illinois."[92]

After winning its first three games, Loyola faced a crucial test when it played the defending national champions, La Salle College of Philadelphia, on 5 December 1954. As the first interracial basketball game played in the history of the city of New Orleans and the state of Louisiana, the game had special significance both on and off the court. Alonzo Lewis, a black player for La Salle was scheduled to start.[93]

In attendance for the game that evening were approximately one thousand black fans, many from Xavier University. They had come to see the black athlete from up North playing with white teammates, and they were not disappointed when Al Lewis scored the first points of the game. Sitting wherever they wanted in Loyola's new Field House, the black fans attending the game were making history of their own. The 5,000 white fans would not forget this historic evening either; it was, for most of them, their first encounter with the New South.[94]

While there were basketball games being played on the courts of Loyola's new Field House, there were also games being played on campus. The race question was still a source of contention, and not all members of the Loyola Jesuit community supported President Donnelly's, or the province's, decision to desegregate. Among those who opposed the decision were William J. Harty, S.J., the pastor of Holy Name of Jesus Church, a Jesuit parish located on the campus of Loyola University, and one of his assistants, Lawrence Toups, S.J., who, as one of the province consultors reported, publicly attacked province policy. In January 1955 university board member and consultor Edward A. Doyle, S.J., informed the provincial, William Crandell, that there was "a general and persistent spirit of criticism and lack of cooperation on the part of the Pastor and this particular assistant who challenge and condemn with regularity the policies of the University, the local Ordinary [Rummel], and the teaching of the Church on social questions." After listening to these clerics preach, Doyle considered their words "extremely serious breaches of discipline and loyalty to the Church and Society [of Jesus]." Doyle also informed Crandell that the senior ethics professor in Loyola's philosophy department, Martin Burke, S.J., refused to support the province's racial policy. "In fact," Doyle stated, "he [Burke] is teaching a doctrine contrary to that outlined by your Reverence." The situation was such that Doyle believed Burke's stance was "the source of much confusion and disedification to students in whose judgment he is losing the influence, prestige, and effectiveness in teaching which he formerly enjoyed."[95]

Writing that same January, Aloysius Goodspeed had a different impression of the situation in New Orleans. While the race issue was dividing the Jesuit community, he believed that those members favoring segregation were "to be commended highly for bending all the forces of their understanding and will in obeying the instructions of your Reverence's letter as some few of the Integrationists waive [sic] the red flag of conquest before them."[96]

TALKING ABOUT CATHOLIC DESEGREGATION

Had members of the Loyola community attended the meeting of the Young Men's Business Club of New Orleans in January 1955 or read the article in the Catholic newspaper about the address given at the meeting, they would have heard the chancellor of the archdiocese of New Orleans, Monsignor Charles J.

Plauche, declare that segregation was a "totally inadequate means of permanent social adjustment consonant with the demands of justice and charity." He argued that permanent segregation of blacks naturally would degenerate into discrimination, which was a violation of human dignity. "As an American citizen and as a Catholic," he continued, "I submit that there is no acceptable moral alternative to the condemnation of segregation of the Negro and the acceptance of integration of the races in public and semi-public institutions and agencies."[97]

While Plauche spoke forcibly and directly in calling for an end to segregation, he acknowledged that it would be difficult for some whites to change their attitudes regarding the race question because of "the deep-seated, ingrained aversion to a change in our Southern social pattern that has been instilled into us from earliest childhood." Be that as it might, the chancellor still called upon New Orleanians, and especially the leaders listening to his remarks, to do their duty, to follow the directives of the courts and the law of the land. In closing he appealed to "all responsible members of the community not to rebel against constituted authority or waste time in useless gestures of defiance, but to face the problem resolutely, calmly, and honestly, striving to bring about in orderly fashion the elimination of that blot on our escutcheon which is segregation."[98] For the Catholic populace in New Orleans there should have been no doubt that the leadership of the archdiocese favored an end to segregationist practices. There was, however, a difference between favoring policy change and changing policy.

As New Orleanians came to terms with desegregation, interracial activities in the archdiocese continued as usual. The first post-*Brown* Interracial Sunday gathering was held in March 1955 at Xavier University. A departure from the previous events, with no guest speakers, collegians' speech contest, or high school poster contest, ten panel discussions covering educational, economic, legal, moral, and sociological aspects of segregation and integration replaced the traditional agenda.[99] The various panel members agreed that discriminatory practices in the United States were morally bankrupting the country and its people. Urban League member Prather Hauser, sitting on the panel entitled "What Price Discriminatory Employment Practices," told his listeners that the goal of racial equality should be just opportunity. Rather than trying to equalize all of society, he argued, the real objective of equal opportunity in the job market should be "to enable each man to attain the level of his ability." Fellow panel member Paul Downey, S.S.J., assistant pastor of Joan of Arc Church, reminded the audience that "the denial of the equality of human nature was a denial of one of the fundamental truths of the Catholic Church." Such a denial, he asserted, led to "moral bankruptcy." Frederick Routh of the Southern Regional Council, another member of the panel, stated that strong Fair Employment Practices Commission measures were needed to ensure just treatment in the workplace.[100]

Another noteworthy panel discussion was one titled "Integration in Inter-collegiate Athletics." Anthony O'Flynn, S.J., athletic director at Loyola University of the South, pointed out that segregation was disappearing from the athletic world; an athlete was required to "stand on his own ability." Recounting Loyola's experience in competing against La Salle College in basketball earlier that aca-demic year, O'Flynn noted that only one ticket was returned for a refund. While Xavier University and Loyola University did not compete against each other in basketball, O'Flynn informed his listeners that he would "accept a qualified Negro player on his basketball team."[101] What O'Flynn did not address was whether Loyola University's undergraduate program would accept a black student in order to allow the qualified ball player to be a member of a Wolfpack team.

THE PROBLEM OF SOCIAL INTEGRATION

The struggle between racial separation and social integration became an issue for Loyola University officials in the spring of 1955 when Loyola law students Ben Johnson and Norman Francis and their dates attended an affair sponsored by Loyola's Alumni Association. A minority of the alumni membership, led by Emile Wagner, protested the presence of blacks at the social. At a subsequent meeting of the alumni, Patrick Donnelly, the president of Loyola, attempted to resolve the controversy by reading to those present the province policy regarding race rela-tions. Wagner later accused the Jesuits of attempting to force integration whether the Catholic community wanted it or not.[102]

In light of the protest, university officials had to decide what course of action to take. Either Loyola would accede to the demands of the alumni by excluding blacks from all functions, or the university could take a more drastic step and dis-band the alumni association.[103] As a compromise, the Jesuits of Loyola decided to allow each university-sponsored organization to determine the racial makeup of its social gatherings. Blacks, however, could not be excluded from any univer-sity organization or event other than social functions.[104]

Tension among the alumni regarding the race question was matched by con-tinued tension within the Jesuit community at Loyola. Promulgation of the province policy statement regarding interracial relations did not quiet dissenters. Once again Crandell had to admonish the men at the university. "Caustic remarks and criticisms of other members of the community, name calling and other signs of bitterness and personal animosity," he wrote, "are to be sedulously avoided by all, with due regard being given to the possibility of an honest differ-ence of opinion concerning the practical solution of some of the more intricate social problems of the day." In order to create harmony in the community, the provincial strongly recommended that the Loyola Jesuits "should carefully read and closely follow" the province policy regarding the race question. He deplored the making of "intemperate remarks in teaching or preaching"—no matter which side of the issue was being defended. And he also cautioned against imputing sinfulness regarding segregation, as such action could "be a source of great harm to souls."[105]

In a nuanced evaluation of the situation, Crandell wrote in his annual letter to his religious superior in Rome, John Janssens, that community living at Loyola appeared to have improved; the uncharitable behavior, so often manifested when discussing social issues, had dissipated. However, he still detected an undercurrent of unrest regarding the race question and implementation of the province policy statement. "Loyola is now the only community in the Province," he wrote, "in which I have noticed such tensions to be still in existence." The strain, he surmised, was due to the circumstances of people, place, and attitude. "Loyola was the first of our two colleges to accept Negroes," he explained, and "unlike Spring Hill, the vast majority of the Loyola students are from New Orleans and the immediate surrounding area, where opposition to integration is quite strong."[106]

The acceptance of a few black students in particular programs had agitated Loyola alumni, students, and the parents of students. While opposition to this token effort at integration was not too strong, neither had it died down. The resistance evidenced by the alumni's vocal displeasure at the situation, Crandell noted, led some Jesuits to question the logic of implementing the interracial policy. "[S]ince Loyola, unlike Spring Hill, is situated in the very midst of the community which it serves," he explained, "the opinions of Ours are more likely to be swayed by the opinions and the constant talk of those who surround us." Culpability for the heightened tension on campus lay not with those who favored segregation, as far as Crandell was concerned, but with those who advocated integration; he blamed "the imprudence of certain zealots" who had agitated for the acceptance of black alumni at social functions. In spite of the current problems, however, with time, Crandell offered, "the problem presented by integration will be solved even though it may take a few years to obtain perfect peace and harmony among Ours."[107]

Opposition to integration, heretofore confined to individual acts of resistance, was about to spread. Organized resistance soon developed within and without the church as a ten-year struggle to realize racial equality in the United States was about to begin. White southern Catholics were in the forefront of opposition to integration.

Benjamin Johnson (left) and Philip Ogilvie (right), both members of the Commission on Human Rights (CHR), were the main speakers at the 3rd annual Interracial Sunday gathering in 1951. Ben Johnson, along with Norman Francis, integrated Loyola University's school of law in 1952. (Photo courtesy of Special Collections & Archives, Monroe Library, Loyola University, New Orleans.)

A collegiate oratorical contest was held each year at the Interracial Sunday gathering. Here participants admire the first place trophy held by the president of Loyola University, Thomas J. Shields, S.J. The contestants in 1951 were (back row, left to right) Louella Patin from Sacred Heart College, Whitney LeBlanc of Xavier University, and Mary de Beilby, Ursuline College; (front row, left to right) Lydia Patin from St. Mary's Dominican College, Fr. Shields, and Norris Fitzmorris of Loyola University. (Photo courtesy of Special Collections & Archives, Monroe Library, Loyola University, New Orleans.)

Norman Francis of Xavier University (left) and Thomas Tierney of Loyola University (right) confer with SERINCO faculty moderator and chaplain Joseph Fichter (center). Norman Francis, along with Benjamin Johnson, would desegregate Loyola's school of law in the fall of 1952. In 1968 Francis was appointed the president of Xavier University; in 2005, he was still in office. When his brother, Joseph A. Francis, S.V. D., was made an auxiliary bishop in the archdiocese of Newark, New Jersey, in 1976, it was only the second time in the history of the Roman Catholic Church in the United States that two black Catholic brothers held such offices at the same time. The Healy brothers, Patrick and James, were the first to do so in the 1870s with Patrick F. Healy, S.J., serving as president of Georgetown University, while James A. Healy was bishop of Portland, Maine. (Photo courtesy of Special Collections & Archives, Monroe Library, Loyola University, New Orleans.)

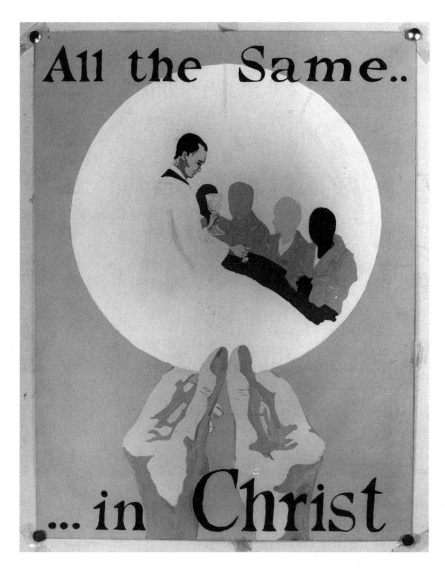

High school students were encouraged to take part in SERINCO's annual Interracial Sunday gathering by participating in a poster contest. Dorothy MacCandless of Mt. Carmel Academy won the contest in 1952. (Photo courtesy of Special Collections & Archives, Monroe Library, Loyola University, New Orleans.)

At the 6th annual Interracial Sunday gathering held in March 1954, one panel discussed the legal aspects of racial segregation. (Left to right) Ernest "Dutch" Morial, who would serve as the first black mayor of New Orleans from 1978 to 1986; A. P. Tureaud, attorney for the National Association for the Advancement of Colored People (NAACP) who successfully brought suit against Louisiana State University to desegregate in the 1950s; Janet Riley, the first woman on the faculty at Loyola University of the South; and attorney John P. Nelson, who sued to desegregate Tulane University in the mid-1960s. (Photo courtesy of Special Collections & Archives, Monroe Library, Loyola University, New Orleans.)

XAVIER   LOYOLA

SEVENTH ANNUAL

INTER-RACIAL SUNDAY

CATHOLIC COLLEGE STUDENTS

MARCH 13, 1955

XAVIER

Holy Mass 9:00 A. M.
Breakfast
Panel Discussions
Benediction 12:45 P. M.

DOMINICAN   SACRED HEART

The 7th annual Interracial Sunday gathering was the first one held since the Supreme Court's landmark decision *Brown* v. *Board of Education* was rendered. (Photo courtesy of Special Collections & Archives, Monroe Library, Loyola University, New Orleans.)

CHAPTER VII

The Rise of Southern Catholic Resistance, 1955–1956

ARCHBISHOP JOSEPH FRANCIS RUMMEL'S CALL in 1953 to end segregation practices within the archdiocese of New Orleans coupled with the Supreme Court's *Brown* v. *Board of Education et al.* decision in 1954 altered religious practices in the city of New Orleans and the state of Louisiana. Nonetheless, in 1955 Catholics in the archdiocese of New Orleans, who were not ready to embrace this new social order within or without the church, began a series of public challenges to thwart desegregation efforts. The faithful of the archdiocese questioned the implementation of racial integration on the grounds that segregation was a social rather than moral issue. They opposed desegregation, charging that it was Communist inspired. They petitioned for a delay in effecting any changes and, failing that, organized an opposition body to challenge church leaders and policy. In one instance the Catholic laity resorted to physical threat to keep a black cleric from presiding at church services. Only ecclesiastical intervention at the highest levels eventually broke the opposition in 1956 and again in 1962. Catholic dissent against church teachings regarding segregation, nevertheless, set the tone for later challenges to church authority on a variety of issues, from birth control, the Vietnam War, and abortion to the ordination of women.

The rise of southern Catholic resistance coincided with the development of other Southern antisegregation organizations, especially the White Citizens' Council (WCC). Founded in July 1954 in Indianola, Mississippi, the WCC established its first chapter in Louisiana in the spring of 1955. Other prosegregation organizations established in Louisiana at this time were the Southern Gentlemen, Inc., the Knights of White Christians, and the Society for the Preservation of State Government and Racial Integrity. In the fall of 1955, New Orleans became the site of the second WCC chapter established in the state. Within a year the Crescent City would be home to half of Louisiana's WCC members—mostly Catholic New Orleanians. WCC efforts to thwart desegregation by legal and extralegal means, including intimidation, would lead directly to the demise of the Commission on Human Rights (CHR).[1]

The Supreme Court's *Brown* decision of 1954 and the Court's rendering of *Brown II* the following year spurred interest in the WCC. While the original decision outlawed racial segregation in the public school system, the companion decision instructed school boards to begin the process of desegregation "with all deliberate speed." For many southerners, the Court's directive meant "take one's time" in effecting change, if at all.[2]

RUMMEL AND DESEGREGATION

Before the Citizens' Councils and other prosegregation organizations could attack and silence pro-integration associations, Southeastern Regional Interracial Commission (SERINCO) and CHR members continued their efforts to promote interracial harmony. Archbishop Joseph Francis Rummel, for his part, established a committee to examine the Supreme Court's desegregation decisions as they applied to church policy. With twelve representative members of the clergy and laity chaired by Auxiliary Bishop L. Abel Caillouet, the committee began its deliberations in early 1955. The archbishop instructed this ecclesiastical committee to take into consideration not only the spiritual and moral obligations of the desegregation issue but also temporal questions: difficulties arising from the long-term practice of segregation, crowded conditions in the black and white Catholic schools, the cost of establishing and maintaining integrated schools, and "the general effect which premature de-segregation may have upon the present favorable attitude of our people towards Catholic education."[3]

After holding several meetings and soliciting the opinions and attitudes of pastors, principals, and other interested Catholics, the committee, in August 1955, reported back to Rummel recommending:

> [A]t the earliest practical moment, a notice should be sent by [Rummel] . . . to all pastors and principals of schools that integration will be introduced as of the opening of the 1956 school session: such integration *to commence only with the first grade (or kindergarten)*. As early as possible prior to the opening date an educational campaign as to the moral obligation, propriety, helpfulness and patriotic ideal of true Americanism with regard to integration [should] be developed throughout the Archdiocese.[4]

The committee report also clarified the relation of archdiocesan policy regarding desegregation to Louisiana state law. Because parochial schools did not receive financial assistance from state, parish (i.e., county), or municipal agencies, the decision to integrate Catholic schools in the New Orleans archdiocese, the committee report concluded, would not be affected by the recently passed segregation laws. Bishop Caillouet, commenting on the difficulties presented by this issue, observed that "if it were only a matter of policy not involving any moral principle, it would be more prudent not to de-segregate. If, however, the moral principle of love of neighbor is involved, then it certainly becomes more prudent to de-segregate: custom and tradition to the contrary notwithstanding." On 10 August 1955, at their regular monthly meeting, Rummel and his advisers unanimously approved the report.[5]

Later that month the archbishop reported the results of the committee's findings to pastors and Catholic school officials. While the recommendations would apply to all archdiocesan schools, the archbishop informed Catholic educators that no steps to desegregate would be taken prior to September 1956. During the 1955–1956 school year, the archdiocese would further clarify impending policy changes for all school administrators. In justifying the delay, Rummel stated that "a decision to integrate immediately and hastily would be imprudent and impractical." He understood that several factors worked against rapid change, the first being the practice of segregation itself: "Behind segregation there is the tradition and emotional background of a century and a half that must be superceded by Christian principles of justice and charity." It would take time to change attitudes. Also faced with overcrowded schools, black and white, Archbishop Rummel needed time to formulate a plan for desegregating schools as well as accommodating students who would be moving from one school to another. For the future well-being of Catholic education, he wanted to preserve and strengthen parental support for Catholic education among black and white parents alike.[6]

"These and other considerations," Rummel continued, "explain why *at least a year of suspense* is proposed to allow time and opportunity for explaining the mind of the Church on this important issue and thus preparing the way for a ready acceptance of the solution." During the year, the archbishop would present the Catholic position on desegregation through pastoral letters and other forms of communication. He hoped that through these efforts he could "solve the difficulties which exist in some minds" regarding segregation. Rummel wanted to "counter the agitations of those to whom any change of the old system is anathema, chiefly because of inborn prejudice." He expected the clergy and religious of his archdiocese to assist in this process of change. As he explained, the priests, sisters, and brothers of the archdiocese shared in "the duty of promoting the welfare and just rights of all beings who bear upon their souls the image of God, the baptismal seal of children of God and of membership in Christ's Mystical Body."[7]

Thus, in the summer of 1955, four months before the Montgomery bus boycott began, the leaders of the Archdiocese of New Orleans agreed that segregation in the parochial schools would come to an end. The archbishop of New Orleans decided to delay implementation until the 1956–1957 school year in order to prepare the Catholics of his archdiocese for this change; however, Archbishop Rummel did not expect or anticipate the various forms of Catholic protest that soon visited New Orleans regarding this issue.

While not completely surprised by the announcement, the laity did react strongly to the archbishop's desegregation news. In New Orleans, opposition took the form of public resolutions presented and passed at many of the Catholic parents' club meetings. A heated debate took place between parents at the Jesuit-run Holy Name of Jesus parish school in October when the resolution was presented for discussion and voted upon.[8] Located in an affluent section of New Orleans, Holy Name of Jesus Church counted among its parishioners many of the most influential Catholics in New Orleans. Most parishioners, including Loyola alumnus Emile Wagner, sent their children to the parochial school. In late October 1955, a large majority of the Holy Name parents passed a resolution, sponsored by Wagner, calling upon Archbishop Rummel to defer, for an indefinite period of time, the integration of the parochial school system.[9] So agitated did the parents become at this meeting that, after the meeting, "the fathers of two of the school-children engaged in a fist fight."[10]

Two of the parish priests of Holy Name of Jesus Church, both Jesuits, were present at the meeting and did not speak during the debate. Later the clerics explained that they did not want to become "personally involved in the discussion" and thereby lose "the respect of the people."[11] A member of the Loyola University board of directors, Edward A. Doyle, S.J., contradicted the clerics' excuse, in particular the actions of the acting pastor, Lawrence Toups, S.J. According to Doyle, Toups "fully approved and encouraged a resolution of the Parents' Club of the Parish protesting to the Archbishop any attempt at integration of the races in the parochial schools." This same Jesuit, Doyle continued, had "stirred up the local parish with rather inane yet earnest sermons attacking the racial program of the Archbishop."[12]

JESUIT BEND: A CHALLENGE TO CHURCH AUTHORITY

The anti-integration protests were not limited to the city parishes; there were troubles in other parts of the archdiocese. In early October 1955, in Jesuit Bend, a hamlet named for land formerly held by the Society of Jesus in the eighteenth century and located some twenty miles downriver from New Orleans in Plaquemines Parish, the Reverend Gerald Lewis, S.V.D., a black priest of the Society of the Divine Word, was sent to St. Cecilia's Chapel, a mission of Our Lady of Perpetual Help Church in Belle Chasse, to celebrate Sunday Mass. As he attempted to enter the chapel, Lewis was barred entry by three white members of the congregation. The black priest left without saying Mass that morning and reported the incident to the pastor responsible for the chapel, who in turn informed Archbishop Rummel of the incident.[13]

After learning of the behavior of the St. Cecilia parishioners, Rummel placed the chapel under an interdict; that is, he suspended services there and sent a letter to the people of Jesuit Bend calling upon the faithful to repudiate their actions. The archbishop expressed his disappointment and viewed the incident clearly "as a violation of the obligation of reverence and devotion which Catholics owe to every priest of God, regardless of race, color, or nationality." And since the only apparent reason the members of St. Cecilia's Chapel refused Lewis entry into their sanctuary was his race, Rummel reminded the faithful that the church taught that "every human being, regardless of race, color or nationality, is created after the image and likeness of God"; therefore, "every human being, regardless of race, color, or nationality, is entitled to individual respect and consideration."[14]

The offenders, the archbishop emphasized, were guilty of committing acts of "injustice, uncharitableness and irreverence." These Catholics, moreover, were subject to "severe penalties" because they violated church law by interfering with "the exercise of ecclesiastical authority or functions." Rummel also wrote that he had met with a committee of five representatives from the parish and missions, informing them of the seriousness of the situation. Unfortunately, the archbishop noted, the committee did not take his warning seriously but rather had been canvassing their fellow parishioners, encouraging them to resist any future attempts to have a black priest say Mass in their church. "Such conduct," Rummel stated, was "in itself a clear violation of a true Catholic spirit and deserving of severe censure and even penalty." Until the Jesuit Bend congregation repented and all the Catholics in the area expressed "their willingness to accept for service in these churches whatever priest or priests we find it possible to send them," the archbishop declared, he would keep the chapel closed and reduce the number of liturgies held in the area.[15]

The Vatican newspaper *L'Osservatore Romano* praised Rummel's forthright stand in a 15 October editorial titled "Touches of Color." Concerning racial discrimination within the church, the editorial board stated: "Racial exclusiveness is a sin against the nature of Catholicism. It is a negation of it and a blasphemy against it." The writers argued that in the universal church there was no room for any kind of exclusion and made it quite clear that any individual who would deny a priest, because of his race, the right to offer the sacrifice of the Mass, was committing a sacrilege. To counter impressions that the church promoted discrimination, the editors recounted the many ways in which, over the centuries, the Roman Catholic Church had advanced racial justice and was continuing to do so. The editorial concluded by reminding all Catholics that they were "obliged by their religion and patriotism to aid and cooperate in this struggle [against prejudice] by all available means."[16]

In early November the people of Belle Chasse, Jesuit Bend, and Myrtle Grove formed a Citizens' Council chapter in order to organize a body to resist any form of integration in the church. In addition, some 250 residents of the area allegedly signed a petition to be sent to Archbishop Rummel expressing their opposition to the assignment of a black priest to preside at Sunday services. They argued that integration was contrary to church teachings and that Lewis's presence was part of a plan to end segregation. The archbishop quickly responded, claiming that there was "[e]vidence of misunderstanding or misinterpretation." Contrary to the rumors circulating among the parishioners, the archbishop denied that he had ever "discussed or contemplated assigning a Negro priest to the parish as an assistant. . . . We merely were supplying an extra priest to help out on the weekends."[17]

On 2 December 1955, Rummel once again wrote the Catholics of Belle Chasse, Jesuit Bend, and Myrtle Grove asking them to make an act of contrition for their behavior and to express their willingness to accept any priest who might be sent to them to celebrate Mass. Until that time, Rummel explained, services would continue to be curtailed and, in the case of Jesuit Bend, not held at all. "We trust that you will receive this appeal of your shepherd in Christ," the archbishop continued, "speaking to you in the charity of Christ and out of a heart that has a deep concern for your souls." Appealing to the leaders of the community, Rummel pleaded with them "to open their minds to truth and to let justice and charity take the place of hatred and prejudice in their hearts."[18] Apparently Rummel believed that the leaders of the dissent would be able to bring their followers back into the right thinking with the church on this matter.

Three days later, Clement Meyer, S.V.D., the white pastor of Our Lady of Perpetual Help Church and the missions at Jesuit Bend and Myrtle Grove, sent a letter to his parishioners asking them to publicly repudiate their community's act of defiance and to accept any priest sent to administer the sacraments. If they did not, Meyer explained, they were "facing the very serious danger of losing the privilege of receiving the sacraments, of Christian burial and other privileges of the Church. We are in danger of excommunication." As the archbishop had explained the church's position regarding the dignity of the priesthood and the human person, Meyer reminded his parishioners they could not "continue to overlook the request of our Archbishop to repair an offense against the priesthood and the human person committed in our community." To aid the faithful in their act of repentance, Meyer enclosed a form letter that all were to sign and return.

It read: "In conformity with the teaching of the Church on the dignity of the priesthood and the dignity of the human person I regret the offenses committed in our community against this teaching. Henceforth, I will accept any priest appointed to give us Sunday Mass and other services." Most of the faithful refused to sign, and the interdict remained in force.[19]

As the protests continued, archdiocesan officials tried to defend or clarify the church's policy. The political boss of Plaquemines Parish, District Attorney Leander Perez, one of the protest organizers, claimed that desegregation was Communist inspired. He encouraged Catholics in the New Orleans area to join a Citizens' Council to resist efforts at desegregating the archdiocese. A representative of the Belle Chasse Church spoke on New Orleans television explaining that the people of the area did not believe they should submit, under the threat of church sanction, to a policy they did not believe in or agree with. With a large majority of the Catholics of the area unwilling to express some sort of contrition, the Jesuit Bend affair reached an impasse and remained unresolved for two more years.[20]

When a handful of the almost three hundred Catholic families of the area finally signed a letter of repentance in 1958, Rummel lifted the interdict and the chapel doors reopened. Ending the stalemate at Jesuit Bend did not mean a majority of the Catholics in the area had repented or changed their minds regarding segregation within the church; rather, it appears they had been given quiet assurances by members of the Society of the Divine Word that no black priests would be sent to celebrate Mass in their community. While the archbishop was disappointed with the developments and the apparent compromise regarding this matter, there was nothing he could do without plunging the community into turmoil. Later that summer, however, a hurricane destroyed St. Cecilia's Chapel. It was never rebuilt.[21]

CATHOLIC DISSENT AND THE RACE QUESTION

In January 1956 another act of southern Catholic dissent occurred in the archdiocese. That month, at a Jesuit High School Parents' Club meeting, a group of adults, numbering five or six dozen, apparently strangers to the institution, moved that the organization pass a resolution denouncing integration. The principal of Jesuit High School, Claude Stallworth, S.J., forewarned of possible trouble, ruled the motion to be out of order because the faculty and administration were not consulted prior to the meeting and the constitution of the parents' club did not allow these outsiders to determine school policy. Recounting the affair, Stallworth explained that he "could not allow any organization connected with Jesuit High School to take any action that might be construed as giving the slightest approval to an organized movement that is just un-American, un-Christian and un-Catholic as Nazism, Ku Klux Klanism or Communism."[22] A vast majority of the parents were relieved that the motion failed, not because they favored integration, but because they did not wish to publicly oppose Archbishop Rummel.[23]

That same month, at a tumultuous meeting of the Council of Catholic School Cooperative Clubs held at St. Mary's Dominican College, council members asked Monsignor Henry Bezou, superintendent of the archdiocesan school system, if he favored integration. Council members, who were past and present Catholic parents' club presidents, raised the question because they felt that the church and, more specifically, the archbishop were avoiding the issue. Three months earlier at their October meeting, the members passed by an overwhelming majority (70 to 4) a resolution opposing integration and had requested a meeting with the archbishop to discuss the matter; they were still waiting for a response.[24]

Monsignor Bezou answered their first question by stating that he believed integration was going to follow "just like night follows the day," but he did not have a specific timetable for that eventuality. The audience did not accept his ambiguous answer. Members of the council charged that Archbishop Rummel was "not being fair to white people" and was "trying to shove integration down our throats." Bezou informed his listeners that integration would neither be sprung on them nor would it "be put off until the last minute."[25]

At Loyola, the chaplain of the university, Harold Cooper, S.J.,[26] concerned that college students were being led astray by their elders, addressed the race question through a series of articles in the student newspaper, the *Maroon*. Cooper's articles addressed not only the teaching authority of the church (that is, as granted by Holy Scripture, authorized by church councils, and exercised by bishops and the papacy) but also the development of racial segregation in the United States.

Quoting from Scripture and church councils, specifically the Council of Trent (sixteenth century) and the First Vatican Council (nineteenth century), in his first article Cooper outlined the historical development of Christian leadership and obedience. The chaplain reminded his readers that the bishops, as successors and heirs of the Apostles, were responsible for governing and instructing the Christian community. "We Catholics," he wrote, "must accept the teaching and obey the regulations of our bishops. We have no right to prefer even any priest's private opinion to the contrary."[27] Cooper most likely intended to refute the opinions and teachings of his fellow Jesuits such as Sam Hill Ray and Martin Burke regarding the morality of segregation. Cooper also addressed the argument that an individual bishop's statement or teaching on a moral issue was not infallible and, therefore, not binding on the faithful. Cooper noted that the question at hand had nothing to do with infallibility. He acknowledged "Every Catholic is aware that no individual bishop is infallible," and then asked, "But whoever claimed that our submission is limited to those rare instances of infallible pronouncement?" To reject a bishop's statement on church practices or doctrine, Cooper argued, was "tantamount to rejecting Christ Himself." If "the bishop of the diocese is not competent to speak for the Church," he asked, "then who in the diocese is?"[28]

In subsequent writings, Cooper continued to discuss teaching authority in the church. Again he appealed to Scripture and church teachings to support his claim that the bishops and the pope had the moral authority to speak to the faithful concerning the social and moral issues of the day. What he feared most, however, was that Catholic thought, policy, and doctrine would become subject to the whims of public opinion. Cooper cited the Jesuit Bend incident and the larger question of integration as examples of selective Catholicism, that is, individuals' believing they could pick and choose those teachings they liked and agreed with and reject those with which they disagreed. The chaplain of Loyola University stated what was obvious to 1950s Catholics: "The Catholic Church is not a democracy. There is no doubt about it—authoritarian. Authoritarian, not with the authority of men but of Christ." There was little room for selective observance. Cooper would continue to write on the subject throughout the rest of the semester, addressing the development of segregation in the United States and, later, analyzing the archbishop's pastoral letter on the morality of racial segregation.[29]

RUMMEL AND THE MORALITY OF SEGREGATION

Both as part of the educational process to enlighten the faithful regarding the moral ramifications of segregation and as a way to reduce the tension in the archdiocese concerning the race question, Archbishop Rummel promulgated a pastoral letter titled "The Morality of Racial Segregation," which was read from every pulpit in New Orleans on Sunday morning, 19 February 1956. Drafted with the assistance of Louis Twomey, S.J., this pastoral letter was based on the New Orleans Province policy statement regarding interracial relations.[30]

Members of SERINCO and the CHR directly influenced the development of the archbishop's letter, for it was their interracial activities that forced the Jesuits to draft a statement on the race question in 1952. Now, four years later, in 1956, Archbishop Rummel was using that very document to formulate his own position on race matters. From all indications, SERINCO and CHR activities did not, however, encourage the archbishop to produce such a document;

rather the organized protests among Catholic parents in New Orleans and the intransigency of the parishioners at Jesuit Bend more likely forced the issue.

In the cover missive accompanying his pastoral, Archbishop Rummel wrote his priests that he hoped his letter would be of some benefit to parish leaders "in guiding the faithful regarding their attitudes towards the momentous controversy which has been characterized by much bitterness, recrimination and at least the threat of insubordination on the part of some souls." But in what appeared to be a change from the information he presented to pastors and superiors of Catholic schools in August 1955, the archbishop announced that his episcopal pronouncement was not the final decision on the matter of school desegregation; a group of competent attorneys, physicians, priests, religious educators, and sociologists were studying the objections to integration and would report to him in the near future. Rummel expressed the hope that his efforts to examine the issue carefully would "convince extreme segregationists that we are not guilty of trying 'to cram integration down the throats' of our people or play the part of a dictator." In closing this cover letter, he called on all the faithful to pray for guidance during these deliberations.[31]

The pastoral letter began with the archbishop's acknowledging the difficulty of reaching a socially acceptable solution for all those concerned about racial integration, especially, he stated, "in the Deep South where for more than a century and a half segregation has been accepted without serious question or challenge." Though this statement concerning the lack of challenges and questions to segregation was open to debate, Rummel now challenged and questioned the moral rectitude of the current social practices. In subsequent paragraphs he outlined the moral implications of segregation, the reasons for rejecting the practice, and the teaching authority of a bishop to address such an issue. He concluded with a plea for prayers and understanding as the process unfolded.[32]

Racial segregation was morally wrong and sinful, he explained, because it denied "the unity and solidarity of the human race as conceived by God," because it denied "the unity and universality of Redemption" and because it violated

> the dictates of justice and the mandate of love, which in obedience to God's will must regulate the relations between all men. To deny to members of a certain race, just because they are members of that race, certain rights and opportunities, civic or economic, educational or religious, recreational or social, imposes upon them definite hardships and humiliations, frustrations and impediments to progress which condemn them to perpetual degradation which is only a step removed from slavery. Such indignities are grievous violations of Christian justice and charity, which cannot be justified in this modern age of enlightenment and loudly proclaimed democracy.[33]

While the archbishop excused the development of racial segregation in southern society by explaining that it was the result of the physical and economic hardships after Emancipation, he noted that the situation had been tolerated but never viewed as a long-term solution. Segregation within the Roman Catholic Church, he explained, developed in order to give black Catholics "the opportunity to practice their faith more freely and educate their children more fully than was often possible in mixed congregations, but this arrangement was never intended to be permanent."[34] Rummel, however, failed to mention that the development of segregated parishes began in the 1890s and was not made a permanent arrangement until the 1920s. Listening to the archbishop's letter, one could be left with the impression that racial segregation developed immediately after the Civil War.

Arguments for continuing segregation within the school system, Rummel posited, were based on "unwarranted generalizations in which it is aimed to give the impression that all members of the Negro race and especially all Negro children are tainted with virtually all the alleged defects," which included mental deficiency, immoral behavior, lack of hygiene, and predisposition to crime. The archbishop was amazed that black people were not worse off "as a race" given the neglect and barriers they encountered and endured. The laws and customs of segregation, he noted, "have practically relegated Negroes to an island-like existence. They emerge to work, toil and serve even in the intimacy of the white home and family, but 'segregation' cuts off the free avenue to progress in the better things of life that are synonymous with Christian civilization." He concluded, "This condition in itself is an indictment against continuing segregation 'indefinitely' as its advocates envision."[35]

On what authority did Rummel presume to teach on the morality of segregation? This was the heart of the controversy regarding the church's challenge to social customs and traditions, for if the archbishop could not demonstrate that he had the prerogative to speak on this issue, the cause would be lost. Citing Pope Pius XII, Archbishop Rummel made it quite clear to his audience that a bishop, as a successor of the Apostles, shared in the teaching authority of the church in union with the Holy See. He had the right to speak because he was empowered by the Christian community to do so.[36]

As he had in his cover letter accompanying this text, Rummel stated that no final decision regarding desegregation had been reached; the matter was still under investigation. "Nothing would please us more," he informed his listeners, "than to be able at the present moment to render a decision that would serve as a guide for priests, teachers and parents" regarding desegregation. He explained that he was unable to do so because there were "still many vital circumstances which require further study and consideration if our decision is to be based upon wisdom, prudence and the genuine spiritual welfare of all concerned." Asking for patience and prayers as the process unfolded, the archbishop hoped that when a decision was reached, it would "be accepted in the spirit of Christian charity and justice and in that unity of mind, heart and will which must always characterize the family of God."[37] Only time would tell if the faithful would accept the decision in a spirit of charity and justice or in one of contention and discord.

New Orleans papers, the *Item, Times-Picayune,* and *States,* all printed Rummel's pastoral letter in full.[38] What had been considered a social issue now had become a moral one. The concern of a limited number of Catholics participating in interracial activities now involved all Catholics in the archdiocese. The Catholic narrative regarding the race question was being rewritten by the integrationists.

Noteworthy in the archbishop's letter was the apparent reversal in policy regarding school desegregation. In his letter of August 1955, Rummel had made it quite clear that the highest archdiocesan authority, the archbishop and his consultors, had accepted the recommendation to integrate the parochial schools. Now, six months later, the language and tone had changed. The Jesuit Bend incident and the Catholic parents' clubs' protest, account in part for the less forceful language of the February 1956 letter.

Commenting on Rummel's pastoral, one New Orleanian posited sarcastically that Christian and Jewish leaders "discovered" that segregation was a moral issue only after the Supreme Court's *Brown* decision of 1954. This *Times-Picayune* reader argued that it was quite reasonable for various racial and ethnic groups to want to associate with their "own kind," which made segregation a reasonable way of ordering society. While he did not believe segregation deprived anyone of any rights, he did find that integration deprived individuals "the simple right of free association." This reader also specifically challenged the arguments presented in Rummel's pastoral. He wondered why parents were urged to send their children to parochial schools if, quoting the archbishop, "segregation was sinful," as such schools segregated Catholic students from "pagans, protestants and Jews." From his perspective, God had ordained that blacks live in Africa; it was "the wickedness of man that defeated this purpose—commencing with the betrayal of Negroes by Negroes into the hands of Arab slave-traders, then Yankee slaveships, then Southern planters buying human beings, and finally the signers of the Declaration of Independence." The author of this letter to the editor concluded by predicting that only trouble lay ahead for those who advocated integrated schools.[39]

HULAN JACK AND THE RISE OF CATHOLIC RESISTANCE

One week after the archbishop's letter was promulgated, the eighth annual Interracial Sunday gathering was held. Just as interest in SERINCO had been waning, the timing of this event brought more attention to the organization than any prior function. Interest in this particular convocation was due to the main speaker: Hulan Jack of New York City.

As part of an education project undertaken by the CHR to prepare Catholic New Orleanians for desegregation, Hulan Jack's appearance at the Interracial Sunday gathering was underwritten by a grant from the Fund for the Republic.[40] With Archbishop Rummel's approval, the CHR sponsored a series of Catholic forums which focused on the race question and desegregation. The Fund for the Republic grant paid for the New Orleans interracial organization to sponsor speakers and events, to print and mail literature regarding race relations, and to organize any other program or event that would further equitable race relations in the city.[41] Hulan Jack's appearance was one such sponsored event.

As president of the borough of Manhattan, Jack was the highest elected black official in the United States in 1956. A few days prior to Jack's arrival in New Orleans, Loyola alumnus Emile Wagner presented information to Archbishop Rummel's office and to Loyola University officials concerning Jack's prior political affiliations. Without directly accusing him, Wagner intimated that the New York City politician was a Communist sympathizer and a subversive. Claiming that he only wanted to protect the good name of the university, this Loyola alumnus was responsible for turning the SERINCO forum into a *cause célèbre*.[42] Estimates at the time placed attendance at well over nine hundred people, approximately 20 percent of whom were white. By all accounts this forum was the best attended in the eight-year history of this SERINCO-sponsored event. It would also be the last Interracial Sunday ever held.[43]

Addressing his interracial audience in the auditorium of Holy Name of Jesus Elementary School adjacent to Loyola University's campus, Jack began his address, titled "God and Human Relations," by commending Archbishop Rummel for his courageous leadership in speaking out against segregation. "The future history books," he stated, "will long record his name as one of the chief architects of true democracy dedicated to the ideals of freedom and justice to ensure that these United States of America remain forever the symbol of hope to all men everywhere."[44]

Digressing from his text, Jack described his personal odyssey to the United States. As a sixteen-year-old immigrant from Jamaica, he did not imagine that "one day I would be freely chosen by the peoples of all races, creeds, color, and national origin as the president of the borough of Manhattan." His election as borough president in 1953, he noted, was a "practical demonstration of democracy in action," as 83 percent of the New Yorkers who voted for him were not black. Just four days prior to his arrival in New Orleans, he pointed out, he had been the Grand Marshal of the Annual Knights of Columbus parade, which traveled up Fifth Avenue to St. Patrick's Cathedral to be received by the Cardinal-

Archbishop of New York City, Francis Spellman. He cited these few incidents for the crowd "as proof positive that it is possible for all people to dwell side by side as friendly neighbors."[45]

Returning to his main theme of equality and human freedom, Jack informed his listeners, "The equality of freedom is not only a basic freedom of our democracy but it is also a part of the household of God; we are not alone in believing in these fundamentals of equality." Citing the first epistle of St. Peter, the Vatican newspaper, and the Supreme Court's 1954 *Brown* v. *Board of Education* desegregation decision to support his claim of equality, he rhetorically asked if "the opponents of equality in education are sincere when they attempt to declare that the Bible is wrong, that the Vatican is wrong, that . . . members of the Supreme Court are also wrong in asserting that all men are children of God and born with the status of equality."[46]

Jack expressed concern that religion would become a victim of persecution because of its innate message of freedom under God. "With all the courage and faith it is possible for man to possess, with all the spiritual guidance given to us by our church, we must resolve," he told his listeners, "to become the messengers to carry the word of God to the high road which leads to the true brotherhood of men and the fatherhood of God."[47]

A country founded on liberty, justice, and equality, he argued, should not have to face a period of emotional tyranny. "We have always been a nation of law-abiding men and women," he continued, "with a responsibility of handing down to our children the heritage that freedom is the right and privilege of everyone who believes in the basic and inspirational fundamentals of our American democracy." He wondered how we could teach children the history of democracy and its benefits while denying them the concomitant philosophy of equality. He warned the audience, "If emotional tyranny is permitted to exist, you will find its proponents spreading out into other fields of our American society." Jack cited recent attempts by the state legislatures of Mississippi and Georgia to curb freedom of the press as examples of how emotional and political tyranny function. Gratified that the newspaper owners in those states were challenging the constitutionality of such legislation, he posited that "the freedom of the press has always been our first defense against any kind of totalitarian thinking, whether it be on a peanut-minded scale or on any other related level."[48]

Jack believed that resolution of the segregation issue was of international importance. The peoples of Africa, Asia, and Eastern Europe, he argued, were watching the United States, "the citadel of hope and inspiration for every land whose people have been dreaming of self- independence," to see if true democracy would be practiced. The propaganda war that had developed between the democratic West and the Communist East could be won, he noted, by our society's "becoming the outstanding example of true democracy." If the United States failed to practice what it preached, Jack asserted, "the ugly forces of Communism will have gained substantial victory." The stakes were too high, he concluded, because the future of the United States was at risk, "for we will need the friendship, confidence, and cooperation of these liberty-seeking countries" in the future. He closed his talk by quoting the Gospel of John: "I am the light of the world; he that followeth me walketh not in darkness but shall have the light of life."[49]

After Hulan Jack addressed the crowd, Archbishop Rummel rose to speak. He thanked Jack for coming to speak and for his words of praise. The archbishop spoke for several minutes on the merits of the borough of Manhattan, where he had grown up, and on Jack's role in the administration of the borough. Halfway through his remarks, Rummel turned to the issue of segregation and the role Communism played in maintaining it. The archbishop began this portion of his address by discussing the attention the United States had received in the foreign press concerning segregation. He informed the crowd that he had heard from many parts of the world regarding this issue and that many foreign writers were bewildered with the situation in the United States. They questioned how a country that professed to be Christian and democratic could justify racial segregation. "The controversy over segregation has not only created astonishment in many parts of the world," he elaborated, "but has also lessened the respect of a great many abroad for the sincerity and the honesty of our dedication to the democratic way of life. . . . [T]hat's deplorable, that's deplorable."[50]

He took issue with the arguments put forth by the segregationists, especially the argument that Communists were responsible for promoting desegregation. "Among the allegations that have been proposed as being sources of inspiration for integration is the charge that integration is being fostered and promoted by Communism [and that] whether they are conscious of it or not, the leaders of integration are actually doing the work of the Communists." Raising his voice the archbishop thundered, "Sometimes I wonder who is doing the work of the Communists—whether we are doing the work of the Communists when we speak for honesty and sincerity in the interpretation of the democratic way of life and the assertion of human rights for all our American citizens, or whether those are doing the work of the Communists who are striving to keep up, just because of the difference of color, certain inhibitions and restrictions and privations of the Negro race." The crowd responded with loud applause. He continued:

> I think it would be well for the gentlemen that are loudest in their
> advocacy of the continuation of segregation, contrary to the rulings
> of the Supreme Court of the United States [and] contrary to the

opinions that have been expressed on several issues that have been referred to district courts of the federal government, [to consider] whether or not they are really acting as genuine Americans that believe in American principles and the American way of life for all Americans, or whether they are not, consciously or unconsciously as they say, doing the work of those who sow discord and are striving to introduce the principles of atheism and infidelity and the general principles of Communism into the United States of America. I think that is a thought that is deserving of consideration by many.[51]

Rummel was pleased with the gathering, stating that he was "very grateful for the spirit that . . . [had] been manifested. . . . I wish indeed that that spirit could be generalized, that it could be contagious and communicated to more and more of our fellow citizens and especially of our fellow Catholics." He lamented that "many of them have reached a state of obstinacy on this question that makes them almost repudiate any thought or any desire of being informed and enlightened on the true principles that are involved in the equality of all our fellow citizens regardless of race, creed, or color." Concerned that the disregard for principles of justice might jeopardize other aspects of American life, the archbishop asked "if the inroads [by segregationists] are allowed to creep into one department of our American way of life . . . where will they stop? What will become of American democracy when they stop or when they think they ought to stop? So let us again pray for unity of thought, unity of conviction, unity of principle." Indirectly addressing opponents of his and the church's teachings regarding desegregation, he asked that all Catholics "strive to accept the teachings especially of our Church, as we have tried to expose them, and as they will be exposed more fully in the days to come." In conclusion, he prayed that "the day will come when rights and justice and charity will prevail to the peace and to the happiness and to the prosperity of all our people that constitute the population of our great Republic, the United States of America."[52]

The next day the New Orleans newspapers ran lead stories concerning Rummel's comments at the Interracial Sunday gathering, but the real story was Emile Wagner's charge that Loyola University had knowingly allowed an individual with subversive leanings, if not actual subversive ties, to speak at a university gathering.[53] In a public statement released to the press that Sunday evening, Wagner stated, "As a Catholic and an alumnus of Loyola University of the South, I consider it most regrettable and unfortunate that the university should act as host for Sacred Heart, Dominican and Spring Hill colleges and Loyola and Xavier universities should participate in, and the archbishop of New Orleans should approve an 'interracial day' at which Hulan Jack was the featured speaker and honored guest." Wagner based his denouncement of Loyola's sponsorship of the event on information he had received from the House of Representatives Un-American Activities Committee (HUAC). Through the assistance of Leander Perez and Senator James Eastland of Mississippi, Wagner had obtained HUAC files containing lists of organizations with which Hulan Jack had been associated and which were later deemed subversive by the Attorney General of the United States.[54]

Wagner charged that Loyola University as well as the other Catholic institutions of higher learning and the archdiocese of New Orleans were being duped by subversives. He alleged that Communists or Communist sympathizers were behind the efforts to force integration. "It is sad but nevertheless true," he stated, "that certain institutions and agencies in their zeal to foist integration upon an unwilling and intellectually sincere majority may be unwittingly aligning themselves with sinister forces which are working to bring about not only their own destruction but also the destruction of the democratic way of life."[55]

The president of Loyola, Patrick Donnelly, S.J., publicly criticized Wagner's decision to release the HUAC information to the press rather than approaching university officials with the information. "As a loyal alumnus concerned with the good name of the university, which Sunday acted as host for the SERINCO meeting, it would seem that Mr. Wagner might have come directly to the university with his charges against Mr. Hulan Jack, whether true or false. Instead of presenting the results of his study to the university, he gave them to the press." Donnelly explained that "it was because of Mr. Jack's outstanding record as a Catholic that he was selected by SERINCO as yesterday's speaker. His record as a Catholic is well known."[56]

Responding to Donnelly's criticism, Wagner released his own statement challenging the president's assertions. Wagner countered Donnelly's claim that he had no prior knowledge of Jack's background prior to his Sunday appearance by claiming that he, Wagner, had sent a summary of Jack's personal history to the president of Loyola and the archbishop. The information, Wagner stated, had been transmitted to church officials through the Reverend Carl Schutten, editor in chief of *Catholic Action of the South*. According to Wagner, Schutten later confirmed reception of the material by both parties, President Donnelly and Archbishop Rummel.[57]

Not wanting to be caught in a lie, Donnelly admitted having received the Schutten information prior to the Sunday forum, but he reiterated his basic criticism of the manner in which Wagner handled dissemination of the HUAC information. Donnelly explained that he had received the Jack information but that Schutten would not state who was making the accusation against the Interracial Sunday speaker. "Thereupon, in Father's Schutten's presence I immediately telephoned New York and the office of *America* magazine [a national

Jesuit weekly] . . . to check upon the unauthorized charges. From a member of the *America* staff I received reassurances that Mr. Hulan Jack was a Catholic in good standing and quite capable of addressing the meeting." Schutten seemed satisfied, Donnelly concluded, and so "I thought the matter ended." It was only with the press release on Sunday night, the president explained, that he had learned for the first time "that Mr. Wagner was making the complaint."[58]

For several days the Hulan Jack controversy received news coverage both in New Orleans and New York City. The mayor of New York, Robert F. Wagner, publicly defended Jack, calling him "the highest grade of American that I know of." The mayor knew nothing of the accusations against Jack, and as far as Wagner was concerned, the "purpose of these charges obviously was to degrade him [Jack]."[59] For his part, Hulan Jack categorically denied that he had ever been a member of any subversive organization and said the charges were "a diabolical scheme . . . an outgrowth of the White Citizens Council which is staging a rearguard action to disobey the decision handed-down by the Supreme Court on desegregation in schools."[60] He even contemplated litigation against his detractors.[61] From his New York office Jack explained that "unauthorized use" of his name by the America Labor Party resulted in his name then being linked with organizations deemed to be subversive: "You never know where anybody will put your name. But these never had my approval."[62]

On 28 February 1956, Wagner publicly attacked the president of Loyola for the last time regarding the Hulan Jack affair. Wagner accused the president of not adequately investigating the validity of the charges against Jack. "I do not consider a telephone call to the officials of 'America' an adequate investigation in so serious a matter," he stated. "I also believe that Loyola university, on its own, should have taken the same pains as I took in checking on Mr. Jack." Donnelly did not respond to this latest charge. This, however, would not be the last time Wagner would be at odds with church officials over race matters.[63]

The New Orleans provincial, William Crandell, immediately reviewed the Hulan Jack case for his Jesuit superior in Rome, John B. Janssens. While Crandell believed that the attacks on Hulan Jack, Archbishop Rummel, and Loyola University were unfair, he informed Janssens that he did not feel that "it was a prudent thing to have an interracial meeting addressed by a Negro speaker in the midst of the present turmoil. It served to convert no one, but only to keep their case before the eye of the public."[64] The position of the Jesuit provincial contrasts with the tactics later employed by civil rights organizations. The Southern Christian Leadership Conference, the Congress of Racial Equality, and the Student Non-Violent Coordinating Committee relied on direct confrontation to keep the race question before the public. For those groups, the issue was not conversion but demanding inalienable rights granted by the Constitution of the United States.[65]

Letters to the editor of the *Times-Picayune* commenting on the Interracial Sunday gathering and Hulan Jack's appearance were decidedly prosegregation. One writer asked rhetorically why the panel discussions at Loyola did not go "to the logical and inevitable result and discuss intermarriage." Perhaps that was to come later, she answered, "creeping insidiously into the existing social system, destroying the color barrier by dissolving the white race?"[66] Another writer charged that the Interracial Sunday gathering was helping the Communist cause, asserting that "communism strives to make all men equal. But this is contrary to nature." Physical, intellectual, and economic differences between peoples resulted in a division of rights and duties, the writer explained. The natural order of life, therefore, was being disrupted by Communists.[67]

The *Louisiana Weekly* came to Jack's defense in an editorial that appeared 10 March 1956. The editor wanted to know how a black Catholic with such a dubious past could have been elected in New York City. "Surely the people in New York as well as the Catholics," the author noted, "would have known long before now if there was any truth in the files." The paper doubted that Jack's political opponents would have refrained from using such information in one of his many campaigns for elective office if it were true. Nor could the writer believe that the Catholics of New York would have allowed Jack to head the Knights of Columbus parade down Fifth Avenue just days prior to his New Orleans appearance if he were a Communist.[68]

The editorialist took Emile Wagner and his associates to task for their shameful behavior. Echoing the observation made by Archbishop Rummel at the Interracial Sunday gathering, the writer noted that prosegregationists and white supremacists were "making a mockery of democracy" with their continued defiance of the Supreme Court's *Brown* decision. By refusing to accept the Court's ruling, these individuals were presenting "the world on a silver platter" to the Communists. Furthermore, the continued oppression of black Americans by whites proved to the world that democracy was not practiced as it was preached: "In the battle for the mind of the peoples of the world, two-thirds of whom are colored, as to which is best, democracy or Communism, the pro-segregationists are giving the Commies a big assist in raising doubt in the eyes of the world as to whether we are morally suited to lead the world, whether the democracy and Christian principles we espouse are worth following." The current state of affairs in the United States was both tragic and pathetic in the eyes of the author. Internationally the country was promoting democracy and fighting Communism, while domestically Americans were undermining their very cause. "At a time when this country so desperately needs all of its human resources to combat the menace of Communism," the author concluded, "it is indeed tragic and pathetic that the pro-segregationists are so blind in their prejudice and hatred they have not the capacity to see what a destructive force they are to democracy today."[69]

REFUTING THE OPPOSITION

As the Hulan Jack controversy evolved, Loyola's chaplain, Harold Cooper, S.J., was entrusted with the responsibility of replying to Emile Wagner's recently articulated position on segregation.[70] As Wagner questioned the teaching authority of a bishop, challenged the theological foundations for integration, and promoted racial segregation, Cooper would have to refute these positions.[71] Regarding the teaching authority within the church, Cooper questioned Wagner's apparent lack of understanding of the issue. The Loyola chaplain challenged the notion that only when the papacy had made an infallible pronouncement were Catholics required to assent to the teaching. Cooper asked rhetorically what would become of church and papal teachings if every utterance by a pope had to be defined as infallible. Citing Pius XII's encyclical *Humani generis* (August 1950), the university chaplain explained that whenever a pontiff spoke on a disputed issue in the ordinary course of events in a papal encyclical, decree, public address, or some other form of communication, and in a capacity as leader and teacher of the faithful, the issue could no longer be "considered a question open to discussion among theologians." Ordinary teachings of the church, therefore, called for a certain degree of acceptance among the faithful.[72]

Loyola's chaplain followed up his discourse on papal infallibility with a discussion of the teaching authority of bishops. He questioned Wagner's selective use of canon law. Canon 1326, Cooper pointed out, presented an affirmative proposition rather than a negative or limited interpretation as Wagner would have had his readers believe. The canon read in part: "Although they do not possess, either individually or when assembled in particular councils, infallibility in their teachings, the bishops are truly doctors and teachers of the faithful committed to their care under the authority of the Roman pontiff." As far as Cooper was concerned, the bishops did have the right to speak. Furthermore, the chaplain argued, the church had the right to address social issues when they involved moral issues. Archbishop Rummel, Cooper noted, was speaking and teaching on a social matter that fell clearly within the realm of morals. Cooper informed Wagner that even though the arguments presented for a particular teaching might not be satisfactory to some Catholics, the obligation to accept the teaching remained, which is why the clergy were not willing to speak against Rummel's position on race relations.[73]

Cooper then addressed the most difficult portion of Wagner's letter and the most demanding question that would face church leaders regarding the race issue. He explained the apparent shift in racial attitudes and policies by church officials.

Wagner claimed that Catholics were entitled to a rational explanation for the change in thinking. While Cooper conceded that there had been no dogmatic teachings or promulgations on precise matters of faith regarding segregation, he explained that the papacy normally spoke to universal norm and practices. Because the practice of segregation in the southern United States was a local problem, Cooper stated that the Holy See allowed the local ordinary, or bishop, to address the issue.[74]

The Loyola official then questioned the alumnus's ability to understand church documents and the principles contained therein, citing Pius XII's encyclical *Summi pontificatus* regarding human solidarity as an example of Wagner's inability to do so. An error which Pius XII found in human society and one which he wanted to see uprooted was the "forgetfulness of that law of human solidarity and charity which is dictated and imposed by our own common origin and by the equality of rational nature in all men, to whatever people they belong." Pius drew attention to the unity of the human race found in a common origin, to a unity found in the means to develop and sustain life, and to a unity found in their supernatural end: God. This unity did not allow for discrimination.[75]

Basing his argument on Pius's words, Cooper asked Wagner whether or not segregation had denied blacks Americans the rights and means to develop themselves as human beings and to attain their supernatural end. The Loyola chaplain pointed to the inequalities in educational, economic, medical, legal, and social opportunities for blacks, and wondered how this had occurred. For Cooper, the source of the race problem rested with the "society the white man has built up around his pride of race."[76]

Cooper questioned the validity of Wagner's definition of segregation, calling it an "arbitrary" one. As far as the chaplain was concerned, Wagner had presented an abstract concept of segregation but failed to define the actual practice of segregation as found in the southern United States. The southern practice, Cooper posited, could not be justified on moral grounds because it was nothing more than an extension of the practice of slavery from the nineteenth century—a practice based on racial pride. Cooper cited other papal writings to support his assertion that the church had spoken against the exaltation of race. For example, Pius XI, in his 1937 address to the church in Germany (*Mit brennender Sorge*), stated:

> Whoever exalts race, or the people . . . or any other fundamental value of the human community—however necessary and honorable be their function in worldly things—whoever raises these notions above their standard value . . . distorts and perverts an order of the world planned and created by God: He is far from the true faith and from the concept of life which that faith upholds.[77]

Pius XII did likewise in an address to the people of Rome in 1945: "There remains no other way to salvation than that of repudiating definitely . . . the pride of race and blood . . . and to turn resolutely to that spirit of sincere fraternity which is founded on the worship of the Divine Father of all."[78]

Finally Cooper addressed Wagner's complaint that the church was teaching something new regarding segregation. If segregation was wrong, then it always had been wrong and should never have been tolerated, Wagner argued. But since the church had tolerated it, he wanted to know why the church had taken so long to discover this moral error. The chaplain began his answer by reviewing the precepts of the moral law. Knowing and understanding these precepts depended on the capacity of a people to learn and comprehend right from wrong. Social, cultural, and educational developments, he explained, influenced the ability of a people to know and understand the moral life. As the human race advanced in the areas of knowledge and learning, human beings also grew in moral understanding. Aided by the spirit of God, the faithful developed and defined their belief system. Cooper cited the development of church teachings regarding Jesus as the Son of God, Mary as the Mother of God, and papal infallibility as examples of the development of church doctrine. These statements of faith, he noted, arose over time as individuals grew in faith and understanding of God's plan for the world and its inhabitants. The same happened, he explained, with the church's understanding of racial segregation.[79]

Cooper argued that, far from being an age-old practice, racial segregation in the United States was a recent development, citing the recently published work by historian C. Vann Woodward, *The Strange Career of Jim Crow,* to prove his point. Woodward's research demonstrated that there had been competing political viewpoints regarding race relations in the postbellum South. While the conservative (i.e., white, upper-class, and paternalistic) voices prevailed during the 1870s and 1880s, there was a history of southern acceptance of interracial relations. Only when the conservatives' socioeconomic and political position was threatened by a biracial coalition of the lower classes in the 1890s did racial segregation emerge.[80]

Returning to the theological and philosophical presuppositions underlying the race question, the chaplain explained that segregation was morally wrong and could no longer be tolerated because it violated the moral precepts of justice and charity. Catholics, Cooper noted, had come to understand the immorality of the practice and were now trying to correct the error. Within a time span of sixty years, roughly 1890 to 1950, he pointed out, the policy of segregation had been developed and now was being dismantled. Given this historical development, Cooper warned Wagner not to "exaggerate the time-element in the Church's coming to a clear perception of the evil of segregation."[81]

The assault on Catholic principles and those who practiced them would continue, even if those responsible for it had no theological or philosophical basis for doing so. The relentless barrage of attacks, direct and indirect, on pro-integration bodies would eventually force them into submission and extinction. Only firm resolve and leadership could have prevented fear and intimidation from crushing Catholic interracialism.

CHAPTER VIII

The Death of Southern Catholic Interracialism, 1956

BY 1956 PRO-INTEGRATION ORGANIZATIONS in the South were coming under attack, and were often accused of being subversives or under the influence of subversive elements. White Citizens' Councils, state governments, and members of Congress, among others, attempted to thwart desegregation efforts. In March of that year, southern members of the United States Congress issued their "Southern Manifesto," calling for resistance to court-ordered desegregation. In Alabama, chapters of the National Association for the Advancement of Colored People (NAACP) ceased operations because of state harassment, and in Louisiana many chapters faced a similar fate. Furthermore, the state legislature in Louisiana passed laws penalizing educators who encouraged students to attend integrated institutions, and, in an ironic twist, using an anti–Klu Klux Klan statute, legislators forced pro–civil rights organizations to make their membership rolls public, thus exposing individuals to intimidation and retribution.[1]

Subjected to similar tactics and attacks, the Catholic interracial organizations in New Orleans, both the Commission on Human Rights (CHR) and Southeastern Regional Interracial Commission (SERINCO) ceased functioning in the fall of 1956—victims of fear and intimidation. The CHR was a casualty of state pressure, but SERINCO was suppressed by forces from within the very church whose principles SERINCO had sought to put into practice. The Catholic educators at Loyola University of the South had tolerated the collegians' interracial activities for several years, but they had also tried, on occasion, to suppress the organization. In 1956 they decided that the student-sponsored events, which had drawn undue attention to their institution, were becoming a threat to institutional viability.

OPPOSITION AND RESPONSE

By 1956 integration was being resisted by priests, politicians, and Catholic laity alike. The battle to maintain segregation within the Catholic Church was fought not only with pen and paper but with state legislation. In 1956 in an effort to prevent the integration of the Catholic school system in Louisiana, state legislators again proposed bringing parochial schools under state control by invoking the police powers of the state.[2] Emboldened by the example of the prosegregation members of the U.S. Congress, Louisiana state senator William "Willie" Rainach, chairman of the Joint Committee on Segregation and founding member of the Citizens' Council of Louisiana, helped orchestrate the protest in Baton Rouge by using both legislative and extralegal means to thwart the federal mandate to integrate.[3]

Just as he had done in 1954, Millard F. Everett, editor of the archdiocesan newspaper *Catholic Action of the South,* explained the gravity of the situation in a front-page editorial on 26 February 1956. Everett warned the Catholic authors of the pending legislation that passage of their bill would automatically result in their excommunication. The grounds for such a drastic measure was Canon 2334 of church law, which called for the excommunication of anyone who impeded the exercise of ecclesiastical authority. As Everett explained, "The Catholic school system of any diocese operates under the direction of the Ordinary. . . . He is assisted in its supervision by a school board composed of responsible clerical and lay persons. No other group has any right to dictate the operation of the schools . . . least of all the state."[4] The following day, state legislators Joseph F. Casey, Frank X. Huerstel, and E. W. Gravolet issued a joint statement claiming that Catholic canon law had no relevance to their legislative initiative. The three Catholic laymen argued, "The Catholic Church has not required and does not require integration under penalty of censure." As far as these men were concerned, the pending legislation in no way impeded "the church in its ecclesiastical jurisdiction with respect to education."[5] They saw no conflict between their support of Rainach's bill and church authority.

In the following Sunday's edition of *Catholic Action,* Everett again addressed the conflict between church and state. He explained in his front-page editorial that the bishop of the diocese was the head of the Catholic school system and that he alone determined policy. "Once the Ordinary decides," he asked rhetorically, "that the diocesan seminary shall be conducted on a racially integrated basis, who has the right to challenge this decision? Surely not the legislators of the state."[6]

In the same editorial, Everett also addressed the practice of racial segregation within the church. Speaking to the larger community, he denounced segregation, informing his readers that the concept of "separate but equal" institutions went against Christian ideals, democratic justice, and human needs. He explained that racial segregation "was never at any time favored by the Church. It has been reluctantly tolerated in this country simply to avoid the possibility of a greater evil."

Any predictions that disaster would follow integration, the editor continued, did not follow conventional wisdom and practice. Everett noted that "in Louisiana there has been integration in both state and private colleges and universities without incident or excitement." Everett concluded by warning that passage of this legislation regarding private school education could be the first step toward "domination of religion by the state and even totalitarianism." This had happened elsewhere in the world, he noted, and there was no reason it could not happen in America.[7]

OPEN DEFIANCE: ASSOCIATION OF CATHOLIC LAYMEN

Threats to church unity also came from within as thirty white Catholic males formed the Association of Catholic Laymen on 16 March 1956.[8] It was the second major anti-integration movement organized in New Orleans that year, the first being the White Citizens' Council. This new church-related alliance was established without the knowledge, consent, or approval of the archbishop of New Orleans and, as stated in their Articles of Incorporation, was founded

> [t]o foster, promote and protect the moral, physical, cultural and educational welfare and the general interests of all the people by an investigation and study, in all of its aspects, of the problem of compulsory integration of the black and white races; to keep the public fully informed and alerted on all matters related thereto; to seek out, make known and denounce Communist infiltration, if any there be in the integration movement; to unite thoughtful and sincere persons in an organization which seeks to attain a prudent, just and peaceful solution to this racial problem; and to unite all Catholics in daily prayer to the end that the Holy Spirit may enlighten and guide this Association, its members, and all other persons concerned with the issue of racial integration.

Membership was limited "to persons of the Caucasian race who profess the faith of the Holy Roman Catholic Church." Emile Wagner was elected president of the organization and Jackson Ricau, executive secretary.[9]

In a newspaper interview, Wagner explained that he conceived the idea of forming the laymen's association after receiving hundreds of letters and many phone calls praising him for his stance against Hulan Jack's appearance at SERINCO's annual Interracial Sunday gathering at Loyola University. "These people," according to Wagner, "were requesting leadership of some type to fairly clarify the question of compulsory integration." When asked if his organization would consult church officials, he responded: "On questions of dogmas we would certainly consult with a spiritual advisor."[10]

The identity of that spiritual adviser would never be revealed. Rumors circulated at the time that Martin Burke, S.J., and/or Lawrence Toups, S.J., were assisting the Catholic resistance movement. When questioned, both Jesuits denied any involvement. Yet one wonders how Wagner, not a theologian by training, became so well versed in church teachings and doctrine without professional help. William Crandell, provincial of the New Orleans Province, wrote to John B. Janssens, his Jesuit superior in Rome:

> Accusations have been made against Father Burke, professor of Philosophy at Loyola, and against Father Toups, administrator of the Holy Name parish, stating that they have been making statements opposed to integration, and have secretly been advising Mr. Wagner in some of his writings. I have checked into this matter as carefully as possible. Both men vigorously deny the charges, although both are admittedly pro-segregation in sentiment. Father Toups admits that some of the remarks that have been attributed to him were made by him in passing some two years ago, but that he has now ceased talking publicly about the matter. Fr. Burke admits that he has expressed his sentiments in class occasionally, but states that he has not been disloyal to the Archbishop, nor has he co-operated with Mr. Wagner. Since the accusations were made mainly on suspicion and with no solid proof to substantiate them, I have accepted the statements of both men and have warned them to be careful of their teachings in the future. I have always found Father Toups most obedient to directives that have been given him, Fr. Burke a little more reluctant to respond, a little more ready to "distinguish" in order to save his own opinion.[11]

The day after announcing the formation of the association, Wagner sent a letter of introduction to Archbishop Rummel, explaining that "a group of well-intentioned Catholics have banded together for the purpose of the serious study of compulsory integration." He enclosed a copy of the act of incorporation for the archbishop's edification.[12] The archbishop lost no time in responding to President Wagner's letter. "My immediate reaction," he wrote, "is that such an organization seems unnecessary, ill-advised and capable of causing much scandal, confusion and dissension among our Catholic people." Rummel pointed out that the organization was "without parallel among the religious denominations of our city and State" and would be understood by Catholics and non-Catholics alike as an attempt to undermine the authority of church leaders. He expressed his willingness to speak with the charter members of the association in the near future, but in the meantime he strongly urged the members "to refrain from further action and publicity" for the good of all concerned. Furthermore, he asked that the association refrain from divulging the contents of the letter to the press and asked that no reporters be invited to the proposed meeting when it was finally held.[13]

A few days later, Archbishop Rummel sent out a directive to the clergy of his archdiocese, especially those who served as confessors and spiritual directors, on pastoral care and the question of segregation. He wanted to tell his priests that while the pastoral letter of 19 February exposed the sinfulness of segregation, it did not impute guilt to those who had practiced various forms of it in the past carried out "in good faith as a prevailing custom." However, now that conditions had changed and the church has spoken on the issue, he clarified the grievous nature of continuing segregationist practices. He instructed the clergy to explain to the faithful, "tactfully" and on an individual basis, that "the individual Catholic who still adheres to segregation must examine his motives and manner of practicing segregation and must submit the matter to his or her Confessor for guidance and decision." This directive, he concluded, was "definitely" not for publication.[14]

On 28 March, an advertisement encouraging "Roman Catholics of the Caucasian race" to join the Association of Catholic Laymen appeared in a New Orleans newspaper.[15] That same day, Rummel requested Wagner's presence at the archbishop's residence to discuss the advertisement.[16] At that meeting Wagner and two members of the association's executive committee agreed to cease, for the moment, soliciting for membership and processing membership applications. The laymen informed the archbishop that a decision would be made regarding the membership drive at the next general meeting of the association.[17] Several days later, on 5 April, Archbishop Joseph Francis Rummel; his assistant Bishop Abel Caillouet; Monsignor Charles Plauche, chancellor of the archdiocese; and Monsignor Lucien Caillouet, vicar general of the archdiocese met with twenty-eight board members of the Association of Catholic Laymen. The four clerics expressed their opposition to the formation of the organization in no uncertain terms, and the laymen voiced their concerns regarding compulsory integration. Association members feared that the integration movement was a Communist-inspired plot and thus believed their organization served a moral and patriotic service. They denounced the imprudence of "over-zealous integrationists" who praised individuals "whose connection with subversive organizations was well known." The reference to the Hulan Jack affair was obvious. The members also presented a list of questions regarding integration for which they could find no answers. Until Rummel's archives are opened, one can only speculate that the most likely question asked of the archbishop would have been to explain the apparent change in church thinking involving segregation. For his part, the archbishop wanted to know whether or not these Catholic laymen intended to continue recruiting members.[18]

A week later the executive secretary of the association, Jackson Ricau, informed the archbishop that the organization had voted "to continue its policies . . . and not to restrict itself in the securing of additional active members." The membership was convinced, Ricau wrote, that they "could render a valuable and needed service to the community in assisting to resolve the problem of compulsory integration and in the exposure of Communists in the integration movement."[19] Wanting to emphasize the serious nature of the situation, Rummel immediately sent Ricau a telegram informing him that the members' decision "to continue the formation of an active membership group is unacceptable." A detailed reply was forthcoming, the archbishop continued, and in the "meanwhile all activity relative to such membership shall remain suspended."[20]

Archbishop Rummel responded on 23 April. In his letter, he reviewed the series of events that had led to his writing. He reiterated his concern that the Association of Catholic Laymen was causing "scandal, confusion and dissension among our Catholic people." The failure of the organization to heed his request to cease recruiting members, the archbishop believed, was evidence of its disregard for ecclesiastical authority. Given these developments, Rummel deemed it his "duty to define and decree that the Association of Catholic Laymen shall be entirely discontinued and that there shall be no further solicitation, public or private, for membership." The archbishop also rescinded "the provisional tolerance of the Charter group as a recognized body of Catholic laymen." The only reason he had tolerated the organization up until then was that he had expected the group to abide by his request not to recruit additional members. Failure to accept this ruling by 1 May, Rummel informed each member of the board of directors, would make them "liable to the penalty of excommunication promulgated in Canon 2331, paragraphs 1 and 2, of the Code of Canon Law." Each member was expected to submit in writing his pledge of compliance with the archbishop's ruling; failure to do so would result in excommunication.[21]

A three-man delegation from the laymen's association met with church officials on 26 April asking for a two week extension in order "to study and reflect upon our future course of action." Fearing that none of the clergy in the archdiocese would want to advise members of the association as they contemplated their future, the delegates also requested that the archbishop issue a letter "authorizing any member of the clergy to consult with and advise us concerning . . . our duties with reference to your letter of April 23."[22] Writing for the archbishop, Monsignor

Charles Plauche rejected the laymen's request for an extension. He informed the Association of Catholic Laymen that Archbishop Rummel was convinced that his letter required "no additional clarification or extension of time to permit members to make a decision that will do justice to their Catholic spirit and sincerity." Plauche added that his letter did "not preclude the possibility of seeking advice either from the pastors of the individual directors or from competent ecclesiastical authority to be invited to address the group as a unit." The chancellor assured the group of the archbishop's concern for the spiritual welfare of the group and trusted that this letter would receive a sympathetic reception.[23]

On 1 May, Wagner, writing on behalf of the entire membership of the Association of Catholic Laymen, informed the archbishop of their decision to stop recruiting members and to disband. Wagner assured Rummel that their intention for organizing had never been to embarrass him or to challenge his teaching authority, and, therefore, the association would "obey" his command and "acknowledge" his episcopal authority. But as the board of directors of the association questioned the propriety of the archbishop's decision, Wagner informed Rummel that the group was going to avail itself of its "right as Catholics to appeal this matter to higher authority, and this letter will serve notice of our intention to prosecute an appeal to the Holy See."[24] Four days later, the *Times-Picayune* reported the archbishop's directive to the Association of Catholic Laymen to disband.[25] Initially church officials and association officials declined to comment on the issue, but on the following day, Emile Wagner informed the press that only the threat of excommunication had brought an end to the organization. When asked about appealing to the Holy See, Wagner replied that an appeal was "in the process of being prepared. Possibly within a week it will have been prepared in the proper fashion and forwarded to the proper party." The association president concluded his remarks by questioning the propriety of the archbishop's action and wondering if "the dread threat of excommunication could have been made against the Association of Catholic Laymen, then why was it not made against the Catholic members of the citizens' councils?"[26]

CHALLENGE AND COUNTER-CHALLENGE

In the midst of the Catholic laymen's controversy, Jesuit provincial William Crandell made his last official visit to Loyola University 16–27 April 1956. In his letter of exhortation to the community, he called on all to meditate on the rules and regulations of the Society of Jesus in order to gain spiritual benefits and praised the community members for their untiring labors on behalf of the university. Concerning the race question, the provincial stated emphatically: "[T]he moral principles enunciated in the Province Policy on Interracial Relations are to be strictly followed by all, neither belittling nor exaggerating the obligations involved." Crandell also advised the members of the Loyola community to avoid making statements or taking action that would confuse and aggravate rather than convince individuals of the correctness of the new approach regarding integration. Acknowledging that there might be a difference of opinion on the issue, Crandell stated quite clearly, "loyalty to the Archbishop and to his program must be stressed in our statements for the instruction and guidance of others." He concluded by asking that all be mindful of "the deep-rooted emotional problems that exist among the people [regarding this issue] and that can be overcome only by tactful, yet firm, leadership in the right direction accompanied by patience, kindness and Christlike charity."[27]

In his report to the superior general of the order, John B. Janssens, Crandell noted that community life at Loyola had improved since "[e]xtremists on both sides of the [race] question have been checked by Father Rector [Patrick Donnelly]." Public pronouncements concerning racial matters, in his opinion, were much more moderate. Through religious discipline and moderation, the provincial believed that the Loyola University community was approaching "the desired united front in our teachings on the matter." Notably, he failed to mention that there were still problems with some Jesuits, especially with Martin Burke and the staff at Holy Name of Jesus Church, and he made no mention of the Association of Catholic Laymen crisis.[28]

While Jesuits were encouraged to present a united front concerning race relations in the province, the members of the CHR attempted to do the same for the Catholic faithful in New Orleans by sponsoring an essay contest promoting the Supreme Court's desegregation rulings. Southern Catholics were asked to write on the theme "Why an integrated school is better than a segregated one." Instead of student contestants, only Catholic parents with children currently attending Catholic schools were eligible to compete, with cash prizes for the three winning essays. In their entries, contestants focused on the harmful effect of segregation on their children, the hypocritical lessons their children were learning in segregated schools, and the consequent undermining of Christian values.[29]

In her winning essay, Mrs. Francis X. Waguespack of St. Agnes Parish juxtaposed the lessons of Christian love and democratic equality taught at church and in school with the practice of racial segregation. By preaching democracy and love but sanctioning racial segregation, American society was sending a contradictory message to its children, thus inflicting "harm" on them. This harm was dwarfing "the mind and spirit" of children by engendering prejudice and hatred for others. "Our attempts at educating are in vain so long as we keep contradicting our efforts to allow our children to open their minds to the brotherhood of men."[30] Dr. Gerald Eberle's essay noted that children were sent to school to learn "to live as intelligent members of the human community." The pursuit of truth and the elevation of reason over passion and impulse, he argued, were aims of education. Hence, he concluded, "a segregated school is a living lie. For segregation is based upon prejudice . . . [and] prejudice is simply unintelligent. It certainly has no place in the schools."[31] Another respondent, Peter Clark, had "seen the great sea of bitterness built up by discriminatory walls." As long as the effects of segregation remained, he argued, there would be "a great gulf of difference existing [between the races]." The best way to address the situation, therefore, was to allow all school children to attend class together, thus giving them all an equal opportunity to succeed "regardless of race, color or creed." He did not think that racial equality would ever be achieved "as long as a segregated system of schools . . . [was] perpetuated."[32]

While several parents linked Christian teachings and democracy in arguing for integrated schools, others pointed to the morals and values integrated schools would preserve. "Integrated schools will be an example of democracy in action," argued Mrs. C. D. Olivier, "and also will follow more closely the Gospel of love and Christian charity."[33] Mrs. William H. Syll wondered what right society had to foster a segregationist mentality among its youth if it "is neither morally right nor in accord with our democratic principles."[34] And Naomi Branch presented America as a melting pot to assert that a child should attend an integrated school, for it is in the classroom that a child first comes in contact with other races and nationalities. "The living example of democracy," she concluded, "can be seen within the walls of an integrated school. Side by side, the children prepare to transfer this democratic training into the community in which they live."[35] Mrs. Milton O. Fee wrote, "A school is only as good as the principles it instills in the pupils, and the characters it moulds. . . . The much touted Brotherhood of Man can come about only by taking away the color barrier. Integration in the schools will give our next generation a clear, open mind, barring no one for reasons of race or other superficial attributes. Children have no prejudices—they copy their elders; it is to our great shame if we leave our children a heritage of hatred."[36]

While the CHR received entries favoring integration, some Catholics used the contest to present contrary views. These individuals objected to "race mixing," while others viewed integration as a cause influenced and dominated by Communist agitation. Most submissions were signed; however, one submitted a copy of the CHR essay contest advertisement with the following inscription written over it: "This is the cheapest and most stupid type of bribery yet attempted—appeal to reason and nature. If we want prizes we'll enter soap contests for $50,000." It was signed, "A Jesuit trained Catholic with a child in parochial school." In the margins was added: "If this [segregation] is wrong today, it was wrong centuries ago. Let's keep the church out of politics, please." And a further postscript stated that the individual had never been insulting or unfair to anyone of any race but did want to choose his own friends. "As a child and through my life until now," the writer concluded, "such organizations [as the CHR] have been silent . . . why?"[37]

"Segregated schools are our way of living," wrote Mrs. A. Tesvich. Attendance in a racially segregated school was a way of inculcating "the ways and habits of our white ancestors" and means for preserving "the white race." Through segregation, she believed that the "Catholic race" would grow rather than decline through integration."[38] Parents of a child attending St. Agnes Catholic School in Baton Rouge could not think of any reasons, "not even one," why schools should be integrated. They did, however, present a familiar argument by claiming that everyone was satisfied with the system as it currently operated, where "[t]he white children are happy the way it is and the colored children are also."[39] Some whites opposed school integration but professed personal regard for blacks. Mrs. E. R. Morris had "no ill feeling toward my colored brethren [sic]," but she could not accept racial mixing, as she did not believe it was part of the divine plan: "I am strictly against integration. If God had intended it differently he would not have made different races."[40]

George L. James represented the "Catholic dilemma" faced by the Roman Catholic leadership in New Orleans—practice versus principle. On the one hand, church doctrine presented the unity of the human race, but on the other hand, it practiced segregation. Catholic officials feared whites would leave Catholic schools because of the church's promotion of racial integration. James, a Catholic and a member of the Knights of Columbus, had a daughter graduating from one of the local Catholic high schools. As he explained in his letter to the CHR, he was not going to allow his daughter to "mix" with blacks, and therefore he and his wife had changed their minds regarding college choices for her: "We had planned to send her to Loyola of the South but that is now out since they have negros [sic], & the Jesuits are so dead bent on living with & wanting you to live with the negro."[41]

William Davenport suggested that if CHR chaplain Father Joseph Fichter was not satisfied with the segregated South, he should move "north where you can eat & sleep with the negroes [sic] if you like."[42] Donald J. Plaisance wanted Fichter to answer the parental dilemma regarding interracial marriage: "Who is going to draw the line when your's or my daughters ask for permission to marry a member of the colored race?"[43] And some individuals were surprised that the CHR even existed and that it was sanctioned by the church. One of those surprised individuals, Kathy Schmidt, informed Fichter that she and her friends, all "white, young, convent bred," did not "know anyone who belongs or who even knows about your group." She doubted that the organization was very old because CHR's promotion of integration would have contradicted the church's stance just a few years prior.[44]

More important, Schmidt's letter provides insight into the influence and power a priest could wield when dispensing God's forgiveness through the sacrament of reconciliation as well as the limits of church authority. She explained that, on occasion, she and her friends had "come in contact with a 'mixer' [a priest who advocates integration] in the confessional." Obviously she and others had been asked specifically about their racial attitudes and were told that holding a segregationist position was unacceptable. Nevertheless, Schmidt and her friends maintained their position even though they understood that in doing so the priest would not grant them absolution for their sins. She believed that these experiences "only succeeded in making lukewarm Catholics of former fervent ones, and ice cold Catholics out of former practicing ones." Furthermore, she justified her actions by the following rationalization: "When told that if we refuse to take in the black birds there will be no absolution, we simply tell God that we have done our part—we have come to confession, confessed our sins and are truly sorry. If the priest attempts to force his personal beliefs on us we pray for him and just receive as though it were a normal confession." A pro-integration priest was not keeping her or her friends from God but only "keeping them away from the collection baskets."[45]

One Catholic opponent of integration viewed the church's promotion of desegregation as mimicking the heavy-handedness of a Communist regime. "It amazes and sickens me," wrote William Brady, Sr., "to see Catholic organizations adopting communistic methods to successfully force integration on the Catholics in this archdiocese; pour out the propaganda, truths, half-truths and distorted truths and then wield the big stick. In this case the threat of excommunication, name calling and vilification for those opposed to this movement." Although Brady did not see segregation as a moral issue, he argued that if it were, church officials would find it difficult to justify past actions when changing church policy. "If the practice of racial segregation is a sin," Brady stated, "then our religious leaders and teachers have been condoning sinful practices for generations."[46] Church credibility was called into question; the accommodationist approach to racial segregation, practiced for many decades, left Catholic leaders exposed to the charges of hypocrisy, selectivity, and immorality.

Brady's response was typical of the challenge presented by desegregation and was made manifest in the rise of the Association of Catholic Laymen as well as the Citizens' Council. White Catholics such as Brady felt helpless individually against the Supreme Court and the NAACP, so they sought strength in numbers. "I became a member of the Citizens Council of New Orleans and of the Catholic Laymen's League [i.e., Association of Catholic Laymen]," he explained, "because

I know that the only way to preserve peace and decency in our community is by organizing the responsible white elements to fight the influence exerted by the Communist dominated N.A.A.C.P. Individual opposition can accomplish nothing in this situation as has been proven by the success enjoyed by this group up to this time."[47] John Cummins echoed Brady's sentiments concerning the subversive nature of integrationists when he wrote requesting that his name be removed from CHR's mailing list. Cummins had no idea how or why he was receiving "unsolicited" literature concerning integration, but he wanted such mailings to stop. As he explained, he was not going to condone "the cruelty and harm and ridicule brought upon the heads of our good Southern Negroes by the communistic activities of any perverted organization posing under the name *Catholic*."[48]

Nevertheless, the CHR continued to advance the integration cause. The Fund for the Republic grant enabled the CHR to sponsored a series of Catholic forums focusing on the race question and desegregation during the first half of 1956.[49] Experts from various academic disciplines addressed such issues as integration and disease, race and intelligence, the Constitution and school integration, the Scriptures and segregation, as well as delinquency and race.[50] Hulan Jack's visit to New Orleans in February of that year also was sponsored by the grant.[51]

In addition to the presentations, the grant provided funds for CHR members to prepare fliers, newsletters, press releases and pamphlets to distribute to all Catholics of the archdiocese. The expectation was that Catholic New Orleanians, having been educated on the issues, would be better prepared to accept the transition to an integrated society. Furthermore, these forums and the information generated by them would help counter prosegregationist sentiment among Catholics and society as a whole. The CHR launched a propaganda war to convert individuals to the cause of integration.[52]

DIRECT ATTACK

But as members of CHR tried to educate and inform their fellow Catholics about integration, the organization came under attack. Originally spared public scrutiny, the interracial group now fell victim to state policy. In the process of crushing the NAACP and silencing pro- integration public school teachers, the Louisiana State Legislature and the White Citizens' Council were able to quash the CHR.

With the support of state senator William Rainach in 1956, Louisiana state attorney general Fred LeBlanc accused the NAACP of subversion and violation of state law. LeBlanc charged that the organization had failed to file membership rolls with the office of secretary of state in compliance with the rarely enforced anti-Ku Klux Klan law of 1924, the "Fuqua law." Deriving its name from then Governor Henry Fuqua, the law was intended to unmask secret societies. Refusal to obey the Fuqua law would mean the end of NAACP activities in Louisiana because the organization would violate a state ordinance, but disclosure of NAACP rolls would also damn the organization because disclosure of names was certain to invite acts of individual reprisal against members. By the end of the year only seven of the sixty-five branches had filed their membership lists with the state, resulting in a decline in membership from 13,190 to 1,698, of whom 1,300 were members of the New Orleans chapter.[53]

In May 1956 the state legislature of Louisiana, in order to thwart integration efforts, began passing a series of bills proposed by Rainach's Joint Committee on Segregation mandating or reinforcing racial segregation: there were to be separate waiting rooms, restrooms, water fountains, and diners at train and bus stations; all interracial social and sporting events were outlawed; and school boards were granted immunity from desegregation lawsuits. Particularly troublesome for high school educators were Acts 15 and 249: Act 15 required all students applying to state institutions of higher learning to obtain certificates of academic eligibility and moral rectitude from their respective schools, while Act 249 made advocacy of racial integration grounds for dismissal from state employment. This was a catch-22: students had to have a certificate to attend the now-desegregated Louisiana institutions but in producing the document, a school employee would risk losing his or her job by advocating integration.[54]

In light of this pending legislation, CHR members A. P. Tureaud, Janet Riley, Clarence Laws, and Francis Weller advised those who were employed by a public school board to resign from the commission if continued affiliation would compromise their jobs. Monsignor Charles Plauche personally advised Nora Wallbillich to resign her CHR membership if she could not afford to lose her job. Hence, members of the CHR of the Catholic Committee of the South (CCS) unanimously decided "to accept provisional resignation dated 24 June 1956, of all C.H.R. members who are public school employees."[55]

Even before the commission made its formal decision, however, Lucile Cherbonnier, a founding member of CHR, tendered her resignation, explaining, "Because of the legislation on segregation it will not be possible to continue my membership in this organization."[56] Several weeks later Clare Andrews wrote the commission to confirm her resignation from the CHR. "*If* there is any doubt," she wrote, "that my absence from meetings and my failure to pay dues during the last year has constituted a resignation, as I intended that it should, I wish to make it very clear that I *have* resigned." With passage of the teacher tenure legislation, Andrews wanted "to make doubly certain that I am not considered a member of the Commission."[57] Luella Cavalier followed suit, resigning for the same reason.[58]

The resignations came as the Citizens' Council took aim at the remaining interracial organizations in New Orleans: the Urban League and the CHR. At a Citizens' Council rally held at Pelican Stadium in the spring of 1956, members of the Urban League were denounced, resulting in several resignations shortly thereafter.[59] When Archbishop Rummel's name was mentioned (he was a board member of the Urban League), the crowd booed loudly, and the rally culminated with a cross-burning on the grounds of the archdiocesan seminary, located just a few blocks from the stadium.[60] In response, the CHR publicly criticized those who had attended the rally and those who were members of segregationist organizations, characterizing them as "anti-American, anti-Southern, anti-Catholic and irreligious people."[61]

The New Orleans chapter of the Citizens' Council quickly retaliated when chapter chairman Dr. Emmett Lee Irwin called for the disclosure of the membership roll of the CHR and a full investigation of the CCS. "What is the commission of human rights of the Catholic Committee of the South?" he asked. "Do these organizations speak with the authority of the Church and for the churches?" he wanted to know, and "[f]rom what source is derived the right to speak for all members of the Church?" Too often, he noted, "these organizations have made pronouncements in the press, but no one seems to know who composes these groups. Are they secret authoritative bodies?" He reasoned that "[i]t may be revealing to give the names of the persons composing the commission of human rights as well as the names of those composing the Catholic Committee of the South."[62]

In his letter to J. Edgar Hoover, director of the Federal Bureau of Investigation (FBI), Irwin requested that the FBI "make a searching investigation of the activities of the Rev. Joseph H. Fichter, S.J., and his secret organization, the Catholic Committee of the South [and the CHR] of which he is reported to be the founder."[63] Irwin also pointed out to Hoover that the CHR was "operating illegally within the State" because it failed to divulge its membership rolls. According to Irwin, the CHR fell "within the category of institutions of secret membership and sound[s] off from beyond the dark curtain of mystery."[64]

The director of the FBI politely informed Irwin that the bureau would be unable to carry out an investigation. As Hoover explained, "[T]he FBI operates solely as a fact-gathering agency. It is not within our prescribed functions to evaluate, nor do we recommend or endorse, any organization or individual irrespective of the circumstances." If Irwin had additional information that might demonstrate clearly that the CHR had violated a particular federal law or statute, Hoover asked that he send it to him.[65]

Because the CHR was a church-sponsored organization, its members decided to adopt a "wait-and-see" policy regarding state-mandated disclosure. The commission did decide, however, to cease issuing press releases "in the name of the CHR under CHR letterhead unless adopted by membership." The rationale for this decision was that members should be aware of statements being made in their name "before publication in order that they can amend significant positions—or reconcile themselves to the aftermath."[66]

Joseph Fichter, having accepted a Distinguished Visiting Professor Fellowship in the department of sociology at the University of Notre Dame beginning in the summer of 1956 and continuing through the academic year 1956–1957, was not present at the 20 June 1956 CHR meeting when the issue of membership disclosure was discussed and the publicity prohibition was decided.[67] Fichter's departure was a blow to interracial activities in the archdiocese of New Orleans, for without his forceful leadership, CHR and SERINCO could not withstand the growing storm of protest.

From South Bend, Fichter, informed of the developments in New Orleans, offered his measured advice to CHR.[68] "In the face of the racist legislation against public school teachers," he wrote commission member Gladys Williams, "it is difficult to see how an individual member of an integration group can offer defiance of it. . . . I have always believed that personal decisions must be left up to individuals in any group, to belong or not to belong, to cooperate or not to cooperate. Group decisions are another thing." Fichter continued by chastising CHR members for their lack of group action. Their decision of 20 June (i.e., to cease producing press releases) was particularly irksome: "[I]f the only point on which you can get complete agreement is the decision to do nothing, then, of course the decision is absurd and futile. Nothing would please the racists more than to have the CHR become a hard-praying, non-action, organization. It may as well fold up in a dignified way and make its obeisance at the feet of Dr. Irwin and his WCC."[69]

Meanwhile, Fichter came under attack from the Caribbean Division of the Anti-Communist Committee of the Americas, a group of predominately Catholic New Orleans businessmen and professionals. Writing to Jesuit provincial William Crandell, Maurice B. Gatlin, general counsel of the organization, requested that the provincial "arrange for the transfer of Father Ficte [sic] to some other part of the nation or the world." Gatlin and his associates felt that Fichter's "actions and utterances tend to bring the Church and the Jesuit Order into disrepute and to the extent that he brings disrepute to our Christian Religion, he injures our American way of life."[70]

In his response, Crandell acknowledged that Fichter had made mistakes, "just as we all do," and he was "not ready to defend all that Father Fichter has said and done." The provincial informed Gatlin, however, that he was "ready to defend his [Fichter's] integrity, his wholehearted opposition to Communism and the things for which it stands, and his very sincere zeal for the establishment of social justice." Crandell also advised Gatlin that for "reasons quite different from those mentioned in your letter, reasons which bring honor rather than manifest disrepute, Father Fichter will not be in New Orleans next year."[71]

Gatlin followed up by thanking Crandell for his prompt response. "I am indeed happy with the information given to me, which will be kept confidential," he wrote. Gatlin also wanted to clarify that neither he nor his clients believed that "the cleric in question was motivated by other than the best subjective intentions." They evaluated Fichter's activities from the "layman's standpoint, and in the context of the present situation with which we are faced" and determined that the best course of action was for Fichter to be sent away. While their letter did not influence the decision-making process of the Society of Jesus, the members of the Anti-Communist Committee of the Americas were grateful a major nemesis was gone.[72]

As Fichter and the CHR came under attack, church officials were also drawn into the Citizens' Council's quest to obtain CHR membership rolls. A month after Irwin contacted the FBI, Archbishop Rummel received a request "for information regarding the present membership and officers of the Catholic Committee of the South and also the membership and responsible direction of the Commission on Human Rights." Writing to Fichter in South Bend, Rummel explained that the "request comes to me from a Catholic source in good standing but I believe that it is intended to meet the pressure which is apparently being exerted by other individuals well-known to you for information regarding this dual organization." The archbishop did not reject the request outright and told Fichter, "[A]ny information that you will be able to give me regarding its [the CHR's] direction and a list of the local membership will be welcome."[73]

Fichter sent a guarded response to Rummel. In general, Fichter was under the impression that most of the members, black and white, were "well-known to Your Excellency.'" He characterized these individuals as "active Catholics, not only in their parishes, but also in various supra-parochial organizations." Prior to the Teacher Tenure Act, Fichter informed Rummel, CHR membership numbered approximately one hundred, but in light of recent state action, approximately thirty individuals had resigned. Fichter then gave the archbishop his own assessment of the situation: "The racists have been trying desperately to obtain our list of members, and I suspect that they will stop at nothing to get their hands on it." Because of their "viciousness and the kind of reprisals they visit on their opponents," he wrote, "I am completely unwilling that they know the names of members," citing fear for the members' well-being. He asked the archbishop's pardon in begging him "also to be suspicious of the 'Catholic source of good standing' which is requesting this information from you."[74]

Fichter then forwarded his and the archbishop's correspondence to Henry Montecino, S.J., acting chaplain to the CHR, with words of advice. "I suggest that you call Charlie Plauche [chancellor of the archdiocese]," Fichter began, "and impress on him (to impress on the Archbishop) the fact that you want these people fully protected." He suggested that Montecino make a personal appointment to see the archbishop, at which time he could provide Rummel with the membership list, and then, Fichter concluded, Montecino could "explain to him why we are cautious, and tell him in general about the importance of the CHR as his lay right hand in this whole messy business of racism."[75] Montecino took Fichter's advice and arranged to meet with the archbishop. In the course of the conversation, the archbishop "identified the Catholic source of good standing as Mr. William Guste, Jr." Montecino learned that the Citizens' Council had been pressuring Guste, who would later become attorney general of the state of Louisiana, to acquire the CHR membership rolls from the archdiocese. Rummel did not believe the list had to be turned over, and when Montecino offered it to him, he declined to keep a copy for his own files. The archbishop wanted to be able to state honestly, if asked, that he did not possess one.[76]

Despite Fichter's and the archbishop's efforts to protect CHR members, however, by all indications, the CHR had ceased to function by the fall of 1956. It was a casualty of a concerted effort by archsegregationists to silence all those who promoted integration. Threat and intimidation had won over principle and righteousness. SERINCO suffered a similar fate.

CATHOLIC SILENCE

In May 1956 Loyola University of the South's board of directors reviewed the status of the National Federation of Catholic College Students (NFCCS) at the university, ostensibly to determine its viability as a campus organization.[77] Having tolerated the federation's interracial commission for several years, Loyola University officials had been particularly embarrassed by the eighth annual Interracial Sunday gathering (the Hulan Jack affair). The Jesuits did not want to draw attention to themselves or their institutions. Change in racial policy was supposed to come without fanfare, as mandated by the Jesuits' 1952 policy statement, but the Hulan Jack incident had violated that mandate. Hence the time had come for the university leadership to act.

At the May meeting of the board of directors of Loyola University, Anthony O'Flynn, S.J., dean of students, reported that the NFCCS was "practically dormant on campus except for one aspect," SERINCO. Board members expressed concern regarding the commission's newsletter, the *Christian Conscience,* because it "often had news notices or items which were so presented as to tend to rub salt into open wounds in re. the racial question." Discussion among the directors focused on whether the newsletter should be controlled or abolished. O'Flynn pointed out that the interracial commission was not composed solely of Loyola students but also included students from Xavier University and the less-active St. Mary's Dominican College. If the newsletter was banned by Loyola, O'Flynn informed the board, "it would continue to be published either by Dominican or more probably by Xavier." The directors also contemplated withdrawing from the NFCCS, with the understanding that "once out of membership the said publication would automatically be off campus."[78]

After further discussion a vote was taken whether Loyola University should remain in the NFCCS. Two directors, Aloysius Goodspeed and James Whelan, voted for withdrawal, while one, Edward Doyle, joined by President Patrick Donnelly, voted to remain; the final director, Edward Shields, abstained asking for more time to consider the question. The discussion of the interracial commission, the directors noted, did not signal rejection of the university's endorsement of and adherence to the fundamental principle of racial integration. The discussion, however, did reflect serious concern on the part of the directors about the manner in which that goal should be achieved. They feared that "over-enthusiastic and, perhaps, sometimes offensive statements or comments" might hinder the "orderly and peaceful progress of the university in pursuit of its declared policy."[79]

As Loyola directors debated the fate of the interracial commission, Louis Boyer, a graduate of Jesuit High School of New Orleans, wrote an old acquaintance of his, New Orleans Province provincial William Crandell, S.J. Boyer contacted Crandell to raise serious questions regarding the *Christian Conscience.* In the May issue of the newsletter, the editors highlighted the recently held Interracial Sunday gathering featuring Hulan Jack. This issue also contained a quote from Clarence Laws of the *Louisiana Weekly.* Boyer wondered why these two men were mentioned in a Catholic publication, as he thought that their political sympathies contradicted the teachings of the church:

> I was frankly puzzled as well as amazed when I read the attached. I know, of course, that the Church is an avowed enemy of Communism, or even anything that has a red tinge. How could the Church, therefore, countenance this type of literature which seeks to glorify these men? Is this the work of misguided zealots within the Church who are so busy crusading in an integration movement that they fail to realize that the whole issue is Communist inspired? As a Catholic I do not like to see the Church duped in any way and hardly by so sinister and evil a force.[80]

In his reply to Boyer, Crandell gave his analysis of the interracial situation. He lamented the fact that there were "so many wild, immoderate and ill-considered statements being made by extremists on both sides of the question that it becomes very hard to cope with the situation." As for the newsletter, the provincial noted that he had been concerned with the utterances of the *Christian Conscience:* "I personally consider it [the newsletter] unrepresentative, undignified and inaccurate in its statements." Wanting to disassociate the Society of Jesus from the publication, Crandell informed Boyer that only two or three Jesuits were involved with the work and that he was taking steps "to see to it that the publication improves or that all Jesuits immediately disassociate themselves from it." Crandell explained to Boyer that, since the *Christian Conscience* was not a Jesuit publication, the Society of Jesus did not have complete control over its content. In closing, the provincial asked his Jesuit high school friend to consider the correspondence personal and private and "not [to] pass my remarks to anyone else."[81]

CONTINUED CATHOLIC OPPOSITION

With SERINCO under review, Joseph Fichter under attack, and the CHR under investigation, Emile Wagner, Loyola alumnus and erstwhile president of the Association of Catholic Laymen, once again publicly challenged the archbishop's position on desegregation in his letter-pamphlet of May 1956 titled "An Analysis by Emile A. Wagner, Jr., Catholic Layman of Archbishop Joseph Francis Rummel's Pastoral Letter Entitled 'Morality of Racial Segregation.'" In part his letter was also a response to the letter produced by Harold Cooper just a few months before.

In his writing, Wagner claimed that the archbishop's pastoral letter of February 1956 had not proven that racial segregation was morally wrong and sinful. He took issue with the archbishop's assertion that "racial segregation as such is a denial of the unity and solidarity of the human race as conceived by God in the creation of Adam and Eve." If segregation based on one's race was wrong, Wagner argued, then segregation based one's nationality, sex, class, or consanguinity was also prohibited. Organizations, societies, clubs, and the like, whether secular or religious, he concluded, should also be proscribed. "Judged by these criteria . . . it would be morally wrong and sinful to exclude women from ordination to the priesthood solely because of sex!"[82]

According to Wagner, the type of segregation he and his fellow Catholics were advocating was not based solely on race. They did not care to see people denied their "God-given rights to develop their talents, to live their lives in peace and to save their immortal souls." He and his associates, however, did not believe that Rummel had "demonstrated in any manner that segregation deprives the Negro of his right and duty to serve God here, nor of his privilege of finding eternal happiness with Him in the world to come."[83]

Using somewhat biased data concerning health standards and academic achievement among black Americans, Wagner argued in favor of maintaining segregation. He believed that a parent had the right to protect his or her child from undesirable situations and individuals, in this case association with black children. The black child, because he or she came from a home that did not measure up to the standard of living of the average white family (Wagner did not examine why there was a disparity between the black and white families), was a moral and physical menace to a white child. Blacks lacked the social, civil, and moral values, in Wagner's estimation, necessary for associating with whites, hence the need for segregation. With regard to education, he claimed:

> [A]n overwhelming majority of white parents are convinced that racial segregation is necessary, not on the basis of race alone, not indeed on the basis of race at all, but because only through racial segregation can they be assured that their children will not be exposed to an environment that could be dangerous, and possibly seriously harmful to the fulfillment of their objective in life. Viewed in this light racial segregation is not only not morally wrong and sinful, but on the contrary, morally right and meritorious.[84]

As for the immorality of segregation, Wagner presented a distinction between the political and social order on the one hand and the spiritual and supernatural order on the other. He acknowledged that Catholics, and for that matter all people, must recognize the rights of individuals to the spiritual and supernatural goods in life, such as the right to worship God, to receive the sacraments, to seek spiritual enrichment, but he and his fellows did not feel obligated to concede, nor did they recognize, equality of rights within the physical and social order.

That the white man did not want to associate with the black man on a social or physical basis, he contended, did not mean the white man was denying a black man the right to save his immortal soul. He did not see how the black man was denied the church's spiritual grace offered all Christians, through the death and resurrection of Christ, just because the white man refused to socialize with the black. Segregation was not a violation of justice and love as far as he was concerned. Furthermore, he did not believe that racial segregation "by definition" denied similar rights and opportunities for blacks or whites. Blacks could join their own organizations, establish their businesses, and work with their own people. To Wagner there was "no requirement in justice or charity that he [a black man] enjoy the same rights as white persons." Public officials, taxpayers, priests, ministers, and other professionals, Wagner posited, should see to it that the medical, education, and living standards for blacks were improved. He believed that when the black man and woman had obtained the same moral principles and social responsibilities as a white man or woman, then segregation would become "a shade of the past without legislation, compulsion, rebellion and bloodshed."[85]

Finally, Wagner once again challenged Archbishop Rummel's authority to teach on this matter. Since the pope had not spoken on the issue of racial segregation, how could the archbishop? If Rummel were repeating what the papacy had already proclaimed, Wagner maintained, then there would be no problem understanding and submitting to such a position. The archbishop's teaching appeared to be something new and unsupported by church authority. Since segregation was practiced in the past, Wagner wanted to know why the church was changing her thinking on the matter. He accused the archbishop of taking "an inflexible position in racial segregation, despite all that well-intentioned and sincere Catholics here have done to persuade you to the contrary." Rummel's position, he charged, has caused "confusion and division" among the clergy and laity. Behind this move toward racial integration Wagner found Communist hands at work: "Marxism urges integration in the United States because of the strife it will engender." Even though the archbishop urged integration based on Christian justice and charity, Wagner wondered "just whose purpose is being served?" He concluded by begging Rummel not to order the integration of the schools: "Call upon your Catholic men to work for the material betterment of the Negro. Call upon your clergy to care for his spiritual needs. Let us solve the fundamental problems first, and, if they can be solved, there will be no need to bludgeon Catholics into acceptance of integration."[86]

Throughout, Wagner failed to acknowledge that integration had already taken place at the graduate and undergraduate levels in Catholic higher education. He also failed to make reference to papal pronouncements condemning the "pride of race." Whether he was aware of these declarations is unclear; however, given his close scrutiny of the situation, it is hard to imagine that he was unaware of church teachings on the matter.

DEMISE OF SERINCO

The closing of the College of the Sacred Heart in Grand Coteau, Louisiana, in the summer of 1956 was not predicated on the events taking place in New Orleans that year. Rather, it ceased operations for lack of funds. Throughout the 1950s financial difficulties had plagued the college even though it tried to increase student enrollment and reduce expenses. When the undergraduates received the news of the college's imminent demise, they attempted to entice more young women to attend Sacred Heart and thereby keep the institution open. Their plans, however, came to naught.[87]

News of the closing received sensational coverage in the local newspaper and on the local radio station and television station.[88] Segregationists used the closing of Sacred Heart College as an example of what happened to an institution when it accepted black students. Accusations that the college was forced to close because of its racial policy were refuted. The *Southwest Louisiana Register,* the official newspaper of the diocese of Lafayette, printed the following account of the closure: "Sacred Heart College was known for its forthright stand on Catholic social problems and was the first college in the deep South to integrate effectively. Negro day students of the area were allowed to enroll in the college some three years ago and were accepted readily by both faculty and student body. College authorities reported that enrollment problems were serious even then and that integration was not the cause of closure."[89]

With the closing of Sacred Heart College, SERINCO was reduced to Loyola University of the South, St. Mary's Dominican College, and Xavier University. The fate of the collegians' interracial commission, however, rested with five men at Loyola. In July 1956 the issue of Loyola's membership in the NFCCS was again reviewed by the university directors. The board was asked whether it wanted to withdraw from the national federation as the best way to control SERINCO's publication the *Christian Conscience* or, if the organization should remain on campus, have SERINCO's faculty moderator control (i.e., censor) the publication. Board members Aloysius Goodspeed and James Whelan again voted for withdrawal, but this time they were joined by Edward Shields and Edward Doyle, the latter explaining that he was voting for withdrawal because "the organization was beyond University control," as it "was seemingly an outside organization which the University could not exercise adequate control [over] even through the moderator." Only Loyola President Patrick Donnelly, who had long been a champion of integration, wanted Loyola to remain in the NFCCS. Since all the board members voted against the president, the matter was referred to the provincial, who advised Donnelly that "under the circumstances of the sentiments of the Fathers Consultors, Loyola should withdraw from N.F.C.C.S. which would effectively terminate the University's responsibility for the 'Christian Conscience.'"[90]

Thus, Loyola University of the South officially withdrew from the NFCCS in September 1956. Without Joseph Fichter's support and guidance as director of the interracial commission during the summer and fall of 1956, SERINCO disbanded. The last issue of the *Christian Conscience* was published in October 1956. This issue gave no indication that the newsletter would no longer be published or that the organization would cease to function; on the contrary, the October *Christian Conscience* announced that the next SERINCO meeting would be held at Loyola on 10 November. In one of their last editorials, the editors worried that segregation would persist due to indifference and that no one would strive to change society. In response they issued what turned out to be a last call to action: "Indifference is the enemy of progress and justice. Christians cannot be satisfied with the belief that eventually racial problems will work out by themselves. Such a belief is usually a bit of specious reasoning which has been designed to justify inaction. Only through persistent effort can the stain of segregation be removed. Every effect must have a cause."[91]

RETREAT AND DEFEAT

Loyola officials also capitulated to prosegregation forces by revoking the 1954 integration policy for the university's Field House. In July 1956 the Louisiana state legislature passed Act 597, which banned interracial collegiate athletic competition and ordered separate facilities for blacks and whites attending athletic events. Ostensibly this law was directed at the Sugar Bowl committee, which had sponsored an integrated football game earlier that year, but the legislation affected colleges as well, including Loyola.[92]

At a September meeting of the board of directors of Loyola University, members discussed the ramifications of the act. Even though this new state law conflicted with federal decrees, the Jesuits of Loyola decided to "observe the local laws until they are declared unconstitutional." Furthermore, university officials agreed, "the University could not, under present circumstances despite its past policy, play teams at present which had Negro players."[93] The Jesuits debated the merits of excluding blacks from the Field House as a form of protest; they concluded such a policy would penalize the very people the university was trying to support. Instead, they decided to display "signs, as inconspicuous as possible, . . . to designate a section for Negro spectators as well as other signs designating facilities for Negroes in accordance with the laws." Given the circumstances and the prospects that the state law would eventually be overturned, the Loyola board members believed that this interim action was the "the prudent and right thing for the University to do."[94] The decision should have pleased board member Aloysius Goodspeed, who believed that Donnelly's pro-integration policy had hurt the university financially. In his letter to the provincial, Goodspeed maintained that "because of his [Donnelly's] backing of Fr. Louis Twomey's [pro-]labor ideology and of the negro [sic] question, he has lost thousands of dollars for the university. He is not only not liked, but strongly disliked by businessmen that count in the city, many of them up to this time staunch backers of the Jesuits in New Orleans."[95]

Proponents of segregation, or at least those reluctant to confront it, also would have been gratified that there would be no Interracial Sunday gathering in 1957. Writing to President Donnelly from the University of Notre Dame in the winter of 1957, Joseph Fichter inquired about plans for the ninth annual Inter-racial Sunday. He was "a little worried" by the lack of news and asked the president if "this apostolate [had] been de-emphasized at Loyola." Fichter feared that the organization had in fact disbanded, just as many of the NAACP chapters in Louisiana had folded, due to pressure from prosegregation forces. "It would be a shame," he wrote with deep concern, if the segregationists "could score up a victory over the Catholics, the Jesuits and Loyola by pointing out that they 'silenced' the student group, the *Christian Conscience,* and forced the abandonment of the Catholic Inter-Racial Sunday."[96]

Donnelly replied, explaining to Fichter that the interracial activities were "now back under the control of the sodalities where I sincerely believe they ought to be."[97] Fichter praised Donnelly for getting the sodalities involved with interracial affairs, but he was disappointed that the president's letter said nothing about the annual Sunday gathering or the student interracial commission. This distinguished sociologist urged the president to use his influence to keep the students involved and active. With no news about the interracial commission, Fichter suspected, "the weight of racist opposition, both internal and external, may be slowing down even the more zealous students." Keeping the student organization going would be a victory of sorts for Fichter, as he knew that the "racial bigots would like nothing better than to brag that they closed down this annual affair. And especially the inter-collegiate (Loyola, Xavier and Dominican and Spring Hill) Inter-racial Commission . . . with its monthly paper, the *Christian Conscience.*"[98]

Realizing that something had gone awry, Fichter contacted officials at Dominican College and Xavier University concerning interracial activities. He asked the executive vice president at Dominican, Philip Des Marais, if he would mind getting "behind some of the students at least to put on a small token celebration to keep the tradition of Catholic Interracial Sunday going."[99] Fichter asked the president of Xavier, Sister Mary Josephina, S.B.S., if she could arrange an interracial program and, more important, if a group of students at Xavier would continue publishing the *Christian Conscience.*[100] The president sent a brief note to South Bend explaining to Fichter that she was leaving town on business and could not look into the situation at the moment. "On my return," she informed him, "I shall give the matter consideration and see if something can be done."[101] In April, Des Marais wrote Fichter explaining that "an attempt was made to have a student committee commemorating Interracial Sunday, but for some reason unknown to me, Loyola was unable to participate, which made it impractical to go ahead at this time."[102]

When Fichter completed his guest professorship at Notre Dame, Donnelly did not want him to return to New Orleans. The Loyola president so informed the provincial, William Crandell, but the provincial wanted Fichter back at the university. Donnelly argued for a moderate policy of racial integration, although he did not explain what this meant; Fichter's presence on campus, he feared, would create more agitation and disunity. "The wiser policy," the president stated, "would certainly have been to keep him [Fichter] out of stirring up the situation." Continuing, Donnelly warned the provincial, "I can only say that if your Reverence insists on placing him here you must not be surprised nor complain at the inevitable difficulties which will come up in the inter-racial field as a consequence." He argued that "the real solution in the present circumstances is to use Fr. Fichter elsewhere as the only way to achieve our desired goal (and Fr. Fichter's also) peacefully, and with due consideration to living on after integration fruitfully."[103] The provincial prevailed, and Fichter returned to Loyola in the fall of 1957. He resumed teaching in the sociology department but no longer directed interracial activities. He and the institution would have to wait five more years before integration took place at the undergraduate level.[104]

CHAPTER IX

Southern Catholics, Martin Luther King, Jr., and "Letter from Birmingham Jail"

"I commend the Catholic leaders of this state for integrating Spring Hill College several years ago."
—MARTIN LUTHER KING, JR.,
"LETTER FROM BIRMINGHAM JAIL"

IN POST–WORLD WAR II NEW ORLEANS, the establishment of Catholic interracial organizations was a sign of hope and expectations: hope for a better day in American race relations and expectations that that day was at hand. For these southerners, interracialism was seen as a concrete manifestation of the Christian belief in the unity of the human race and the dignity due all peoples regardless of race. Through interracialism the world would be transformed: segregation would end and a new social order would emerge.

The Southeastern Regional Interracial Commission (SERINCO) and the Commission on Human Rights (CHR) promoted the Christian principles regarding human unity and dignity. Belief in these religious tenets sustained these interracial organizations throughout their existence. Catholic interracial activities underlined the inherent contradiction between the theory and the practice of the faith. Christian teachings called for loving one another, for loving one's neighbor, yet Christians discriminated against one another based on the color of their skin. Such contradictions, unfortunately, can be found throughout the history of Christianity.

The development and acceptance of racial segregation in the southern states, less pernicious than slavery but oppressive nonetheless, forced Christians to try to reconcile their principles of justice, charity, equality, and human solidarity with a social, economic, and political system that advocated discrimination, oppression, and subjugation. However, those Christians who could neither accept nor justify the values and practices of racial segregation were motivated to challenge and overturn it.

A small but enthusiastic group of southern Catholics undertook measured and gradual efforts to improve race relations in New Orleans beginning in the late 1940s and continuing well into the 1950s. They acted out of a religious conviction that the promotion of prejudice and racial discrimination could be neither embraced nor condoned by Christians. Their religious beliefs were reinforced by a faith in American values and the rule of law, according to which segregation and discrimination came to be seen as unjust. The establishment of SERINCO and CHR threatened the accepted racial customs and traditions of the South. White and black Catholics, male and female, demonstrated through word and deed their belief in the Christian values of justice and charity and the American political doctrine of equality for all.

While these organizations' activities were grounded in Catholic principles, they threatened the institutional viability of Catholic establishments, especially schools on all levels. Could any institution that rejected the accepted customs and traditions of southern race relations survive if the very people who constituted its student body felt threatened by such a change? On the other hand, could an institution allow, even for a limited period of time, an injustice to persist with the understanding that it eventually would be eliminated? Does one advance a principle at any cost or accept an unjust status quo, at least for a time? These questions go to the heart of the matter regarding civil rights and the Roman Catholic Church. Advancing the cause of human rights in the South through the formation of interracial groups forced individuals to choose between principle or expediency. There was some progress, followed by reversals, but throughout the period of segregation, some Roman Catholics in New Orleans and Louisiana actively strove to advance human rights.

A CATHOLIC CONTRIBUTION TO CIVIL RIGHTS

In evaluating the contribution of the CHR to the cause of civil rights in the city of New Orleans and the Catholic Archdiocese of New Orleans as a whole, one must consider that the commission survived for over seven years in a climate that developed from indifference to open oppression. Its very existence was a tribute to the black and white Catholic men and women who came together as one to put Christian principles into practice in an often unfavorable setting. Although it only averaged a hundred members at any given time, the CHR's open challenge to prevailing concepts of racial superiority was a powerful witness to authentic Catholic and American values.

The CHR agitated for the desegregation of archdiocesan organizations and events in New Orleans. Members expressed their displeasure to Archbishop

Rummel over segregation practices in religious ceremonies, especially the Holy Name Hour, which the archbishop canceled in 1949. Activism by CHR members helped hasten the merger of formerly separate black and white religious organizations. The CHR's efforts to raise Catholic consciousness through talks, presentations, forums, and essay competitions made it much more difficult for New Orleans Catholics to plead ignorance about the moral implications of the race question. The commission's failure to obtain permission to attend Sunday church services as an integrated body at various parishes in New Orleans indicated, however, the depth of Catholic racial prejudice in the city. In some respects, the demise of the CHR should have been anticipated because the organization was never fully embraced by the Catholics of the archdiocese. Custom proved stronger than religious principles.

Catholic efforts to promote interracial justice aroused opposition both within the church and beyond it. Within months of its founding in 1948, college-sponsored SERINCO faced suppression from religious leaders. On several other occasions, the student organization faced proscription until its ultimate demise, eight years later, at the hands of ecclesiastical authorities. This small but energetic organization (the average attendance at SERINCO's monthly meetings was thirty students) and the values it promoted compelled church leaders to address the conflict between principle and expediency. Profound disagreements among students and faculty at Loyola University of the South over the segregation issue forced the Jesuits of the New Orleans Province of the Society of Jesus to address the issue. The student organization played a direct role in the development of a racial policy for southern Jesuits.

Louis Twomey, S.J., Joseph Fichter, S.J., and the activities of the Catholic interracial commissions directly influenced the drafting of the New Orleans Province's policy statement on race relations in 1952, which the archdiocese of New Orleans used, in turn, in drafting the archbishop's statement on racial segregation four years later. Having decided to desegregate, the Jesuits began a gradual process of integration: in 1950 blacks were admitted into select programs at Loyola; in 1952 Loyola's law school integrated; in 1954 Loyola's graduate school of education and its evening division were desegregated, as was the undergraduate program at Spring Hill College in Mobile, Alabama; in the fall of 1954 Loyola held the first interracial basketball game in the history of the state of Louisiana; Dallas Jesuit College Preparatory (one of the New Orleans Province high schools in Texas) desegregated in the fall of 1955; and finally, in the summer of 1956 the first black candidate for the priesthood was admitted into the New Orleans Province of the Society of Jesus. Because of a fear of a drop in enrollment and other problems associated with desegregation, the Jesuits of the New Orleans Province, however, did not integrate the undergraduate program at Loyola University of the South or Jesuit High School of New Orleans until

1962—the year the archdiocese desegregated parochial schools. Failure to take the lead in desegregating the largest Catholic institution of higher learning in a predominately Catholic city, one could argue, demonstrated a lack of resolve by the religious men of the Society of Jesus to effect real change. Catholic leadership from Loyola University of the South might have positively influenced events during the New Orleans public school desegregation crisis during the early 1960s.

Those Jesuit institutions that did undertake desegregation did so with little fanfare over the change in the racial customs and practices of the day, but that is how the members of the Society of Jesus wanted it. The Jesuits said as much in their 1952 policy statement on race relations. Perhaps that is why historians know so little of this history. When Dallas Jesuit High School admitted its first black students, Arthur Allen and Charles Edmond, in the fall of 1955, the local newspaper reports of the story caused only a minor disturbance.[1] Many people even praised the Jesuits for their decision; the white students at the school accepted the change without incident.[2]

In July 1956, Numa Rousseve, Jr., a French Creole Catholic from New Orleans, became the first black accepted into the New Orleans Province of the Society of Jesus. Rousseve was the son of a Xavier University of New Orleans professor and the nephew to both a religious sister, Theresa Vincent, S.S.F., a member of the Sisters of the Holy Family, the second religious order founded in the United States for black women, and a religious priest, Maurice Rousseve, S.V.D., a member of the Society of the Divine Word. Maurice Rousseve had been ordained in 1937, only the twenty-second black Catholic to become a priest in the history of United States Roman Catholicism.[3] Just as there was no publicity surrounding the integration of Loyola's law school or the integration of Spring Hill College, the admission of Numa Rousseve into the Jesuit novitiate in 1956 occurred without notice. No special meetings were held to advise those already living in Grand Coteau that a black novice would be among their number. None of the entering white novices was informed ahead of time that a person of color was also admitted to the novitiate, and no special attention was given to his presence once he had arrived.[4]

The Jesuits were not alone in addressing the desegregation issue before the Supreme Court's historic *Brown* decision of 1954. The religious women of the Sacred Heart desegregated their college in Grand Coteau, Louisiana, in 1953. While the college desegregated as a matter of principle, it did so, also, on practical grounds, because white enrollment had declined and black students could help the college's precarious finances. The sisters could take some satisfaction, nevertheless, in knowing that their institution was the first Catholic undergraduate program in the state to integrate.

St. Mary's Dominican College was a different story. The fact that the institution never hosted an Interracial Sunday gathering and its students effectively abandoned SERINCO after a couple of years of involvement speaks volumes. Concerning integration, the college would not jeopardize its viability by admitting blacks before the other Catholic institutions did. As one of the college's former chaplains and instructors commented in 1953, "By way of supposition, to admit Negroes to Dominican College would be all but disastrous to the college and would serve no real purpose."[5] Blacks were admitted to Dominican College in the late 1960s.

Xavier University has survived segregation, desegregation, and integration. Its graduates have played significant roles in American society. Aaron Henry, a member of SERINCO, was one of two delegates representing the Mississippi Freedom Democratic Party who were seated at the 1964 Democratic National Convention. Richard Gumbel, SERINCO member and national treasurer of the National Federation of Catholic College Students, served as a judge in Cook County, Illinois; his sons, Bryant and Greg, are national broadcasters. Since 1968 Xavier University has been headed by Norman Francis, former SERINCO chairman and one of the first blacks to integrate Loyola University School of Law. Today, Xavier University of New Orleans has had twice as many of its undergraduates accepted into medical school as other historically black colleges such as Howard University, Fisk University, and Atlanta University, and currently 25 percent of all black pharmacists in the United States are Xavier graduates.[6]

The suppression of the Southeastern Regional Interracial Commission of the National Federation of Catholic College Students in 1956 in order to terminate its monthly newsletter, the *Christian Conscience,* silenced Catholic college debate and discussion concerning the highly controversial issue of southern race relations. SERINCO's demise, along with the simultaneous collapse of the CHR, signaled a retreat from interracial justice. An opportunity to present Catholic precepts and principles was lost. The legacy of Catholic interracial groups of the 1940s and 1950s was one of unfulfilled promises.

The demise of the CHR was especially regrettable, as it was a forum for developing lay leadership capable of leading and training fellow Catholics in biracial cooperation. Instead of acquiescing in the face of segregationist opposition, Catholics in New Orleans could have taken a stand for racial justice and Christian charity. They did not. The assault on the CHR by fellow Catholics as well as the lack of support from religious leaders indicated the depth of animosity and indifference within the archdiocese regarding the race question. The next Catholic attempt to promote interracial cooperation and harmony came only in 1961, seven months after the first black students, amid daily taunting from malicious protestors, began desegregating the public schools in New Orleans.[7]

Joseph Fichter, S.J., and Louis Twomey, S.J., continued their work at Loyola University of the South through the 1950s and beyond. Twomey headed the

Institute of Industrial Relations, later called the Human Relations Institute, promoting the cause of labor and human rights until his death in 1969. Loyola University of the South honored Twomey's memory by renaming the institute the "Twomey Center for Peace through Justice" in 1991. Until his death in 1994, Fichter continued to research and write on various sociological topics. His work received recognition during his lifetime as well as after. From 1965 to 1970, Fichter was the Stillman Professor of Theology at Harvard Divinity School, and the Association for the Sociology of Religion honored Fichter by establishing the Fichter Research Grants, which allow scholars the opportunity to conduct research on topics that figured prominently in Fichter's own scholarly work.

THE CHURCH AND RACIAL SEGREGATION

Until all the archival material concerning Archbishop Joseph Francis Rummel's tenure is made available to the public, a definitive assessment of the influences on archdiocesan policy and Rummel's own opinions on the race question must wait. One can draw some conclusions, however, from his public statements and policies.

In 1948 Rummel indicated to SERINCO members that the desegregation of the Catholic school system would not occur in the near future. The archbishop was concerned about parental response to such a move. Would Catholic parents continue to support Catholic educational institutions if desegregation occurred before the public schools integrated? At the time, the archbishop did not indicate that he thought that racial segregation was an intrinsic evil. He was willing to live with the status quo, taking measured steps to change social policy.[8]

In 1949 Rummel canceled the Holy Hour Procession in City Park rather than let civil authorities dictate church policy and practice. The archbishop had been pressured by Holy Name society and CHR members to conduct the service on an integrated basis; however, this meant obtaining city permission to do so. When municipal government officials refused to grant a waiver, the archbishop called off the service. The issue here was not the intrinsic immorality of racial segregation, which at this point the archbishop was not ready to concede. Rather, he was asserting that the church would not permit secular authorities to dictate the conditions for church-sponsored events.[9]

The following year, however, the archdiocese began a gradual process of desegregation. At a diocesan synod, archdiocesan officials called for an end of segregation within the church.[10] In 1951, Rummel made reference to this policy in an annual financial appeal letter for the Indian and Negro missions.[11] In 1953, the archbishop ordained the first black man as a priest for the archdiocese of New Orleans.[12] Also that year he wrote a pastoral letter calling for an end to racial segregation in the archdiocese.[13] This formally prohibited Jim Crow Catholicism. Now the archbishop had to win the hearts and minds of his flock.

The *Brown* decision in 1954, which the archdiocese supported, made many Catholics worry that the archdiocesan schools and other institutions soon would be integrated. The archdiocesan policy regarding desegregation is unclear. It appears that Archbishop Rummel and his advisors favored desegregation but delayed, and later were forced to delay, implementation.[14] Catholic dissent caused the postponement. Parental protest against desegregation, expressed in the form of petitions,[15] the Jesuit Bend incident,[16] and the Hulan Jack affair and the founding of the Catholic Laymen's Associations[17] all reflected Catholic displeasure with any changes in the racial status quo in the archdiocese. Rummel's pastoral letter of 1956 concerning the morality of segregation did not convince those opposed to desegregation.[18] The situation in New Orleans would only get worse before it got better.[19]

Rummel did not always provide strong, firm, and decisive leadership during these years. In some cases he equivocated and, apparently, reversed policy. In the Jesuit Bend incident he took half measures, which sent mixed signals to the Catholics of the archdiocese regarding his teaching authority and his position on racial matters. The possible loss of white parental support for Catholic education apparently forced the archbishop to reconsider his commitment to desegregation. On the other hand, Rummel was decisive when dealing with members of the Association of Catholic Laymen; his threat of excommunication quickly put an end to the organization. These mixed signals, however, left many Catholics unsure of the church's stance on the race question. Furthermore, Catholics who did not approve of desegregation were not going to follow church policy no matter what was stated. Unfortunately, Archbishop Rummel would have to contend with prosegregation Catholics throughout the remainder of his episcopal reign.

Southern Catholic resistance to desegregation, furthermore, points to future problems within the Roman Catholic Church in the post–Second Vatican Council era. While all too often conservative Catholics of the late twentieth century argue that Vatican II ushered in an era of liberalism and "cafeteria Catholicism," all one has to do is examine this period of history to find the origins of twentieth-century Catholic lay dissent. The irony of the situation is this: in the pre–Vatican II church, the liberals were the most loyal to church teachings and church authority, while in the post–Vatican II church, the conservatives have assumed that role.

KING AND CATHOLIC INTERRACIALISM

Martin Luther King, Jr., in his 1963 "Letter from Birmingham Jail" criticized the "white moderate" who did not understand the black person's struggle, who wanted blacks to go slowly in their pursuit of constitutional rights, who claimed the leaders and participants in the Civil Rights Movement were extremists. King asked rhetorically whether he was an extremist for hate or for love. If the former, he deserved to be criticized; if the latter, he merited support and approval. Overall, he was disappointed with the white churches and their leaders, their unwillingness to stand up for a righteous cause being "more cautious than courageous." King made an exception, however, and commended the Catholic leaders of Alabama for integrating Spring Hill College in Mobile "several years ago." In doing so King honored the Catholic interracialists of New Orleans, namely members of SERINCO, who brought about that change in Mobile and directly influenced the Jesuit decision to desegregate the college in 1954.[20]

SERINCO and CHR members were not moderates. They were extremists for love—love of neighbor, love of the human person, and love of the human race. They were willing to stand up for a righteous cause; they demonstrated more courage than caution. Had the organizations survived beyond 1956, they would have found common cause with the Southern Christian Leadership Conference and the Student Non-Violent Coordinating Committee. They could have played a significant role in transforming Catholic New Orleans.

Members of the CHR and SERINCO, Catholics, black and white, challenged racial segregation as immoral and unjust before Montgomery, before Birmingham, before Selma. Thwarted by fear and intimidation at the time, their victories were few. But they remain as heralds of the integrated future for which their Christian and democratic principles inspired them to fight.

APPENDIX A

POPULATION OF CATHOLIC COLLEGE
STUDENTS IN NEW ORLEANS, 1947–1956

	MALE	FEMALE	TOTAL
1947			
Loyola University (white)	2,049	625	2,674
Xavier University (black)	579	451	1,030
Dominican College (white)		225	225
Ursuline College (white)		101	101
Sacred Heart College (white)		89	89
1948			
Loyola University	2,572	611	3,183
Xavier University	670	435	1,105
Dominican College		225	225
Ursuline College		94	94
Sacred Heart College		92	92
1949			
Loyola University	2,510	584	3,094
Xavier University	623	378	1,001
Dominican College		180	180
Ursuline College		92	92
Sacred Heart College		91	91
1950			
Loyola University	2,271	706	2,977
Xavier University	563	395	958
Dominican College		202	202
Ursuline College		90	90
Sacred Heart College		93	93
1951			
Loyola University	2,011	672	2,683
Xavier University	586	444	1,030
Dominican College		205	205
Ursuline College		82	82
Sacred Heart College		73	73

	MALE	FEMALE	TOTAL
1952			
Loyola University	1,302	967	2,269
Xavier University	493	533	1,026
Dominican College		197	197
Ursuline College		72	72
Sacred Heart College		73	73
1953			
Loyola University	1,638	713	2,351
Xavier University	465	575	1,040
Dominican College		222	222
Ursuline College		75	75
Sacred Heart College		65	65
1954			
Loyola University	1,701	776	2,477
Xavier University	500	551	1,051
Dominican College		253	253
Sacred Heart College		72	72
1955			
Loyola University	1,887	911	2,798
Xavier University	532	581	1,113
Dominican College		320	320
Sacred Heart College		78	78
1956			
Loyola University	1,907	953	2,860
Xavier University	576	609	1,285
Dominican College		320	320
Sacred Heart College		56	56

Sources: Student population statistics from the *Official Catholic Directory* (New York: P. J. Kenedy, 1947–1956). The average attendance at a Southeastern Regional Interracial Commission (SERINCO) monthly meeting was 30, and the average annual membership of the Commission on Human Rights (CHR) was 100; see SERINCO minutes, 1947–1956, and CHR minutes, 1949–1956, Joseph H. Fichter Papers. The Catholic population of the archdiocese of New Orleans, which included areas outside the city proper, increased from 421,262 in 1947 to 549,371 in 1956. *Official Catholic Directory* (1947), 173; ibid. (1956), 150.

APPENDIX B
Manhattanville Resolutions

WHEREAS: I am enjoying the privileges of a Catholic higher education, I recognize that I have certain duties and obligations toward my fellow man, among which I must consider my conduct and attitude toward the American Negro. I therefore resolve to carry out and adhere to the following resolutions:

1. To maintain that the Negro as a human being and as a citizen is entitled to the rights of life, liberty and pursuit of happiness and to the essential opportunities of life and the full measure of social justice.
2. To be courteous and kind to every colored person, remembering the heavy yoke of injustice and discrimination he is bearing. To remember that no race or group in America has endured the many handicaps that are his today.
3. To speak a kind word for him on every occasion.
4. Not to speak slightly or use nick names which tend to humiliate, offend or discourage him.
5. To remember that the Catholic Church and the Catholic program of social justice have been called "The Greatest Hope of Colored People."
6. To recognize that the Negro shares by membership in the Mystical Body of Christ and the privileges that flow therefrom and to conduct myself in accordance therewith.
7. To give liberally on Sundays of the year when the collections are devoted to the heroic missionaries laboring among the Negro group.
8. To become increasingly interested in the welfare of the Negro; to engage actively in some form of Catholic Action looking to the betterment of his condition, spiritually and materially.

From the archives of the National Federation of Catholic College Students, Manhattanville College. Also found in John LaFarge, *No Postponement: U.S. Moral Leadership and the Problem of Racial Minorities* (New York: Longmans, Green and Co., 1950) 74–75.

APPENDIX C

RESOLUTION PASSED BY MEMBERS OF THE SOUTHEASTERN REGIONAL INTERRACIAL COMMISSION, SUMMER, 1948

We, the members of the regional inter-racial commission have carefully considered the educational situation as it exists here in Louisiana. We know that the statues of the Constitution of the State of Louisiana concerning separate school systems apply only to institutions supported by public funds. Since there is no legal restriction on our Catholic school system, whether primary or secondary, whether parochial or private, we realize that only the long-imbedded unchristian custom of segregation stands as an obstacle to the destruction of the segregated Catholicism which exists in our midst.

We feel that under the inspiring and encouraging leadership of His Excellency, the Archbishop of New Orleans, we must overcome the anti-Christian custom with Christian principles. We therefore, go on record as heartily endorsing any step, even the least practical measure, that will lead to the abolition of segregation in the Catholic schools of Louisiana.

As individuals, we welcome the opportunity to share the experience of Catholic instruction side by side with members of both races. We should like to have the pleasure of participating in the full life of the Mystical Body without embarrassment, without reference to, or worry about, the pagan customs which would separate the brethren of Christ from each other.

We humbly submit this statement to His Excellency, as expressing the minds of the delegates to the Louisiana regional commission, having approved it in open meeting, Monday, July 12, 1948.

Christian Conscience 1, no. 6 (summer 1948), Joseph H. Fichter Papers.

APPENDIX D

RESOLUTION 5C 48-10 PASSED BY THE DELEGATES TO THE
FIFTH NATIONAL CONGRESS OF THE NATIONAL FEDERATION
OF CATHOLIC COLLEGE STUDENTS HELD IN PHILADELPHIA,
PENNSYLVANIA, APRIL 22–25, 1948

WHEREAS: we who profess to be Catholics and Americans believe that among those rights belonging to all, regardless of race, color or creed, is that of equal opportunity in education; and

WHEREAS: we deplore the fact that in the past, owing to conditions, which have prevailed in the United States, there have been comparatively few negro students in Catholic institutions of higher learning; and

WHEREAS: we recognize and deplore the fact that in some states, because of legal restrictions and unamerican social attitudes Catholic institutions are not allowed to admit negro students; therefore

BE IT RESOLVED: That the NFCCS not only recommend a standard policy of non-discrimination in regard to the race or color of students applying for admission to Catholic colleges, but furthermore looks forward to the day when in Catholic Institutions of Higher Learning those students shall be present in good numbers, thereby manifesting American thinking as well as Catholic theory in practice.

Resolution 5C 48–10, NFCCS Fifth National Congress, April 22–25, 1948, National Federation of Catholic College Students, records, Manhattanville College Archives, Pleasantville, NY.

APPENDIX E
RESOLUTION 5C 48-17 PASSED BY THE DELEGATES TO THE
FIFTH NATIONAL CONGRESS OF THE NATIONAL FEDERATION
OF CATHOLIC COLLEGE STUDENTS HELD IN PHILADELPHIA,
PENNSYLVANIA, APRIL 22–25, 1948

WHEREAS: racial segregation in any form, whether practiced by a Government management, the armed forces, or on the college campus, is a direct denial of the basic equality of man, and;

WHEREAS: it is evident that civil rights is now an issue of paramount and immediate practical significance to all Americans and;

WHEREAS: the necessity of providing for the protection of the Basic Freedoms of millions of American citizens transcends any alleged violations of states rights and legality, and considerations of politics and expedience, therefore;

BE IT RESOLVED: That the NFCCS endorse the report of the President's Commission on Civil Rights and recommends enactment of its recommendations into law by the Congress of the United States.

Resolution 5C 48–17, NFCCS Fifth National Congress, April 22–25, 1948, National Federation of Catholic College Students. records, Manhattanville College Archives, Pleasantville, NY.

APPENDIX F
CONCERNING INTER-RACIAL RELATIONS AT LOYOLA UNIVERSITY

Preamble

1. It has become increasingly evident that an official policy on the matter of inter-racial relations must be issued by the administration of Loyola University for the guidance of Ours.
2. While aiming at the ideal, all must be aware of the necessity of being practical. Well-intentioned efforts for the ideal may retard, and de facto have hindered, progress towards betterment of inter-racial relations.
3. In this, as in other matters, Ours are to be guided by strict obedience and full loyalty to the directives of the Superior charged with the administration of Loyola University.
4. The following are the result of much prayer, study and consultation and are to be taken as the norms most suitable to the purpose of Loyola University and the betterment of inter-racial relations within the framework of human society in this section of the country.

Doctrine

According to our Constitutions and Rules diversity of doctrine cannot and will not be permitted. All are to conform to the following doctrine, teaching what is certain as certain, what is probable as probable.

1. It is certain that all men are equal, in that each man is an end unto himself, and hence has an *inalienable* right to the pursuit of happiness, which ultimately is the gaining of Heaven. Hence the colored man has equal rights with the white man as to liberty of conscience, freedom of worship, etc., and all requisite means thereto.
2. It is certain that the colored citizen has equal rights with the white citizen *politically.* This implies the right to vote, to hold office, elective and appointive, etc. Some question the Negro's right to vote in a *white primary,* but the Supreme Court of the U.S.A. by an 8 to 1 vote decided the Negro has this right. Distributive justice requires that State funds for education etc., be proportionately equally distributed among the white and colored citizens.
3. It is certain that the colored man had equal rights economically in that he has a right to a fair opportunity to make a decent living wage, to be paid an

Archives of the New Orleans Province of the Society of Jesus.

equal salary for equal work, etc; however, the F.E.P.C. seems to extend this too far by denying to an employer the right to hire a white man in preference to a colored.

4. It is no means certain that there is social equality between the races. As is obvious, different groups of men, even of the same race, tend to form their own social units. Hence laws of segregation in means of transportation, hotels, stores, places of amusement, schools, etc., if approved by a majority, probably are not unethical or un-Christian. The same holds with regard to zoning laws restricting white or colored residential districts. Of course in all these cases the supposition is that equal service is given for equal price, i.e., if the colored man is charged the same as the white for riding the streetcar, he be given equal convenience with the white.

In conclusion, it would seem if each race were given equal opportunity to develop itself separated socially from the other, this system would work out to the greater advantage of both than a system which would attempt to impose *social* equality by a fiat of civil law.

Practical Rules

In the practical efforts to better inter-racial relations the following are to be observed:

a. The abolition of segregation seems to be the immediate aim and objective of some. Because of local conditions precipitate action may, and has, delayed the attainment of this objective. Let every effort be made toward the betterment of the religious, moral, economic, educational and living conditions of the Negro race. Raise the standard of the Negro people and segregation will not be an issue. Therefore, let Ours de-emphasize the matter of segregation and intensify efforts to better the condition of the Negro as above stated. This will not get you publicity and acclaim as a hero, but will be more effective to an attainment of the objective of every sincere promoter of inter-racial relations.

b. From actual experience it is evident that signs on the campus do not help better race relations, are not good publicity for the cause, but rather engender resentment, suspicion, and race dissension. Therefore, no signs dealing with inter-racial matters or activities are to be posted any place at Loyola.

c. The mimeographed sheet called "Christian Conscience" had not sided in betterment of race relations. Therefore, it is not to be distributed directly or indirectly to any Loyola student or faculty member except those who are members of the Inter-racial Committee of the N.F.C.C.S.

d. Negro lecturers or speakers are not to be invited to address classes or groups at Loyola except very rarely and with the permission of the Rector or Dean.

e. It is highly imprudent, unfair to both races and detrimental to overall improvement of inter-racial relations at the present time to suggest, encourage or foster the white students to make "dates" with Negroes of the opposite sex. Ours must abstain from this.

f. Recent emphasis on inter-racial relations has created an unhappy situation at Loyola, has set back greatly the progress hitherto made towards better race relations; briefly, has failed to attain its objective. Therefore, until local conditions are bettered, we will not permit further harm to racial relations. Consequently, no meeting of the Inter-racial Committee may be held anywhere on the campus of Loyola.

APPENDIX G
WORKING DRAFT AND FINAL RESOLUTION PASSED AT FIRST REGIONAL CONGRESS OF THE NFCCS, NOVEMBER 13, 1949, XAVIER UNIVERSITY, NEW ORLEANS, LOUISIANA[6]

Working draft:

WHEREAS, In the South many institutions and organizations which conspicuously represent the Church exclude, segregate or otherwise discriminate against even Catholic Negroes and thereby give a false and scandalous impression as to what Catholicism means as a way of life; be it therefore,

RESOLVED, That members of the New Orleans region of the NFCCS deplore such discriminations and will implement the programs and policies adopted by the NFCCS so that our every act may be a charitable act, and the truth and goodness of Catholic doctrine may be diffused without compromise or ambiguity.

RESOLVED, That the New Orleans Region of the NFCCS shall endorse any Christian effort that will lead to the abolition of segregation in the Catholic Colleges of New Orleans Region and to the admission of qualified students without racial discrimination.

RESOLVED, That practical efforts will be made by a special committee of the Inter-Racial Commission to develop a spirit of Christian integration among all the members of the New Orleans Region and this integration should be achieved by a program of group work and recreation.

Resolution adopted:

WHEREAS, the Southeastern Regional Inter-Racial Commission through the N.F.C.C.S. has done much to further the cause of Inter-Racial justice and charity in the South, and whereas we feel the need for continued efforts toward this end, be it therefore:

RESOLVED, That members of the Southeastern Region of the N.F.C.C.S. will implement the programs and policies adopted by the N.F.C.C.S. so that our

SERINCO minutes, 13 November 1949, Box 51, folder 8, Joseph H. Fichter Papers.

every act may be a charitable act, and truth and goodness of Catholic doctrine may be diffused without compromise or ambiguity.

RESOLVED, That the Southeastern Region of the N.F.C.C.S. shall endorse any Christian effort that will lead to the abolition of segregation in the Catholic Colleges of the Southeastern Region and to the admission of qualified students without racial discrimination.

RESOLVED, That practical efforts will be made by a special committee of the Inter-Racial Commission to develop a spirit of Christian integration among all the members of the Southeastern Region and this integration should be achieved by a program of work and recreation.

APPENDIX H
RESOLUTION INTRODUCED BY THE DELEGATES FROM THE NEW YORK-NEW JERSEY REGION AT THE TENTH NATIONAL CONGRESS OF THE NFCCS, 25–30 AUGUST 1953, CINCINNATI, OHIO

WHEREAS segregation in its many forms is inimical to justice and charity, and

WHEREAS it behooves us as Catholic students to introduce Christian social principles in institutions as well as individuals, and

WHEREAS segregation is incompatible with the Christian teaching that all men are destined by Christ to form a close unity in brotherhood of man under the Fatherhood of Christ,

BE IT THEREFORE RESOLVED that the NFCCS, as a voice for the Catholic College youth of the nation, go on record as being unalterably opposed in principle to racial discrimination in all its forms and to segregation in employment, housing, education, and church, and

BE IT FURTHER RESOLVED that we dedicate ourselves to do everything in our power to end discrimination in all forms in campus student life, and

BE IT FURTHER RESOLVED that we recognize precisely as students and members of the lay apostolate that institutions as well as individuals must be Christianized and to this end we comment in principle efforts to promote integration both by education and by law.

Draft Resolution, NFCCS Tenth National Congress, 25–30 August 1953, National Federation of Catholic College Students, records, Manhattanville College Archives, Pleasantville, NY..

APPENDIX I

RESOLUTION TO BE PRESENTED TO THE DADS' CLUB OF THE
HOLY NAME OF JESUS SCHOOL ON OCTOBER 24, 1955

WHEREAS, the Committee appointed by His Excellence, the Archbishop, to study the question of integration, has concluded that the White and Negro children attending Catholic schools in the Archdiocese of New Orleans should be integrated:

WHEREAS, notwithstanding the Dads' Club of Holy Name of Jesus School is convinced that it would be seriously harmful to the welfare of both the White and Negro children to integrate them because of the great disparity that exists between the races in the areas of moralty [sic], culture, education and health;

WHEREAS, since it is self-evident that fraternization cannot be separated from education, the integration of White and Negro students in the Catholic schools would bring about the fraternization of the White and Negro students, not only of the same sex, but of opposite sexes; a condition, particularly during adolescence, which this organization deems extremely imprudent and undesirable, and to be avoided at almost any cost;

WHEREAS, the Dads' Club is certain that the integration of the children would completely disrupt the organization of our Dads' Club and other Dads' Clubs, as well as that of the various Cooperative Clubs throughout the Archdiocese by making it possible for Negro parents to become members of such organizations in which until now membership has been totally non-Negro;

WHEREAS, because the majority of White parents do not wish to intermingle with Negroes on a social basis, this organization is convinced that the introduction of Negro members into the various Dads' and Cooperative Clubs would bring to an end all social functions, as well as all fund raising projects, such as fairs, drives for money and the like, which projects have so substantially aided the parishes of the Archdiocese in carrying the heavy financial burden of Catholic education;

WHEREAS, in view of the fact that almost all of the White Catholic schools in the Archdiocese are already overcrowded to the point where approval by the State of Louisiana could be withdrawn, it is unnecessary and therefore unjustifiable, by

Archives of the New Orleans Province of the Society of Jesus.

compelling integration, to impose a burden in conscience on those devout Catholic parents, who, through intellectual conviction or emotional reaction, will remove their children from the Catholic schools;

WHEREAS, as parents of children attending a Catholic school, we believe that we have not only the right, but the serious obligation, to inform His Excellency, the Archbishop, of our convictions, attitudes and opinions, so that he might duly weigh them before making any decision in this most vital matter;

NOW THEREFORE, IN CONSIDERATION OF THE FOREGOING, BE IT RESOLVED:

1. That the Dads' Club of the Holy Name of Jesus School go on record as most strongly disapproving and opposing the integration of White and Negro children in the Catholic schools throughout the Archdiocese of New Orleans at any time in the foreseeable future;
2. That this organization respectfully petitions His Excellency, Archbishop Joseph Francis Rummel to defer the integration of White and Negro children in Catholic schools for an indefinite period;
3. That His Excellency be presented with a copy, duly certified, of this resolution.

NOTES

Abbreviations

LORINCO	*Annual Report of Meetings and Activities of the Louisiana Regional Inter-Racial Commission*
ALUNO	Special Collections and Archives, Monroe Library, Loyola University, New Orleans
ANOSJ	Archives of the New Orleans Province of the Society of Jesus
ARC-CCS	Amistad Research Center, Tulane University, Catholic Committee of the South collection
ARSCJ-College	College Journal 1939–1956, National Archives of the Society of the Sacred Heart
ARSCJ-House	House Journals: 1941–1953, National Archives of the Society of the Sacred Heart
ARSI	*Archivum Romanum Societatis Iesu* (Roman Archive of the Society of Jesus)
CC	*Christian Conscience*
CCM	Commission for Catholic Missions among Colored People and Indians
CHR	Commission on Human Rights of the Catholic Committee of the South
CI	*Christian Impact*
DCA	Archives of St. Mary's Dominican College
DJA	Dallas Jesuit College Preparatory School Archives
DSA	Archives of the Dominican Congregation of St. Mary, Dominican Center, New Orleans
JFRP	Joseph Francis Rummel Papers
JHFP	Joseph H. Fichter Papers, Special Collections and Archives, Monroe Library, Loyola University, New Orleans
LJTP	Louis J. Twomey Papers, Special Collections and Archives, Monroe Library, Loyola University, New Orleans
LUBD	Loyola University of the South's board of directors' minutes
RNFCCS	Records of the National Federation of Catholic College Students
SERINCO	Southeastern Regional Interracial Commission
XUA	Archives of Xavier University

Preface

1. James Hennesey, *American Catholics: A History of the Roman Catholic Community in the United States* (New York: Oxford University Press, 1981), 304–6; John Tracey Ellis, *American Catholicism,* 2d ed. (Chicago: University of Chicago Press, 1969), 147–48; Jay Dolan, *The American Catholic Experience: A History from Colonial Times to the Present* (Notre Dame: University of Notre Dame Press, 1992), 365–71.

2. Roger Baudier, *The Catholic Church in Louisiana* (New Orleans: A. W. Hyatt Stationery Manufacturing, 1939), 421. St. Mary's was founded by the Dominican sisters from Cabra, Ireland, in 1910 on a parcel of land located in uptown New Orleans, an afflu-ent area upriver from the city's downtown. With a curriculum that stressed the liberal arts,

science, religion, and philosophy, Dominican College was the first Catholic institution of higher learning for women in New Orleans. Course offerings were limited because the student body was small. The college did not obtain accreditation until the late 1940s.

3. Baudier, *Catholic Church*, 498–99, 557. Established by the Society of Jesus in 1904 as Loyola College, Loyola University of the South was granted a state charter as a degree-granting institution of higher learning in 1912. The university stressed the traditional liberal arts program, but it also had a business school, dental school, and school of law. Admission was limited to white males, with white women having limited access to professional programs and course work there.

4. Baudier, *Catholic Church*, 520–21. Ursuline College was established in 1927 by the Ursuline sisters, who had been ministering to New Orleans Catholics since 1727. Like the Dominican institution, Ursuline College offered courses in the liberal arts for the young white Catholic women of New Orleans. Unlike Dominican, Ursuline never obtained accreditation, which ultimately resulted in its closing in the early 1950s.

5. The Religious of the Sacred Heart of Jesus arrived in Grand Coteau in 1821 and established a boarding school for young women that same year; the Academy of the Sacred Heart is still in operation. The College of the Sacred Heart opened in 1939 and closed in 1956.

6. In 1917 the Blessed Sacrament Sisters, a religious order of women founded by St. Katharine Drexel to work among blacks and Indians, established a "normal school" in New Orleans to produce black teachers who would work in the Louisiana countryside. Eight years later, in 1925, the normal school became a teachers' training college and Xavier College of Liberal Arts with an enrollment of forty-seven. The next year a premedical department was opened, followed by a school of pharmacy in 1927. Baudier, *Catholic Church*, 519; Katherine Burton, *The Golden Door, The Life of Katharine Drexel* (New York: P. J. Kenedy and Sons, 1957), 259–79; Consuela Marie Duffy, *Katharine Drexel: A Biography* (Philadelphia: P. Reilly Co., 1966), 324–29; Kim Lacy Rogers, *Righteous Lives: Narratives of the New Orleans Civil Rights Movement* (New York: New York University Press, 1993), 6; Betty Porter, "The History of Negro Education In Louisiana," *Louisiana Historical Quarterly* 25 (July 1942): 728–821.

7. For statistics concerning the New Orleans Catholic college student populations between 1947 and 1956, see Appendix A.

8. For statistics of the size of the interracial organizations and the Catholic population of the archdiocese of New Orleans, see Appendix A.

9. *Brown v. Board of Education of Topeka et al.*, 347 U.S. 483 (1954).

10. Dolan, *American Catholic Experience*, 349–83; Ellis, *American Catholicism*, 124–254; Hennesey, *American Catholics*, 280–306; Thomas T. McAvoy, *A History of the Catholic Church in the United States* (Notre Dame: University of Notre Dame, 1969), 402–68.

11. McAvoy, *History of the Catholic Church*, 464.

12. Ellis, *American Catholicism*, 147–48, 170–75.

13. Martin E. Marty, *A Short History of American Catholicism* (Allen, TX: Thomas More, 1995), 184.

14. Hennesey, *American Catholics*, 305–6.

15. Richard A. Lamanna and Jay J. Coakley, "The Catholic Church and the Negro" in

Contemporary Catholicism in the United States, ed. Philip Gleason (Notre Dame: University of Notre Dame Press, 1969), 147–93.

16. Charles Morris, *American Catholic: The Saints and Sinners Who Built America's Most Powerful Church* (New York: Times Books, 1997).

17. For example, see John Egerton, *Speak Now Against the Day: The Generation before the Civil Rights Movement in the South* (New York: Alfred A. Knopf, 1994), and Adam Fairclough, *Race and Democracy: The Civil Rights Struggle in Louisiana, 1915–1972* (Athens: University of Georgia Press, 1995).

18. See John T. McGreevy, *Parish Boundaries: The Catholic Encounter with Race in the Twentieth-Century Urban North* (Chicago: The University of Chicago Press, 1996); Eileen McMahon, *What Parish Are You From?: A Chicago Irish Community and Race Relations* (Lexington: University Press of Kentucky, 1995); Dorothy A. Blatnica, *At The Altar Of Their God: African American Catholics in Cleveland, 1922–1961* (New York: Garland Pub., 1995); Gary W. McDonogh, *Black and Catholic in Savannah, Georgia* (Knoxville: University of Tennessee Press, 1993); Stephen Ochs, *Desegregating the Altar: The Josephites and the Struggle for Black Priests, 1871–1960* (Baton Rouge: Louisiana State University Press, 1990); William A. Osborne, *The Segregated Covenant: Race Relations and American Catholics* (New York: Herder and Herder, 1967); and David Southern, *John LaFarge and the Limits of Catholic Interracialism, 1911–1963* (Baton Rouge: Louisiana State University Press, 1996). McGreevy and McMahon are concerned with northern urban Euro-American Catholics and their encounter with people of color, while Blatnica deals with northern black Catholics and McDonogh, southern. William Osborne and Stephen Ochs examine the struggle within the church to break the color barrier, and David Southern examines the efforts by northern liberal Catholics to provide an environment in which race relations could be discussed among coreligionists.

19. Katherine Martensen, "Region, Religion, and Social Action: The Catholic Committee of the South, 1939–1956," *Church History* 68 (April 1982): 249–67; Gregory Hite, "The Hottest Places in Hell: The Catholic Church and Civil Rights in Selma, Alabama, 1937–1965" (Ph.D. dissertation, University of Virginia, 2002); and Joseph Kight, "'How about September?': Archbishop Joseph F. Rummel and the Desegregation of the Roman Catholic Parochial Schools in New Orleans, 1962" (M.A. thesis, University of New Orleans, 1997).

20. Leslie Woodcock Tentler, "On the Margins: The State of American Catholic History," *American Quarterly* 45 (March 1993): 104–27.

21. *Smith* v. *Allwright,* 321 U.S. 649 (1944).

Introduction

1. Derived from the Portuguese word *crioulo,* the term *Creole* was originally used to designate slaves born in the New World. By the twentieth century, the term *Creole* was used in New Orleans to identify blacks of French and Spanish descent. Arnold R. Hirsch and Joseph Logsdon, ed., *Creole New Orleans: Race and Americanization* (Baton Rouge: Louisiana State University Press, 1992); Joseph G. Tregle, Jr., "On That Word 'Creole' Again: A Note," *Journal of Louisiana History,* (Spring 1982): 193–98.

2. Robert Emmett Curran, "Rome, the American Church and Slavery," in *Building the Church in America: Studies in Honor of Monsignor Robert F. Trisco on the Occasion of His*

Seventieth Birthday, ed. Joseph C. Linck and Raymond J. Kupke (Washington, D.C.: Catholic University of America Press, 1999), 30–49; dates of establishment from the *Official Catholic Directory* (New York: P. J. Kenedy and Sons, 2000).

3. Cyprian Davis, "Black Catholics in Nineteenth-Century America," *U.S. Catholic Historian* 5 (1986): 1–18; Kenneth J. Zanca, ed., *American Catholics and Slavery: 1789–1866, An Anthology of Primary Documents* (New York: University Press of America, 1994), 110–12.

4. Madeleine H. Rice, *American Catholic Opinion in the Slavery Controversy* (New York: Columbia University Press, 1944), 66–69, 84–85, 88–89, 92–96, 102–3, 124, 137.

5. Ibid., 155–58.

6. Cyprian Davis, *The History of Black Catholics in the United States* (New York: Crossroad, 1990), 58–61.

7. Curran, "Rome, the American Church and Slavery," 30–49; Davis, *History of Black Catholics,* 39–57; Zanca, *American Catholics and Slavery,* 27.

8. John B. Alberts, "Black Schools: The Josephite Parishes during the Jim Crow Era," *U.S. Catholic Historian* 12 (winter 1994): 78–80; Davis, *History of Black Catholics,* 118–21; Jay P. Dolan, *The American Catholic Experience: A History from Colonial Times to the Present* (Garden City, NY: Doubleday, 1985; reprint, Notre Dame: Notre Dame University Press, 1992), 268–76; John Tracy Ellis, *American Catholicism,* 2d ed. (Chicago: University of Chicago Press, 1969), 100–104; John T. Gillard, *Colored Catholics in the United States* (Baltimore: Josephite Press, 1941), 113–14; James Hennesey, *American Catholics: A History of the Roman Catholic Community in the United States* (New York: Oxford University Press, 1981), 161–63; Richard A. Lamanna and Jay J. Coakley, "The Catholic Church and the Negro," in *Contemporary Catholicism in the United States,* ed. Philip Gleason (Notre Dame: University of Notre Dame Press, 1969), 151; Thomas T. McAvoy, *A History of the Catholic Church in the United States* (Garden City, NY: Doubleday., 1985; reprint, Notre Dame: University of Notre Dame Press, 1969), 202; Stephen J. Ochs, *Desegregating the Altar: The Josephites and the Struggle for Black Priests, 1871–1960* (Baton Rouge: Louisiana State University Press, 1990), 39–41.

9. H. Shelton Smith, *In His Image, but . . . : Racism in the Southern Religion, 1780–1910* (Durham: Duke University Press, 1972), 248–51; Alberts, "Black Schools," 78–80; Davis, *History of Black Catholics,* 132–33; Gillard, *Colored Catholics,* 115–16, 121–22; Lamanna and Coakley, "The Catholic Church and the Negro," 152; McAvoy, *History of the Catholic Church,* 259–60; Ochs, *Desegregating the Altar,* 59–63.

10. Alberts, "Black Schools," 78–80; Dolan, *Catholic Experience,* 268–76; Ellis, *American Catholicism,* 104; Gillard, *Colored Catholics,* 115–16, 121–22; Hennesey, *American Catholics,* 185–87; McAvoy, *History of the Catholic Church,* 259–60; Ochs, *Desegregating the Altar,* 59–63.

11. Dolores E. Labbé, *Jim Crow Comes to Church: The Establishment of Segregated Parishes in South Louisiana,* USL History Series (Lafayette: University of Southwestern Louisiana, 1971).

12. Roger Baudier, *The Catholic Church in Louisiana* (New Orleans: A. W. Hyatt Stationery Manufacturing, 1939), 473; Annemarie Kasteel, *Francis Janssens, 1843–1897: A Dutch-American Prelate* (Lafayette: Center for Louisiana Studies, University of Southwestern Louisiana, 1992), 1–130; Labbé, *Jim Crow Comes to Church,* 27–28.

13. Kasteel, *Janssens*, 133–42; Labbé, *Jim Crow Comes to Church*, 30; Ochs, *Desegregating the Altar*, 68.

14. Kasteel, *Janssens*, 275; Gillard, *Colored Catholics*, 95–109; Labbé, *Jim Crow Comes to Church*, 31–33.

15. Smith, *In His Image*, 248–50.

16. Letter from Francis Janssens to William Elder, 11 February 1889, quoted in Kasteel, *Janssens*, 280, emphasis in original; Labbé, *Jim Crow Comes to Church*, 33, 38–41. At the time, Elder was archbishop of Cincinnati, but he had been bishop of Natchez. Janssens succeed him in Natchez.

17. The Negro and Indian Commission was established in 1884 on the recommendation of the bishops gathered at the Third Plenary Council. It oversaw the administration of funds used for black evangelization. Ochs, *Desegregating the Altar*, 62.

18. Francis Janssens, 1892 report to the Commission for Catholic Missions among Colored People and Indians (hereafter referred to as CCM), quoted in Gillard, *Colored Catholics*, 122; Labbé, *Jim Crow Comes to Church*, 50, 53–54.

19. Janssens, 1894 report, CCM, quoted in Gillard, *Colored Catholics*, 122, and in Labbé, *Jim Crow Comes to Church*, 53.

20. Labbé, *Jim Crow Comes to Church*, 18, 40.

21. For a life of Drexel, see Katherine Burton, *The Golden Door: The Life of Katharine Drexel* (New York: P. J. Kenedy and Sons, 1957); Consuela Marie Duffy, *Katharine Drexel: A Biography* (Philadelphia: Peter Reilly Co., 1965); and Patricia Lynch, *Sharing the Bread in Service: Sisters of the Blessed Sacrament, 1891–1991* (Bensalem, PA: Sisters of the Blessed Sacrament, 1998).

22. Labbé, *Jim Crow Comes to Church*, 24, 51.

23. Historically, during the nineteenth century "national" churches were created in response to the huge influx of European immigrants into Louisiana as well as eastern and midwestern sections of the United States. Catholic immigrants were grouped by national origin in order to ease the transition into America's English-speaking and Protestant world.

24. John B. Alberts, "Origins of Black Catholic Parishes in the Archdiocese of New Orleans, 1718–1920" (Ph.D. diss., Louisiana State University, 1998), 239–63; Kasteel, *Janssens*, 297; Labbé, *Jim Crow Church*, 53–54; Charles B. Rousseve, *The Negro in Louisiana* (New Orleans: Xavier University Press, 1937; reprint, New York: Johnson Reprint Corp., 1970), 139–40.

25. Janssens, 1895, CCM, quoted in Gillard, *Colored Catholics*, 122, and in Labbé, *Jim Crow Comes to Church*, 53.

26. Quoted from the New Orleans *Times-Democrat*, 20 May 1895, in Rousseve, *Negro in Louisiana*, 139–40; Labbé, *Jim Crow Church*, 54–55.

27. Baudier, *Catholic Church*, 493–501; Labbé, *Jim Crow Comes to Church*, 63.

28. Alberts, "Black Catholic Parishes," 313–16; Baudier, *Catholic Church*, 507; Labbé, *Jim Crow Comes to Church*, 63–64.

29. Baudier, *Catholic Church*, 508; Alberts, "Black Schools," 77–98; Labbé, *Jim Crow Comes to Church*, 69–70, 78–84.

30. Baudier, *Catholic Church*, 509, 516–17, 519; Mary B. Deggs, *No Cross, No Crown: Black Nuns in Nineteenth-Century New Orleans*, ed. Virginia M. Gould and Charles E.

Nolan (Bloomington: Indiana University Press, 2001); Virginia M. Gould and Charles E. Nolan, *Henriette Delille: 'Servant of Slaves'* (New Orleans: Sisters of the Holy Family, 1998); Joseph H. Fichter, *The Sociology of Good Works: Research in Catholic America* (Chicago: Loyola University Press, 1993), 95–111; Labbé, *Jim Crow Comes to Church,* 69–70, 78–84.

31. Baudier, *Catholic Church,* 523–35.

32. Baudier, *Catholic Church,* 555.

33. *A Catechism of Christian Doctrine, Prepared and Enjoined by Order of the Third Plenary Council of Baltimore* (New York, Cincinnati: Benzinger Brothers, 1933; reprint, Rockford, IL: Tan Books and Publishers, 1977); Heribert Jone, *Moral Theology,* 18th ed., trans. Urban S. Adelman (Westminster, MD: Newman Press, 1962); Mark S. Massa, *Catholics and American Culture: Fulton Sheen, Dorothy Day, and the Notre Dame Football Team* (New York: Crossroad, 1999); Charles R. Morris, *American Catholic: The Saints and Sinners Who Built America's Most Powerful Church* (New York: Times Books, 1997).

34. Joan deBilby Norris, interview by author, tape recording, Birmingham, AL, 21 December 1998; Paula Begnaud Roden, interview by author, tape recording, Buffalo, NY, 21 June 1999; Wilbert Sykes, interview with author, tape recording, New York, NY, 6 January 1999; Lenora Chandler, interview by author, tape recording, New Orleans, LA, 18 October 1998; Jerry Mialaret and Ida [née Chirieleison] Mialaret, interview by author, tape recording, New Orleans, 25 June 1997.

35. Joseph H. Fichter, *Southern Parish,* vol. 1, *Dynamics of a City Church* (Chicago: University of Chicago Press, 1951), 70–84, 188–97. For Catholic devotional practices, see Janice T. Connell, *Praying with Mary: a Treasury for All Occasions* (San Francisco: HarperSanFrancisco, 1997); John D. Miller, *Beads and Prayers: The Rosary in History and Devotion* (London: Burns and Oates, 2001); Alfred A. Sinnott, *The Watch: 14 Holy Hours, for Each Month of the Year, for Holy Thursday, and for Forty Hours* (Milwaukee: Bruce Pub. Co., 1947).

36. "Religion—Not Just in Church," *Catholic Action of the South,* 29 July 1948, 4, 5.

37. By 1947 there were eleven "colored" parishes in the archdiocese of New Orleans: All Saints (formed in 1919), Blessed Sacrament (1917), Corpus Christi (1916), St. David's (1938), Holy Ghost (1915), Holy Redeemer (1919), St. Joan of Arc (1909), St. Katherine (1895), St. Monica (1923), St. Peter Claver (1920), and St. Raymond (1927). All these parishes except St. David's had parochial schools, with a total enrollment of 4,427 pupils. *The Official Catholic Directory* (New York: P. J. Kenedy and Sons, 1947), 164–73.

38. The following articles are all from *Catholic Action of the South:* "Minstrel Scheduled," 8 June 1950, 23; "Redemptorist Minstrel" and "Minstrels Elect Officers," 21 September 1950, 13; "KC Minstrel Show," 5 October 1950, 23; "Minstrel Show Given at Dominican College," 7 December 1950, 21; "Club Slates Minstrel" and "Set Minstrel Practice," 25 January 1951, 19; "Slate Minstrel Show," 5 April 1951, 19; "Minstrel Show," 13 December 1951, 23; "Minstrels Sought," 20 December 1951, 13; "Two-Day Minstrel," 17 January 1952, 10; "To Sponsor Minstrel," 24 January 1952, 19; "Mothers Plan Minstrel," 10 April 1952, 16; "Show in Baton Rouge" and "Mothers in Minstrels," 8 May 1952, 19; "Reserve KC Gives Show," 29 May 1952, 19; "Plan Minstrel Show" and "Show Dates Set," 5 February 1953, 19; "Minstrel Show," 2 April 1953, 19. For a history of minstrel shows in New Orleans see John Smith Kendall, "New Orleans' Negro Minstrels," *Louisiana Historical Quarterly* 30 (January 1947): 128–48.

39. William A. Osborne, *The Segregated Covenant: Race Relations and American Catholics* (New York: Herder and Herder, 1967), 71.

40. Fichter, *Southern Parish,* 265–66; Adam Fairclough, *Race and Democracy: The Civil Rights Struggle in Louisiana, 1915-1972* (Athens: University of Georgia Press, 1995) 172–73.

Chapter I

1. Cyprian Davis, *The History of Black Catholics in the United States* (New York: Crossroad, 1990), 214–15; James J. Hennesey, *American Catholics: A History of the Roman Catholic Community in the United States* (New York: Oxford University Press, 1981), 223–30; Marilyn W. Nickels, *Black Catholic Protest and the Federated Colored Catholics, 1917–1933: Three Perspectives on Racial Justice* (New York: Garland Pub., 1988), 31–32; Thomas W. Spalding, *The Premier See: A History of the Archdiocese of Baltimore, 1789–1989* (Baltimore: Johns Hopkins University Press, 1989), 315; David W. Southern, *John LaFarge and the Limits of Catholic Interracialism, 1911–1963* (Baton Rouge: Louisiana State University Press, 1996), 77–78.

2. Davis, *History of Black Catholics,* 215–16; Southern, *John LaFarge,* 76–77.

3. Davis, *History of Black Catholics,* 217–20; Southern, *John LaFarge,* 77–79.

4. Davis, *History of Black Catholics,* 217–20.

5. For a discussion of these organizations, see W. E. B. Du Bois, "Race Relations in the United States, 1917–1947," *Phylon* 9 (3rd quarter 1948): 234–47; August Meier and John H. Bracey, Jr., "The NAACP as a Reform Movement, 1909–1965: 'To Reach the Conscience of America,'" *Journal of Southern History,* 59 (February 1993): 3–30; Jesse Thomas Moore, Jr., *A Search for Equality: The National Urban League, 1910–1961* (University Park: Pennsylvania State University Press, 1981); Nancy J. Weiss, *The National Urban League, 1910–1940* (New York: Oxford University Press, 1974).

6. John LaFarge (1880–1963), Harvard educated, joined the Society of Jesus after ordination to the priesthood in 1905. From 1911 to 1926, he was assigned to work among the black Catholics in southern Maryland, an experience that profoundly influenced his later interracial work. LaFarge believed that the Roman Catholic church offered the best solution to the race question as its universal outlook provided the proper philosophical and theological foundation for belief in the oneness of the human race. By the mid-1930s, John LaFarge would be the leading Catholic spokesman concerning race matters. Davis, *History of Black Catholics,* 225–27; Southern, *John LaFarge,* 8–48.

7. William Markoe (1892–1969), entered in the Society of Jesus in 1913, ordained a priest in 1926. He began working with black Catholics soon after joining the Society. His concern for their plight had inspired him, along with three other Jesuits, including his brother John, to take a vow in 1917 "to give and dedicate our whole lives and all our energies, as far as we are able and it is not contrary to a pure spirit of perfect indifference and obedience, for the work of the salvation of the Negroes in the United States." As pastor of St. Elizabeth's, a black church in St. Louis, Markoe fulfilled his vow by laboring exclusively for the blacks of the area and, with the assistance of his brother, published a newsletter, the *St. Elizabeth's Chronicle.* Davis, *History of Black Catholics,* 222–25; Southern, *John LaFarge,* 110–17. For the text of the vow, see Wisconsin Province, record group SJ Names, folder Markoe, Wm. M., Midwest Jesuit Archives, St. Louis.

8. Davis, *History of Black Catholics,* 221–29; Southern, *John LaFarge,* 103–46.

9. Davis, *History of Black Catholics,* 224–25; Southern, *John LaFarge,* 109–17; Martin A. Zielinski, "Working for Interracial Justice: The Catholic Council of New York, 1934–1964," *U.S. Catholic Historian* 7 (spring/summer 1988): 235.

10. Aaron I. Abell, *American Catholicism and Social Action: A Search for Social Action, 1865–1950* (Garden City, NY: Hanover House, 1960); Daniel Lord, "The Sacrament of Catholic Action," pamphlet (St. Louis: The Queen's Work, 1936); "What Does the Pope Say about Catholic Action?: Some Papal Pronouncements," pamphlet (Sydney: Pellegrini, 1937).

11. Southern, *John LaFarge,* 124–25, 141. Turner's group, which retained the name of Federated Colored Catholics, now was effectively marginalized. It survived in vestigial form until 1952.

12. Southern, *John LaFarge,* 130–46.

13. Spalding, *Premier See,* 345–56; Zielinski, "Interracial Justice," 234–36, CICNY purpose statement quoted on 236; Southern, *John LaFarge,* 124–46, 178–85.

14. Zielinski, "Interracial Justice," 237–47; Davis, *History of Black Catholics,* 252–54; Southern, *John LaFarge,* 186–288; George K. Hunton, *All of Which I Saw, Part of Which I Was: The Autobiography of George Hunton* (Garden City, NY: Doubleday, 1967).

15. Katherine Martensen, "Region, Religion and Social Action: The Catholic Committee of the South, 1939–1956," *Catholic Historical Review* 68 (April 1982): 249–67; Thomas J. Harte, *Catholic Organizations Promoting Negro-White Race Relations in the United States,* (Washington, D.C.: Catholic University of America Press, 1947), 145–54.

16. Catholic Conference of the South, Report of the Proceedings and Addresses of the First Annual Meeting, Atlanta, 14–16 April 1941, iii.

17. Philip Ogilvie, "The Catholic Committee of the South?" pamphlet (n.p., n.d.), Box 45, folder 1, Joseph H. Fichter Papers, Special Collections and Archives, Monroe Library, Loyola University, New Orleans (hereafter referred to as JHFP). The "lay apostolate" refers to Catholic lay involvement in church programs and projects of a spiritual and temporal nature.

18. Fifty invitations to the inaugural meeting were sent out. The early members of the CHR included Iona Berteaux, Lucile Cherbonnier, Inez DeGruy, Mrs. Alphonso del Marmol, Clarence East, Joseph H. Fichter, S.J., Edward Gillen, Ellis Henican, Mr. and Mrs. Philip Hornung, Clarence Laws, Mrs. Dagmar Le Breton, Vernon X. Miller, John McCann, Vincent O'Connell, S.M., Geraldine O'Conner, Janet Riley, Joseph Rouchell, Numa Rousseve, Sr., Mr. and Mrs. Stephen Ryan, Edna St. Cyr, Joseph Schenthal, Lucille Soniat, Joan Stanley, A. P. Tureaud, Sr., and Henry Werner, Jr. Among them, there were four members of the faculty at Xavier University, three lawyers, three homemakers, two social workers, two businessmen, a physician, an engineer, and a law librarian. Joseph H. Fichter to Vernon X. Miller, 24 February 1949, Box 45, folder 5, JHFP.

19. Letter from Vernon Miller to potential CHR members, 14 February 1949, Box 45, folder 5, JHFP. This was a closed meeting with no public announcement regarding the gathering, nor would there be any news of the establishment of the CHR for several months to come.

20. "Statement of the Commission on Human Rights, 1950," Box 48, folder 4, JHFP. Emphasis in original.

21. CHR statement in "Commission on Human Rights of the Catholic Committee of the South: Its Principles, Objectives and Achievements," pamphlet (n.p., n.d.), Amistad Research Center, Tulane University, Catholic Committee of the South collection (hereafter referred to as ARC-CCS).

22. Pope Pius XII, "On the Mystical Body of Christ," 29 June 1943; Daniel A. Lord, *Our Part in the Mystical Body* (St. Louis: Queen's Work, 1935); Emile Mersch, *The Theology of the Mystical Body*, trans. Cyril Vollert (London: B. Herder Book Co., 1951); Ernest Mura, *The Nature of the Mystical Body*, trans. Angeline Bouchard (London: B. Herder Book Co., 1963).

23. 1 Corinthians 12:13.

24. Colossians 1:18.

25. CHR statement, ARC-CCS.

26. John McCann to Janet Riley, 28 February 1949, Box 45, folder 5, JHFP; "CHR Statement, 1950," Box 48, folder 4, JHFP.

27. "Brief history of the CHR," Box 48, folder 4, JHFP.

28. Thomas J. Shields (1900–1975), entered the New Orleans Province of the Society of Jesus in 1918. He was ordained a priest in 1931. From 1937 to 1944 he served as provincial (regional religious superior) of the New Orleans Province of the Society of Jesus, and from 1945 to 1952 he served as rector (local religious superior) and president of Loyola University of the South.

29. Thomas J. Shields to Joseph H. Fichter, 27 April 1949, Box 45, folder 5, JHFP.

30. "Brief History of the CHR," Box 48, folder 4, JHFP.

31. "Negro Employment: A Progress Report," *Christian Impact* (hereafter referred to as *CI*) 3, no. 1 (October 1952), JHFP; "Washington's Split Personality," *CI* 3, no. 5 (March 1953), JHFP; "The Way with Children," *CI* 3, no. 2 (November 1953), JHFP; "Steps toward Desegregation in the Schools," *CI* 5, no. 1 (September 1954), JHFP.

32. Minutes of the Commission on Human Rights of the Catholic Committee of the South (hereafter referred to as CHR minutes), 27 March 1949, Box 47, folder 16, JHFP.

33. Mrs. Stephen P. Ryan, "A Talk Delivered before the Race Relations Workshop at the Mid-Century Convention of the Catholic Committee of the South," Columbia, South Carolina, 23 January 1951, Box 48, folder 4, JHFP.

34. Winifred Byles, student of Manhattanville College, attended the Sixteenth World Congress of Pax Romana (1937) held in Paris. She was asked to undertake the task of establishing a national federation in the United States with ties to the international organization. Roger Goebel, *A Brief History of the National Federation of Catholic College Students* (n.p., n.d.), Records of the National Federation of Catholic College Students (hereafter referred to as RNFCCS), Manhattanville College Archives, Pleasantville, New York.

35. Ibid., Emphasis in original.

36. *History, Interpretations, Questions, and Constitution of the National Federation of Catholic College Students* (n.p., n.d.), RNFCCS. The American Student Union (ASU) was an influential leftist-led youth organ founded in 1935 as a result of the amalgamation of the communist-led National Student League and the socialist-led Student League for Industrial Democracy. See Robert Cohen, *When the Old Left Was Young: Student Radicals and America's First Mass Student Movement, 1929–1941* (New York: Oxford University Press, 1993), 134–42.

37. Goebel, *Brief History,* RNFCCS.

38. Constitution of the National Federation of Catholic College Students (Washington, DC: National Office NFCCS, 1947), RNFCCS.

39. Ibid.

40. *Activities of the National Federation of Catholic College Students—1938–1939* (n.p.), RNFCCS. The resolutions were drafted by the women of Manhattanville College of the Sacred Heart in January 1933 and adopted by the students of Manhattanville in May of the same year as a way to improve American race relations. See John LaFarge, *No Postponement: U.S. Moral Leadership and the Problem of Racial Minorities* (New York: Longmans, Green and Co., 1950), 74–76. See Appendix B of the present volume for a full text of the resolutions.

41. Minutes of the 1944 Annual Meeting of the National Council of the National Federation of Catholic College Students, 1–2 January 1944, Loyola University, Chicago, RNFCCS; Harte, "Catholic Organizations Promoting Negro-White Race Relations," 124–34.

42. Michal R. Belknap, ed., *Urban Race Riots* (New York: Garland Pub., 1991); Thomas J. Sugrue, *The Origins of the Urban Crisis: Race and Inequality in Postwar Detroit* (Princeton: Princeton University Press, 1996); Sheldon Danziger, Reynolds Farley and Harry J. Holzer, *Detroit Divided* (New York: Russell Sage Foundation, 2000); Harvard Sitkoff, "Racial Militancy and Interracial Violence in the Second World War," *Journal of American History* 58 (December 1971): 661–81.

43. Minutes of the 1944 Annual NFCCS Meeting, RNFCCS.

44. Gunnar Myrdal, *An American Dilemma: The Negro Problem and Modern Democracy* (New York: Harper and Row, 1944).

45. In 1946, twenty-one of the twenty-eight Jesuit-run institutions of higher learning reported they had a nondiscriminatory policy regarding the admission of black students. Of the more than 80,000 individuals attending a Jesuit college or university that academic year, 436 were black. St. Louis University and Fordham University in New York City had the largest numbers of African Americans, 150 and 102, respectively. See Francis K. Drolet, "Negro Students in Jesuit Schools and Colleges, 1946–1947," *Social Order* 1 (1947–48): 145–48. By 1953, twenty-six Jesuit colleges and universities reported having black enrollment. The total number of black students attending Jesuit-run schools was 1,085. See Bartholomew Lahiff, "Negro Students in Jesuit Schools, 1952–1953," *Jesuit Educational Quarterly* 16 (October 1953): 123–26.

46. In the "Vita Auctoria" (i.e., "Life of the Author") in his master's thesis, Fichter stated that he spent the years 1920 through 1924 at a minor seminary, the Pontifical Josephinum College, in Worthington, Ohio. And yet there is no indication in his transcript from the school that he graduated, let alone spent four years there. Course credits from the minor seminary, which were accepted by the Jesuits in fulfillment of church educational requirements, only date from the 1921–22 and 1922–23 school years. See Joseph H. Fichter, "The Wage-Earner in the Consumer Cooperative System" (M.A. thesis, St. Louis University, 1939), 88, and "Transcripts," Series VI, JHFP.

47. Carmelo Graffagnini , interview by author, tape recording, Madison, AL, 19 December 1998.

48. According to the Josephinum transcript, Fichter took Latin during the 1921–1922 and 1922–1923 academic years, receiving marks of seventy-three and seventy-two, respec-

tively. In Greek, taken during the 1922–1923 academic year, he received a seventy-eight. This lack of extensive course work as well as the poor performance in the classical languages may explain why the New York Province advised him to apply elsewhere. "Transcripts," Series VI, JHFP.

49. There first two years of training take place at the novitiate, where one is known as a novice. The novitiate is the second "probation," or test, for an individual desiring to become a Jesuit; the first is postulancy, a trial period lasting eight to ten days immediately prior to acceptance into the novitiate. Unlike most other religious orders, the Jesuit novitiate lasts two years rather than one.

50. In order to be ordained a priest in the Roman Catholic Church, four years of theological studies are required. Because of the lengthy formation process within the Society of Jesus, the tradition had been for Jesuits to be ordained after three years of theology. The newly ordained Jesuit would still take a fourth year of studies to fulfill church requirements. Fichter did not complete his theological studies at St. Mary's until 1943.

51. Fichter's doctoral dissertation, "The Social Implications of the *Lex Iulia et Papia Poppaea*," dealt with family law in ancient Rome.

52. Sociology 32, "Seminar in Group Prejudice and Conflict," Box 1, folder 4, course material, Gordon Allport Papers, Harvard University Archives (hereafter referred to as GAP); Alfred M. Lee and Norman D. Humphrey, *Race Riot* (New York: The Dryden Press, 1943); Joseph H. Fichter, *One-Man Research: Reminiscences of a Catholic Sociologist* (New York: John Wiley and Sons, 1973), 112, n. 1.

53. The lives examined included: Vincent de Paul, Bernard Mandeville, Jean-Jacques Rousseau, Thomas Paine, Robert Owen, Antoine Frederic Ozanam, Charles Kingsley, Wilhelm von Kettler, Karl Marx, Henry Edward Manning, Leo XIII, Carl Schurz, Leo Tolstoy, and Sidney and Beatrice Webb.

54. Joseph H. Fichter, *Roots of Change* (New York: D. Appleton-Century Co., 1939), vii.

55. Joseph H. Fichter, *Saint Cecil Cyprian: Early Defender of the Faith* (St. Louis: B. Herder Book Co., 1942), 267.

56. Fichter, *One-Man Research,* 77.

57. Joseph Fichter to Gordon Allport, 14 October 1947, Box 14, folder F-Fl, 1946–50, miscellaneous correspondence, GAP; Fichter, *One-Man Research,* 76–78.

58. In his book *The Sociology of Good Works,* Fichter recounts the first attempts at integrating Loyola University of the South. Between 1921 and 1937, the university allowed black religious women, members of the Sisters of the Holy Family, to attend summer school courses through Loyola's extension program, thereby receiving course credits and teaching certifications according to the standards set by the State of Louisiana. This arrangement ceased in 1937 when a new administration took office at Loyola. Fearing reprisals at the hands of state educational officials, the Jesuits of Loyola University discontinued the summer program and recommended that the Holy Family sisters take courses at Xavier University. See Joseph H. Fichter, *The Sociology of Good Works: Research in Catholic America* (Chicago: Loyola University Press, 1993), 95–102.

59. Louisiana State University was forced to integrate its law school in 1950 *(Wilson v. Board of Supervisors of Louisiana State University),* its other graduate schools in 1951, and its undergraduate program in 1953. See Liva Baker, *The Second Battle of New Orleans: The Hundred-Year Struggle to Integrate the Schools* (New York: HarperCollins, 1996), 122–37, 199–208.

60. Fichter, *One-Man Research*, 76, 112, n. 2. As explained in his autobiography, Fichter modeled the "top down" approach to desegregation on Jesuit-run St. Louis University, which began the process of integration at the graduate school level. There was, however, a great deal of controversy surrounding the integration of the St. Louis school. See Peter McDonough, *Men Astutely Trained: A History of the Jesuits in the American Century* (New York: Free Press, 1992), 182–85, 190–91, 196; Donald Kemper, "Catholic Integration in St. Louis, 1935–1947," *Missouri Historical Review* 73 (October 1978): 1–22; John McCarthy, "Facing the Race Problem at St. Louis University," *Jesuit Educational Quarterly* (October 1951): 69–80; Daniel Van Slyke, "Claude Heithaus and the Integration of Saint Louis University: The Mystical Body of Christ and Jesuit Politics," in *Theology and Lived Christianity*, ed. David M. Hammond (Mystic, CT: Twenty-Third Publications/Bayard, 2000), 139–73; Paul Shore, "The Message and the Messenger: The Untold Story of Father Claude Heithaus and the Integration of Saint Louis University" in *Trying Times: Essays on Catholic Higher Education in the 20th Century*, ed. William M. Shea and Daniel Van Slyke (Atlanta: Scholars Press, 1999): 135–52.

61. Vernon X. Miller to Joseph H. Fichter, 6 November 1947, Box 52, folder 14, JHFP.

62. Fichter, *One-Man Research*, 76–78.

63. From its beginnings until the 1970s, Loyola University of the South was headed by a president who also served as the rector, or religious superior, of the university community. Therefore, the official title of all the Jesuit presidents mentioned in this work is actually "rector-president," but they will be referred to simply as "president" to avoid confusion. A Jesuit rector served a maximum of six years in office. Because of the Second World War, however, some men served longer terms in office.

64. From its inception until the 1970s, the board of directors was comprised of the president of the university and four members of the New Orleans Province of the Society of Jesus who worked at Loyola. The four Jesuits also served as advisers or "consultors," commonly referred to as "Father Consultors," to the religious superior (i.e., rector-president) of the community assisting him in governing the community. Their titles would change depending on whether they were discussing matters that pertained solely to the university or strictly to the life of the religious community. Often these men would meet first with the president as members of the board of directors and then as consultors with the rector—same men, different titles. Throughout this work, these advisers will be referred to as either as consultors or board members depending on the circumstances herein described (in some cases it is not easy to differentiate between the roles). Members of the board during the 1947–1948 academic year were William O'Leary, S.J., Hilton A. Crane, S.J., William Crandell, S.J., and Thomas A. Carey, S.J.

65. Loyola University of the South's board of directors' minutes (hereafter referred to as LUBD minutes), 29 November 1947, Special Collections and Archives, Monroe Library, Loyola University, New Orleans (hereafter referred to as ALUNO).

66. "Thumbnail History of SERINCO," Box 51, folder 15, JHFP.

67. During the 1946–1947 academic year, St. Mary's Dominican College joined the NFCCS, becoming one of the first institutions of higher learning in New Orleans to do so. Minutes of the Administrative Board of St. Mary's Dominican College, 22 May 1946, 17 November 1946, 17 and 26 March 1947, Archives of St. Mary's Dominican College (hereafter referred to as DCA). Xavier University was asked to join the federation prior to the war, but an incident at a meeting in Cincinnati forced the president of the institution

to decline. With the formation of a national interracial commission in 1944, Xavier officials reversed their decision and joined. Sr. Mary Francis, S.B.S., to Margaret Conway, 26 August 1944, Office of the President Series, Archives of Xavier University (hereafter referred to as XUA). During the early postwar period, Ursuline, Loyola, and Sacred Heart expressed interest and joined the federation. Robert Smith Shea to "The Dean, St. Mary's Dominican College," c.1946, DCA; "NFCCS Congress Accepts Charter for Local Regional: Delegates Back from Meet," *Maroon,* 30 April 1948, 1; "Southern Region of N.F.C.C.S. Formed April 17, M. Kingsmill Elected 1947–48 Treasurer," *U-Topia,* April 1948, 1.

68. Minutes of the Southeastern Regional Interracial Commission (hereafter referred to as SERINCO minutes), 23 April 1948, Box 51, folder 6, JHFP.

69. Xavier, Ursuline, and Dominican students indicated that their institutions could establish interracial commissions on their respective campuses, Dominican being the one college that expressed the most hesitancy because of a lack of interest in the race question. SERINCO minutes, 23 April 1948, Box 51, folder 6, JHFP.

70. Minutes of the Southeastern Regional Council of the NFCCS, 11 February 1950, DCA. To avoid confusing the reader with a "Rooseveltesque" alphabet soup listing of organizational name changes, either the acronym "SERINCO" or the generic title "interracial commission" will be used throughout this work to refer to the student organization. In late 1949, New Orleans officers of the Southeastern Region of the NFCCS visited Spring Hill College to discuss with students leaders the possibility of joining the organization. "N.F.C.C.S. Group Meets Council Men to Lay Plans for Hill Cooperation," *Springhillian,* 17 December 1949, 3.

71. "Application for Approval Form," Box 51, folder 16, JHFP. Charter members included Donald Nicodemus, Mary Kathleen Lumsden, T. Kloppner, Frank Trouier, Eugene Murret, Roy Riche, Peter Duffy, and Glen Armautrout. All were white Loyola students.

Chapter II

1. Edward F. Haas, *DeLesseps S. Morrison and the Image of Reform: New Orleans Politics, 1946–1961* (Baton Rouge: Louisiana State University Press, 1974), 41–48, 67–81.

2. "Special Message to the Congress on Civil Rights," 2 February 1948. *Public Papers of the President of the United States: Harry S. Truman, 1947* (Washington, DC: U.S. Government Printing Office, 1962), 121–26.

3. Numan V. Bartley, *The New South, 1945–1980* (Baton Rouge: Louisiana State University Press, 1995), 74–104; William C. Berman, *The Politics of Civil Rights in the Truman Administration* (Columbus: Ohio State University Press, 1970), 79–135; Monroe Billington, "Civil Rights, President Truman and the South," *Journal of Negro History* 58 (April 1973): 127–39; Robert Mann, *The Walls of Jericho: Lyndon Johnson, Hubert Humphrey, Richard Russell, and the Struggle for Civil Rights* (New York: Harcourt Brace, 1996), 16–21; Harvard Sitkoff, "Harry Truman and the Election of 1948: The Coming of Age of Civil Rights in American Politics," *Journal of Southern History* 37 (November 1971): 597–616.

4. Bartley, *The New South,* 74–104; Berman, *Politics of Civil Rights,* 79–135; Mann, *Walls of Jericho,* 16–21; Sitkoff, "Harry Truman and the Election of 1948," 597–616.

5. Daniel G. Quinn to Joseph Francis Rummel, 29 June 1948, Box 49, folder 2, JHFP.

6. The president of the university also served as the local religious superior of the Jesuits at Loyola. The term of office for both positions was usually six years, served concurrently.

7. The Society of Jesus, headquartered in Rome and governed by a superior general commonly referred to as "Father General," is divided into worldwide territories known as provinces. Each province is headed by a religious superior, or provincial, who serves a term of office of six years. The New Orleans Province of the Society of Jesus includes the states of New Mexico, Texas, Arkansas, Louisiana, Mississippi, Alabama, Tennessee, Georgia, South Carolina, and Florida.

8. Quinn had sent Rummel an advance copy of the resolution several days before the meeting. Daniel G. Quinn to Joseph Francis Rummel, 13 July 1948, Box 49, folder 2, JHFP. See Appendix C for a copy of the SERINCO resolution.

9. "Memorandum by Thomas J. Shields," 20 July 1948, Archives of the New Orleans Province of the Society of Jesus (hereafter referred to as ANOSJ).

10. Ibid.

11. Ibid.

12. Ibid.

13. Ibid.

14. Ibid.

15. Ibid.

16. While the president made reference to the hardships endured by Irish immigrants, he did not mention the prejudiced feelings many Irish had toward blacks. Recent scholarship on this phenomenon includes David Roediger, *The Wages of Whiteness: Race and the Making of the American Working Class* (New York: Verso, 1991), and Noel Ignatiev, *How the Irish Became White* (New York: Routledge, 1995).

17. Shields, memorandum, 20 July 1948.

18. Ibid.

19. Ibid.

20. Thomas J. Shields to Harry L. Crane, 20 July 1948, ANOSJ.

21. Ibid.

22. Ibid.

23. Louis Twomey (1905–1969) entered the Society of Jesus in 1929 and was ordained in 1939. He arrived at Loyola in 1947 to begin the IIR, and in 1948 he was appointed regent of the law school. For those schools or colleges of a university that did not have a Jesuit as a dean, a "regent" was designated. The regent was the Jesuit presence for that school or college and functioned as the personal representative of the president (before the office of academic vice president assumed that responsibility) and possibly as chaplain as well. While this person had considerable influence in his particular school or college, he could not set policy. See John Robert Payne, "A Jesuit's Search for Social Justice: The Public Career of Louis J. Twomey, S.J., 1947–1969" (Ph.D. diss., University of Texas at Austin, 1976).

24. Shields to Crane, 20 July 1948.

25. Ibid.

26. Carmelo Graffagnini to Joseph Francis Rummel, 22 July 1948, Box 49, folder 2, JHFP.

27. Carmelo Graffagnini to Thomas J. Shields, 22 July 1948, Box 49, folder 2, JHFP.

28. Thomas J. Shields to John B. Janssens, 1 August 1948, New Orleans Province files, *Archivum Romanum Societatis Iesu* (Roman Archive of the Society of Jesus; hereafter referred to as *ARSI*). The superior general of the Society of Jesus from 1949 to 1965, John B. Janssens, should not be confused with archbishop of New Orleans Francis Janssens, who was in office from 1888 to 1897.

29. Harry L. Crane to John B. Janssens, 24 July 1948, New Orleans Province files, *ARSI*.

30. Achée served as a consultor or adviser to the provincial of the New Orleans Province.

31. Anthony J. Achée to John B. Janssens, 22 July 1948, New Orleans Province files, *ARSI*.

32. Thomas J. Shields to Joseph H. Fichter, 9 September 1948, ANOSJ. The "other officials" at Loyola were the members of the board of directors, all Jesuits. For the academic year 1948–1949, they were William D. O'Leary, S.J., William Crandell, S.J., Thomas A. Carey, S.J., and Theodore A. Ray, S.J. As previously explained, board members also served as consultors for the local religious community.

33. Ibid. Emphasis in original.

34. Ibid.

35. LUBD minutes, 24 September 1948, ALUNO.

36. Ibid.

37. Clarence Howard, a member of the Society of the Divine Word (S.V.D.), was ordained a priest in 1937. At the time of his ordination, only twenty-three black men had previously been ordained to the priesthood in the whole history of the United States. See Stephen Ochs, *Desegregating the Altar: The Josephites and the Struggle for Black Priests, 1871–1960* (Baton Rouge: Louisiana State University Press, 1990), 284–85, 292, 457.

38. Joseph H. Fichter to Clarence J. Howard, 23 February 1948; Box 1, folder 3, JHFP.

39. LUBD minutes, 23 February 1948, ALUNO.

40. Thomas J. Shields to Joseph H. Fichter, 24 February 1948; Box 1, folder 3, JHFP. Emphasis in original. The term "Ours" is a term used by a Jesuit to refer to a member of the order whether specifically or generically.

41. Shields to Fichter, 9 September 1948.

42. Ibid.

43. Joseph H. Fichter to Thomas J. Shields, 10 September 1948, Box 49, folder 2, JHFP. Emphasis in original.

44. Ibid. Emphasis in original.

45. Joseph H. Fichter to Harry L. Crane, 9 September 1948, ANOSJ.

46. Harry L. Crane to Joseph H. Fichter, 15 September 1948, ANOSJ. "Offer up" or "offer it up" was a common Catholic expression used, and notion embraced, at the time to justify one's enduring an unjust situation as in imitation of Christ.

47. Joseph H. Fichter to Thomas J. Shields, 13 September 1948, Box 1, folder 3, JHFP.

48. Ibid.

49. Joseph H. Fichter to Harry L. Crane, 5 October 1948, ANOSJ. Emphasis in original.

50. Mary Agatha, S.B.S., to Joseph Fichter, 29 November 1948, Box 49, folder 2, JHFP.

51. Joseph H. Fichter to Harry L. Crane, 27 October 1948, ANOSJ.

52. Adam Fairclough, *Race and Democracy: The Civil Rights Struggle in Louisiana, 1915–1972* (Athens: University of Georgia Press, 1995), 174.

53. Henry Montecino, S.J., interviews by author, tape recording, Grand Coteau, LA, 29 June 1997, and interview by author, handwritten notes, Grand Coteau, LA, 11 March 1999.

54. Electronic message from Gregory Choppin to the author, 23 February 2000, personal files.

55. "Solon to Tell Loyolans about 'Red' Activities," *Maroon,* 22 October 1948, 1.

56. Harry L. Crane to Joseph H. Fichter, 13 October 1948, ANOSJ.

57. "Truman Backers Capture Debate," *Maroon,* 8 October 1948, 1; "To Debate Civil Rights Wednesday Evening," *Maroon,* 15 October 1948, 4.

58. *Christian Conscience* (hereafter referred to as *CC*) 1, no. 3 (summer 1948). "What Shall You Say?," *Veritas,* 23 November 1948. Margaret Campbell most probably wrote the editorial, as she was the associate editor of *Veritas* and a member of the interracial commission during the 1948–1949 academic year.

59. SERINCO minutes , 23 September 1948, in *Annual Report of Meetings and Activities of the Louisiana Regional Inter-Racial Commission,* 11 April 1949, Box 51, folder 24, JHFP (hereafter referred to as 1949 *LORINCO* Report).

60. SERINCO minutes, 4 October 1948, in 1949 *LORINCO* Report.

61. SERINCO minutes, 6 December 1948, Box 51, folder 6, and 10 January 1949, Box 51, folder 7, JHFP.

62. SERINCO minutes, 10 January 1949, Box 51, folder 7, JHFP.

63. *Resolutions Adopted at the Fifth National Congress NFCCS,* Resolution 5C 48-10. RNFCCS. See Appendix D for full text.

64. *Resolutions Adopted at the Fifth National Congress NFCCS,* Resolution 5C 48–17. RNFCCS. See Appendix E for full text.

65. *CC* 1, no. 7 (fall 1948).

66. *CC* 1, no. 10 (fall 1948). Emphasis in original.

67. *CC* 1, nos. 2, 3, and 5 (summer 1948).

68. Clare Boothe Luce (1903–1987) was an author, playwright, ambassador, and member of Congress. In 1946 she was baptized into the Roman Catholic Church and subsequently wrote several articles about her conversion.

69. "Christian Ideals Stressed by Forum Speaker," *Maroon,* 24 September 1948, 1.

70. David R. Goldfield, *Black, White, and Southern: Race Relations and Southern Culture, 1940 to the Present* (Baton Rouge: Louisiana State University Press, 1991), 45–62.

71. Jeanne Alger, "Interracial Justice Week in Catholic Colleges," *Interracial Review* (April 1946): 58–59.

72. SERINCO minutes, 23 September 1948, and 4 October 1948, *LORINCO* Report, 11 April 1949, Box 51, folder 24, JHFP. On the day Loyola hosted the Inter-American

Day celebration, which was attended by students of the area Catholic colleges and universities including Xavier, some of the Loyola students refused to attend classes that day, while others just ignored the black students. The office of the president received numerous phone calls questioning university policy. Some callers wondered if this was the beginning of integration at Loyola, while others called to express their disapproval. Someone, displeased with the presence of black students on Loyola's campus, phoned the police reporting a disturbance. William Crandell to John B. Janssens, 22 January 1950, New Orleans Province files, *ARSI.*

73. SERINCO minutes, 20 October 1948, Box 51, folder 6, and 1 November 1949, Box 51, folder 8, JHFP.

74. "Ursuline Slates Interracial Day," *Catholic Action of the South,* 20 January 1949, 15; "NFCCS Interracial Commission to Sponsor Oratorical Contest," *Xavier Herald,* February 1949, 1; "Negro Priest to Address Students on Interracial Day," *Catholic Action of the South,* 17 February 1949, 13; "Interracial Day Observance at Ursuline Mar. 13," *Louisiana Weekly,* 26 February 1949, 11; "Interracial Day Program Observed on U.C. Campus," *U-Topia,* March 1949, 1; "Interracial Planners," *Catholic Action of the South,* 3 March 1949, 12; "Interracial Day to Be Observed," *New Orleans Item,* 4 March 1949, 11; "NFCCS to Sponsor Interracial Day; Theme, 'Spiritual Price of Prejudice,'" *Veritas,* 9 March 1949, 1; "Archbishop to Give Prizes for Interracial Day," *Catholic Action of the South,* 10 March 1949, 6; "Archbishop Rummel Endorses Interracial Day, March 13th," *Louisiana Weekly,* 12 March 1949, 1, 8.

75. Joseph Francis Rummel, "Collection: Indian and Negro Missions," pastoral letter, 24 February 1949, Joseph Francis Rummel papers (hereafter referred to as JFRP), Archives of the Archdiocese of New Orleans. When first approached for his endorsement, Rummel wrote that the "suggestion regarding the designation of this Day as Catholic Interracial Sunday throughout the Archdiocese will require some deliberation, but I am considering the matter sympathetically." Daniel Quinn to Joseph Francis Rummel, 6 January 1949, Box 49, folder 3, JHFP, and Joseph Francis Rummel to Daniel Quinn, 12 January 1949, Box 49, folder 3, JHFP.

76. *Outline for Speeches to High School Students,* n.d., Box 51, folder 18, JHFP. Peolita Begnaud and Marilyn Kingsmill of Ursuline; Margaret Campbell and Mary Cahn of Dominican; Charles Felton, Harry Alexander, and Marcel Trudeau of Xavier; and Dan Quinn, Pat Schott, and Carmelo Graffagnini of Loyola were the founding members of the speakers bureau. SERINCO minutes, Box 51, folder 21, JHFP.

77. James Impastato was president of the St. Vincent de Paul Society and a past president of the Metropolitan Council of the Holy Name Society.

78. Address by Clarence J. Howard as reported in the proceedings of the First Interracial Sunday gathering, 13 March 1949, Box 50, folder 17, JHFP.

79. Ibid.

80. Ibid.

81. Address by James Impastato as reported in the proceedings of the First Interracial Sunday gathering, 13 March 1949, Box 50, folder 17, JHFP.

82. Ibid.

83. SERINCO minutes, 7 March 1949, Box 51, folder 7, JHFP.

84. "Xavierites Win Speech, Poster Honors at Interracial Day Meet," *Xavier Herald,* March 1949, 1.

85. Doris Walker, "The Spiritual Price of Prejudice," speech delivered at the First Interracial Sunday gathering, 13 March 1949, Box 50, folder 20, JHFP.

86. Ibid.

87. "Xavier Students Win in Interracial Day Contest," *Catholic Action of the South,* 17 March 1949, 15; "Significant Gains Outlined at Impressive Catholic Interracial Day Observances Here," *Louisiana Weekly,* 19 March 1949, 3; Interracial Day Program Observed on U.C. Campus," *U-Topia,* March 1949, 1.

88. Anonymous letter to the Ursuline sisters, c. March 1949, Box 49, folder 4, JHFP. Nonstandard spelling and grammar in original.

89. Ibid. Emphasis in original.

90. Edward D. Rapier to Louis J. Twomey, 7 February 1949, Box 19, folder 3, Louis J. Twomey Papers, Special Collections and Archives, Monroe Library, Loyola University, New Orleans (hereafter referred to as LJTP).

91. LUBD minutes, 11 March 1949, ALUNO.

92. Ibid.

93. David W. Southern, "But Think of the Kids: Catholic Interracialists and the Great American Taboo of Race Mixing," *U.S. Catholic Historian* 16 (summer 1998): 67–93.

94. LUBD minutes, 11 March 1949, ALUNO.

95. Ibid.

96. Ibid.

97. Ibid.

98. Ibid.

99. Harry L. Crane to the Jesuit Community of Loyola University of the South, 18 March 1949, ANOSJ; Consultors' minutes of the New Orleans Province of the Society of Jesus (hereafter referred to as Consultors' minutes), 31 March 1949, ANOSJ .

100. Harry L. Crane to John B. Janssens, 4 June 1949, New Orleans Province files, *ARSI.*

101. Draft of policy statement "Concerning Inter-racial Relations," 17 March 1949, ANOSJ. See Appendix F for the complete draft.

102. Ibid. Emphasis added.

103. Thomas Shields to Harry L. Crane, 17 March 1949, ANOSJ.

104. Policy statement draft, 17 March 1949, ANOSJ. Emphasis in original.

105. Ibid. Emphasis in original.

106. Ibid.

107. Ibid. Emphasis in original.

108. Ibid.

109. Harry L. Crane to Thomas J. Shields, 1 April 1949, ANOSJ.

Chapter III

1. For a general review of Truman's civil rights record, see William C. Berman, *The Politics of Civil Rights in the Truman Administration* (Columbus: Ohio State University Press, 1970); Monroe Billington, "Civil Rights, President Truman and the South," *Journal of Negro History* 58 (April 1973): 127–39; Michael R. Gardner, *Harry Truman and Civil*

Rights: Moral Courage and Political Risks (Carbondale: Southern Illinois University Press, 2002); Donald R. McCoy and Richard T. Ruetten, *Quest and Response: Minority Rights and the Truman Administration* (Lawrence: University Press of Kansas, 1973).

2. Gardner, *Truman and Civil Rights,* 144–54; Gary A. Donaldson, *Truman Defeats Dewey* (Lexington: University Press of Kentucky, 1999), 205; Robert J. Donovan, *Conflict and Crisis: The Presidency of Harry S. Truman, 1945–1948* (New York: Norton, 1977; reprint, Columbia: University of Missouri Press, 1996), 347–439; Donald R. McCoy, *The Presidency of Harry S. Truman* (Lawrence: University Press of Kansas, 1984), 143–62.

3. CHR minutes, 18 December 1949, Box 47, folder 17, JHFP; CHR minutes, 16 January 1950, Box 47, folder 13, JHFP; CHR minutes, 13 February 1950, Box 47, folder 18, JHFP.

4. CHR minutes, 18 December 1949, Box 47, folder 17, JHFP; CHR minutes, 16 January 1950, Box 47, folder 13, JHFP; CHR minutes, 13 February 1950, Box 47, folder 18, JHFP.

5. Joseph H. Fichter to Thomas J. Shields, 26 November 1948, Box 49, folder 2, JHFP; Joseph H. Fichter to Lester F. X. Guterl, 26 November 1948, Box 49, folder 2, JHFP.

6. *Wolf,* 1948; *Wolf,* 1949, 220, ALUNO.

7. CHR minutes, 23 October 1949, Box 47, folder 17, JHFP; CHR minutes, 11 November 1949, Box 47, folder 13, JHFP; CHR minutes, 16 November 1949, Box 47, folder 17, JHFP.

8. CHR minutes, 27 November 1949, Box 47, folder 17, JHFP; CHR minutes, 16 January 1950, Box 47, folder 13, JHFP.

9. "Archbishop Will Sponsor Full-Scale Passion Play," *Catholic Action of the South,* 24 March 1949, 8. A sodality was a church organization (or club) that Roman Catholics belonged to for spiritual growth and development. The main activities of a sodality consisted of attending Mass together and reciting the rosary and other prayers in honor of the Blessed Virgin Mary. The Sodality Union was the umbrella organization, which included all the sodalities in the city.

10. Ray entered the New Orleans Province of the Society of Jesus in 1910, and after studying for the priesthood, he was ordained in 1925. In the 1930s he was instrumental in establishing a retreat house, Our Lady of the Oaks, in Grand Coteau, Louisiana. He also worked at Loyola University of the South from 1934 to 1937. During World War II he served as a naval chaplain, returning to Loyola in 1946 as director of student counseling. By all accounts he was very popular with the students because he was readily available for advising or talking. Regarding the race question, he favored maintaining the status quo, which was not completely surprising, since he was born and reared in Titusville, Florida.

11. "Sodalities, Schools Have Tickets for Passion Play," *Catholic Action of the South,* 31 March 1949, 9; "Passion Play to Re-Enact Church's Hallowed Pageant," *Catholic Action of the South,* 7 April 1949, 13; "Passion Play Will Open Week Run," *Maroon,* 8 April 1949, 1. The student newspapers at Xavier, Ursuline, and Dominican did not report on the play.

12. SERINCO minutes, 11 April 1949, Box 51, folder 7, JHFP.

13. Ibid. Members of the CHR also protested to Archbishop Rummel about the passion play. CHR minutes, 14 and 25 January 1953, Box 47, folder 15, JHFP.

14. Elizabeth Smith, interview by author, tape recording, New Orleans, 6 March 1999.

15. Daniel G. Quinn to Samuel H. Ray, 11 April 1949, Box 49, folder 5, JHFP.

16. Joseph Francis Rummel to Daniel G. Quinn, 14 April 1949, Box 49, folder 5, JHFP.

17. Daniel G. Quinn to Joseph Francis Rummel, 26 April 1949, Box 49, folder 5, JHFP.

18. Sam Hill Ray to Daniel Quinn, 18 April 1949, Box 49, folder 5, JHFP.

19. Thomas J. Shields to Daniel Quinn, 19 April 1949, Box 49, folder 5, JHFP.

20. Sam Hill Ray to Harry L. Crane, 20 April 1949, ANOSJ.

21. As defined in Chapter 1, Catholic Action consisted of Catholic laity working in union with the bishop to promote faith and build up the church.

22. SERINCO minutes, 7 February 1949, Box 51, folder 7, JHFP.

23. Guy Lemieux (1908–1967) entered the Society of Jesus in 1930. He was ordained a priest in 1941 and began teaching philosophy at Loyola in 1947.

24. SERINCO minutes, 7 March 1949, Box 51, folder 7, JHFP.

25. CHR minutes, 22 May 1949, Box 47, folder 16, JHFP. According to Stephen Ochs, Rummel had been asked between 1937 and 1942 to end the practice of making black parishes march at the end of the Holy Name parade. See Stephen Ochs, *Desegregating the Altar: The Josephites and the Struggle for Black Priests, 1871–1960* (Baton Rouge: Louisiana State University Press, 1990), 368.

26. "No Negroes in Holy Hour Procession, Park Rules," *Catholic Action of the South,* 22 September 1949, 1, 6; "Decision on Holy Hour March Waits Archbishop," *Catholic Action of the South,* 29 September 1949, 1, 20. Archbishop Rummel wrote City Park officials on 19 July, receiving a negative response on the 27 July, and he wrote again on 2 August. Louisiana law forbade racially mixed gatherings in hotels, circuses, and tent shows, but state law did not forbid interracial gatherings such as the one sponsored by the archdiocesan Holy Name societies.

27. "Decision on Holy Hour March Waits Archbishop," 1, 20. Caillouet wrote the third time on 4 September 1949. Park officials responded on 7 September.

28. "Decision on Holy Hour March Waits Archbishop," 1, 20. The Interracial committee for Holy Name activities was established in the spring of 1948. See "Interracial Group Formed by Holy Name Officials," *Catholic Action of the South,* 20 May 1948, 9. The black and white Holy Name societies merged into one organization in the fall of 1952.

29. CHR minutes, 25 September 1949, Box 47, folder 17, JHFP. Four days later, on 29 September 1949, a special meeting of the CHR was held. At that time Tureaud informed commission members that "it was too late to file a suit," and so no legal action was taken. CHR minutes, 29 September 1949, Box 47, folder 17, JHFP.

30. On 27 September 1949, A. P. Tureaud lodged a formal complaint with the mayor of New Orleans regarding the use of City Park. In early 1950, Tureaud, representing the National Association for the Advancement of Colored People, filed suit to desegregate City Park. Blacks gained access to the park golf course in 1952, and the park itself was desegregated in 1958. See Adam Fairclough, *Race and Democracy: The Civil Rights Struggle in Louisiana, 1915–1972* (Athens: University of Georgia Press, 1995), 111, 152, 219; and Edward F. Haas, *DeLesseps S. Morrison and the Image of Reform: New Orleans Politics, 1946–1961* (Baton Rouge: Louisiana State University Press, 1974), 74–75, 255–56.

31. "Holy Hour Is Cancelled Because of Segregation," *Times-Picayune,* 2 October 1949, 1, 6; "Cancel Holy Hour over Segregation," *New Orleans Item,* 3 October 1949, 3.

32. "Holy Hour Is Cancelled"; "Cancel Holy Hour"; "Catholics Refuse to Bow to City Park Bias," *Louisiana Weekly,* 8 October 1949, 1, 2.

33. Commission on Human Rights to Joseph Francis Rummel, dated "Feast of the Holy Rosary" [7 October 1949], Box 46, folder 11, JHFP; Commission on Human Rights to Clarence P. Thomas, 30 September 1949, Box 45, folder 6, JHFP; Commission on Human Rights to Elliot Sheehan, 30 September 1949, Box 45, folder 6, JHFP.

34. Joseph Francis Rummel to Commission on Human Rights, 25 October 1949, Box 45, folder 6, JHFP.

35. Clarence P. Thomas to Commission on Human Rights, 14 October 1949, Box 45, folder 6, JHFP.

36. "Catholic Church's Stance on Segregation," *Louisiana Weekly,* 15 October 1949, 14.

37. CHR minutes, 24 September 1952, Box 47, folder 14, JHFP; CHR minutes, 28 September 1952, Box 48, folder 1, JHFP; CHR minutes, 14 November 1952, Box 48, folder 1, JHFP; "2 Archdiocesan HN Units Will Merge," *Catholic Action of the South,* 6 November 1952, 1, 7.

38. Joseph H. Fichter, sermon at Mater Dolorosa Church, 2 October 1949, Sermons, 1948–50, Box 65, folder 16, JHFP.

39. Ibid.

40. Ibid.

41. William Crandell to John B. Janssens, 22 January 1950, New Orleans Province files, *ARSI.*

42. Personnel file, Office of the President Series, XUA. One year after her presentation, Mugrauer founded a local chapter of Caritas, a lay women's organization dedicated to living and working among the materially poor. In many respects, her talk to the interracial group was an outline of the lifestyle and work she wanted to undertake. Jeanette White, "Caritas, Founded by Dr. Mugrauer, Is Dynamic Catholic Action Group," *Xavier Herald,* November 1953, 7.

43. The previous summer, Tureaud filed the suit *Rosana Aubert* v. *Orleans Parish School Board* in United States Federal District Court for the Eastern District of Louisiana to demand equal educational facilities for black students. See Liva Baker, *The Second Battle of New Orleans: The Hundred-Year Struggle to Integrate the Schools* (New York: HarperCollins, 1996), 154–58, 168–70, 176; Juliette Landphair, "Sewerage, Sidewalks, and Schools: The New Orleans Ninth Ward and Public School Desegregation," *Louisiana History* 40 (winter 1999): 35–62.

44. SERINCO minutes, 30 June 1949, Box 51, folder 7, JHFP.

45. Ibid.

46. The Knights of Columbus were often accused of being a racist organization in part because of the blackball system they employed for rejecting potential members; until 1963, it took only five negative votes to reject a prospective candidate. Very few blacks gained entrance into the organization under this system. In 1964 the Knights rewrote their admissions rules and regulations so that one-third of the membership had to vote for the rejection of a candidate in order to exclude; even with this change, blacks were still being rejected. In the 1970s the voting regulations changed again: rejection of a candidate required a negative vote by a majority of the members. See Christopher Kauffman, *Faith and Fraternalism: The History of the Knights of Columbus, 1882–1982* (New York: Harper and Row, 1982), 396–401.

47. SERINCO minutes, 22 July 1949, Box 51, folder 8, JHFP.

48. St. Augustine's was administered by members of the Society of the Divine Word (S.V.D.). For a thorough history of the efforts to have black Catholics ordained priests in the Roman Catholic Church, see Stephen Ochs, *Desegregating the Altar*.

49. SERINCO minutes, 22 July 1949, Box 51, folder 8, JHFP.

50. "Former Editor of 'AMERICA' Talks to Loyola Groups," *Maroon*, 29 April 1949, 1; "Father LaFarge Talks to CCS Race Unit," *Catholic Action of the South*, 5 May 1949, 17; SERINCO minutes, 25 April 1949, Box 51, folder 7, JHFP.

51. Percy A. Roy (1889–1949), entered the Society of Jesus in 1908 and was ordained a priest in 1922. He served as the superior of the Jesuit community at Loyola and president of the university during the wars years, 1939 to 1945.

52. LUBD minutes, 16 June 1942, ALUNO.

53. Harry Alexander, interview by author, tape recording, Washington, D C, 2 January 1999.

54. "Xavier Graduates Enter Georgetown and St. Louis," *Xavier Herald*, July 1949, 1.

55. See Chapter 2, note 23, for a full explanation of the role of a regent.

56. Louis Twomey to Vincent McCormick, 18 September 1951, Box 19, folder 8, LJTP. Though written in 1951, Twomey's letter recounts the 1949 law school situation and the actions of the Loyola board of directors.

57. Ibid. The "Assistancy" to which Twomey refers is a regional administrative division of the Society of Jesus, comprising several provinces. In this case, the "American Assistancy" (now referred to as the "United States Assistancy") comprises all the Jesuit provinces in the United States. In 1951 there were eight provinces in the American Assistancy.

58. The consultors/board of directors during the 1948–1949 academic year were William O'Leary, S.J., Theodore Ray, S.J., William Crandell, S.J., and Thomas Carey, S.J.

59. Twomey to McCormick, 18 September 1951.

60. Ibid.

61. Louis J. Twomey to Francis E. Lucey, 9 June 1949, Box 19, folder 3, LJTP.

62. Ibid.

63. Francis E. Lucey to Louis J. Twomey, 26 July 1949, Box 19, folder 3, LJTP.

Chapter IV

1. Harry S. Ashmore, *Civil Rights and Wrongs: A Memoir of Race and Politics, 1944–1996*, rev. ed. (Columbia: University of South Carolina Press, 1997); William M. Boyd, "Southern Politics, 1948–1952," *Phylon Quarterly* 13 (3d quarter 1952): 226–35; Douglas J. Ficker, "From *Roberts* to *Plessy:* Educational Segregation and the 'Separate but Equal' Doctrine," *Journal of Negro History* 84 (autumn 1999): 301–14; Whitting B. Johnson, "The Vinson Court and Racial Segregation, 1946–1953," *Journal of Negro History* 63 (July 1978): 220–30.

2. Donald F. Crosby, *God, Church, and Flag: Senator Joseph R. McCarthy and the Catholic Church, 1950–1957* (Chapel Hill: University of North Carolina Press, 1978); Richard Fried, *Nightmare in Red: The McCarthy Era in Perspective* (New York: Oxford

University Press, 1990); Robert Griffith, *The Politics of Fear: Joseph McCarthy and the Senate,* 2d ed. (Amherst: University of Massachusetts Press, 1987); Arnold A. Offner, *Another Such Victory: President Truman and the Cold War, 1945–1953* (Stanford: Stanford University Press, 2002); Michael E. Parrish, "Cold War Justice: The Supreme Court and the Rosenbergs," *American Historical Review* 82 (October 1977): 805–42; James T. Patterson, *Grand Expectations: The United States, 1945–1974* (New York: Oxford University Press, 1996); Stephen Whitfield, *The Culture of the Cold War* (Baltimore: Johns Hopkins University Press, 1991).

3. Dorothy Blatnica, *At the Altar of Their God: African Americans in Cleveland, 1922–1961* (New York: Garland, 1995); James Hennesey, *America Catholics: A History of the Roman Catholic Community in the United States* (New York: Oxford University Press, 1981); Peter C. Kent, *The Lonely Cold War of Pope Pius XII: The Roman Catholic Church and the Division of Europe, 1943–1950* (Montreal: McGill-Queen's University Press, 2002); Jonathan Luxmoore and Jolanta Babiuch, *The Vatican and the Red Flag: The Struggle for the Soul of Eastern Europe* (New York: G. Chapman, 1999); John T. McGreevy, *Parish Boundaries: The Catholic Encounter with Race in the Twentieth-Century Urban North* (Chicago: University of Chicago Press, 1996); Eileen M. McMahon, *What Parish Are You From?: A Chicago Irish Community and Race Relations* (Lexington: University Press of Kentucky, 1995); Joseph Mindszenty, *Memoirs,* trans. Richard Winston and Clara Winston (New York: Macmillan, 1974); David W. Southern, *John LaFarge and the Limits of Catholic Interracialism, 1911–1963* (Baton Rouge: Louisiana State University Press, 1996).

4. SERINCO minutes, 3 October 1949, Box 51, folder 8, JHFP. For an explanation of the role of a "regent," see Chapter 2, note 23.

5. The Holy Name Society was established in 1564 in Europe as a way of honoring the name of God. This devotion was exported with European settlers to the New World and eventually took hold in Louisiana.

6. J. W. Mason to Joan Forshag, 21 October 1949, Box 49, folder 7, JHFP.

7. SERINCO minutes, 1 November 1949, Box 51, folder 8, JHFP.

8. Ibid.

9. SERINCO minutes, 13 November 1949, Box 51, folder 8, JHFP; "NFCCS Schedules Congress Nov. 13th," *U-Topia,* October 1949, 1; "NFCCS in Regional Meet at XU Sunday," *Catholic Action of the South,* 10 November 1950, 2; "Southern Region of NFCCS Holds First Annual Congress," *Veritas,* 18 November 1950, 4; "X.U. Hosts First Regional NFCCS Congress Nov. 13," *Xavier Herald,* November 1949, 5, 6; "NFCCS Group Holds Congress at Xavier University," *Maroon,* 2 December 1949, 2.

10. "Resolution of the First Annual Congress of the New Orleans Region of the National Federation of Catholic College Students," SERINCO minutes, 13 November 1949, Box 51, folder 8, JHFP. See Appendix G for the complete text.

11. Ibid.

12. Ibid.

13. SERINCO minutes, 13 November 1949, Box 51, folder 8, JHFP.

14. SERINCO Report, September 15–November 15, 1949, Box 49, folder 7, JHFP; SERINCO Report, November 16, 1949–January 15, 1950, Box 51, folder 9, JHFP.

15. SERINCO minutes, 29 January 1950, Box 51, folder 9, JHFP; "Slate Second

Interracial Day," *Catholic Action of the South,* 26 January 1950, 14; "Inter-racial Day Set for March 12 in Grand Coteau," *Maroon,* 10 February 1950, 1; "Xavier Joins Interracial Day," *New Orleans Item,* 8 March 1950, 11; "Students Set Program for 2nd Interracial Day," *Catholic Action of the South,* 9 March 1950, 22; "Inter-Racial Day Slated for Sunday," *New Orleans Item,* 9 March 1950, 9; "Fr. Guterl to open Grand Coteau Meet," *Maroon,* 10 March 1950, 4; "Interracial Day XU Student in Speech Contest," *Louisiana Weekly,* 11 March 1950, 3.

16. "Bishop Jeanmard Presides at Second Interracial Day," *Catholic Action,* 16 March 1950, 24; "Fifty Loyolans Attend Second Interracial Day," *Maroon,* 17 March 1950, 4; "Students Urged to Hasten Day of Brotherhood," *Louisiana Weekly,* 18 March 1950, 1, 3; "Xavierite Wins Interracial Day Speech Cup," *Xavier Herald,* March 1950, 1, 8; "Campus Briefs," *U-Topia,* April 1950, 4.

17. "Catholics Hold Interracial Day," *Louisiana Weekly,* 25 March 1950, 10.

18. "Extract of Diocesan Synod, Archdiocese of New Orleans, 1950," Box 47, folder 18, JHFP. Emphasis in original.

19. Ibid.

20. SERINCO minutes, 10 and 21 May 1950, Box 51, folder 9, JHFP.

21. Anna May Kingsmill, Betty Prillmayer, and Rosemary Wingrave represented St. Mary's Dominican College, and Doris Walker, Norman Francis, Larry Brown, and Richard Gumbel were Xavier delegates. "Xavierite Richard Gumbel Is Named to NFCCS Post," *Xavier Herald,* May 1950, 2.

22. Betty Prillmayer Krebs, interview by author, tape recording, New Orleans, 16 March 1999.

23. "Xavierite Richard Gumbel Is Named to NFCCS Post," 2.

24. CHR minutes, 6 July 1950, Box 47, folder 18, JHFP.

25. For LSU law school desegregation, see Liva Baker, *The Second Battle of New Orleans: The Hundred-Year Struggle to Integrate the Schools* (New York: HarperCollins, 1996), 124–37; for Du Bois, see David L. Lewis, *W. E. B. Du Bois,* vol. 1, *Biography of a Race, 1868–1919* (New York: Henry Holt, 1993); for the Korean War, Richard Whelan, *Drawing the Line: The Korean War, 1950–1953* (Boston: Little, Brown, 1990).

26. Thomas J. Shields to John B. Janssens, 17 July 1950, New Orleans Province files, *ARSI.*

27. Thomas J. Shields to John B. Janssens, 12 October 1950, New Orleans Province files, *ARSI.* In *One-Man Research* Fichter wrote, "The first Negro students, 'officially' registered to obtain academic credits, were two religious Sisters of the Holy Family, who began taking Saturday courses at Loyola in September 1951." Joseph H. Fichter, *One-Man Research: Reminiscences of a Catholic Sociologist* (New York: John Wiley and Sons, 1973), 113, n. 3. In *The Sociology of Good Works* he stated, "In August 1951, the trustees of Loyola University took the first timid step toward the racial desegregation of the student body by authorizing a number of tuition-free scholarships to the Sisters of the Holy Family. President Thomas Shields asked me to visit the Mother Provincial and arrange for two of her sisters to take up the offer." Joseph H. Fichter, *The Sociology of Good Works: Research in Catholic America* (Chicago: Loyola University Press, 1993), 95. Given that Thomas Shields and Andrew Smith both wrote their Jesuit superior Rome in the fall of 1950 concerning the admission of the Holy Family Sisters, Fichter must have confused the

dates by one year. See Thomas J. Shields to John B. Janssens, 12 October 1950, New Orleans Province files, *ARSI;* Andrew C. Smith to John B. Janssens, 29 December 1950, New Orleans Province files, *ARSI.*

28. Shields to Janssens, 12 October 1950.

29. CHR minutes, 17 December 1950, Box 47, folder 19, JHFP. Louis Twomey, director of the IIR, confirmed the difficulties when he spoke to members of the CHR in January 1951 (see CHR minutes, 16 January 1951, Box 47, folder 19, JHFP).

30. Recall that a consultor was an advisor to a Jesuit superior. At the time he was writing, Smith was a consultor to the provincial—also known as a province consultor.

31. Andrew C. Smith to John B. Janssens, 29 December 1950, New Orleans Province files, *ARSI.* Emphasis in original.

32. Joseph H. Reising, S.J., interview by author, written notes, 22 April 1999, New Orleans. Reising was one of Crandell's nephews.

33. William Crandell to John B. Janssens, 22 January 1950, New Orleans Province files, *ARSI.*

34. Ibid.

35. Ibid.

36. "Southern Collegians Resist Racism," *Catholic World* (December 1950): 180–85.

37. Ibid., 181–82. The use of the term "social sin" at this time is significant because Catholics were not used to speaking about sinful behavior in such a manner. Sin, for Catholics, was personal, individual. To determine if a situation was sinful, one had to take into consideration the person, the act, and the intention. The notion of "social sin" brought the actions of a community into question. Evaluating such behavior would be more difficult.

38. Ibid.

39. Sam Hill Ray to William Crandell, 28 December 1950, ANOSJ.

40. Sam Hill Ray to William Crandell, n.d. [c. November–December 1950], ANOSJ.

41. Ibid.

42. SERINCO minutes, 10 January 1951, Box 51, folder 10, JHFP.

43. Edward Kammerer to Dawn Proteau, 8 November 1951, Box 49, folder 18, JHFP.

44. For student attendance, see SERINCO minutes, 1948–1956, JHFP.

45. James A. McInerney, O.P., to Mother Mary Dominic, O.P., 9 May 1953, Archives of the Dominican Congregation of St. Mary, Dominican Center, New Orleans (hereafter referred to as DSA).

46. William O'Leary, S.J., began serving as regent of the dental school during the 1947-1948 academic year, having been president of Spring Hill College in Mobile, Alabama, from 1938 to 1946. The consultors/board members of the university for the 1950–1951 academic year were O'Leary, Theodore Ray, S.J., George Bergen, S.J., and John Fuss, S.J.

47. William D. O'Leary to William Crandell, 2 January 1951, ANOSJ.

48. George T. Bergen to William Crandell, 5 January 1951, ANOSJ.

49. John J. Fuss to William Crandell, 4 January 1951, ANOSJ.

50. Sam Hill Ray to William Crandell, 6 February 1951, ANOSJ.

51. Ibid. For a definition of a "sodality" see Chapter 3, note 9. Lack of capitalization in original.

52. Maurice Rousseve, S.V.D., was ordained in 1934 along with five other black seminarians. Their class brought the total number of black priests ordained in the United States since 1854 to twenty-one. For statistics concerning black priests, see Stephen Ochs, *Desegregating the Altar: The Josephites and the Struggle for Black Priests, 1871–1960* (Baton Rouge: Louisiana State University Press, 1990), 456–58.

53. "Interracial Day at Loyola Feb. 18," *Catholic Action of the South,* 11 January 1951, 8; "Interracial Day," *Xavier Herald,* January 1951 2; "Ogilvie to Talk at N.O. Students' Interracial Day," *Catholic Action of the South,* 1 February 1951, 14; "Interracial Day to Tackle Problem of 'Jim Crow,'" *Catholic Action of the South,* 15 February 1951, 4; "Interracial Day Subject of Meet," *Catholic Action of the South,* 15 February 1951, 6; "Third Annual Interracial Day Planned Here," *Maroon,* 16 February 1951, 1; "Students Seek to End Discrimination," *Xavier Herald,* February 1951, 1; "SERINCO Meeting Held," *U-Topia,* February-March 1951, 1, 4; "Students Seek End to Discrimination," *New Orleans States,* 19 February 1951, 10.

54. Norman Francis, "Interracial Day," prepared text, Box 50, folder 18, JHFP.

55. Benjamin J. Johnson, speech delivered third annual Interracial Sunday, 18 February 1951, Box 50, folder 16, JHFP. Portions of Johnson's speech were reprinted in "Catholics Level New Blows at Bias: Segregation within Church Is Hit Hard by Speakers at Annual Interracial Meeting," *Louisiana Weekly,* 24 February 1951.

56. Ibid.

57. Philip Ogilvie, speech to third annual Interracial Sunday, 18 February 1951, Box 50, folder 16, JHFP. Portions of Ogilvie's talk were reprinted in "Catholics Level New Blows at Bias."

58. Sam Hill Ray, memorandum, 13 March 1951, ANOSJ.

59. Thomas J. Shields to William Crandell, 13 March 1951, ANOSJ. In his letter to the provincial, Shields wrote, "When you were here for visitation, the question of Fr. [Franklin] Lynette's 'Catholic Action Group' was agitated and I told him it was not approved, so he dropped said organization. I recently discovered that there is another group forming on the campus which organization is known as Catholic Youth Society. This has no approval, and Fr. Lynette will be informed that it is to be dropped. I had a visit from Fathers [Sam Hill] Ray and [Elmo J.] Rogero concerning the threat to the Sodality by such organizations and have informed Father Ray that he is authorized to tell the Prefects [faculty moderators] of the Sodality that any one belonging to the N.F.C.C.S., the so-called Catholic Action Group, or the Catholic Youth Society will be dropped from the Sodality." Ray was not only annoyed that the "Catholic Action Group" sponsored a Day of Recollection (a day of spiritual reflection) without his permission, but he was also displeased that it was interracial in composition, as he reported to the president. Shields relayed this information to Crandell stating, "I understand from Fr. Ray that those making the Day of Recollection consisted of both Blacks and Whites but I have not been able to check on the accuracy of this except for the fact that I did see Fr. Fichter with three Negroes on that day."

60. Sam Hill Ray to Thomas J. Shields, 9 March 1951, ANOSJ; Thomas J. Shields to William Crandell, 13 March 1951, ANOSJ.

61. Joseph H. Fichter to William Crandell, 16 March 1951, ANOSJ; Joseph H. Fichter to John B. Janssens, 6 March 1951, New Orleans Province files, *ARSI.*

62. Thomas J. Shields to Sam Hill Ray, 16 March 1951 (1), ANOSJ. Shields sent Ray two letters dated 16 March 1951. The one cited here is the longer of the two, in which Shields chastised Ray for publishing the directive concerning the removal of students from their respective sodalities.

63. Thomas J. Shields to Sam Hill Ray, 16 March 1951 (2), ANOSJ. This 16 March 1951 letter is the shorter letter, which directed Ray not to "molest any student who is a member of the N.F.C.C.S."

64. Sam Hill Ray to William Crandell, 1 May 1951, ANOSJ.

65. Sam Hill Ray to William Crandell, 28 July 1951, ANOSJ

66. Blanche Mouledoux, "NFCCS Offers Puzzle to Student Members," *Maroon,* 2 March 1951, 2; Norris Fitzmorris, "The Mystery," *Maroon,* 7 November 1952, 4. The following fall Mary Truxillo of Dominican College wrote a signed editorial encouraging club presidents to take advantage of the benefits of the NFCCS whether the problem dealt with organization and planning or projects and activities. The national federation was viewed as a positive force on her campus. See "NFCCS: Club Tonic," *Veritas,* 31 October 1953, 2.

67. Anthony C. O'Flynn to Joseph H. Fichter, 29 September 1951, Box 49, folder 18, JHFP.

68. Ibid.

69. Rev. James F. Benedict, memorandum 28 January 1952, Box 49, folder 19, JHFP. In January 1952, SERINCO chairman Ed Kammerer paid Tulane University's Newman Club (i.e., Catholic club) forty dollars for printing 10,000 copies of the *Christian Conscience.*

70. Charles S. Palazzolo to Mary Columba, O.S.U., 13 January 1953, Box 49, folder 23, JHFP.

71. Mary Agatha Ryan to Thomas J. Shields, 31 May 1951, XUA.

72. Ibid. Emphasis in original.

73. Ibid.

74. Antonio Papale to Richard Gumbel, 7 June 1951, XUA.

75. Richard Gumbel, Jr., to Thomas Shields, 21 June 1951, ANOSJ. In February 1951 Gumbel attended a national conference on discrimination in higher education, sponsored by the American Council on Education and held in Earlham, Indiana. Its purpose was "to enable student leaders to study the problems of discrimination in higher education, and to encourage and promote the equalization and expansion of opportunities for all persons to share in the experience of higher education without restriction beyond that of individual capacity." Richard B. Anliot to Richard Gumbel, 22 February 1951, XUA. I would like to thank Greg and Bryant Gumbel for granting permission to use their father's correspondence.

76. Ibid.

77. For a discussion of the Louisiana case, *Wilson v. Board of Supervisors* (1951), see Baker, *Second Battle of New Orleans,* 127–38, and Adam Fairclough, *Race and Democracy: The Civil Rights Struggle in Louisiana, 1915–1972* (Athens: University of Georgia Press, 1995), 154–55. For the Oklahoma cases, George L. Cross, *Blacks in White Colleges: Oklahoma's Landmark Cases* (Norman: University of Oklahoma Press, 1975), and Robert M.

Sawyer, "The Gaines Case: Its Background and Influence on the University of Missouri and Lincoln University 1936–1950," (Ph.D. diss., University of Missouri, 1966). For the Texas case, see Amilcar Shabazz, *Advancing Democracy: African Americans and the Struggle for Access and Equity in Higher Education in Texas* (Chapel Hill: University of North Carolina Press, 2004).

78. Gumbel to Shields, 21 June 1951.

79. Ibid.

80. Thomas Shields to Richard Gumbel, Jr., 25 June 1951, ANOSJ. Emphasis in original.

81. Ibid. Even though Shields had enacted token integration, law school regent Louis Twomey believed that the president failed to move forward on Gumbel's application because of the influence of the Jesuit provincial, William Crandell. "The Provincial's mind," Twomey wrote a Jesuit official in Rome, "seems to be that Loyola should receive Negroes only after it has been made safe to do so by their [blacks] also being received by Tulane University in New Orleans and Louisiana State University in Baton Rouge. In other words, and this I believe fairly reflects the Provincial's view, Loyola should not act in this regard as long as there is risk, but that when the risk has been removed, we should go ahead." Louis Twomey to Andrew McCormick, 18 September 1951, Box 19, folder 8, LJTP.

82. Shields to Gumbel, 25 June 1951.

83. Ibid.

84. In the summer of 1951, Shields asked permission of his Jesuit superiors to allow women into Loyola University's premedical, predental, prelegal, and journalism programs. The problem with such a request was that Ursuline College and Dominican College both offered courses in these same fields of study, and therefore the Jesuits would be competing with the Ursulines and Dominicans for a limited number of students. Ill will had been generated over this issue in years past; not wishing to reopen old wounds, the Jesuits denied his request. Thomas J. Shields to William Crandell, 27 July 1951, ANOSJ; Consultors' minutes of the New Orleans Province of the Society of Jesus, 30 August 1951, ANOSJ, and William Crandell to Thomas J. Shields, 1 September 1951, ANOSJ.

85. Shields to Gumbel, 25 June 1951. Despite this gender inequality, Jesuit officials did not allow Loyola University to change its policy. St. Mary's Dominican College gained accreditation in 1949, thus remedying the situation. Crandell to Shields, 1 September 1951.

86. Thomas J. Shields to John B. Janssens, 17 July 1950, New Orleans Province files, *ARSI.*

87. Francis Lucey to Louis Twomey, 15 June 1951, Box 2, folder 2, LJTP.

88. *Who's Who In The Midwest,* 9th ed., s.v. "Richard Dunbar Gumbel, Jr."

89. "Interracial Contest Here March 9," *Xavier Herald,* February 1952, 1; "Archbishop Urges Laity to Back Interracial Day," *Catholic Action of the South,* 6 March 1952, 2; "Catholic University Students to Observe 4th Inter-racial Sunday, March 9, at Xavier U," *Louisiana Weekly,* 8 March 1952, 1, 6.

90. Joyce LaBorde, "All The Same in Christ," speech delivered at the fourth annual Interracial Sunday gathering, 9 March 1952, Box 50, folder 16, JHFP.

91. "Archbishop Hits Race Prejudices," *Times-Picayune,* 10 March 1952, 7; "400 Collegians Challenged to Break Race Prejudice," *Catholic Action of the South,* 13 March 1952, 7; "'Truth, Love Demand No Iron Curtain between Races'—Archbishop Rummel,"

Louisiana Weekly, 15 March 1952, 1, 6; "Archbishop Declares No 'Curtain' between the Races," *Xavier Herald,* March 1952, 1, 8; "Interracial Day Trophy Awarded," *Catholic Action of the South,* 27 March 1952, 13.

92. "A Heart Warming Occasion," *Louisiana Weekly,* 29 March 1952, 6-b.

Chapter V

1. Louis J. Twomey to Patrick Donnelly, 1 June 1952, Box 19, folder 10, LJTP.

2. Quoted in Michael Cardozo, "Racial Discrimination in Legal Schools, 1950–1963," *Journal of Legal Education* 43 (March 1993): 79–84.

3. Patrick Donnelly, S.J., was born in August, Georgia, in 1908. He entered the Jesuits in 1927 and, after studying for the priesthood, was ordained a priest in 1940. Shields had to step down as president when his term of office as rector ended.

4. Patrick Donnelly, "World Citizenship and the Unfinished Business of Democracy," Address of the President of Spring Hill College, Commencement Exercises, Mobile, Alabama, 25 May 1948, ANOSJ.

5. Twomey to Donnelly, 1 June 1952.

6. Louis Twomey to Vincent McCormick, 18 September 1951, Box 19, folder 8, LJTP.

7. For a more complete discussion of this issue, see R. Bentley Anderson, "Black, White, and Catholic: Southern Jesuits Confront the Race Question, 1952," *Catholic Historical Review* 91 (July 2005): 484–505.

8. William Crandell to Jesuit Community, Loyola University, 2 March 1951, ANOSJ. At a province consultors' meeting in May 1951, Crandell asked his advisors if they "thought the time [was] ripe for a meeting of Superiors and other interested Jesuits for the purpose of working out a province policy on the Negro question." Consultors' minutes, 22 May 1951, ANOSJ. The following month the issue was revisited. Again Crandell asked whether "he should try to get the superiors together the 15th of August to try to determine some policy." Some of the consultors wanted to wait till Christmas of 1951 or even the following year. "All agreed," however, "that a carefully arranged program would have to [be] thought out before the meeting in order to accomplish something constructive." Consultors' minutes, 18 June 1951, ANOSJ.

9. William Crandell to John B. Janssens, 20 November 1951, New Orleans Province files, *ARSI.*

10. Ibid.

11. William Crandell to Patrick Donnelly, 5 January 1952, ANOSJ; Consultors' minutes, 11 February 1952, ANOSJ.

12. Consultors' minutes, 3 July 1952, ANOSJ.

13. "Minutes of the Province Meeting on Interracial Relations, 28–29 August 1952," ANOSJ.

14. "Minutes of the Province Meeting," emphasis in original. In the promulgated version, the document states that racial segregation is "morally" rather than intrinsically evil. For further explanation see, Anderson, "Black, White, and Catholic, 1952."

15. "Minutes of the Province Meeting." Complete desegregation of Loyola University of the South did not result, because the Grand Coteau delegates decided not to accept black applicants into any of Loyola's academic programs that were already offered by

Xavier University. The concern was Xavier's viability and not the continuation of segregation. This decision would be considered by some to be a compromise and equivocation of principles.

16. Ibid.

17. LUBD minutes, 6 September 1952, ALUNO.

18. For an account of McLaurin's experience, see George L. Cross, *Blacks in White Colleges: Oklahoma's Landmark Cases* (Norman: University of Oklahoma Press, 1975).

19. Robert A. Leflar to Antonio E. Papale, 21 August 1951, Box 19, folder 10, LJTP.

20. Michael O'Keefe, interview by author, tape recording, New Orleans, 13 June 1996. The grandson of a former mayor of New Orleans and a son of former state senator, Michael O'Keefe was first elected to the Louisiana state senate in 1959 and served until 1984; he was president of the senate from 1972 to 1984.

21. "Freshmen Week Is Set at Loyola," *Times-Picayune–New Orleans States,* 21 September 1952, 4. (The two papers were combined for Sunday editions.)

22. "Loyola Gives 24 Degrees in Law," *Times-Picayune,* 1 October 1952, 5. Because of the Korean conflict, university courses were offered year-round. Law school students finished their degree work in the summer, and commencement was held in the early fall.

23. "Loyola to Confer Degrees of Law," *Times-Picayune,* 3 October 1952, 29.

24. "Law Graduates Hear Fr. Sheen," *Times-Picayune-New Orleans States,* 5 October 1952, 28.

25. Norman Francis, interview by author, tape recording, New Orleans, 13 June 1996. Maurice "Moon" Landrieu later became mayor of New Orleans, secretary of Housing and Urban Development, and father of United States Senator Mary Landrieu (D-LA).

26. O'Keefe interview.

27. Francis interview, June 1996.

28. Norman Francis, interview by author, tape recording, New Orleans, 26 March 1998.

29. Robert Shea to Louis Twomey, 7 October 1952, Box 19, folder 11, LJTP.

30. Richard Gumbel to Louis Twomey, 13 September 1952, Box 19, folder 10, LJTP.

31. Ibid.

32. Ibid.

33. Harry Alexander to Louis J. Twomey, 1 February 1953, Box 19, folder 11, LJTP; Louis J. Twomey to Harry Alexander, 24 February 1953, Box 19, folder 11, LJTP.

34. Hugh St. Paul to William Crandell, 5 November 1952, ANOSJ.

35. Ibid. Emphasis in original.

36. Patrick Donnelly to John B. Janssens, 11 February 1953, New Orleans Province files, *ARSI.* In his letter Donnelly stated, "The policy of integrating Negroes into the University should be continued and extended to other schools of the University. Next year we would like to admit two to the School of Dentistry, if Fr. Provincial will give his permission."

37. Consultors' minutes, 28 March 1953, ALUNO.

38. Ernest Boykins, interview by author, tape recording, Hattiesburg, MS, 10 December 1998. In a human interest story published early in his college career, Boykins expressed interest in becoming a dentist. See "Familiar Faces," *Xavier Herald,* March 1951, 10.

39. William D. O'Leary to Ernest A. Boykins, 27 April 1953, Box: Office of the President Series, folder: Loyola University 1951–53, XUA.

40. Boykins interview. He did, however, continue his studies, receiving his master's degree in biology from Texas Southern University in 1958 and his doctorate in zoology from Michigan State University in 1964. He taught at Alcorn College from 1956 until 1971, when he was appointed president of Mississippi Valley University. He served in that position from 1971 to 1981. Boykins was the second Xavier graduate to become a university president.

41. LUBD minutes, 3 May 1953, ALUNO.

42. Consultors' minutes, 3 May 1953, ANOSJ.

43. William O'Leary to William Crandell, 10 July 1953, ANOSJ.

44. LUBD minutes, 3 May 1953, ALUNO.

45. College Journal entry of 14 September 1953, Series IV: St. Louis Province, E) Grand Coteau, 3) Ministry: College, College Journal 1939–1956, National Archives of the Society of the Sacred Heart (hereafter referred to as ARSCJ-College). Also mentioned in the Sisters' House Journal: "To date we accepted students, seven of whom are day students. Among them is our first colored student." Minutes of the House Council, 9 September 1953, Series IV: St. Louis Province, E) Grand Coteau, 1) Community, A) History, Box 2, House Journals: 1941–1953 (hereafter referred to as ARSCJ-House).

46. College Journal, 10 October 1953, ARSCJ-College. Also mentioned in the Sisters' House Journal: "Saturday [October 10]—Meeting of the Alumnae. The schedule will be the same as last year. . . . The Question of the presence of Negroes in the College will be answered at the beginning of the meeting by Rev. Mother," Minutes of the House Council, October 5, 1953, ARSCJ-House.

47. Minutes, 14 October 1953, ARSCJ-House.

48. Minutes, 9 January 1949, ARSCJ-House.

49. Minutes, 6 December 1949, ARSCJ-House.

50. Minutes, 2 May 1950, ARSCJ-House.

51. Minutes, 27 February 1951, ARSCJ-House.

52. Minutes, 26 October 1953, 2 November 1953, and 25 January 1954, ARSCJ-House.

53. Minutes, 2 August 1954, ARSCJ-House.

Chapter VI

1. For a look at the 1950s, see Pete Daniel, *Lost Revolutions: The South in the 1950s* (Chapel Hill: University of North Carolina Press for Smithsonian National Museum of American History, Washington, D.C., 2000); David Halberstam, *The Fifties* (New York : Villard Books, 1993); J. Ronald Oakley, *God's Country: America in the Fifties* (New York: Dembner Books, 1986); James T. Patterson, *Great Expectations: The United States, 1945–1974* (New York: Oxford University Press, 1996).

2. Stephen E. Ambrose, *Eisenhower* (New York: Simon and Schuster, 1984); Numan V. Bartley, *The New South, 1945–1980* (Baton Rouge: Louisiana State University Press, 1995); Stuart G. Brown *Conscience in Politics: Adlai Stevenson in the 1950s* (Syracuse: Syracuse University Press, 1961); Kenneth S. Davis, *The Politics of Honor: A Biography of Adlai E. Stevenson* (New York: Putnam's Sons, 1967); L. Vaughan Howard and David R.

Deener, *Presidential Politics in Louisiana, 1952* Tulane Studies in Political Science, vol. 1 (New Orleans: Tulane University, 1954).

3. For an overview of this period, see William Berman, *The Politics of Civil Rights in the Truman Administration* (Columbus: Ohio State University Press, 1970); Richard Kluger, *Simple Justice: The History of Brown v. Board of Education and Black America's Struggle for Equality* (New York: Knopf, 1976); Robert Fredrick Burk, *The Eisenhower Administration and Black Civil Rights* (Knoxville: University of Tennessee Press, 1984); Taylor Branch, *Parting the Waters: America in the King Years, 1954–1963* (New York: Simon and Schuster, 1988).

4. Liva Baker, *The Second Battle of New Orleans: The Hundred-Year Struggle to Integrate the Schools* (New York: HarperCollins, 1996), 225, 274–76; Jay Dolan, *The American Catholic Experience: A History from Colonial Times to the Present* (Garden City, NY: Doubleday, 1985; reprint, Notre Dame: University of Notre Dame Press, 1992), 371; Adam Fairclough, *Race and Democracy: The Civil Rights Struggle in Louisiana, 1915–1972* (Athens: University of Georgia Press, 1995), 151–53,158–63, 193; Edward F. Haas, *DeLesseps S. Morrison and the Image of Reform: New Orleans Politics, 1946–1961* (Baton Rouge: Louisiana State University Press, 1974), 154–76, 218–26; James Hennesey, *America Catholics: A History of the Roman Catholic Community in the United States* (New York: Oxford University Press, 1981), 286, 306; A. J. Liebling, *The Earl of Louisiana* (Baton Rouge: Louisiana State University Press, 1961); 171–87; David W. Southern, *John LaFarge and the Limits of Catholic Interracialism, 1911–1963* (Baton Rouge: Louisiana State University Press, 1996), 315.

5. For a survey of this period, see David Caute, *The Great Fear: The Anti-Communist Purge under Truman and Eisenhower* (New York: Simon and Schuster, 1978); Richard Fried, *Nightmare in Red: The McCarthy Era in Perspective* (New York: Oxford University Press, 1990); Jeff Woods, *Black Struggle, Red Scare: Segregation and Anti-Communism in the South, 1948–1968* (Baton Rouge: Louisiana State University Press, 2004).

6. SERINCO minutes, 19 April 1950, 10 May 1950, 14 June 1950, 11 April 1951, 28 June 1951, 22 October 1951, 20 November 1951, 1 April 1952, 13 May 1952, 10 July 1952, 8 May 1953, Box 51, folders 9–13, JHFP; CHR minutes, 21 April 1950, 19 May 1950, 21 September 1950, 21 June 1951, Box 47, folder 8, JHFP.

7. SERINCO minutes, 7 October 1952, 4 November 1952, 7 January 1953, Box 51, folders 12–13, JHFP.

8. "Skit, Jazz Combo Set for Interracial Day," *Catholic Action of the South,* 26 February 1953, 6; "Observe Catholic Interracial Day Sunday, Mar. 1st," *Louisiana Weekly,* 28 February 1953, 1, 6; "Interracial Day," *U-Topia,* March 1953, 1, 2; "Wilbert Sykes is Oratorical Winner," *Xavier Herald,* March 1953, 1.

9. "Race Justice Pays Off in Improved Society," *Catholic Action of the South,* 5 March 1953, 20; "Judge Leo Blessings Cites Race Relations Progress," *Louisiana Weekly,* 7 March 1953, 2. In 1956 Blessings succumbed to the forces of fear and intimidation and abandoned the cause of interracial justice. Denounced at a May 1956 rally of the prosegregation Citizens' Council of New Orleans for being a member of the board of the Urban League, Judge Blessings disclosed the very next day that he had resigned from the organization some two months prior. He explained in a letter to the chairman of the Citizens' Council that he had resigned because he was "opposed to integration and, therefore, could not conscientiously continue to support the action of the Urban League toward that end."

Furthermore, Blessings asked the chairman that in "view of the wide publicity that was given to your erroneous statement, I believe it only fair that you should inform the members of the Citizens' Council of my true status and trust that you will take whatever action is necessary to do so." The chairman obliged. "Blessings Quits Urban League," *Times-Picayune*, 19 May 1956, 10.

10. The "border" archdioceses of St. Louis and Washington, D.C., had ended segregation in 1947 and 1948, respectively. New Orleans was the first "Deep South" diocese to act. In 1953 Rummel ordained the first black priest for the archdiocese of New Orleans, Aubrey Osborne, who had entered the seminary in 1948. There was no publicity surrounding this event. See Stephen Ochs, *Desegregating the Altar: The Josephite Struggle for Black Priests, 1871–1960* (Baton Rouge: Louisiana State University Press, 1990), 404–6.

11. Joseph Francis Rummel, "Blessed Are the Peacemakers," pastoral letter, 15 March 1953, JFRP.

12. Joseph Francis Rummel, "Collection: Indian and Negro Missions," pastoral letter, 29 January 1951, JFRP. As a postscript to this letter, the archbishop asked the pastors "to solicit the prayers of your congregation for God's blessing on 'INTERRACIAL DAY' which will be observed by our Catholic college students, White and Colored, male and female, on Sunday, February 18."

13. "Archbishop Rummel Calls on Orleans to End Segregation in Catholic Church," *Louisiana Weekly*, 17 February 1951, 1, 8; "A Sense of 'Belonging,'" *Louisiana Weekly*, 24 February 1951, 10; "No Unity without End of Segregation," *Louisiana Weekly*, 3 March 1951, 10.

14. "Better Opportunity for Colored Urged," *Catholic Action of the South*, 8 February 1951, 1, 6.

15. Rummel, "Peacemakers." Bishop Vincent S. Waters of the diocese of Raleigh, North Carolina, banned segregation in his diocese three months after Rummel's directive. See "No Segregation Will Be Tolerated in Churches," *Catholic Action of the South*, 25 June 1953, 18.

16. R. Bentley Anderson, "Prelates, Protest and Public Opinion: Catholic Opposition to Desegregation, 1947–1956," *Journal of Church and State* 46 (Summer 2004): 617–44.

17. Sam Hill Ray to members of the New Orleans Province of the Society of Jesus, c. April 1953, ANOSJ.

18. Ibid.

19. Exchange Clubs are civic organizations dedicated to community service projects. In New Orleans, this organization must have been segregated; Ray would not have accepted an invitation to speak at a biracial gathering.

20. "Father Ray Flays Licentious Works," *Times-Picayune*, 3 February 1954, 3.

21. "Minutes of a Special Meeting for the NFCCS Convention," 15 August 1953, Box 51, folder 13, JHFP.

22. Minutes of the Tenth National Congress of the NFCCS, 25–30 August 1953, Cincinnati, Ohio, RNFCCS. See Appendix H for the full text.

23. "The Best of the *Christian Conscience* for Five Years," 1953, JHFP.

24. Ibid., 22. Emphasis in original.

25. Ibid., 15. For an extensive analysis of the effects racial segregation had on foreign affairs, see Mary Dudziak, *Cold War Civil Rights: Race and the Image of American*

Democracy (Princeton: Princeton University Press, 2000), and Azza S. Layton, *International Politics and Civil Rights Policies in the United States, 1941–1960* (New York: Cambridge University Press, 2000).

26. "The Best of the *Christian Conscience* for Five Years," 14, JHFP.

27. CHR minutes, 4 June 1953 and 28 June 1953, Box 47, folder 10, JHFP; 9 July 1953, Box 47, folder 15, JHFP; 26 July 1953, Box 48, folder 2, JHFP; 27 September 1953, Box 48, folder 2, JHFP.

28. Edmund Vales to Joseph Francis Rummel, 9 November 1953, Box 45, folder 17, JHFP.

29. CHR minutes, 25 October 1953, Box 48, folder 2, JHFP; "Commission Notes," *CI,* November 1953, JHFP; "Commission Notes," *CI,* December 1953, JHFP.

30. CHR agenda, 24 November 1953, Box 47, folder 10, JHFP; Vales to Rummel, 9 November 1953, JHFP.

31. CHR minutes, 29 November 1953, Box 48, folder 2, JHFP.

32. For the rest of the 1953–1954 academic year, the hour of reparation prayer service was held at Xavier University. Attendance was always an issue, and the records do not indicate that the practice continued into 1955. CHR minutes, 9 February 1954 and 28 March 1954, Box 48, folder 3, JHFP.

33. *CC* 6, no. 2 (August 1953); *CC* 6, no. 4 (October 1953).

34. SERINCO minutes, 24 June 1953, Box 51, folder 13, JHFP.

35. Ibid.

36. SERINCO minutes, 19 October 1953, Box 51, folder 13, JHFP. Tureaud had also presented the highlights of the case to CHR members the previous month. CHR minutes, 27 September 1953, Box 48, folder 2, JHFP.

37. *Tureaud* v. *Board of Supervisors,* 116 F. Supp. 248 (E.D. La.), *rev'd,* 207 F.2d 807 (5th Cir. 1953), *vacated per curiam,* 347 U.S. 971 (1954).

38. Baker, *Second Battle of New Orleans,* 126–37, 200 204.

39. Perez would also become an outspoken critic of Archbishop Rummel's racial policies, which resulted in his excommunication. See Glen Jeansonne, *Leander Perez: Boss of the Delta* (Baton Rouge : Louisiana State University Press, 1977); James Conaway, *Judge: The Life and Times of Leander Perez* (New York: Knopf, 1973).

40. Quoted in Baker, *Second Battle of New Orleans,* 202–3.

41. SERINCO minutes, 19 October 1953, Box 51, folder 13, JHFP.

42. Baker, *Second Battle of New Orleans,* 207–8; Fairclough, *Race and Democracy,* 155.

43. SERINCO minutes, 23 September 1953, 19 October 1953, Box 51, folder 13, JHFP; *CI,* "Commission Notes," November 1953.

44. Eugene Murret, interview by author, tape recording, Boston, 8 May 1998; Eugene Murret, "Reflections of a SERINCO Member," personal tape recording, Micronesia, c. 1998. While living and working in Micronesia, Murret sent the author a tape recording of his recollections in early 1998; later in the spring of 1998 Murret visited the United States and granted an interview.

45. Murret interview, May 1998.

46. "Xavier Student Places First in Talent Contest," *Catholic Action of the South,* 5 November 1953, 17.

47. SERINCO minutes, 12 October 1954, 9 November 1954, 13 October 1955, Box 51, folder 14, JHFP.

48. SERINCO minutes, 12 January 1954, Box 51, folder 13, JHFP; "Students to Mark Interracial Day," *Catholic Action of the South,* 25 February 1954, 19; "NFCCS Sets Interracial Day for March 14," *Maroon,* 26 February 1954, 3; "Serinco to Host Interracial Day," *Catholic Action of the South,* 4 March 1954, 18; "Mass at Loyola U. to Open 6th Annual Interracial Sunday," *Catholic Action of the South,* 11 March 1954, 1; "Group to Hold Interracial Day Here Sunday," *Maroon,* 12 March 1954, 1.

49. "Interracial Day Emphasizes Need of Moral Action," *Catholic Action of the South,* 18 March 1954, 4; "'Brotherhood Is Full Time Job' Speaker Tells SERINCO," *Maroon,* 19 March 1954, 6; "Students Talk at Interracial Meet," *Xavier Herald,* March 1954, 1; Laws quoted in "'Practice Brotherhood Daily or It Will Die' Laws Tells Catholic Interracial Meet," *Louisiana Weekly,* 20 March 1954, 1, 7.

50. Patricia Ryan to U. S. Pate, 27 June 1951, Box 45, folder 10, JHFP.

51. In 1956 Laws was again targeted by Perez. In a letter written to Mayor Morrison in March, Perez requested that Laws, now field secretary of the NAACP, be investigated for communistic and subversive organizational ties. "NAACP Field Sec'y Laws: Labels Perez Request As 'Smear and Scare' Attack," *Louisiana Weekly,* 31 March 1956, 1.

52. Fairclough, *Race and Democracy,* 144.

53. John Egerton, *Speak Now against the Day: The Generation before the Civil Rights Movement in the South* (New York: Knopf, 1995), 568; Fairclough, *Race and Democracy,* 136–45; Irwin Klibaner, "The Travail of Southern Radicals: The Southern Conference Educational Fund, 1946–1976," *Journal of Southern History* 49 (May 1983): 179–202; Kim Lacy Rogers, *Righteous Lives: Narratives of the New Orleans Civil Rights Movement* (New York: New York University Press, 1993), 40–41; Pamela Jean Turner, "Civil Rights and Anti-Communism in New Orleans, 1946–1965" (M.A. thesis, University of New Orleans, 1981), 26–31; Woods, *Black Struggle, Red Scare,* 56–58, 99–103.

54. Egerton, *Speak Now,* 569–71; Fairclough, *Race and Democracy,* 136–45; Rogers, *Righteous Lives,* 40–41; Turner, "Civil Rights and Anti-Communism in New Orleans," 26–31; Woods, *Black Struggle, Red Scare,* 104–9.

55. William Crandell to the Jesuit Community, Loyola University, 29 April 1954, ANOSJ.

56. William Crandell to John Janssens, 16 August 1954, New Orleans Province files, *ARSI.*

57. Kluger, *Simple Justice;* James T. Patterson, *Brown* v. *Board of Education: A Civil Rights Milestone and Its Troubled Legacy* (New York: Oxford University Press, 2001); John Howard, *The Shifting Wind: The Supreme Court and Civil Rights from Reconstruction to Brown* (Albany: State University of New York, 1999).

58. "Segregation Decision," *Times-Picayune,* 18 May 1954, 8.

59. "The U. S. Supreme Court Decision," *Louisiana Weekly,* 29 May 1954, 4-B.

60. "Louisiana House for Segregation," *Times-Picayune,* 21 May 1954, 7.

61. CHR minutes, 30 May 1954, Box 48, folder 3, JHFP; quoted in "'I Acted as Catholic, Not a Politician'–Rep. Engert," *Louisiana Weekly,* 5 June 1954, 1; "Statesmanship in Legislature," *Louisiana Weekly,* 5 June 1954, 4; "Approval Voted on Segregation," *Times-Picayune,* 27 May 1954, 8; Stephen P. Ryan, "Why a Man Voted," *New Leader,* 12 July 1954, 20.

62. Tom Brenan, "Views of Readers," *Times-Picayune*, 21 May 1954, 8.

63. W. R. Gilfoil, "Views of Readers," *Times-Picayune*, 25 May 1954, 8.

64. Mr. and Mrs. J. M. Dudley, "Views of Readers," *Times-Picayune*, 27 May 1954, 8.

65. Mabel B. Sheldon, "Views of Readers," *Times-Picayune*, 31 May 1954, 8.

66. John K. Baringer, "Views of Readers," *Times-Picayune*, 29 May 1954, 8.

67. The nine winning essays were written by Anne Schekeler, Mary Anne Mume, Margie Fastring, Arletta Dornier, Albert J. Jung, Kay Viellion, Digby Barriops, Stephen Collins, and Elaine Hartel. Essay Contest Tally Sheet, 2 November 1954, Box 46, folder 14, JHFP.

68. Anne Schekeler, student essay contest submission, 1954, Box 46, folder 14, JHFP.

69. "Segregation Banned in Public Schools," *Catholic Action of the South*, 20 May 1954, 1, 21.

70. "The Great Taboo," *Catholic Action of the South*, 27 May 1954, 10.

71. "Catholic Board Favors Ruling," *Times-Picayune*, 28 May 1954, 1; "N.O. School Board Okays Court Segregation Ban," *Catholic Action of the South*, 3 June 1954, 24.

72. Baker, *Second Battle of New Orleans*, 224–26.

73. "Despotic Police State Seen as Result of School Control Acts," *Catholic Action of the South*, 1 July 1954, 1, 5 and 6.

74. "Prelate Denies School Change," *Times-Picayune*, 9 July 1954, 1.

75. Ibid.

76. Ibid.

77. "Prejudice Is Exposed as Mental Blindness," *Catholic Action of the South*, 9 September 1954, 1, 20; "Color Is Accidental, Not Basic Quality," *Catholic Action of the South*, 16 September 1954, 1, 20; "Segregation Exacts Heavy Cost in U.S.," *Catholic Action of the South*, 23 September 1954, 1, 20; "Law of Love Must Extend to All Men," *Catholic Action of the South*, 30 September 1954, 1, 24; "True Equality Ideal Basic to Democracy," *Catholic Action of the South*, 7 October 1954, 1, 24; "Non-Catholic Vote for Racial Justice," *Catholic Action of the South*, 14 October 1954, 1, 20; "School Segregation Is Unconstitutional," *Catholic Action of the South*, 21 October 1954, 1, 24; "What Price Justice?" *Catholic Action of the South*, 28 October 1954, 1, 24.

78. See Baker, *Second Battle of New Orleans*, 226; Fairclough, *Race and Democracy,* 169–70.

79. Consultors of the Jesuit community and members of the board of directors for the 1953–1954 academic year were William O'Leary, John Fuss, Edward Doyle, and Theodore Ray. Aloysius Goodspeed, replaced Ray the following year.

80. LUBD minutes, 23 May 1954, ALUNO.

81. LUBD minutes, 1 November 1954, ALUNO.

82. For a history of the integration process at Spring Hill see, Charles S. Padgett, "'Without Hysteria or Unnecessary Disturbance': Desegregation at Spring Hill College, Mobile, Alabama, 1948–1954," *History of Education Quarterly* (summer 2001): 167–88; Charles S. Padgett, "Schooled in Invisibility: The Desegregation of Spring Hill College, Mobile, Alabama, 1948–1963" (Ph.D. diss., University of Georgia, 2000); Preston Valien, "Desegregation in Higher Education: A Critical Summary," *Journal of Negro Education* 27 (Summer 1958): 373–80.

83. Andrew Smith to John Janssens, 6 July 1952, New Orleans Province files, *ARSI*.

84. Andrew Smith to John Janssens, 2 July 1954, New Orleans Province files, *ARSI*. See also Lewis W. Jones, "The Desegregation Decision—One Year Afterward," *Journal of Negro Education* 24 (Summer 1955): 165–71; Leon Bouvier, "The Spring Hill College Integration Story," *Interracial Review* (May 1961): 128–30. A few years later, the dean of Spring Hill College presented a progress report concerning integration at the school to the faculty; the students, black and white, had to adjust to the new situation. See George T. Bergen to Faculty, "Progress Report of Integration at Spring Hill College," 5 April 1956, Spring Hill College Archives.

85. Smith to Janssens, 2 July 1954.

86. Andrew Smith to John B. Janssens, 2 January 1955, New Orleans Province files, *ARSI*.

87. Andrew Smith to John B. Janssens, 1 July 1955, New Orleans Province files, *ARSI*.

88. Patrick Donnelly to John B. Janssens, 6 January 1955, New Orleans Province files, *ARSI*. Donnelly explained to Janssens, "Loyola, in pursuit of this goal [integration], announced from the beginning that it would follow a policy of non-segregation in the use of its Field House." Those wishing to rent the field house, however, could impose their own standards concerning seating. In January 1955 the Knights of Columbus did just that, requiring segregated seating during a Knights-sponsored event. The CHR sent letters of disapproval to the president of Loyola and the promoter of the event. See Gladys Williams to Patrick Donnelly, 17 January 1955, Box 45, folder 20, JHFP; Gladys Williams to Charles Delfahy, 17 January 1955, Box 45, folder 20, JHFP.

89. Aloysius Goodspeed to William Crandell, 5 January 1955, ANOSJ. Goodspeed must have been referring to the article "Nonsegregation Policy for Sports at Loyola Set," *Times-Picayune*, 25 November 1954, 38.

90. "The Human Race Gets a Chance," *Louisiana Weekly*, 4 December 1954, 6-B.

91. "Orchids to Loyola," *Xavier Herald*, December 1954, 2.

92. "*The Sportlife:* Month of Destiny," *Maroon*, 3 December 1954, 6; "La Salle Here Sunday: Tom Gola & Co. Dedicate New Gym," *Maroon*, 3 December 1954, 1; "Field House Dedication Highlight of Ball Game," *Catholic Action of the South*, 5 December 1954, 9.

93. Jack Wilkinson, "Gola and Co. Solid Choice," *Times-Picayune–New Orleans States*, 5 December 1954, section 6, 1. Wilkinson reported in his column that "one major sidelight of the [Loyola-La Salle] contest is centered around the fact that this will be the first collegiate interracial basketball game in the history of Louisiana. LaSalle's Al Lewis, a Negro, is listed to start at a guard slot."

94. "La Salle Here Sunday: Tom Gola & Co. Dedicate New Gym," *Maroon*, 3 December 1954, 1; "Gola Paces Team to 85–71 Victory," *Philadelphia Daily News*, 6 December 1954, 40; "La Salle Wins, 85–71, over Loyola as Gola Pours in 27 Points," *Philadelphia Inquirer*, 6 December 1954, 39; "Gola Paces Mighty La Salle to 85–71 Victory over Loyola," *Times-Picayune*, 6 December 1954, 28; "La Salle Hurdles Loyola, Faces Big Test at Niagara," Philadelphia *Evening Bulletin*, 6 December 1954, 39. The following year Loyola played another integrated team, facing future NBA Boston Celtics star Bill Russell and the University of San Francisco. The Wolfpack lost to the defending NCAA champs. "Russell, Baxter and Co. to Face Loyola 5 Fri.," *Louisiana Weekly*, 24 December 1955, 1,6; "Russell Sets Pace as San Francisco Overwhelms Loyola, 61–43,"

Times-Picayune, 24 December 1955; "Bill Russell, Dons Outclass Loyola 61–43," *Louisiana Weekly,* 31 December 1955, 1–2b.

95. E. A. Doyle to William Crandell, 10 January 1955, ANOSJ.

96. Aloysius Goodspeed to William Crandell, 8 January 1955, ANOSJ.

97. "Segregation Violates Both Americanism, Christianity," *Catholic Action of the South,* 5 January 1955, 5.

98. Ibid.

99. "Seventh Annual Catholic Interracial Day Mar. 13," *Louisiana Weekly,* 26 February 1955, 3; "Interracial Day Slated March 13," *Catholic Action of the South,* 27 February 1955, 6; "SERINCO Holds Interracial Day," *Veritas,* February 1955, 4; "Interracial Commission Meeting Slated for March 13 at Xavier," *Xavier Herald,* February 1955, 1; "Timely Panel Discussions to Highlight 7th Annual Catholic Interracial Day," *Louisiana Weekly,* 5 March 1955, 3; "SERINCO Slates Interracial Day at XU," *Maroon,* 11 March 1955, 3; "Interracial Day Discussion Set," *Times-Picayune,* 11 March 1955, 35; "Father Lewis to Say Mass at XU Sunday," *Louisiana Weekly,* 12 March 1955, 3; "Mass, Panel Sessions to Feature Interracial Day," *Catholic Action of the South,* 13 March 1955, 6.

100. "Interracial Sunday Proves Success," *Xavier Herald,* March 1955, 8; "Catholic Interracial Day Panelists Agree Bias Is Morally Bankrupting US," *Louisiana Weekly,* 19 March 1955, 1, 2; "Cites Moral Implications of Racial Discrimination," *Catholic Action of the South,* 27 March 1955, 14. Quotes as found in press accounts.

101. "Catholic Interracial Day Panelists Agree"; "Cites Moral Implications". Remarks as quoted in articles.

102. William Crandell to John B. Janssens, 2 March 1956, New Orleans Province files, *ARSI;* Joseph Fichter to Patrick Donnelly, 18 June 1955, Box 52, folder 15, JHFP.

103. Aloysius Goodspeed to William Crandell, 10 July 1955, ANOSJ; John Fuss to William Crandell, 9 July 1955, ANOSJ; E. A. Doyle to William Crandell, 24 July 1955, ANOSJ; Consultors' minutes, 18 August and 16 September 1955, ANOSJ.

104. Crandell to Janssens, 2 March 1956; Fichter to Donnelly, 18 June 1955.

105. William Crandell to the Jesuit Community at Loyola University of the South, 24 April 1955, ANOSJ.

106. William Crandell to John B. Janssens, 12 September 1955, New Orleans Province files, *ARSI.*

107. Ibid.

Chapter VII

1. Numan V. Bartley and Hugh D. Graham, *Southern Politics and the Second Reconstruction* (Baltimore: Johns Hopkins University Press, 1975); Hodding Carter, *The South Strikes Back* (Garden City, NY: Doubleday, 1959); V. O. Key, Jr., with Alexander Heard, *Southern Politics in State and Nation* (New York: Alfred A. Knopf, 1949; reprint, Knoxville: University of Tennessee Press, 1984); Neil R. McMillen, *The Citizens' Council: Organized Resistance to the Second Reconstruction, 1954–1964* (Urbana: University of Illinois Press, 1971), 59–72; Frederick B. Routh and Paul Anthony, "Southern Resistance Forces," *Phylon Quarterly* 18 (first quarter 1957): 50–58; James W. Vander Zanden, *Race Relations in Transition: The Segregation Crisis in the South* (New York: Random House, 1965).

2. Mark Tushnet, "The Significance of *Brown* v. *Board of Education,*" *Virginia Law Review* 80 (February 1994): 173–84; Christopher Vasillopulos, "Prevailing Upon the American Dream: Thurgood Marshall and *Brown* v. *Board of Education,*" *Journal of Negro Education* 63 (summer 1994): 289–96.

3. Joseph Francis Rummel to Pastors and Superiors of Schools of the Archdiocese of New Orleans, 19 August 1955, JFRP. The letter was also reported in the local newspaper: "Archdiocesan Schools Will Postpone Initiation of Integration," *Times-Picayune,* 27 August 1955, 10.

4. Rummel to Pastors and Superiors of Schools, 19 August 1955. Emphasis in original.

5. Ibid.

6. Ibid.

7. Ibid. Emphasis in original.

8. William Crandell to John B. Janssens, 2 March 1956, New Orleans Province files, *ARSI.*

9. "Holy Name Dads Reject Integration," *New Orleans States,* 26 October 1955, 15; "Catholic Dads Hit Integration," *New Orleans Item,* 26 October 1955, 2; "Dads' Club Hits at Integration," *Times-Picayune,* 26 October 1955, 40; "Catholic Group Shows Defiance to Archbishop," *Louisiana Weekly,* 29 October 1955, 1. See Appendix I for full text of the resolution. The Dads' Club initiative came one month after members of the White Citizens' Council began circulating a petition they were going to present to the Orleans School Board that fall opposing public school desegregation. "Petition to Hit at Integration," *Times-Picayune,* 14 September 1955, 22. On 30 November 1955, the Dads' Club of St. Francis Xavier School, located in Metairie, Louisiana, passed a similar resolution. ANOSJ. Ku Klux Klan Grand Wizard David Duke would represent this area in the state legislature in the 1980s.

10. Crandell to Janssens, 2 March 1956.

11. Ibid.

12. Edward A. Doyle to William Crandell, 21 January 1956, ANOSJ.

13. R. Bentley Anderson, "Prelates, Protest, and Public Opinion: Catholic Opposition to Desegregation, 1947–1955," *Journal of Church and State* 46 (July 2004): 617–44; Adam Fairclough, *Race and Democracy: The Civil Rights Struggle in Louisiana, 1915–1972* (Athens: University of Georgia Press, 1995), 178–79; Michael B. Friedland, *Lift Up Your Voice like a Trumpet: White Clergy and the Civil Rights and Antiwar Movements, 1954–1973,* (Chapel Hill: University of North Carolina Press, 1998), 41–43; Stephen Ochs, *Desegregating the Altar: The Josephites and the Struggle for Black Priests, 1871–1960* (Baton Rouge: Louisiana State University Press, 1990), 433–34; "Negro Priest Barred, Mission Is Rebuked," *New York Times,* 15 October 1955; "Parishes Placid in Racial Dispute," *New York Times,* 16 October 1955; "Jesuits' Bend Had Origin in French Colonial Days," *Catholic Action of the South,* 30 October 1955; "Attitude in Jesuit Bend Not Seen in Other Places," *Catholic Action of the South,* 6 November 1955.

14. Joseph Francis Rummel to the congregations of Our Lady of Perpetual Help Church, Belle Chasse, and its missions of St. Cecilia, Jesuit Bend, and St. Joseph, Myrtle Grove, 7 October 1955, reprinted in "Church Services Are Suspended for Irreverence to Priest," *Catholic Action of the South,* 16 October 1955; "Archbishop Punishes 'Bias' Catholics," *Louisiana Weekly,* 22 October 1955; Ochs, *Desegregating the Altar,* 435.

15. Rummel to the congregations of Our Lady of Perpetual Help Church and its missions, 7 October 1955; Ochs, *Desegregating the Altar,* 435.

16. "Touches of Color," *L'Osservatore Romano,* 15 October 1955, Box 52, folder 20, JHFP; "Faithful Divided in Closed Church," *New York Times,* 17 October 1955; "Vatican Commends New Orleans Prelate," *New York Times,* 18 October 1955; "Archbishop Punishes 'Bias' Catholics," *Louisiana Weekly,* 22 October 1955; "Vatican City Praises Archbishop's Action in Condemning Racial Prejudice," *Catholic Action of the South,* 23 October 1955; "Vatican Denounces Race Bias in Catholic Church," *Louisiana Weekly,* 29 October 1955; "Complete Text of 'Touches Of Color,'" *Catholic Action of the South,* 6 November 1955; Ochs, *Desegregating the Altar,* 435–36.

17. "Action at Jesuit Bend Misinterpreted by Group," *Catholic Action of the South,* 20 November 1955; Ochs, *Desegregating the Altar,* 436–37.

18. "Full Text of Archbishop's and Pastor's Messages Refutes False Statements," *Catholic Action of the South,* 18 December 1955; Ochs, *Desegregating the Altar,* 437.

19. "Full Text," *Catholic Action,* 18 December 1955; Ochs, *Desegregating the Altar,* 437–38.

20. "Full Text," *Catholic Action,* 18 December 1955; Ochs, *Desegregating the Altar,* 438.

21. Ochs, *Desegregating the Altar,* 439–40.

22. Claude J. Stallworth to William Crandell, 14 January 1956, ANOSJ.

23. William Crandell to John B. Janssens, 2 March 1956, New Orleans Province files, *ARSI.*

24. "School Integration Time Undecided—Msgr. Bezou," *Times-Picayune,* 24 January 1956, 3; "Catholic Parent Group Opposes Desegregation," *New Orleans States,* 11 October 1955, 2.

25. "School Integration Time Undecided," *Times-Picayune,* 24 January 1956; "Catholic Parent Group," *New Orleans States,* 11 October 1955.

26. Cooper was born and raised in Mobile, Alabama, where he attended Cathedral Boys School. He traveled north to study at Maryknoll Minor Seminary in Clark Summit, Pennsylvania. Upon completion of his high school training, he entered the New Orleans Province of the Society of Jesus in 1936 at the age of twenty; thirteen years later he was ordained a priest. During the 1950s, he was a member of the theology and philosophy departments at Loyola and served as chaplain of the university. Harold Cooper, S.J., interview by author, tape recording, Algiers, LA, 24 May 1996.

27. Harold Cooper, "Chaplain's Corner," *Maroon,* 3 February 1956, 6.

28. Ibid.

29. Ibid. See also Cooper's columns in the *Maroon,* 10 February 1956, 4; 24 February 1956, 3; 2 March 1956, 6; 9 March 1956, 4; 16 March 1956 5; and 6 April 1956, 4.

30. Crandell to Janssens, 2 March 1956. "Before writing his recent letter on the moral implications of segregation," wrote Crandell, "His Excellency [Rummel] called Fr. Louis Twomey (Loyola University) to help him in its preparation. He received from Father Twomey, with my permission, a copy of our Province letter on the same subject."

31. Joseph Francis Rummel to the Clergy, Religious and Laity of the Archdiocese of New Orleans, 15 February 1956, JFRP.

32. Joseph Francis Rummel, "The Morality of Racial Segregation," pastoral letter, 19 February 1956, JFRP.

33. Ibid.

34. Ibid.

35. Ibid.

36. Ibid.

37. Ibid.

38. "Segregation Sinful, Says Archbishop," *New Orleans Item,* 20 February 1956; "Prelate Plans Further Study," *Times-Picayune,* 20 February 1956, 1, 10; "N.O. Archbishop Raps Segregation," *New Orleans States,* 20 February 1956, 3

39. Walter C. Carey, "Views of Readers," *Times-Picayune,* 29 February 1956, 12.

40. The Fund for the Republic was established by the Ford Foundation in 1952 to promote and defend American civil liberties; funding for Hulan Jack's appearance was part of the American Legacy of Liberty Project of the fund. *The Fund for the Republic: A Report on Three Years' Work, May 31, 1956* (New York: Fund for the Republic, 1956), 9–12, 29. See also Frank K. Kelly, *Court of Reason: Robert Hutchins and the Fund for the Republic* (New York: Free Press, 1981); Thomas C. Reeves, *Freedom and the Foundation: the Fund for the Republic in the era of McCarthyism* (New York: Knopf, 1969).

41. Joseph H. Fichter to David Freeman, 31 December 1955, Box 45, folder 23, JHFP; Joseph Francis Rummel to David Freeman, 3 January 1956, Box 45, folder 24, JHFP; David Freeman to Joseph H. Fichter, 16 January 1956, Box 45, folder 24, JHFP; Joseph H. Fichter to David Freeman, 20 January 1956, Box 45, folder 24, JHFP; Joseph H. Fichter to David E. Freeman, 14 June 1956, Box 1, folder 14, JHFP; Joseph H. Fichter, *One-Man Research: Reminiscences of a Catholic Sociologist* (New York: John Wiley and Sons, 1973), 82–91.

42. "Hulan E. Jack Guest Speaker at Interracial Meet," *Catholic Action of the South,* 26 February 1956, 6; "Hulan Jack Is Catholic Interracial Sun. Speaker," *Louisiana Weekly,* 25 February 1956, 1, 6.

43. "Observe Catholic Interracial Sunday," *Catholic Action of the South,* 26 February 1956, 6.

44. Hulan Jack, address to Eighth Annual Interracial Sunday gathering, Holy Name of Jesus Elementary School auditorium, tape recording, 26 February 1956, JHFP.

45. Ibid.

46. Ibid.

47. Ibid.

48. Ibid.

49. Ibid.

50. Joseph Francis Rummel, address to the Eighth Annual Interracial Sunday gathering, Holy Name of Jesus Elementary School auditorium, tape recording, 26 February 1956, JHFP.

51. Ibid.

52. Ibid.

53. "Fight May Aid Reds—Rummel," *Times-Picayune,* 27 February 1956, 1, 16; "Integration Foes May Aid Reds, Says Archbishop," *New Orleans States,* 27 February 1956, 1; "Race Fight Helps Reds," *New Orleans Item,* 27 February 1956, 1, 9; "Pro-Segregationist Doing Work of Commies," *Louisiana Weekly,* 3 March 1956, 1, 8.

54. "Wagner attacks Loyola's Invitation to Hulan Jack," *Times-Picayune,* 27 February 1956, 20. Involvement of Spring Hill College students in SERINCO was negligible, if at all, as the minutes reflect they never attended any meetings.

55. "Wagner Attacks Loyola's Invitation," *Times-Picayune,* 27 February 1956, 20.

56. "Head of Loyola Hits Procedure Used by Wagner," *Times-Picayune,* 28 February 1956, 1, 3.

57. Ibid.

58. Ibid.

59. "New York Mayor Backs Loyola Program Speaker," *New Orleans States,* 27 February 1956, 14.

60. "Hulan Jack Denies Red Links," *New York World-Telegram and Sun,* 27 February 1956; "Jack Condemns 'Link' to Red Fronts as 'Sneak Attack' by Citizens Council," *New York Post,* 27 February 1956; "Jack, in South, Scores Bias; Denies Charge of Red Link," *New York Times,* 27 February 1956; "Jack Back, Indignant over Red Charges," *New York Daily News,* 28 February 1956. Articles from newspaper clippings file, Hulan Jack Papers, Schomburg Center for Research in Black Culture, New York Public Library, New York.

61. "Jack Weighs Suit against Detractors," *New York Times,* 28 February 1956, 1, 14; "Hulan Jack Row Still Unresolved," *New Orleans Item,* 28 February 1956, 3.

62. "Jack Charges Name 'Used,'" *New Orleans States,* 28 February 1956, 2; "Misuse of Name Charged by Jack," *Times-Picayune,* 29 February 1956, 8.

63. "Wagner Issues New Statement in Jack Furor," *New Orleans States,* 29 February 1956, 2.

64. Crandell to Janssens, 2 March 1956.

65. For a general overview of these civil rights organizations, see Adam Fairclough, *To Redeem the Soul of America: The Southern Christian Leadership Conference and Martin Luther King, Jr.* (Athens: University of Georgia Press, 1987); Cheryl L. Greenberg, ed., *A Circle of Trust: Remembering SNCC* (New Brunswick, NJ: Rutgers University Press, 1998); August Meier and Elliott Rudwick, *CORE: A Study in the Civil Rights Movement, 1942–1968* (New York: Oxford University Press, 1973).

66. Annie Laurie M. St. Paul, "Interracial Day," *Times-Picayune,* 29 February 1956, 10.

67. W. G. Madary, "Believes Integration Fits with Communism," *Times-Picayune,* 2 March 1956, 8.

68. "Making a Mockery of Democracy," *Louisiana Weekly,* 10 March 1956, 3-B.

69. Ibid.

70. In December 1955, Wagner wrote Edmund B. Bunn, S.J., president of Georgetown University in Washington, DC, regarding the university's race policy. "On the Question 'Morality of Segregation,'" pamphlet, 10 December 1955, private printing, Box 53, folder 3, LJTP. Four days later, Wagner wrote Archbishop Rummel concerning Catholics and the race question. Emile Wagner to Joseph Francis Rummel, 14 December 1955, Box 52, folder 15, JHFP. Cooper was responding to Wagner's position taken in these documents. A fuller examination of Wagner's thought on the race question can be found in Chapter 8.

71. Cooper interview, 24 May 1996.

72. Harold Cooper to Emile Wagner, 28 February 1956, Box 20, folder 2, LJTP.

73. Ibid.

74. Ibid.

75. Pius XII, *Summi pontificatus,* 1939, quoted in Cooper to Wagner, 28 February 1956.

76. Cooper to Wagner, 28 February 1956.

77. Pius XI *Mit brennender Sorge,* 1937, quoted in Cooper to Wagner, 28 February 1956.

78. Pius XII, "To the Citizens of Rome," 18 March 1945, quoted in Cooper to Wagner, 28 February 1956.

79. Cooper to Wagner, 28 February 1956.

80. C. Vann Woodward, *The Strange Career of Jim Crow,* 3d rev. ed. (New York: Oxford University Press, 1974).

81. Cooper to Wagner, 28 February 1956.

Chapter VIII

1. Numan V. Bartley, *The Rise of Massive Resistance: Race and Politics in the South during the 1950s* (Baton Rouge: Louisiana State University Press, 1969), 116–17, 212–16; Kenneth O'Reilly, "Racial Integration: The Battle General Eisenhower Chose Not to Fight," *Journal of Blacks in Higher Education* 18 (winter 1997–1998): 110–19; Kim Lacy Rogers, *Righteous Lives: Narratives of the New Orleans Civil Rights Movement* (New York: New York University Press, 1993), 1–48; Neil McMillen, *The Citizens' Council: Organized Resistance to the Second Reconstruction, 1954–64* (Urbana: University of Illinois Press, 1971), 58–68; Jeff Woods, *Black Struggle, Red Scare: Segregation and Anti-Communism in the South, 1948–1968* (Baton Rouge: Louisiana State University Press, 2004), 49–68; C. Vann Woodward, "Look Away, Look Away," *Journal of Southern History* 59 (August 1993): 487–504.

2. M. F. Everett, "Church Rights Are Threatened," *Catholic Action of the South,* 26 February 1956, 1, 12; reprinted in "Comments Here and There," *Louisiana Weekly,* 3 March 1956, 3-B.

3. Liva Baker, *The Second Battle of New Orleans: The Hundred-Year Struggle to Integrate the Schools* (New York: HarperCollins, 1996), 258–77; Adam Fairclough, *Race and Democracy: The Civil Rights Struggle in Louisiana* (Athens: University of Georgia Press, 1995), 196–203.

4. Everett, "Church Rights." Canon 2334 states that individuals "who issue laws, mandates, or decrees contrary to the freedom or rights of the Church . . . [or] who directly or indirectly impede the exercise of ecclesiastical jurisdiction either of the internal or external forum, and for this purpose have recourse to any lay authority" incur the penalty of excommunication. See T. Lincoln Bouscaren and Adam C. Ellis, *Canon Law: A Text and Commentary,* 2d rev. ed. (Milwaukee: Bruce, 1951), 924; "Catholics Warned on School Measure," *Times-Picayune* 25 February 1956, 1, 7.

5. "3 Deny Canon Affects School Segregation Bid," *New Orleans States,* 27 February 1956, 2; "Race Law Won't Interfere, View," *Times-Picayune,* 27 February 1956, 1, 5.

6. M. F. Everett, "Errors in Statement by Trio Are Pointed Out," *Catholic Action of the South,* 4 March 1956, 1, 12; "Pro-Segregation Legislators Are Hit Again by CAS," *Louisiana Weekly,* 1, 6.

7. Everett, "Errors in Statement."

8. Charter members included William E. Blake, Jr. (Loyola '34), Charles A. Bourgeois,

J. Louis Boyer (Loyola '28), James Everett Brown (Loyola '38), Pat W. Brown, Edward J. Cambre (Loyola '37), Joseph S. Casey (Loyola '37), A. R. Childress, Jr. (Loyola '37), Lucien C. Delery, M.D. (Loyola '35—Dr. Delery delivered this author into the world and was the family physician for many years), Charles T. deMahy (Loyola '37), Albert A. Demarest, Albert J. Derbes, Jr. (Loyola '32), Donald J. Duclaux, H. D. Eaton (Loyola '37), Lloyd J. Fitzpatrick, Vincent C. Jennaro, A. K. Lagarde (Loyola '43), Daniel J. Lyons (Loyola '39), Henry L. Mason, F. Lloyd Monroe, R. Allen Pendleton, Jr., Gerard A. Rault (Loyola '30), Jackson G. Ricau (Loyola '39), James H. Rooney, Jr., Raymond J. Salassi, James T. Skelly (Loyola '42), James E. Steiner (Loyola '33), C. C. Viguerie, Joseph E. Viguerie, and Emile A. Wagner, Jr. (Loyola '30).

9. "Articles of Incorporation of Association of Catholic Laymen," Box 83, folder 9, LJTP.

10. "Racial Problem Study to Be Aim," *The Times-Picayune,* 18 March 1956, 19.

11. William Crandell to John B. Janssens, 2 March 1956, New Orleans Province files, *ARSI.*

12. Emile A. Wagner to Joseph Francis Rummel, 17 March 1956, Box 20, folder 4, LJTP.

13. Joseph Francis Rummel to Emile A. Wagner, 19 March 1956, Box 20, folder 3, LJTP.

14. Joseph Francis Rummel to members of the clergy of the archdiocese of New Orleans, 22 March 1956, JFRP.

15. "CATHOLIC MEN and WOMEN: Join Now!" 28 March 1956, *Times-Picayune,* 5.

16. Joseph Francis Rummel to Emile A. Wagner, 28 March 1956, Box 20, folder 3, LJTP.

17. Emile A. Wagner to members of the Association of Catholic Laymen, 30 April 1956, Box 20, folder 4, LJTP.

18. Joseph Francis Rummel to Jackson G. Ricau, 23 April 1956, Box 20, folder 4, LJTP; Emile A. Wagner to members of the Association of Catholic Laymen, 30 April 1956, Box 20, folder 4, LJTP.

19. Jackson G. Ricau to Joseph Francis Rummel, 12 April 1956, Box 20, folder 4, LJTP.

20. Telegram from Joseph Francis Rummel to Jackson G. Ricau, 14 April 1956, Box 20, folder 4, LJTP.

21. Joseph Francis Rummel to Jackson G. Ricau, 23 April 1956, Box 20, folder 4, LJTP. Canon 2331 states, "Those who obstinately fail to comply when the Roman Pontiff or their own Ordinary lawfully prescribes or forbids something, shall be punished according to the gravity of the fault, with suitable penalties, not excluding censures. Those who conspire against the authority of the Roman Pontiff or of his Legate, or of their own Ordinary, or against the lawful commands of the same, and likewise those who provoke subjects to such disobedience, shall be punished with censures or other penalties." See Bouscaren and Ellis, *Canon Law: A Text and Commentary,* 924. Archbishop Rummel excommunicated Jackson Ricau on 31 March 1962 for his stance against desegregation in the archdiocese of New Orleans. Ricau never reconciled with the church; however, his obituary, which appeared in the *Times-Picayune,* 11 February 2001, stated that he had. The chancellor of the archdiocese denied it, saying, "I am unaware of any reconciliation. I do not know the source of the information printed in the *Times-Picayune.*" See R. Bentley

Anderson, "*Norman Francis Is a Negro:* Race, Religion, and Catholic Higher Education in New Orleans, 1947–1957" (Ph.D. diss., Boston College, 2001), 448 note 17, 476-77; Monsignor Thomas J. Rodi to author, 6 March 2001.

22. James Everett Brown to Joseph Francis Rummel, 26 April 1956, Box 20, folder 4, LJTP.

23. Charles J. Plauche to James Everett Brown, 26 April 1956, Box 20, folder 4, LJTP.

24. Emile A. Wagner to Joseph Francis Rummel, 1 May 1956, Box 20, folder 5, LJTP.

25. "Pro-segregation Catholics Disband on Cleric's Order," *Times-Picayune,* 5 May 1956, 1.

26. "Excommunication Threat Halted Activities–Wagner," *Times-Picayune,* 6 May 1956, 1, 11; "Lay Group to Appeal to Pontiff," *New Orleans Item,* 6 May 1956, 8; "Call Halt to Activity of Laymen," *New Orleans Item,* 7 May 1956, 6; Joseph T. Taylor, "Desegregation in Louisiana, 1956," *Journal of Negro Education* 25 (summer 1956): 262–72.

27. William Crandell to the Jesuit Community at Loyola University of the South, 1 May 1956, ANOSJ.

28. William Crandell to John B. Janssens, 22 August 1956, New Orleans Province files, *ARSI.*

29. In the pamphlet "Southern Catholic Parents Speak Up for Integrated Schools," six of the nine essays presented were written by women, and eight of the ten excerpts cited were from women.

30. Mrs. Francis X. Waguespack, essay submission, March 1956, Box 46, folder 27, JHFP.

31. Dr. Gerald J. Eberle, essay submission, March 1956, Box 46, folder, 27, JHFP.

32. Peter Clark, essay submission, c. February 1956, Box 46, folder 2, JHFP.

33. Mrs. C. D. Olivier, essay submission, March 1956, Box 46, folder 27, JHFP.

34. Mrs. William H. Syll, essay submission, March 1956, Box 46, folder 27, JHFP.

35. Mrs. Naomi [M]cCullum Branch, essay submission, March 1956, Box 46, folder 27, JHFP.

36. Mrs. Milton O. Fee, essay submission, March 1956, Box 46, folder 27, JHFP.

37. Newspaper clipping (n.d.), Box 46, folder 13, JHFP.

38. Mrs. A. Tesvich, essay submission, 7 February 1956, Box 46, folder 13, JHFP.

39. Unsigned essay submission, 13 February 1956, Box 46, folder 2, JHFP.

40. Mrs. E. R. Morris, essay submission, 16 February 1956, Box 46, folder 2, JHFP.

41. George L. James to the Catholic Committee of the South, 24 February 1956, Box 46, folder 2, JHFP. Emphasis in original.

42. William Davenport to Joseph H. Fichter, 12 June 1956, Box 46, folder 7, JHFP.

43. Donald J. Plaisance to the CHR, 9 July 1956, Box 46, folder 8, JHFP.

44. Kathy Schmidt to Joseph H. Fichter, 11 June 1956, Box 46, folder 7, JHFP.

45. Ibid.

46. William Brady, Sr., to CHR, 22 May 1956, Box 46, folder 6, JHFP.

47. Ibid.

48. John Cummins to CHR, 17 June 1956, Box 46, folder 7, JHFP.

49. Joseph H. Fichter to David Freeman, 31 December 1955, Box 45, folder 23, JHFP; Joseph Francis Rummel to David Freeman, 3 January 1956, Box 45, folder 24, JHFP; David Freeman to Joseph H. Fichter, 16 January 1956, Box 45, folder 24, JHFP; Joseph H. Fichter to David Freeman, 20 January 1956, Box 45, folder 24, JHFP; Joseph H. Fichter, *One-Man Research: Reminiscences of a Catholic Sociologist* (New York: John Wiley and Sons, 1973), 82–91.

50. Ross Taggart, "The Facts and Fiction of Health Hazard," *CI,* February 1956, JHFP; Benjamin Pasamanick, "Racial Aspects of Human Intelligence," *CI,* March 1956, JHFP; William Hepburn, "The Constitution and School Integration," *CI,* April 1956, JHFP; National Association for the Advancement of Colored Peoples; Albert Reiss, "Racial Immorality and Delinquency," *CI,* May 1956, JHFP.

51. Fichter to Freeman, 31 December 1955.

52. Joseph Francis Rummel to Joseph Fichter, 26 March 1956, Box 46, folder 4, JHFP; Fichter to Freeman, 31 December 1955; Fichter, *One-Man Research,* 82–91.

53. Baker, *Second Battle,* 271–74; Fairclough, *Race and Democracy,* 196–97, 207–10.

54. Baker, *Second Battle,* 270–71; Fairclough, *Race and Democracy,* 205; Charles A. Reynard, "Legislation Affecting Segregation," *Louisiana Law Review* 17 (1956–1957): 101–22. The laws were ruled unconstitutional early in 1957, but the damage had already been done.

55. CHR minutes, 24 June 1956, Box 48, folder 3.

56. Lucile Cherbonnier to the executive secretary, CHR, 31 May 1956, Box 46, folder 6, JHFP.

57. Clare Andrews to the executive board, CHR, 27 July 1956, Box 46, folder 8, JHFP. Emphasis in original.

58. Luella G. Cavalier to the executive board, CHR, 31 July 1956, Box 46, folder 8, JHFP.

59. "Citizens Council to Rally May 17," *Times-Picayune–New Orleans States,* 6 May 1956, 20; "Citizens' Group Sets Rally Here," *New Orleans Item,* 7 May 1956, 6; "South Is Ready to 'Battle for Rights,' Griffin Says," *Times-Picayune,* 18 May 1956, 1, 3; "Griffin Raps Supreme Court at Rally," *New Orleans Item,* 18 May 1956, 1, 6. See also Chapter 6, n. 9, on Judge Leo Blessings' resignation from the Urban League.

60. "Council Denies Church Insult," *Times-Picayune,* 25 May 1956, 6; "Booing of Archbishop Irks Church," *New Orleans Item,* 21 May 1956, 11; "Burning Cross Brings Firemen," *Times-Picayune,* 18 May 1956, 3; Fairclough, *Race and Democracy,* 200–203; Rogers, *Righteous Lives,* 45; McMillen, *Citizens' Council,* 59–72.

61. "Catholic Group Scores 'Insult,'" *Times-Picayune,* 21 May 1956, 23.

62. "Council Denies Church Insult," *Times-Picayune,* 25 May 1956, 6; Irwin quoted in "Human Rights Commission Lists Reasons for Stand," *Times-Picayune,* 11 June 1956, 27. Irwin apparently was not aware that the CHR was a subcommittee of the Catholic Committee of the South.

63. Emmett Lee Irwin to J. Edgar Hoover, 12 June 1956, Freedom of Information Act No. 105-40774, Federal Bureau of Investigation; "Probe Charges, FBI Requested," *Times-Picayune,* 14 June 1956, 2; "Citizen Council Asks FBI to Probe Priest," *New Orleans States,* 14 June 1956, 6.

64. Irwin to Hoover, 12 June 1956.

65. J. Edgar Hoover to Emmett Lee Irwin, 19 June 1956, Freedom of Information Act No. 105-40774.

66. CHR executive committee minutes, 20 June 1956, Box 47, folder 15, JHFP.

67. Notre Dame's attempts to obtain Fichter's services the previous year (1955–1956) had been unsuccessful because the New Orleans Province provincial had disapproved of Fichter living outside a Jesuit community, but the following year Notre Dame officials had made a more substantial offer for Fichter's services, which his superiors accepted. When debating the issue in 1956, Loyola officials argued that his appointment would bring prestige to the university and that "it will be good for Father Fichter to be away from New Orleans next year when the interracial question will surely be hotly debated." William Crandell to John B. Janssens, 27 May 1956, New Orleans Province files, *ARSI*. For a complete review of the Fichter Notre Dame issue, see Joseph H. Fichter to William Crandell, 22 March 1955, ANOSJ; Joseph H. Fichter to William Crandell, 19 April 1955, ANOSJ; William Crandell to Joseph H. Fichter, 20 April 1955, ANOSJ; Joseph H. Fichter to William Crandell, 13 June 1955, ANOSJ; John Kane to Joseph H. Fichter, 30 September 1955, ANOSJ; Joseph H. Fichter to William Crandell, 10 October 1955, ANOSJ; Crandell to Janssens, 27 May 1956.

68. Gladys Williams to Joseph H. Fichter, Feast of St. William [of Vercelli?], June 1956, Box 46, folder 7, JHFP. St. William Vercelli's feast day is June 25th.

69. Joseph H. Fichter to Gladys Williams, 30 June 1956, Box 46, folder 7, JHFP.

70. Maurice B. Gatlin to William Crandell, 24 May 1956, ANOSJ.

71. William Crandell to Maurice Gatlin, 2 June 1956, ANOSJ.

72. Maurice B. Gatlin to William Crandell, 8 June 1956, ANOSJ.

73. Joseph Francis Rummel to Joseph H. Fichter, 23 July 1956, Box 46, folder 8, JHFP. The "dual organization" Rummel refers to is the Catholic Committee of the South and its subcommittee the Commission on Human Rights.

74. Joseph H. Fichter to Joseph Francis Rummel, 26 July 1956, Box 46, folder 8, JHFP.

75. Joseph H. Fichter to Henry Montecino, 26 July 1956, Box 46, folder 8, JHFP.

76. Henry Montecino, memorandum of record, 1 August 1956, Box 46, folder 8, JHFP.

77. Jesuit consultors and board members of Loyola University of the South during the 1956–1957 academic year were Edward Doyle, Aloysius Goodspeed, Edward Shields, and James Whelan.

78. LUBD minutes, 11 May 1956, ALUNO.

79. Ibid.

80. Louis Boyer to William Crandell, 4 May 1956, ANOSJ.

81. William Crandell to Louis Boyer, 2 June 1956, ANOSJ.

82. Emile A. Wagner, "An Analysis by Emile A. Wagner, Jr., Catholic Layman of Archbishop Joseph Francis Rummel's Pastoral Letter Entitled 'Morality of Racial Segregation,'" pamphlet, private printing, 28 May 1956, Box 85, folder 2, LJTP.

83. Ibid.

84. Ibid.

85. Ibid.

86. Ibid.

87. House Council entries of 2 March 1955, 10 June 1955, and 29 January 1956,

Series IV: St. Louis Province, E) Grand Coteau, 1) Community, A) History, Box 2, House Journals: 1941–1953, 1953–1962; Minutes of the House Council, Aug. 2, 1954–May 22, 1957, ARSCJ-House; "Sacred Heart College to Pass Away in June," *Daily Advertiser,* 25 January 1956, 1, 2; "Students Band Together to Help Sacred Heart College Remain Open, "*Southwest Louisiana Register,* 3 February 1956, 1; "Decision to Close Sacred Heart College Final, Superior Tells," *Southwest Louisiana Register,* 17 February 1956, 1; "Last Commencement Is Held at College of Sacred Heart," *Southwest Louisiana Register,* 11 June 1956, 1.

88. College Journal entry, 25 January 1956, SERIES IV: St. Louis Province, E) Grand Coteau, 3) Ministry: College, College Journal 1939–1956, ARSCJ-College.

89. "Sacred Heart to Close in June '56, Failure to Increase Enrollment Is Given as Cause for Action," *Southwest Louisiana Register,* 3 February 1956, 1.

90. LUBD minutes, 24 July 1956, ALUNO.

91. *CC* 9, no. 4 (October, 1956).

92. Russell J. Henderson, "The 1963 Mississippi State University Basketball Controversy and the Repeal of the Unwritten Law: 'Something More Than the Game Was Lost,'" *Journal of Southern History* (November 1997): 827–54. When referring to a basketball game played at Loyola University of the South in 1961, Henderson mistakenly noted that the university "had desegregated its classrooms in the early 1950s."

93. LUBD minutes, 15 September 1956, ALUNO.

94. Ibid. In 1958 the United States District Court for the Eastern District of Louisiana ruled that the law was unconstitutional. The United States Supreme Court upheld the ruling in *State Athletic Commission* v. *Dorsey,* 359 U.S. 533 (1959).

95. Aloysius Goodspeed to William Crandell, 7 July 1956, ANOSJ.

96. Joseph H. Fichter to Patrick Donnelly, 17 February 1957, Box 1, folder 17, JHFP.

97. Patrick Donnelly to Joseph H. Fichter, 21 February 1957, Box 50, folder 13, JHFP.

98. Joseph H. Fichter to Patrick Donnelly, Sexagesima Sunday [24 February], 1957, Box 50, folder 13, JHFP.

99. Joseph H. Fichter to Philip Des Marais, 26 February 1957, Box 50, folder 13, JHFP.

100. Joseph H. Fichter to Mary Josephina, 4 March 1957, Box 50, folder 13, JHFP.

101. Mary Josephina to Joseph H. Fichter, 8 March 1957, Box 50, folder 13, JHFP.

102. Philip Des Marais to Joseph H. Fichter, 4 April 1957, Box 50, folder 13, JHFP. In his autobiography Fichter states that it was only after he had made these inquires that he "learned how Father Donnelly succeeded, where his predecessor Father Thomas Shields had failed, in suppressing both SERINCO and its monthly newssheet, *The Christian Conscience*." Fichter, *One-Man Research,* 105. Evidently Fichter never learned that the only person who voted to keep the interracial commission alive was Patrick Donnelly. Provincial William Crandell made the final determination to terminate the commission based on the vote of Loyola board members.

103. Patrick Donnelly to William Crandell, 2 July 1957, ANOSJ.

104. In a 1959 letter to the then provincial, Lawrence O'Neill, S.J., Fichter commented: "You probably know that we are still pursuing the 'wait-and-see' policy here on the campus in regard to the inter-collegiate, inter-racial commission. This group was officially disbanded while I was at Notre Dame, and the *Christian Conscience* was also killed off." Joseph Fichter to Lawrence O'Neill, 16 March 1959, ANOSJ.

Chapter IX

1. Minister's Diary, Jesuit High School Dallas, 1953–1956, 96, Dallas Jesuit College Preparatory School Archives (hereafter referred to as DJA).

2. House History, Jesuit High School Dallas, 1955, 3, DJA.

3. Numa Rousseve, Jr., interview by author, tape recording, White Plains, NY, 15 January 2000.

4. Philip Postell, S.J., telephone interview by author, written notes, Dallas, TX, 18 January 2000; Gerald Fagin, S.J., interview by author, written notes, New Orleans, 24 January 2000; Edward Buvens, S.J., interview by author, written notes, New Orleans, 26 January 2000.

5. James A. McInerney, O.P., to Mother Mary Dominic, O.P., 9 May 1953, DSA.

6. See Xavier University's Web site, www.xula.edu, for information about its graduates.

7. "Council on Human Relations Is Seen as 'Holy Crusade,'" 2 April 1961, *Catholic Action of the South,* 1, 4–5; Liva Baker, *Second Battle of New Orleans: The Hundred-Year Struggle to Integrate the Schools* (New York: HarperCollins, 1996), 394–436; Kim Lacy Rogers, *Righteous Lives: Narratives of the New Orleans Civil Rights Movement* (New York: New York University Press, 1993), 49–76; Adam Fairclough, *Race and Democracy: The Civil Rights Struggle in Louisiana, 1915–1972* (Athens: University of Georgia Press, 1995), 234–64. The archdiocesan newspaper *Catholic Action of the South* did not cover the desegregation crisis in depth.

8. See pages 27–29.

9. See pages 56–59.

10. See page 77.

11. See page 114.

12. See, page 245, note 10.

13. See pages 113–15.

14. See pages 143–45.

15. See pages 145, 148–49.

16. See pages 145–48.

17. See pages 153–61, 167–71.

18. See pages 150–53.

19. See Liva Baker, *The Second Battle of New Orleans: The Hundred-Year Struggle to Integrate the Schools* (New York: HarperCollins Publishers, 1996); Adam Fairclough, *Race and Democracy: The Civil Rights Struggle in Louisiana, 1915–1972* (Athens: University of Georgia Press, 1995); and Kim Lacy Rogers, *Righteous Lives: Narratives of the New Orleans Civil Rights Movement* (New York: New York University Press, 1993).

20. Martin Luther King, Jr., "Letter from Birmingham Jail," in *Why We Can't Wait* (New York: Harper and Row, 1964), 77–100.

BIBLIOGRAPHY

Papers and Archival Collections

Allport, Gordon. Papers. Harvard University, Cambridge.

Amistad Research Center. Tulane University, New Orleans.

Dallas Jesuit Preparatory College. Archives. Dallas.

Dominican Congregation of St. Mary. Archives. Dominican Center, New Orleans.

Fichter, Joseph H. Papers. Special Collections and Archives, Monroe Library, Loyola University, New Orleans.

Jack, Hulan. Papers. Schomburg Center for Research in Black Culture, New York Public Library.

Loyola University. Archives. Special Collections and Archives, Monroe Library, Loyola University, New Orleans.

Midwest Jesuit Archives. St. Louis.

National Federation of Catholic College Students. Records. Manhattanville College Archives, Pleasantville, NY.

New Orleans Province of the Society of Jesus. Archives. Loyola University, New Orleans.

Rummel, Archbishop Joseph Francis. Pastoral letters, 1935–1962. Archdiocesan Archives, Archdiocese of New Orleans.

Saint Mary's Dominican College. Archives. Dominican Center, New Orleans.

Society of the Sacred Heart. National archives, U.S.A., St. Louis.

Twomey, Louis J. Papers. Special Collections and Archives, Monroe Library, Loyola University, New Orleans.

Ursuline College. Archives. Ursuline Convent Archives and Museum, New Orleans.

Xavier University. Archives and Special Collections. Xavier University, New Orleans.

Federal Archives

Department of Justice. Freedom of Information and Privacy Acts records for Joseph H. Fichter (FOIPA file no. 105-40774) and for National Federation of Catholic College Students (FOIPA file no. 94-37775).

Selected Books

Abell, Aaron I. *American Catholicism and Social Action: A Search for Social Action, 1865–1950.* Garden City, NY: Hanover House, 1960.

Ahmann, Mathew, ed. *Race: Challenge to Religion; Original Essays and an Appeal to Conscience.* Chicago: Henry Regnery Co., 1963. Reprint, Westport, CT: Greenwood Press, 1979.

Allport, Gordon W. *The Nature of Prejudice.* Cambridge, MA: Addison-Wesley Pub. Co., 1954.

Alvis, Joel L. *Religion and Race: Southern Presbyterians, 1946–1983.* Tuscaloosa: University of Alabama Press, 1994.

Ambrose, Stephen E. *Eisenhower.* New York: Simon and Schuster, 1983.

Aptheker, Herbert, ed. *A Documentary History of the Negro People in the United States.* New York: Carol Publishing Group, 1979.

263

Ashmore, Harry S. *Civil Rights and Wrongs: A Memoir of Race and Politics, 1944–1996.* Rev. ed. Columbia: University of South Carolina Press, 1997.

Ayers, Edward L. *The Promise of the New South: Life after Reconstruction.* New York: Oxford University Press, 1992.

Baer, Hans A., and Yvonne Jones, eds. *African Americans in the South: Issues of Race, Class, and Gender.* Athens: University of Georgia Press, 1992.

Baker, Liva. *The Second Battle of New Orleans: The Hundred-Year Struggle to Integrate the Schools.* New York: HarperCollins Publishers, 1996.

Bartley, Numan V. *The Rise of Massive Resistance: Race and Politics in the South during the 1950s.* Baton Rouge: Louisiana State University Press, 1969.

————. *The New South, 1945–1980.* Baton Rouge: Louisiana State University Press, 1995.

Bartley, Numan V., and Hugh D. Graham, *Southern Politics and the Second Reconstruction.* Baltimore: Johns Hopkins University Press, 1975.

Baudier, Roger. *The Catholic Church in Louisiana.* New Orleans: A. W. Hyatt Stationery Manufacturing, 1939.

Belknap, Michal R. ed. *Urban Race Riots.* New York: Garland Pub., 1991.

Bell, Caryn Cossé. *Revolution, Romanticism, and the Afro-Creole Protest Tradition in Louisiana, 1718–1868.* Baton Rouge: Louisiana State University Press, 1997.

Berlin, Ira. *Slaves without Masters: The Free Negro in the Antebellum South.* New York: Pantheon Books, 1975.

Berman, William C. *The Politics of Civil Rights in the Truman Administration.* Columbus: Ohio State University Press, 1970.

Blassingame, John W. *Black New Orleans, 1860–1880.* Chicago: University of Chicago Press, 1973.

Blatnica, Dorothy A. *At the Altar of Their God: African American Catholics in Cleveland, 1922–1961.* New York: Garland Pub., 1995.

Boles, John B. *Masters and Slaves in the House of the Lord: Race and Religion in the American South, 1740–1870.* Lexington: University Press of Kentucky, 1988.

Bolner, James, ed. *Louisiana Politics: Festival in a Labyrinth.* Baton Rouge: Louisiana State University Press, 1982.

Bouscaren, T. Lincoln, and Adam C. Ellis. *Canon Law: A Text and Commentary.* 2d rev. ed. Milwaukee: Bruce, 1951.

Branch, Taylor. *Parting the Water: America in the King Years, 1954–1963.* New York: Simon and Schuster, 1988.

Branyan, Robert L., and Lawrence H. Larsen, eds. *The Eisenhower Administration, 1953–1961: A Documentary History.* New York: Random House, 1971.

Brett, Stephen F. *Slavery and the Catholic Tradition: Rights in the Balance.* New York: Peter Lang, 1994.

Brown, Stuart G. *Conscience in Politics: Adlai Stevenson in the 1950s.* Syracuse: Syracuse University Press, 1961.

Burk, Robert Frederick. *The Eisenhower Administration and Black Civil Rights.* Knoxville: University of Tennessee Press, 1984.

Burton, Katherine. *The Golden Door: The Life of Katharine Drexel.* New York: P. J. Kenedy and Sons, 1957.

Callan, Louise. *Philippine Duchesne, Frontier Missionary of the Sacred Heart, 1769–1852.* Westminster, MD: Newman Press, 1957.

Carter, Hodding. *The South Strikes Back.* Garden City, NY: Doubleday, 1959.

Carter, Hodding, et al., eds. *Past as Prelude: New Orleans, 1718–1968.* New Orleans: Tulane University and Pelican Publishing, 1968.

A Catechism of Christian Doctrine, Prepared and Enjoined by Order of the Third Plenary Council of Baltimore. New York, Cincinnati: Benzinger Brothers, 1933; reprint, Rockford, IL: Tan Books and Publishers, 1977.

Caute, David. *The Great Fear: The Anti-Communist Purge under Truman and Eisenhower.* New York: Simon and Schuster, 1978.

Chappell, David L. *Inside Agitators: White Southerners in the Civil Rights Movement.* Baltimore: Johns Hopkins University Press, 1994.

————. *A Stone of Hope: Prophetic Religion and the Death of Jim Crow.* Chapel Hill: University of North Carolina Press, 2004.

Chase, John Churchill. *Frenchmen, Desire, Good Children and Other Streets of New Orleans.* 3d ed. New York: Collier Books, 1979.

Cohen, Robert. *When the Old Left Was Young: Student Radicals and America's First Mass Student Movement, 1929–1941.* New York: Oxford University Press, 1993.

Coleman, John A., ed. *One Hundred Years of Catholic Social Thought: Celebration and Challenge.* Maryknoll, NY: Orbis Books, 1991.

Colten, Craig E., ed. *Transforming New Orleans and Its Environs: Centuries of Change.* Pittsburgh: University of Pittsburgh Press, 2000.

Conaway, James. *Judge: The Life and Times of Leander Perez.* New York: Alfred A. Knopf, 1973.

Congar, Yves M.-J. *The Catholic Church and the Race Question.* The Race Question and Modern Thought series. Paris: United Nations Educational, Scientific and Cultural Organization, 1953. Reprint, Paris: IFMRP, 1961.

Connell, Janice T. *Praying with Mary: A Treasury for All Occasions.* San Francisco: HarperSanFrancisco, 1997.

Conrad, Glenn R., ed. *Cross, Crozier, and Crucible: A Volume Celebrating the Bicentennial of a Catholic Diocese in Louisiana.* New Orleans: Archdiocese of New Orleans in cooperation with the Center for Louisiana Studies, 1993.

Cowan, Walter G., et al. *New Orleans Yesterday and Today: A Guide to the City.* Baton Rouge: Louisiana State University Press, 1983.

Cronin, John F. *Catholic Social Action.* Milwaukee: Bruce, 1948.

Crosby, Donald F. *God, Church and Flag: Senator Joseph R. McCarthy and the Catholic Church, 1950–1957.* Chapel Hill: University of North Carolina Press, 1978.

Cross, George L. *Blacks in White Colleges: Oklahoma's Landmark Cases.* Norman: University of Oklahoma Press, 1975.

Culver, Dwight W. *Negro Segregation in the Methodist Church.* New Haven: Yale University Press, 1953.

Curran, Charles E., and Richard A. McCormick, eds. *Dissent in the Church.* Moral Theology, no. 6. New York: Paulist Press, 1988.

Dalfiume, Richard M. *Desegregation of the U.S. Armed Forces: Fighting on Two Fronts, 1939–1953.* Columbia: University of Missouri Press, 1969.

Daniel, Pete. *Lost Revolutions: The South in the 1950s.* Chapel Hill: University of North Carolina Press for Smithsonian National Museum of American History, Washington, DC, 2000.

Danziger, Sheldon, Reynolds Farley, and Harry J. Holzer. *Detroit Divided.* New York: Russell Sage Foundation, 2000.

Daues, Dorothy, and Charles E. Nolan, eds. *Religious Pioneers: Building the Faith in the Archdiocese of New Orleans.* Chelsea, MI: Sheridan Books, 2004.

Dauphine, James G. *A Question of Inheritance: Religion, Education, and Louisiana's Cultural Boundaries, 1880–1940.* Lafayette: Center for Louisiana Studies, University of Southwestern Louisiana, 1993.

Davis, Cyprian. *The History of Black Catholics in the United States.* New York: Crossroad, 1991.

Davis, Kenneth S. *The Politics of Honor: A Biography of Adlai E. Stevenson.* New York: Putnam's Sons, 1967.

Deferrari, Roy J., ed. *Essays on Catholic Education in the United States.* Washington, DC: Catholic University of America Press, 1942.

Deggs, Mary Bernard. *No Cross, No Crown: Black Nuns in Nineteenth-Century New Orleans.* Edited by Virginia Meacham Gould and Charles E. Nolan. Bloomington: Indiana University Press, 2001.

Dittmer, John. *Local People: The Struggle for Civil Rights in Mississippi.* Urbana: University of Illinois Press, 1994.

Dolan, Jay. *The American Catholic Experience: A History from Colonial Times to the Present.* Garden City, NY: Doubleday, 1985. Reprint, Notre Dame: Notre Dame University Press, 1992.

Dominguez, Virginia R. *White by Definition: Social Classification in Creole Louisiana.* New Brunswick, NJ: Rutgers University Press, 1986.

Donaldson, Gary A. *Truman Defeats Dewey.* Lexington: University Press of Kentucky, 1999.

Donovan, Robert J. *Conflict and Crisis: The Presidency of Harry S. Truman, 1945–1948.* New York: W.W. Norton, 1977. Reprint, Columbia: University of Missouri Press, 1996.

———. *Tumultuous Years: The Presidency of Harry S. Truman, 1949–1953.* New York: W.W. Norton, 1982.

Dorr, Donald. *Option for the Poor: One Hundred Years of Vatican Social Teaching.* Maryknoll, NY: Orbis Books, 1983.

Doyle, Bertram W. *The Etiquette of Race Relations in the South.* Chicago: University of Chicago Press, 1937.

Dudziak, Mary L. *Cold War Civil Rights: Race and the Image of American Democracy.* Princeton, NJ: Princeton University Press, 2000.

Duffy, Consuela Marie. *Katharine Drexel: A Biography.* Philadelphia: Peter Reilly Co., 1965.

Dulles, Avery Robert. *Models of the Church.* Garden City, NY: Doubleday, 1974.

Ellis, John Tracy. *American Catholicism.* 2d ed. Chicago: University of Chicago Press, 1969.

Egerton, John. *Speak Now against the Day: The Generation before the Civil Rights Movement in the South.* New York: Alfred A. Knopf, 1994.

Fairclough, Adam. *To Redeem the Soul of America : The Southern Christian Leadership Conference and Martin Luther King, Jr.* Athens: University of Georgia Press, 1987.

———. *Race and Democracy: The Civil Rights Struggle in Louisiana, 1915–1972.* Athens: University of Georgia Press, 1995.

Fichter, Joseph H. *Roots of Change.* New York: D. Appleton–Century Co., 1939.

———. *Man of Spain: A Biography of Francis Suarez.* New York: Macmillan Co., 1940.

———. *Saint Cecil Cyprian: Early Defender of the Faith.* St. Louis: B. Herder Book Co., 1942.

———. *James Laynez, Jesuit.* St. Louis: B. Herder Book Co., 1944.

———. *Southern Parish.* Vol. 1, *Dynamics of a City Church.* Chicago: University of Chicago Press, 1951.

———. *Sociology: A Clear and Objective Presentation of the Basic Concepts of Sociology.* Chicago: University of Chicago Press, 1957.

———. *One-Man Research: Reminiscences of a Catholic Sociologist.* New York: John Wiley and Sons, 1973.

———. *The Sociology of Good Work: Research in Catholic America.* Chicago: Loyola University Press, 1993.

Fields, Barbara Jeanne. *Slavery and Freedom on the Middle Ground: Maryland during the Nineteenth Century.* New Haven: Yale University Press, 1985.

Fischer, Roger. *The Segregation Struggle in Louisiana, 1862–77.* Urbana: University of Illinois Press, 1974.

Flannery, Austin, gen. ed. *Vatican Council II: The Conciliar and Post Conciliar Documents.* Rev. ed. Boston: St. Paul Books and Media, 1992.

Foley, Albert S. *God's Men of Color: The Colored Catholic Priests of the United States, 1854–1954.* New York: Farrar, Straus and Co., 1955.

Foner, Eric. *Reconstruction: America's Unfinished Revolution, 1863–1877.* New York: Harper and Row, 1988.

Fortier, Alcèe. *A History of Louisiana.* Vol. 1. New York: Manzi, Joyant and Co., 1904.

Fried, Richard. *Nightmare in Red: The McCarthy Era in Perspective.* New York: Oxford University Press, 1990.

Friedland, Michael B. *Lift Up Your Voice like a Trumpet: White Clergy and the Civil Rights and Antiwar Movements, 1954–1973.* Chapel Hill: University of North Carolina Press, 1998.

Gardner, Michael R. *Harry Truman and Civil Rights: Moral Courage and Political Risks.* Carbondale: Southern Illinois University Press, 2002.

Garson, Robert A. *The Democratic Party and the Politics of Sectionalism, 1941–1948.* Baton Rouge: Louisiana State University Press, 1974.

Garvey, Joan B., and Mary Lou Widmer. *Beautiful Crescent: A History of New Orleans.* New Orleans: Garmer Press, 1982.

Gibson, Ralph. *Social History of French Catholicism, 1789–1914.* New York: Routledge, 1989.

Gill, James. *Lords of Misrule: Mardi Gras and the Politics of Race in New Orleans.* Jackson: University Press of Mississippi, 1997.

Gillard, John T. *The Catholic Church in the United States.* Baltimore: St. Joseph's Society Press, 1929.

———. *Colored Catholics in the United States.* Baltimore: Josephite Press, 1941.

Gleason, Philip, ed. *Contemporary Catholicism in the United States.* Notre Dame: University of Notre Dame Press, 1969.

Goldfield, David R. *Black, White, and Southern: Race Relations and Southern Culture, 1940 to the Present.* Baton Rouge: Louisiana State University Press, 1990.

Gould, Virginia Meacham, and Charles E. Nolan, *Henriette Delille: "Servant of Slaves."* 2d rev. ed. New Orleans: Sisters of the Holy Family, 1998.

Greenberg, Cheryl Lynn, ed. *A Circle of Trust: Remembering SNCC.* New Brunswick, NJ: Rutgers University Press, 1998.

Griffith, Robert. *The Politics of Fear: Joseph McCarthy and the Senate.* 2d ed. Amherst: University of Massachusetts Press, 1987.

Haas, Edward F. *DeLesseps S. Morrison and the Image of Reform: New Orleans Politics, 1946–1961.* Baton Rouge: Louisiana State University Press, 1974.

Halberstam, David. *The Fifties.* New York: Villard Books, 1993.

Hamby, Alonzo L. *Beyond the New Deal: Harry S. Truman and American Liberalism.* New York: Columbia University Press, 1973.

Hammond, David M. *Theology and Lived Christianity: The Annual Publication of the College Theology Society.* Mystic, CT: Twenty-Third Publications/Bayard, 2000.

Hanger, Kimberly S. *Bounded Lives, Bounded Places: Free Black Society in Colonial New Orleans, 1769–1803.* Durham, N.C.: Duke University Press, 1997.

Harte, Thomas Joseph. *Catholic Organizations Promoting Negro-White Race Relations in the United States.* Washington, DC: Catholic University of America Press, 1947.

Haws, Robert, ed. *The Age of Segregation: Race Relations in the South, 1890–1945.* Jackson: University Press of Mississippi, 1978.

Heaney, Jane Francis. *A Century of Pioneering: A History of Ursuline Nuns in New Orleans, 1727–1827.* Chelsea, MI: Bookcraft, 1993.

Hennesey, James. *American Catholics: A History of the Roman Catholic Community in the United States.* New York: Oxford University Press, 1981.

Henry, Aaron, with Constance Curry. *Aaron Henry: The Fire Ever Burning.* Jackson: University Press of Mississippi, 2000.

Higham, John, ed. *Civil Rights and Social Wrongs: Black-White Relations since World War II.* University Park: Pennsylvania State University Press, 1997.

Hirsch, Arnold R., and Joseph Logsdon, eds. *Creole New Orleans: Race and Americanization.* Baton Rouge: Louisiana State University Press, 1992.

Hollandsworth, James G., Jr. *An Absolute Massacre: The New Orleans Race Riot of July 30, 1866.* Baton Rouge: Louisiana State University Press, 2001.

Howard, John. *The Shifting Wind: The Supreme Court and Civil Rights from Reconstruction to Brown.* Albany: State University of New York Press, 1999.

Howard, L. Vaughn, and David R. Deener. *Presidential Politics in Louisiana, 1952.* Tulane Studies in Political Science, vol. 6. New Orleans: Tulane University, 1954.

Hunton, George K. *All of Which I Saw, Part of Which I Was: The Autobiography of George Hunton.* Garden City, NY: Doubleday, 1967.

Ignatiev, Noel. *How the Irish Became White.* New York: Routledge, 1995.

Jack, Hulan E. *Fifty Years a Democrat: The Autobiography of Hulan Jack.* New York: New Benjamin Franklin House, 1983.

Jeansonne, Glen. *Leander Perez: Boss of the Delta.* Baton Rouge: Louisiana State University Press, 1977.

Jezer, Marty. *The Dark Ages: Life in the United States, 1945–1960.* Boston: South End Press, 1982.

Johnson, Walter. *Soul by Soul: Life inside the Antebellum Slave Market.* Cambridge: Harvard University Press, 1999.

Jone, Heribert. *Moral Theology.* 18th ed. Translated by Urban S. Adelman. Westminster, MD: Newman Press, 1962.

Kasteel, Annemarie. *Francis Janssens, 1843–1897: A Dutch-American Prelate.* Lafayette: Center for Louisiana Studies, University of Southwestern Louisiana, 1992.

Kauffman, Christopher. *Faith and Fraternalism: The History of the Knights of Columbus, 1882–1982.* New York: Harper and Row, 1982.

Kein, Sybil, ed. *Creole: The History and Legacy of Louisiana's Free People of Color.* Baton Rouge: Louisiana State University Press, 2000.

Kelly, Frank K. *Court of Reason: Robert Hutchins and the Fund for the Republic*. New York: Free Press, 1981.

Kelsey, George D. *Social Ethics among Southern Baptists, 1917–1969*. Metuchen, NJ: Scarecrow Press, 1973.

Kent, Peter C. *The Lonely Cold War of Pope Pius XII: The Roman Catholic Church and the Division of Europe, 1943–1950*. Montreal: McGill-Queen's University Press, 2002.

Key, V. O., Jr., with Alexander Heard. *Southern Politics in State and Nation*. New York: Alfred A. Knopf, 1949. Reprint, Knoxville: University of Tennessee Press, 1984.

King, Martin Luther, Jr. *Why We Can't Wait*. New York: Harper and Row, 1964.

Klinkner, Philip A., and Rogers M. Smith. *The Unsteady March: The Rise and Decline of Racial Equality in America*. Chicago: University of Chicago Press, 1999.

Kluger, Richard. *Simple Justice: The History of Brown v. Board of Education and Black America's Struggle for Equality*. New York: Alfred A. Knopf, 1976.

Koenig, Louis W., ed. *The Truman Administration: Its Principles and Practice*. New York: New York University Press, 1956.

Kurtz, Michael L., and Morgan D. Peoples. *Earl K. Long: The Saga of Uncle Earl and Louisiana Politics*. Baton Rouge: Louisiana State University Press, 1990.

Labbé, Delores Egger. *Jim Crow Comes to Church: The Establishment of Segregated Parishes in South Louisiana*. USL History Series. Lafayette: University of Southwestern Louisiana, 1971.

LaFarge, John. *Interracial Justice: A Study of the Catholic Doctrine of Race Relations*. New York: American Press, 1937. Reprint, New York: Arno Press, Inc., 1978.

————. *The Race Question and the Negro: A Study of the Catholic Doctrine on Interracial Justice*. New York: Longmans, Green and Co., 1937.

————. *No Postponement: U.S. Moral Leadership and the Problem of Racial Minorities*. New York: Longmans, Green and Co., 1950.

Layton, Azza Salama. *International Politics and Civil Rights Policies in the United States, 1941–1960*. New York: Cambridge University Press, 2000.

Lee, Alfred McClung, and Norman Daymond Humphrey. *Race Riot*. New York: Dryden Press, 1943.

Lewis, David L. *W. E. B. Du Bois*. Vol. 1, *Biography of a Race, 1868–1919*. New York: Henry Holt, 1993.

Liebling, A. J. *The Earl of Louisiana*. 1961. Reprint, Baton Rouge: Louisiana State University Press, 1970.

Linck Joseph C., and Raymond J. Kupke, eds. *Building the Church in America: Studies in Honor of Monsignor Robert F. Trisco on the Occasion of His Seventieth Birthday*. Washington, DC: Catholic University of America Press, 1999.

Lofgen, Charles A. *The Plessy Case: A Legal-Historical Interpretation*. New York: Oxford University Press, 1987.

Lord, Daniel A. *Our Part in the Mystical Body*. Saint Louis: Queen's Work, 1935.

Lott, Eric. *Love and Theft: Blackface Minstrelsy and the American Working Class*. New York: Oxford University Press, 1993.

Luxmoore, Jonathan, and Jolanta Babiuch. *The Vatican and the Red Flag: The Struggle for the Soul of Eastern Europe*. New York: G. Chapman, 1999.

Lynch, Patricia. *Sharing the Bread in Service: Sisters of the Blessed Sacrament*. Bensalem, PA: Sisters of the Blessed Sacrament, 1998.

Mann, Robert. *The Walls of Jericho: Lyndon Johnson, Hubert Humphrey, Richard Russell, and the Struggle for Civil Rights*. New York: Harcourt Brace, 1996.

Marable, Manning. *Race, Reform and Rebellion: The Second Reconstruction in Black America, 1945–1982.* Jackson: University Press of Mississippi, 1984.

Martinez, Elsie, and Margaret LeCorgne. *Uptown/Downtown: Growing Up in New Orleans.* Lafayette: The Center for Louisiana Studies, University of Southwestern Louisiana, 1986.

Marty, Martin E. *A Short History of American Catholicism.* Allen, TX: Thomas More, 1995.

Massa, Mark S. *Catholics and American Culture: Fulton Sheen, Dorothy Day, and the Notre Dame Football Team.* New York: Crossroad, 1999.

Maxwell, John Francis. *Slavery and the Catholic Church: The History of Catholic Teaching Concerning the Moral Legitimacy of the Institution of Slavery.* London: Barry Rose Publishers, 1975.

McAvoy, Thomas T. *A History of the Catholic Church in the United States.* Notre Dame: University of Notre Dame Press, 1969.

McBrien, Richard P. *Catholicism: Completely Revised and Updated.* 2d ed. San Francisco: HarperSanFrancisco, 1994.

McCoy, Donald R. *The Presidency of Harry S. Truman.* Lawrence: University Press of Kansas, 1984.

McCoy, Donald R., and Richard T. Ruetten. *Quest and Response: Minority Rights and the Truman Administration.* Lawrence: University Press of Kansas, 1973.

McDonogh, Gary W. *Black and Catholic in Savannah, Georgia.* Knoxville: University of Tennessee Press, 1993.

McDonough, Peter. *Men Astutely Trained: A History of the Jesuits in the American Century.* New York: Free Press, 1992.

McGinty, Garnie W. *A History of Louisiana.* 2d ed. New York: Exposition Press, 1951.

McGreevy, John T. *Parish Boundaries: The Catholic Encounter with Race in the Twentieth-Century Urban North.* Chicago: University of Chicago Press, 1996.

McKivigan, John R., and Mitchell Snay. *Religion and the Antebellum Debate over Slavery.* Athens: University of Georgia Press, 1998.

McMahon, Eileen. *What Parish Are You From?: A Chicago Irish Community and Race Relations.* Lexington: University Press of Kentucky, 1995.

McManus, Eugene P. *Studies in Race Relations.* Baltimore: Josephite Press, 1961.

McMillen, Neil R. *The Citizens' Council: Organized Resistance to the Second Reconstruction, 1954–64.* Urbana: University of Illinois Press, 1971.

Meier, August, and Elliott Rudwick. *CORE: A Study in the Civil Rights Movement, 1942–1968.* New York: Oxford University Press, 1973.

Mellafe, Rolando. *Negro Slavery in Latin America.* Translated by J. W. S. Judge. Berkeley: University of California Press, 1975.

Mersch, Emile. *The Theology of the Mystical Body.* Translated by Cyril Vollert. London: B. Herder Book Co., 1951.

Miller, John D. *Beads and Prayers: The Rosary in History and Devotion.* London: Burns and Oates, 2001.

Miller, Randall M., and John L. Wakelyn, eds. *Catholics in the Old South: Essays on Church and Culture.* Macon, GA: Mercer University Press, 1983.

Mindszenty, Joseph. *Memoirs.* Translated by Richard Winston and Clara Winston. New York: Macmillan, 1974.

Mitchell, Reid. *All on a Mardi Gras Day: Episodes in the History of New Orleans Carnival.* Cambridge: Harvard University Press, 1995.

Mooney, Catherine M. *Philippine Duchesne: A Woman with the Poor.* New York: Paulist Press, 1990.

Moore, Jesse Thomas, Jr. *A Search for Equality: The National Urban League, 1910–1961.* University Park: Pennsylvania State University Press, 1981.

Morris, Charles. *American Catholic: The Saints and Sinners Who Built America's Most Powerful Church.* New York: Times Books, 1997.

Mura, Ernest. *The Nature of the Mystical Body.* Translated by Angeline Bouchard. London: B. Herder Book Co., 1963.

Myrdal, Gunnar. *An America Dilemma: The Negro Problem and Modern Democracy.* New York: Harper and Row, 1944.

Nickels, Marilyn Wenzke. *Black Catholic Protest and the Federated Colored Catholics, 1917–1933: Three Perspectives on Racial Justice.* New York: Garland Pub., 1988.

Nolan, William A. *Communism versus the Negro.* Chicago: Henry Regnery Co., 1951.

Oakley, J. Ronald. *God's Country: America in the Fifties.* New York: Dembner Books, 1986.

O'Brien, David J., and Thomas A. Shannon, eds. *Renewing the Earth: Catholic Documents on Peace, Justice, and Liberation.* Garden City, NY: Image Books, 1977.

———. *Catholic Social Thought.* Maryknoll: Orbis Books, 1992.

O'Brien, Felicity. *Treasure in Heaven: Katharine Drexel.* Middlegreen, MN: St. Paul Publications, 1991.

O'Brien, Michael. *The Idea of the American South, 1920–1941.* Baltimore: Johns Hopkins University Press, 1979.

Ochs, Stephen. *Desegregating the Altar: The Josephites and the Struggle for Black Priests, 1871–1960.* Baton Rouge: Louisiana State University Press, 1990.

Odum, Howard W. *Race and Rumors of Race: Challenge to American Crisis.* Chapel Hill: University of North Carolina Press, 1943.

Offner, Arnold A. *Another Such Victory: President Truman and the Cold War, 1945–1953.* Stanford: Stanford University Press, 2002.

O'Malley, John. *The First Jesuits.* Cambridge, MA: Harvard University Press, 1993.

O'Neill, Joseph E., ed. *A Catholic Case against Segregation.* New York: Macmillan, 1961.

O'Neill, Charles E. *Church and State in French Colonial Louisiana: Policy and Politics to 1732.* New Haven: Yale University Press, 1966.

O'Neill, William L. *American High: The Years of Confidence, 1945–1960.* New York: Free Press, 1986.

Orsy, Ladislas. *The Church: Learning and Teaching.* Wilmington: Michael Glazer, 1987.

Osborne, William A. *The Segregated Covenant: Race Relations and American Catholics.* New York: Herder and Herder, 1967.

Pach, Chester J., Jr., and Elmo Richardson. *The Presidency of Dwight D. Eisenhower.* Rev. ed. Lawrence: University Press of Kansas, 1991.

Parmet, Herbert S. *Eisenhower and the American Crusades.* New York: Macmillan, 1972.

Patterson, James T. *Grand Expectations: The United States, 1945–1974.* New York: Oxford University Press, 1996.

———. *Brown v. Board of Education: A Civil Rights Milestone and Its Troubled Legacy.* New York: Oxford University Press, 2001.

Reeves, Thomas C. *Freedom and the Foundation: The Fund for the Republic in the Era of McCarthyism.* New York: Knopf, 1969.

Rice, Madeleine H. *American Catholic Opinion in the Slavery Controversy.* New York: Columbia University Press, 1944.

Roediger, David R. *The Wages of Whiteness: Race and the Making of the American Working Class.* New York: Verso, 1991.

Rogers, Kim Lacy. *Righteous Lives: Narratives of the New Orleans Civil Rights Movement.* New York: New York University Press, 1993.

Rousseve, Charles B. *The Negro in Louisiana: Aspects of His History and His Literature.* New Orleans: Xavier University Press, 1937; reprint, New York: Johnson Reprint Corp., 1970.

Rubin, Louis D., Jr., ed. *The American South: Portrait of a Culture.* Baton Rouge: Louisiana State University Press, 1980.

Sanson, Jerry P. *Louisiana during World War II: Politics and Society, 1939–1945.* Baton Rouge: Louisiana State University Press, 1999.

Schafer, Judith Kelleher. *Slavery, the Civil Law, and the Supreme Court of Louisiana.* Baton Rouge: Louisiana State University Press, 1994.

Schuck, Michael J. *That They Be One: The Social Teaching of the Papal Encyclicals 1740–1989.* Washington, DC: Georgetown University Press, 1991.

Senser, Robert. *Primer on Interracial Justice.* Baltimore: Helicon Press, 1962.

Shabazz, Amilcar. *Advancing Democracy: African Americans and the Struggle for Access and Equity in Higher Education in Texas.* Chapel Hill: University of North Carolina Press, 2004.

Shea, William M., with Daniel Van Slyke, ed. *Trying Times: Essays on Catholic Higher Education in the 20th Century.* Atlanta: Scholars Press, 1999.

Sinnott, Alfred A. *The Watch: 14 Holy Hours, for Each Month of the Year, for Holy Thursday, and for Forty Hours.* Milwaukee: Bruce Pub. Co., 1947.

Smith, H. Shelton. *In His Image, but . . . : Racism in the Southern Religion, 1780–1910.* Durham, NC: Duke University Press, 1972.

Smith, T. Lynn, and Homer L. Hitt. *The People of Louisiana.* Baton Rouge: Louisiana State University Press, 1952.

Sosna, Martin. *In Search of the Silent South: Southern Liberals and the Race Issue.* New York: Columbia University Press, 1977.

Southern, David W. *John LaFarge and the Limits of Catholic Interracialism, 1911–1963.* Baton Rouge: Louisiana State University Press, 1996.

Spalding, Thomas W. *The Premier See: A History of the Archdiocese of Baltimore, 1789–1989.* Baltimore: Johns Hopkins University Press, 1989.

Stampp, Kenneth. *The Peculiar Institution: Slavery in the Antebellum South.* New York: Vintage Books, 1956.

Sterkx, H. E. *The Free Negro in Ante-bellum Louisiana.* Cranburg, NJ: Associated University Presses, 1972.

Sugrue, Thomas J. *The Origins of the Urban Crisis: Race and Inequality in Postwar Detroit.* Princeton, NJ: Princeton University Press, 1996.

Tannenbaum, Frank. *Slave and Citizen: The Negro in the Americas.* New York: Alfred A. Knopf, 1947.

Tarry, Ellen. *Katharine Drexel, Friend of the Neglected.* New York: Farrar, Straus and Cudahy, 1958.

Taylor, Joe Gray. *Negro Slavery in Louisiana.* Baton Rouge: Louisiana State University Press, 1963.

———. *Louisiana: A History.* New York: W. W. Norton, 1976.

Thomas, Brook, ed. *Plessy v. Ferguson: A Brief History with Documents.* Boston: Bedford Books, 1997.

Tindall, George B. *The Emergence of the New South, 1913–1945.* Baton Rouge: Louisiana State University Press, 1967.

Tushnet, Mark V. *The NAACP's Legal Strategy against Segregated Education, 1925–1950.* Chapel Hill: University of North Carolina Press, 1987.

Tyler, Pamela. *Silk Stockings and Ballot Boxes: Women and Politics in New Orleans, 1920–1963.* Athens: University of Georgia Press, 1996.

Vander Zanden, James W. *Race Relations in Transition: The Segregation Crisis in the South.* New York: Random House, 1965.

Vyhnanek, Louis. *Unorganized Crime: New Orleans in the 1920s.* Lafayette: Center for Louisiana Studies, University of Southwestern Louisiana, 1998.

Weiss, Nancy J. *The National Urban League, 1910–1940.* New York: Oxford University Press, 1974.

Whelan, Richard. *Drawing the Line: The Korean War, 1950–1953.* Boston: Little, Brown, 1990.

Whitfield, Stephen. *The Culture of the Cold War.* Baltimore: Johns Hopkins University Press, 1991.

Wilds, John, Charles L. Dufour, and Walter G. Cowan. *Louisiana, Yesterday and Today: A Historical Guide to the State.* Baton Rouge: Louisiana State University Press, 1996.

Woods, Jeff. *Black Struggle, Red Scare: Segregation and Anti-Communism in the South, 1948–1968.* Baton Rouge: Louisiana State University Press, 2004.

Woodward, C. Vann. *Origins of the New South, 1877–1913.* Baton Rouge: Louisiana State University Press, 1951.

———. *The Burden of Southern History.* Baton Rouge: Louisiana State University Press, 1960.

———. *The Strange Career of Jim Crow.* 3d rev. ed. New York: Oxford University Press, 1974.

Zanca, Kenneth J., ed. *American Catholics and Slavery, 1789–1866: An Anthology of Primary Documents.* New York: University Press of America, 1994.

Articles

Agathe, Mother M. "Catholic Education and the Negro." In *Essays on Catholic Education in the United States,* ed. Roy J. Deferrari, 500–22. Washington, DC: Catholic University of America Press, 1942.

Alberts, John B. "Black Catholic Schools: The Josephite Parishes during the Jim Crow Era." *U.S. Catholic Historian* 12 (winter 1994): 77–98.

Alger, Jeanne. "Interracial Justice Week in Catholic Colleges." *Interracial Review* (April 1946): 58–59.

Anderson, R. Bentley. "Prelates, Protest, and Public Opinion: Catholic Opposition to Desegregation, 1947–1955." *Journal of Church and State* 46 (summer 2004): 617–44.

———. "Black, White, and Catholic: Southern Jesuits Confront the Race Question, 1952." *Catholic Historical Review* 91 (July 2005): 484–505.

Aycock, Joan Marie. "The Ursuline School in New Orleans, 1727–1771." In *Cross, Crozier, and Crucible,* ed. Glenn R. Conrad, 203–18. New Orleans: Archdiocese of New Orleans in Cooperation with the Center for Louisiana Studies, 1993.

Bell, Caryn Cossé. "French Religious Culture in Afro-Creole New Orleans, 1718–1877." *U.S. Catholic Historian* 17 (spring 1999):1–16.

Bernard, Raymond. "Jim Crow Vocations?" *Social Order* II (1949): 241–43.

Billington, Monroe. "Civil Rights, President Truman and the South." *Journal of Negro History* 58 (1973): 127–39.

Blish, Mary. "Mother Mary Elizabeth Moran (1836–1905): From Grand Coteau to the World." In *Religious Pioneers,* ed. Dorothy Daues and Charles E. Nolan, 89–104. Chelsea, MI: Sheridan Books, 2004.

Bouvier, Leon. "The Spring Hill College Integration Story." *Interracial Review* (May 1961): 128–30.

Boyd, William M. "Southern Politics, 1948–1952." *Phylon Quarterly* 13 (3d quarter 1952): 226–35.

Campion, Donald. "Negro Students in Jesuit Schools, 1950–1951." *Jesuit Educational Quarterly* 13 (March 1951): 223–28.

Cardozo, Michael. "Racial Discrimination in Legal Schools, 1950–1963." *Journal of Legal Education* 43 (March 1993): 79–84.

Connell, Francis J. "Rights of the Catholic Negro." *American Ecclesiastical Review* (June 1946): 459–62.

Curran, Robert Emmett. "'Splendid Poverty': Jesuit Slaveholding in Maryland, 1805–1838." In *Catholics in the Old South,* ed. Randall M. Miller and Jon L. Wakelyn, 125–46. Macon, GA: Mercer University Press, 1983.

———. "Rome, the American Church and Slavery." In *Building the Church in America,* ed. Joseph C. Linck and Raymond J. Kupke, 30–49. Washington, DC: Catholic University of America Press, 1999.

Czuchlewski, Paul E. "Liberal Catholicism and American Racism, 1924–1960." *Records of the American Catholic Historical Society of Philadelphia* 85 (September–December 1974): 144–62.

Dammann, Mother Grace. "The American Catholic College for Women." In *Essays on Catholic Education in the United States,* ed. Roy J. Deferrari, 173–94. Washington, DC: Catholic University of America Press, 1942.

Daues, Dorothy. "Sister Mary O'Brien (1846–1900): Cabra's Gift to New Orleans." In *Religious Pioneers*, ed. Dorothy Daues and Charles E. Nolan, 163–78. Chelsea, MI: Sheridan Books, 2004.

———. "Mother Mary De Ricci Hutchinson (1868–1931): New Orleans Dominicans Come of Age." In *Religious Pioneers,* ed. Dorothy Daues and Charles E. Nolan, 227-42. Chelsea, MI: Sheridan Books, 2004.

Davis, Cyprian. "Black Catholics in Nineteenth-Century America." *U.S. Catholic Historian* 5 (1986):1–18.

———. "The Holy See and American Black Catholics: A Forgotten Chapter in the History of the American Church." *U.S. Catholic Historian* 7 (spring/summer 1988): 157–81.

———. "The Future of African-American Catholic Studies." *U.S. Catholic Historian* 12 (winter 1994): 1–9.

Drolet, Francis K. "Negro Students in Jesuit Schools and Colleges, 1946–1947." *Social Order* 1 (1947–48): 145–48.

Du Bois, W. E. B. "Race Relations in the United States, 1917–1947." *Phylon* 9 (3rd quarter 1948): 234–47.

Dudziak, Mary L. "Desegregation as a Cold War Imperative." *Stanford Law Review* 41 (November 1988): 61–120.

Dunne, George. "Sin of Segregation." *Commonweal* 42 (September 1945): 542–45.

Everett, Donald E. "Free Persons of Color in Colonial Louisiana." *Louisiana History* 7 (winter 1966): 21–50.

Fichter, Joseph H. "Christian Brotherhood." *America* 55 (1936): 202–4.

———. "The Meaning of Prejudice." *Interracial Review* 20 (January 1947): 6–7.

———. "Predictive and Practical Generalizations about Desegregation." In *A Catholic Case against Segregation,* ed. Joseph E. O'Neill, 101–15. New York: Macmillan, 1961.

———. "The Catholic South and Race." *Religious Education* 59 (1964): 30–3.

———. "American Religion and the Negro." *Daedalus* 94 (fall 1965):1085–1106.

———. "The First Black Students at Loyola University: A Strategy to Obtain Teacher Certification." *Journal of Negro Education* 56 (fall 1987): 535–49.

———. "The White Church and the Black Sisters." *U.S. Catholic Historian* 12 (winter 1994): 31–48.

Ficker, Douglas J. "From *Roberts* to *Plessy*: Educational Segregation and the 'Separate but Equal' Doctrine." *Journal of Negro History* 84 (autumn 1999): 301–14

Fischer, Roger. "Racial Segregation in Ante Bellum New Orleans." *American Historical Review* 74 (February 1969): 926–37.

Fitzpatrick, Joseph. "Directions in the Social Apostolate." *Woodstock Letters* 88 (1959): 115–30.

Foley, Albert S. "Blackface Minstrels: 10 Reasons Why They're Not So Funny." *Catholic Interracialist* 11, no. 9 (April 1952): 1–2.

———. "Adventures in Black Catholic History: Research and Writing." *U.S. Catholic Historian* 5 (1986): 103–18.

Gandy, Samuel L. "Desegregation of Higher Education in Louisiana." *Journal of Negro Education* 58 (summer 1958): 269–74.

Gleason, Philip. "The Erosion of Racism in Catholic Colleges in the 40s." *America* 173 (1995): 12–15.

Gould, Virginia M., and Charles E. Nolan. "Mother Henriette Delille (1812–1862): Servant of Slaves." In *Religious Pioneers*, ed. Dorothy Daues and Charles E. Nolan, 25–36. Chelsea, MI: Sheridan Books, 2004.

Haas, Edward F. "New Orleans on the Half Shell: The Maestri Era, 1936–1946." *Louisiana History* 13 (summer 1972): 283–310.

Hall, Gwendolyn Midlo. "The Formation of Afro-Creole Culture." In *Creole New Orleans,* ed. Arnold R. Hirsch and Joseph Logsdon, 58–87. Baton Rouge: Louisiana State University Press, 1992.

Henderson, Russell J. "The 1963 Mississippi State University Basketball Controversy and the Repeal of the Unwritten Law: 'Something More Than the Game Will Be Lost.'" *Journal of Southern History* (November 1997): 827–54.

Hirsch, Arnold R. "Simply a Matter of Black and White: The Transformation of Race and Politics in Twentieth-Century New Orleans." In *Creole New Orleans,* ed. Arnold R. Hirsch and Joseph Logsdon, 262–319. Baton Rouge: Louisiana State University Press, 1992.

Janssens, John B. "War's Aftermath: Communism in Our Day." *Social Order* 1 (1947–1948): 99–102.

———. *De Apostolatu Sociali.* In *The Woodstock Letters.* Woodstock, MD: Woodstock College Press, 1950.

Johnson, Whitting B. "The Vinson Court and Racial Segregation, 1946–1953." *Journal of Negro History* 63 (July 1978): 220–30.

Jones, Lewis W. "The Desegregation Decision—One Year Afterward." *Journal of Negro Education* 24 (summer 1955): 165–71.

Kemper, Donald J. "Catholic Integration in St. Louis, 1935–1947." *Missouri Historical Review* 73 (October 1978): 1–22.

Kendall, John Smith. "New Orleans' Negro Minstrels," *Louisiana Historical Quarterly* 30 (January 1947): 128–48.

Klibaner, Irwin. "The Travail of Southern Radicals: The Southern Conference Educational Fund, 1946–1976." *Journal of Southern History* 49 (May 1983): 179–202.

Korner, Barbara O. "Philippine Duchesne: A Model of Action." *Missouri Historical Review* 81 (July 1986): 341–62.

Korstad, Robert, and Nelson Lichtenstein. "Opportunities Found and Lost: Labor, Radicals and the Early Civil Rights Movement." *Journal of American History* 75 (December 1988): 786–811.

Kunkel, Paul A. "Modifications in Louisiana Negro Legal Status under Louisiana Constitution, 1812–1957." *Journal of Negro History* 44 (January 1959): 1–25.

Kurtz, Michael L. "Earl Long's Political Relations with the City of New Orleans: 1948–1960." *Louisiana History* 10 (summer 1969): 241–60.

———. "DeLesseps S. Morrison: Political Reformer." *Louisiana History* 17 (winter 1976): 19–39.

Lahiff, Bartholomew. "Negro Students in Jesuit Schools, 1952–1953." *Jesuit Educational Quarterly* 16 (October 1953): 123–26.

Lamanna, Richard A., and Jay J. Coakley. "The Catholic Church and the Negro." In *Contemporary Catholicism in the United States,* ed. Philip Gleason, 147–93. Notre Dame: University of Notre Dame Press, 1969.

Landphair, Juliette. "Sewerage, Sidewalks, and Schools: The New Orleans Ninth Ward and Public School Desegregation." *Louisiana History* 40 (winter 1999): 35–62.

Logsdon, Joseph, and Caryn Cossé Bell. "The Americanization of Black New Orleans, 1850–1900." In *Creole New Orleans,* ed. Arnold R. Hirsch and Joseph Logsdon, 201–61. Baton Rouge: Louisiana State University Press, 1992.

Marshall, Patricia. "Sister Mary Francis Buttell (1884–1977): Visionary for Xavier University." In *Religious Pioneers,* ed. Dorothy Daues and Charles E. Nolan, 287–98. Chelsea, MI: Sheridan Books, 2004.

Martensen, Katherine. "Region, Religion and Social Action: The Catholic Committee of the South, 1939–1956." *Catholic Historical Review* 68 (April 1982): 249–67.

McCarthy, John J. "Facing the Race Problem at St. Louis University." *Jesuit Educational Quarterly* (October 1951): 69–80.

McNally, Michael J. "Peculiar Institution: Catholic Parish Life and the Pastoral Mission to the Blacks in the Southeast, 1850–1980." *U.S. Catholic Historian* 5 (winter 1986): 67–80.

Meier, August, and John H. Bracey, Jr. "The NAACP as a Reform Movement, 1909–1965: 'To Reach the Conscience of America.'" *Journal of Southern History,* 59 (February 1993): 3–30.

Miller, Randall M. "A Church in Captivity: Some Speculations on Catholic Identity in the Old South." In *Catholics in the Old South,* ed. Randall Miller and Jon L. Wakelyn, 11–52. Macon, GA: Mercer University Press, 1983.

Morris, Christopher. "Impenetrable but Easy: The French Transformation of the Lower Mississippi Valley and the Founding of New Orleans." In *Transforming New Orleans and Its Environs,* ed. Craig E. Colten, 22–42. Pittsburgh: University of Pittsburgh Press, 2000.

Neary, Timothy B. "Crossing Parochial Boundaries: Interracialism in Chicago's Catholic Youth Organization, 1930–1954." *American Catholic Studies* 114 (fall 2003): 23–38.

O'Reilly, Kenneth. "Racial Integration: The Battle General Eisenhower Chose Not to Fight." *Journal of Blacks in Higher Education* 18 (winter 1997–1998): 110–19.

Padgett, Charles S. "'Without Hysteria or Unnecessary Disturbance': Desegregation at Spring Hill College, Mobile, Alabama, 1948–1954." *History of Education Quarterly* (summer 2001): 167–88.

Parrish, Michael E. "Cold War Justice: The Supreme Court and the Rosenbergs." *American Historical Review* 82 (October 1977): 805–42.

Parsons, Wilfrid. "Commentary on the 29th Decree of the XXIX General Congregation." *Social Order* 1 (1947–1948): 103–4, 138.

Porter, Betty. "The History of Negro Education in Louisiana." *Louisiana Historical Quarterly* 25 (July 1942): 728–821.

Reed, Adolph L. "The Battle of Liberty Place." *Progressive* 57 (June 1993): 32–34.

Reed, Germaine A. "Race Legislation in Louisiana, 1864–1920." *Louisiana History* 6 (fall 1965): 384–85.

Reeves, Sally K. "The Society of the Sacred Heart in New Orleans." In *Cross, Crozier, and Crucible,* ed. Glenn R. Conrad, 219–32. New Orleans: Archdiocese of New Orleans and Center for Louisiana Studies, 1993.

Reinders, Robert C. "The Free Negro in New Orleans Economy, 1850–1860." *Louisiana History* 6 (summer 1965): 273–85.

Reynard, Charles A. "Legislation Affecting Segregation." *Louisiana Law Review* 17 (1956–1957):101–22.

Riddell, William B. "Le Code Noir." *Journal of Negro History* 10 (July 1925): 321–29.

Routh, Frederick B., and Paul Anthony. "Southern Resistance Forces." *Phylon Quarterly* 18 (1st quarter 1957): 50–58.

Ryan, Stephen. "Catholic Activity in New Orleans." *Interracial Review* 23 (January 1950): 7–9.

———. "Why a Man Voted." *New Leader* (July 1954): 20.

Shore, Paul. "The Message and the Messenger: The Untold Story of Father Claude Heithaus and the Integration of Saint Louis University." In *Trying Times,* ed. William M. Shea with Daniel Van Slyke, 135–52. Atlanta: Scholars Press, 1999.

Siefken, Mary Ethel Booker. "Mother Marie St. Augustin Tranchepain (d. 1733): Missionary to the Colonies." In *Religious Pioneers,* ed. Dorothy Daues and Charles E. Nolan, 3–18. Chelsea, MI: Sheridan Books, 2004.

Sitkoff, Harvard. "Harry Truman and the Election of 1948: The Coming of Age of Civil Rights in American Politics." *Journal of Southern History* 37 (November 1971): 597–616.

———. "Racial Militancy and Interracial Violence in the Second World War." *Journal of American History* 58 (December 1971): 661–81.

Slawson, Douglas J. "Segregated Catholicism: The Origins of Saint Katherine's Parish, New Orleans." *Vincentian Heritage,* 17 (fall 1996): 141–84.

Southern, David W. "But Think of the Kids: Catholic Interracialists and the Great American Taboo of Race Mixing." *U.S. Catholic Historian* 16 (summer 1998): 67–93.

"Southern Collegians Resist Racism." *Catholic World* (December 1951): 180–85.

Taylor, Joseph T. "Desegregation in Louisiana: One Year Later." *Journal of Negro Education* 24 (summer 1955): 258–74.

———. "Desegregation in Louisiana, 1956." *Journal of Negro Education* 25 (summer 1956): 262–71.

Tentler, Leslie Woodcock. "On the Margins: The State of American Catholic History." *American Quarterly* 45 (March 1993): 104–27.

Tregle, Joseph G., Jr. "On That Word 'Creole' Again: A Note." *Journal of Louisiana History* (spring 1982): 193–98.

———. "Creoles and Americans." In *Creole New Orleans,* ed. Arnold R. Hirsch and Joseph Logsdon, 131–85. Baton Rouge: Louisiana State University Press, 1992.

Tushnet, Mark. "The Significance of Brown v. Board of Education." *Virginia Law Review* 80 (February 1994): 173–84.

Valien, Preston. "Desegregation in Higher Education: A Critical Summary." *Journal of Negro Education* 27 (summer 1958): 373–80.

Van Slyke, Daniel. "Claude Heithaus and the Integration of Saint Louis University: The Mystical Body of Christ and Jesuit Politics." In *Theology and Lived Christianity,* ed. David M. Hammond, 139–73. Mystic, CT: Twenty-Third Publications/Bayard, 2000.

Vasillopulos, Christopher. "Prevailing Upon the American Dream: Thurgood Marshall and Brown v. Board of Education." *Journal of Negro Education* 63 (summer 1994): 289–96.

Woodward, C. Vann. "Look Away, Look Away." *Journal of Southern History* 59 (August 1993): 487–504.

Zielinski, Martin A. "Working for Interracial Justice: The Catholic Council of New York, 1934–1964." *U.S. Catholic Historian* 7 (spring/summer 1988): 233–60.

Newspapers and Periodicals

America
Blueprint for the South
Catholic Action of the South (New Orleans)
Catholic World
The Christian Conscience
The Christian Impact
Commonweal
Daily Advertiser (Lafayette)
Interracial Review
The Louisiana Weekly
The Maroon (Loyola University, New Orleans)
The New Leader
New Orleans Item
New Orleans States
The New York Times
The Philadelphia Daily News
Philadelphia Evening Bulletin
The Philadelphia Inquirer
Southwest Louisiana Register (Lafayette)
The Springhillian (Spring Hill College, Mobile)
Times-Democrat (New Orleans)
The Times-Picayune (New Orleans)
The U-Topia (Ursuline College, New Orleans)
Veritas (St. Mary's Dominican College, New Orleans)
Woodstock Letters (New York)
The Xavier Herald (Xavier University, New Orleans)

Government and Institutional Documents

Catholic Conference of the South. *Report of the Proceedings and Addresses of the First Annual Meeting, Atlanta, 14–16 April 1941.*

The Fund for the Republic: A Report on Three Years' Work, May 31, 1956. New York: Fund for the Republic, 1956.

The Public Papers of the Presidents: Harry S. Truman, 1947. Washington, DC: Government Printing Office, 1962.

The Public Papers of the Presidents: Harry S. Truman, 1948. Washington, DC: Government Printing Office, 1964.

President's Committee on Civil Rights. *The Report of the President's Committee on Civil Rights: To Secure These Rights.* Washington, DC: Government Printing Office, 1947.

U.S. Congress. House of Representatives. Committee on Un-American Activities. *Investigation of Communist Activities in the New Orleans Area.* 85th Congress, 1st Session, 1957.

Theses and Dissertations

Alberts, John B. "Origins of Black Catholic Parishes in the Archdiocese of New Orleans, 1718–1920." Ph.D. diss., Louisiana State University, 1998.

Anderson, Robert Bentley. "*Norman Francis Is a Negro:* Race, Religion, and Catholic Higher Education in New Orleans, 1947–1957." Ph.D. diss., Boston College, 2001.

Clark, Emily J. "A New World Community: The New Orleans Ursulines and Colonial Society, 1727–1803." Ph.D. diss., Tulane University, 1998.

Dauphine, James G. "Religion, Education and Louisiana's Cultural Boundary, 1880–1940." Ph.D. diss., University of Mississippi, 1989.

DeVore, Donald E. "The Rise from the Nadir: Black New Orleans between the Wars, 1920–1940." M.A. thesis, University of New Orleans, 1983.

Dugas, Carroll J. "The Dismantling of De Jure Segregation in Louisiana, 1954–1974." Ph.D. diss., Louisiana State University, 1989.

Everett, Donald E. "Free Persons of Color in New Orleans, 1803–1860." Ph.D. diss., Indiana University, 1952.

Fichter, Joseph H. "The Wage-Earner in the Consumer Cooperative System." M.A. thesis, St. Louis University, 1939.

———. "The Social Implications of the *Lex Iulia et Papia Poppaea.*" Ph.D. diss., Harvard University, 1947.

Hanigan, Maria G. "The Problem of Higher Education for Negroes in Catholic Colleges, Universities and Seminaries." M.A. thesis, Marquette University, 1940.

Kenney, Mary Josephina. "Contributions of the Sisters of the Blessed Sacrament for Indian and Colored People to Catholic Negro Education in the State of Louisiana." M.A. thesis, Catholic University of America, 1942.

Kight, Joseph A. "'How about September?': Archbishop Joseph F. Rummel and the Desegregation of the Roman Catholic Parochial Schools in New Orleans, 1962." M.A. thesis, University of New Orleans, 1994.

Kimbrell, Joseph Dee. "Joseph Francis Rummel: Archbishop and Teacher of Social Justice." M.A. thesis, Notre Dame Seminary, New Orleans, Louisiana, 1962.

Kurtz, Michael. "The 'Demagogue' and the 'Liberal': A Study of the Political Rivalry of Earl Long and DeLesseps Morrison." Ph.D. diss., Tulane University, 1971.

Lee, M. Florita. "The Efforts of the Archbishop of New Orleans to Put into Effect the Recommendations of the Second and Third Plenary Councils of Baltimore with Regard to Catholic Education (1860–1917)." M.A. thesis, Catholic University of America, 1946.

Martensen, Katherine. "Region, Religion, and Social Action: The Catholic Committee of the South, 1939–1956." M.A. thesis, University of New Orleans, 1978.

McCulla, Ernest Joseph. "Historical Analysis of the Development of Social Justice in the Archdiocese of New Orleans during the Episcopate of Archbishop Joseph Francis Rummel, 1935–1963." M.A. thesis, Notre Dame Seminary, New Orleans, 1972.

McTigue, Geraldine. "Forms of Racial Interaction in Louisiana, 1860–1880." Ph.D. diss., Yale University, 1975.

Miceli, Mary V. "The Influence of the Roman Catholic Church on Slavery in Colonial Louisiana under French Domination, 1718–1763." Ph.D. diss., Tulane University, 1979.

Misch, Edward J. "The American Bishops and the Negro from the Civil War to the Third Plenary Council of Baltimore (1865–1884)." Ph.D. diss., Pontificia Universitas Gregoriana, 1968.

Moore, Andrew S. "Catholics in the Modern South: The Transformation of a Religion and a Region, 1945–1975." Ph.D. diss., University of Florida, 2000.

Nickels, Marilyn Wiezke. "The Federated Colored Catholics: A Study of Three Varied Perspectives of Racial Justice as Represented by John LaFarge, William Markoe, and Thomas Wyatt Turner." Ph.D. diss., Catholic University of America, 1975.

Padgett, Charles S. "Schooled in Invisibility: The Desegregation of Spring Hill College, Mobile, Alabama, 1948–1963." Ph.D. diss., University of Georgia, 2000.

Payne, John Robert. "A Jesuit Search for Social Justice: The Public Career of Louis J. Twomey, S.J., 1947–1969." Ph.D. diss., University of Texas at Austin, 1976.

Rankin, David C. "The Forgotten People: Free People of Color in New Orleans, 1850–1870." Ph.D. diss., Johns Hopkins University, 1976.

Roche, Richard J. "Catholic Colleges and the Negro Student." Ph.D. diss., Catholic University of America, 1948.

Sanson, Jerry Purvis. "A History of Louisiana, 1939–1945." Ph.D. diss., Louisiana State University, 1984.

Sawyer, Robert M. "The Gaines Case: Its Background and Influence on the University of Missouri and Lincoln University, 1936–1950." Ph.D. diss., University of Missouri, 1966.

Stowe, William McFerrin, Jr. "William Rainach and the Defense of Segregation in Louisiana, 1954–1959." Ph.D. diss., Texas Christian University, 1989.

Turner, Pamela Jean. "Civil Rights and Anti-Communism in New Orleans, 1946–1965." M.A. thesis, University of New Orleans, 1981.

Westrick, Benedict. "The History of Catholic Negro Education in the City of New Orleans, La. (1924–1950)." M.A. thesis, St. Mary's University, 1950.

White, Doris M. "The Louisiana Civil Rights Movement's Pre-Brown Period, 1936–1954." M.A. thesis, University of Southwestern Louisiana, 1976.

Young, Mary David. "A History of the Development of Catholic Education for the Negroes in Louisiana." Ph.D. diss., Louisiana State University, 1944.

Pamphlets

Bernard, Raymond E. "Who Is the Negro?" St. Louis: Queen's Work, 1956.

Cantwell, Daniel M. "Catholics Speak on Race Relations." Chicago: Fides Publishers Association, 1952.

"The Catholic Church and Negroes in the United States: A Report." Chicago: Catholic Interracial Council, 1950.

Donnelly, Patrick. "World Citizenship and the Unfinished Business of Democracy." N.p., 1948.

"Facts in Black and White." Notre Dame: Ave Maria Press, 1955.

"Handbook on Catholic School Integration." New Orleans: n.p., 1956.

Lord, Daniel. "The Sacrament of Catholic Action." St. Louis: Queen's Work, 1936.

Madigan, James J. "The Catholic Church and the Negro." St. Louis: Queen's Work, 1941.

Markoe, John P. "A Moral Appraisal of an Individual Act of Racial Discrimination." N.p., 1951.

Riley, Frank A. "Fifty Ways to Improve Race Relations." St. Louis: Queen's Work, 1951.

———. "Race Riddles: The Whys of Discrimination." St. Louis: Queen's Work, 1952.

Twomey, Louis J. "How to Think about Race." St. Louis: Queen's Work, 1952.

"What Does the Pope Say about Catholic Action?: Some Papal Pronouncements." Sydney: Pellegrini, 1937.

Interviews

Alexander, Harry. Interview by author. Tape recording. Washington, DC, 2 January 1999.

Boykins, Ernest. Interview by author. Tape recording. Hattiesburg, MS, 20 November 1998.

Buvens, Edward P., S.J. Interview by author. Written notes. New Orleans, 26 January 2000.

Chandler, Lenora. Interview by author. Tape recording. New Orleans, 18 October 1998.

Cominskey, James. Interview by author. Tape recording. New Orleans, 21 September 1999.

Cooper, Harold., S.J. Interview by author. Tape recording. Algiers, LA, 24 May 1996.

Fagin, Gerald M., S.J. Interview by author, written notes, New Orleans, 24 January 2000.

Francis, Norman C. Interview by author. Tape recording. New Orleans, 16 June 1996 and 26 March 1998.

Graffagnini, Carmelo. Interview by author. Tape recording. Madison, AL, 19 December, 1998.

Krebs, Betty Prillmayer. Interview by author. Tape recording. New Orleans, 16 March 1999.

Mialaret, Gerald, and Ida Mialaret [née Chirieleison]. Interview by author, New Orleans, 25 June 1997.

Montecino, Henry R., S.J. Interview by author. Tape recording. Grand Coteau, LA, 29 June 1997.

———. Interview by author. Handwritten notes. Grand Coteau, LA, 11 March 1999.

Murret, Eugene. Interview by author. Tape recording. Boston, 8 May 1998.

———. "Reflections of a SERINCO Member." Tape recording. 1998.

Norris, Joan deBilby. Interview by author. Tape recording. Birmingham, AL, 21 December 1998.

O'Keefe, Michael. Interview by author. Tape recording. New Orleans, 16 June 1996.

Postell, Philip S., S.J. Telephone interview by author. Written notes. Dallas, 18 January 2000.

Reising, Joseph H., S.J. Interview by author. Written notes. New Orleans, 22 April 1999.

Ricau, Jackson. Interview by author. Written notes. New Orleans, 8 December 1999.

Rivet, Janet M. Interview by author. Written notes. Atlanta, 16 October 2000.

Roden, Paula Begnaud. Interview by author. Tape recording. Buffalo, NY, 21 June 1999.
Rousseve, Numa, Jr. Interview by author. Tape recording. White Plains, NY, 15 January 2000.
Shea, Robert Smith. Interview by author. Tape recording. New York, 14 January 2000.
Smith, Elizabeth. Interview by author. Tape recording. New Orleans, 6 March 1999.
Sykes, Wilbert. Interview by author. Tape recording. New York, 6 January 1999.

INDEX